MARVEL ENCYCLOPEDIA

Spider-Man, A to Z

WRITER/RESEARCHER
Jonathan Couper-Smartt
CONTRIBUTING WRITERS
Syd Barney-Hawke & Seth Biederman

Chapters One through Four

WRITER
Kit Kiefer

EDITOR
Jeff Youngquist
ASSISTANT EDITOR
Jennifer Grünwald
COPY EDITOR
Jake Kornegay
DIRECTOR OF CREATIVE SERVICES
Johnny Greene
CREATIVE DIRECTOR
Tom Marvelli
ART DIRECTOR/DESIGNER
Matty Ryan
DESIGNER/RECOLORING
Victor Gonzalez
DESIGNER
Jeof Vita
EDITOR IN CHIEF
Joe Quesada
PRESIDENT
Bill Jemas

Chapter Four images courtesy the personal collection of Mr. Sy Winnie. Used with permission.

Special thanks: Axel Alonso, Chris Allo, Mark D. Beazley, Tom Brevoort, Michael Doran, Andrew Lis, Ralph Macchio, John Miesegaes, Stefano Perrone Jr., Wilson Ramos Jr., Sean Ryan, Cory Sedlmeier, Joshua Silverman, Warren Simons, Christine Slusarz, Alberta Stuart, Jeffery Suter and Liam Webb.

Kit Kiefer would like to thank: all the Spider-Man fans at McDill Elementary, and Jeff Youngquist for a job well done.

Jonathan Couper-Smartt would like to thank: Jeff Christiansen, Mike Fichera, Ronald Byrd, Henrique Ferreira, Michael Hoskin, Kyle Sims, Rich Green, Bill Lenz, Stuart Vandal, Al Sjoerdsma, Bradley Bradley and Jeanne Burch.

www.spiderfan.org
"The Unofficial Spider-Man Page"

www.marvunapp.com
"The Appendix to the Unofficial Handbook of the Marvel Universe"

MARVEL ENCYCLOPEDIA VOL. 4: SPIDER-MAN. First printing 2003. ISBN# 0-7851-1304-5. Published by MARVEL COMICS, a division of MARVEL ENTERTAINMENT GROUP, INC. OFFICE OF PUBLICATION: 10 East 40th Street, New York, NY 10016. $24.99 per copy in the U.S. and $40.00 in Canada (GST #R127032852); Canadian Agreement #40668537. **Printed in Canada.** ALLEN LIPSON, Chief Executive Officer and General Counsel; AVI ARAD, Chief Creative Officer; GUI KARYO, Chief Information Officer; DAVID BOGART, Managing Editor; STAN LEE, Chairman Emeritus. For information regarding advertising in Marvel Comics or on Marvel.com, please contact Russell Brown, Executive Vice President, Consumer Products, Promotions and Media Sales at rbrown@marvel.com or 212-576-8561.

10 9 8 7 6 5 4 3 2 1

TABLE OF CONTENTS

INTRODUCTION

"And a lean silent figure slowly fades into the gathering darkness, aware at last that in this world, with great power must also come great responsibility."

Those words appeared on the final panel of *Amazing Fantasy #15*, the book that introduced Spider-Man to the world. And that, ladies and gentlemen, could have been the end of the story. But here we are, 40 years later, and we're still talking about him, we're still writing about him, and we're still fascinated with that brainy nerd from Queens who, through the bite of a radioactive spider, got super powers, earned his now famous mantra and began his lifelong quest.

The question is *"Why?"* When trends in fashion and music and movies and television have a half-life of, say, 15 minutes or so, why has Spider-Man remained one of the world's most recognized and beloved characters, more popular today than ever? Spider-Man made his debut in 1962…so why is the character enjoying his heyday some 40 years later?

Let me offer up two words: *"relevance"* and *"timelessness."*

There's just something about Peter Parker and his web-slinging alter ego that resonates through us all no matter how young or old and no matter whether we read his adventures in 1964 or 2004. These aren't tangible things, these are matters of the *in*tangible — ideas and philosophies that relate to our existence instead of appealing to our idea of novelty. Such ideas don't change on the whim of the "trendsetters." Rather, these ideas are as relevant now as they were four decades ago. Like Romeo and Juliet, Spidey is classic in nature.

Think about the challenges Peter Parker has faced over the years. Haven't we all at one time or another had to deal with these same dilemmas? The simple but titanic struggle between what's right and wrong? Between learning how to triumph over mistakes or dooming yourself to repeat them? And as it goes with these themes and issues, there aren't any easy resolutions, and the struggle is ongoing — there are only little stories and minor victories in between. What's more, these are universal themes and issues — not just personal struggles indigenous to Americans, which is probably why Spidey maintains his relevance among cultures and across continents.

(Well, it's either that, or the world won't ever grow tired of a super hero who can sling webs from tall buildings and kick the crap out of deranged villains.)

Spider-Man preserves his relevance because, hey, he's just like us — just trying to do the right thing in a crazy, mixed-up world regardless of the decade, regardless of cultural schisms, regardless of whether he's in the pages of a comic book, on our TV sets or on our movie screens. And until the world isn't crazy or mixed up anymore, Spider-Man's struggle will *always* be relevant.

That first story as it appeared in *Amazing Fantasy #15* could have ended right then and there on that final panel with Peter walking off into that gathering darkness, lesson learned. But we all know it didn't. Because we all knew it couldn't. The story doesn't end with his epiphany — instead, it's really where the story starts. Not just for Peter, not just for Spider-Man, but for us all.

See ya in the funnybooks!

'03

JQ
EEK

Art by Alex Ross

CHAPTER 1

KING SPIDER

Why the Wall-Crawler Rules Comics

Marvel Comics' founding fathers got it right. Scratch that. They got it *perfect.*

Somewhere in the Marvel test kitchens, sometime during the company's transition from a cowboys-'n'-cover-girls comics publisher to a maker of super-hero mags, writer Stan Lee and his all-star artists hit on a recipe so sublime it's still being emulated and copied and ripped off and bent at right angles by every comics creator and Emeril wannabe from here to Ulan Bator. The recipe wasn't for web-fluid or Aunt May's banana bread; it wasn't even a how-to on creating successful comic-book characters. The recipe was the secret for creating pop-culture icons.

Good recipe. A real bake-off winner. Throw away your cookie cutters, boys and girls. Out of Smilin' Stan's lovin' ovens came the quintessential comics characters of the last half-century, characters spun out in a flash of creative genius that makes Mozart look like a dawdler: the Fantastic Four. The Incredible Hulk. The Uncanny X-Men. Daredevil, the Man Without Fear. The Mighty Thor. And the Amazing Spider-Man. By all means, the Amazing Spider-Man.

Stan Lee, Steve Ditko, Jack Kirby and company cranked out Spidey and his pals at about the same time and pace as the Beatles cranked out hit singles — and just like those first blasts of the British Invasion, they're all great. In fact, you can throw all Marvel's classic characters into a cocked hat, and whoever you pull out is going to be a winning combination of power and pathos.

Point well taken, but a six-way tie for first is not allowed. At the end of the story — when the hard choices are made, and there's nothing to look at but the ad for 500 Revolutionary War soldiers for $2.99 — Spider-Man comes out on top. He is the greatest super hero created during the last 50 years. Maybe the greatest super hero ever.

What's interesting about this lofty pronouncement is that what makes Spider-Man great is the exact opposite of what makes his competitors great. Captain America, Superman and Captain Marvel derived greatness from invulnerability. They had no real weaknesses, no Achilles heels that didn't come with an escape clause of a size you can only find at Sam's Club. And we wanted them that way; we were happy about it.

Not Spider-Man. The No. 1 reason for Spider-Man's superiority is that he's not superior at all. Spider-Man is all weaknesses. He's too young. He's an emotional mess, which is to say he's an average 17- to 22-year-old. He's strong, but not *that* strong — not stronger than the Hulk or the Thing, and very often weaker than his opposition. He can tell when danger is afoot, but what super hero can't? The only thing different about Spidey's spider-sense is that it gives vague suspicions a name. He's smart and clever, but those two traits don't illustrate well and don't usually translate into victories on the super-hero circuit.

More weaknesses? Spider-Man is a lightweight on the weaponry front. Instead of ray guns, he wears funky atomizers on his wrists that shoot a derivative of rubber cement. The atomizers are powerful enough to propel the stuff several hundred feet, and the web-goo is strong enough to suspend a half-dozen criminals from a flagpole — but big deal. The rubber-cement cylinders run dry. The webbing can be cut. It dissolves in an hour.

Spider-Man can cling to walls and ceilings — but as a super-power, clinging to walls and 50 cents gets you coffee at the Superpower Café. It's more creepy than useful.

Spider-Man's costume is endowed with no particular talents, powered boots or customized gauntlets. It's a leotard, okay? An uninsulated leotard. No polypro long johns under that spider-suit. The wind blows right through to the thorax when Spidey swings through the canyons of New York. No wonder colds and the flu knock him for a loop. Shoot, anyone with an iota of sense knows

CHAPTER 1

that when you swing through the canyons of New York in February, you wear your coat.

And here's the topper: One of the reasons Spider-Man goes through the gyrations is *to earn a living*. Peter Parker fights crime for the old standbys duty and responsibility, but he also makes sure his camera captures Spider-Man in action, because he needs the bread to buy bread. Literally.

Spider-Man's in a place Batman, Iron Man, the Mighty Thor, the Sub-Mariner and the Fantastic Four can never be: He's a triple jump away from public assistance — and while it's rotten news for him, it's great for the plot. Peter Parker's money troubles fit right in with the rest of his traumas.

With a street life that doubles as a WB series, it's no wonder Peter Parker finds escape in becoming Spider-Man. There's a lot Peter hates about his alter ego: It complicates his relationships with women, makes him look like a coward, wrecks his grades, takes him away from his beloved Aunt May at crucial moments, turns him into the most misunderstood fugitive east of the Incredible Hulk and repeatedly brings him *this* close to being the corpse formerly known as Peter Parker. But sometimes, heading to the rooftops and shooting a little web beats reality eight ways to Sunday.

It's funny. Take all the doubts and girl troubles and money crunches and just plain stupid stuff that goes with being somewhere between 17 and 22 and trying to make sense of it all, take away the webs, add some freckles and yucks, and you know what you've got? Archie.

Sure enough. And the No. 1 thing these two pop-culture icons have in common is this: They're human down to their toe-nails. For all the modern touches added to Spider-Man during the last 40 years, the essential humanness of Peter Parker — the fact that he's more like one of us than any other comic-book alter ego — keeps him right up front on the super-hero hot list.

Art by Steve Ditko

In keeping with his status as a human being, Spider-Man never gets too big not to crack a joke when the situation presents itself — and the situations just keep presenting themselves. Of all the smart-aleck super heroes in all the smart-aleck comic books spun from Stan Lee's irreverent mind, Spider-Man is the most smart-alecky. Anything's fair game, from the Kingpin's belly to the Fantastic Four's self-importance to Jonah Jameson's big fat mouth. It's pure clover to be a writer when you can play a funny scene straight and a straight scene funny, and the artists love the fact that Spidey's light/dark character can handle anything from Powerpuff Girls impressionism to photo-realism without getting so far out of line it would take six weeks at Parris Island to whip him back into shape.

Wisecracks come and go, and the art may change, but the character remains constant. To an amazing degree, Spider-Man has been futzed with less than any 40-year-old comic-book character. Stan Lee and Steve Ditko got it right, right from the start.

Now, about that start. As the Eisenhower '50s swung toward the Kennedy '60s, Marvel Comics was hanging on by the skin of its covers. The company that had started so promisingly in the '40s as Timely Comics, with Captain America punching out Adolf Hitler, was riding a backlog of cowboy and soap-opera comics on a one-way road to the sewage-treatment plant. There was nothing terribly wrong with these Marvel comics technically, nothing that a few more compelling characters at the center couldn't fix. The compelling characters were there, lodged in the brain of Marvel Comics Editor-in-Chief Stan Lee, but comics in the brain represented a whole lot less risk than comics on the hoof — so in the brain they stayed, at least until the backlog of stories ran out.

The stories ran out in 1959. Lee then hired a mess of freelancers — including Steve Ditko and Captain America co-creator Jack Kirby — and turned them loose to create new stories for Marvel's remaining science-fiction titles. They formed the legendary core of the first Marvel Bullpen, and they did good work on so-so titles —

but it took the success of chief competitor DC's multiple-super-hero *Justice League of America* to spur them toward their best work.

The JLA's popularity did not go unnoticed by Marvel Publisher Martin Goodman. Goodman requested a multi-super-hero Marvel comic, only with brand-new super heroes instead of retreads. Stan Lee called up a team of characters from his mental archives, and the Fantastic Four were born in 1961.

Once the Fantastic Four established the brash Marvel style, the new characters came fast and furious: the Hulk, Henry Pym/Ant-Man — and to fill out the pages of a soon-to-be-cancelled title called *Amazing Adult Fantasy* in August 1962, the Amazing Spider-Man.

Right from that first story, Spider-Man staked out his territory. He wasn't overpowered, overendowed or overdrawn. He had problems at school, problems with girls and problems with money. He didn't fit in. He wasn't unlikable, but he definitely wasn't cool. Inside the spider-suit, he was a free-swinging wiseacre; in his civvies, he was a quiet, polite young man.

Liberating as it was for Peter Parker to become Spider-Man, it wasn't his Career Choice A. He didn't bring it upon himself. He wasn't testing the barriers of science when it happened. He didn't come from another planet. He was the victim of an accident that was the victim of an accident. He was bitten by a spider that inadvertently — or not, depending on which book you read — soaked up a dose of radiation. By most accounts, the transformation of Peter Parker into Spider-Man couldn't have been more unintentional.

One of the best things about Spider-Man is that you can pick up an issue of his comics from 1964, 1978, 1986, 1997 or today and find all the essential elements in place. (Just like Archie, come to think of it.) The framework Stan Lee erected for Spider-Man in 1962 still holds strong 40-some years later — whether in the long-running *Amazing Spider-Man* or the semi-revisionist *Ultimate Spider-Man*, in which Peter Parker is portrayed as a 21st-century teenager. It's a strong framework, the geodesic dome of character frameworks. Spider-Man is very easy to care about.

Art by John Romita

Spider-Man's constancy is remarkable, especially when you look at the machinations other characters have been put through. They've been killed and brought back to life, occupied other beings and been occupied themselves, been dispatched to parallel universes, and been out-and-out messed with. Spider-Man's had his out-of-body moments — there was a Peter Parker clone floating around for a while, and Spidey switched to a black suit briefly in the '90s — yet they've been mercifully few and short-lived (even though the black-suit foray turned out pretty good for the plot, spawning a superb third-generation villain named Venom). For now and the foreseeable future, Spider-Man plans to stay close to his skinny-kid roots, and nobody minds a bit.

The reason comic-book characters get dispatched to alternate universes is that this universe has only so many plots, and they're not a renewable resource. The story needs a shakeup, and a trip to some parallel world where an unfathomable existence lies hidden behind a veneer of normality — like France — is just what the plot doctor ordered. Spider-Man's never had that problem, in part because the cast of characters built around him is as solid as a '58 Buick. Jonah Jameson's bluster is hard to fathom in today's Gannettized-for-your-protection newspaper scene, but it's screwball empty bluster — straight out of *The Front Page, It Happened One Night* and *Nothing Sacred.* In her role as vulnerable conscience, Peter's beloved Aunt May is better

CHAPTER 1

than any mom or sidekick or golden retriever or Shirley Temple knockoff could ever be. And Peter Parker's girls — from Betty Brant to Gwen Stacy to Mary Jane Watson — are not only exceptionally easy on the eyes, but good for the story. Given the choice between squaring off with a plug-ugly bird-man like the Vulture and pitching woo to any or all of the above, it's no wonder Parker more than once went with the woo and ditched the leotard. The only surprising thing is that he went back for the suit.

The girls are grand, but the villains are best of all. Spider-Man's villains are the most varied and best-conceived bunch of baddies in the comics canon. Spider-Man doesn't need to go traipsing around alternate universes to find new challenges; he is gifted with all he can handle right here, now and forever.

The flow of plot from one villain to the next to the next to the next over *years* of issues is astonishing — especially in the '60s and '70s, when other comics had their hands full maintaining continuity through a single 12-page story. Spider-Man's stories weave the Vulture, the Green Goblin, Doctor Octopus, the Kingpin, the Beetle, Morbius, Kraven the Hunter and many others in an unbroken tapestry of good and evil, college and girls, and making rent. When the first Green Goblin, troubled industrialist Norman Osborn, dies fighting Spider-Man, the perfect successor is waiting in the wings in the guise of Osborn's son, Harry — who just happens to be Peter Parker's roommate. Doctor Octopus rents Aunt May's spare room. The Kingpin crashes a campus demonstration involving Peter Parker. It just rolls on, with the black humor and deft plotting of *The Sopranos* minus the contract squabbles and Bruce Springsteen guitarists.

What's really knock-you-on-your-tail amazing is that the continuity can even survive a trip to that

comic-book boneyard known as the newspaper funny pages. Spider-Man has been a denizen of the daily funnies since 1977, and it's easy to understand why he made a smooth transition. His stories have always valued character interaction over mindless action, and comic strips are all about character interactions. If they weren't, Charlie Brown getting undressed by a line drive through the box would be the least of his worries.

The villains have aged every bit as well as Spidey, and work in as many different setups and styles. The Rhino packs the same unique wallop when Jim Mahfood draws him with beatnik-cool Yogi Bear lines. The Green Goblin still chills to the bone when Sean Phillips shows him buying drinks for a house of super-villains, or when Mark Bagley draws him as an unripe, drug-shooting devil. The Kingpin is big and bad no matter who's holding the pen. And because Spidey can play small ball as well as Home Run Derby, there'll always be hoods to wink in between the big jobs.

Spider-Man's seamlessness hasn't been hurt by the fact that the people who have drawn and written his adventures through the years make the '27 Yankees look like the '62 Mets. If Stan Lee didn't feel more of an attachment to Spider-Man than any of his other characters, he's got us fooled. Smilin' Stan stayed on the case with Spidey for a decade. His artists for most of the run were original collaborator Steve Ditko and successor John Romita — who, along with Jack Kirby, pretty much defined the Silver Age.

A generation later, a Canadian artist named Todd McFarlane took Spidey back to the top of the charts. McFarlane's *Spider-Man #1* almost single-handedly created the comics boom of the early '90s and helped catapult the writer/artist to the forefront of the creator-owned-comics movement. You may have heard of the creator-owned publishing company McFarlane helped launch. Little thing called Image Comics. Little title called *Spawn*.

And that's just scratching the surface. The legendary Gil Kane penciled the chilling "Death of Gwen Stacy" issues. Erik Larsen took a crack at Spider-Man before creating the modern classic *Savage Dragon*. Paul Jenkins emigrated from the horror-noir of *Hellblazer* to pen *Peter Parker: Spider-Man* and *Spectacular Spider-Man*.

If the current writer/artist combo on *Amazing Spider-Man* isn't a super-team, it'll do until one comes along. John Romita Jr. took over the artist's seat once occupied by his father, and has pushed Spider-Man to new heights of power and expression. Romita's clean-lined work is what all modern comics art aspires to. Lines strike the proper balance between heft and sketchiness. Panels serve the story. Normal people look like normal people; super heroes look like super heroes. Big guys look *really* big. Romita's art looks like Romita's art. It is the real thing.

Art by Mark Bagley

Writer J. Michael Straczynski gives Romita Jr. plenty to work with. His resume includes creating the TV series *Babylon 5, Crusade, The Legend of the Rangers* and *Polaris*; producing a *Murder, She Wrote* TV movie; and adapting his *Rising Stars* comic for the big screen. He has a couple Hugo awards for excellence in science-fiction writing sitting on his mantelpiece. The guy can lay the pen to paper.

On *Amazing Spider-Man,* Straczynski's style is visual, iconic, storyboard-like, fast-paced to the point of breathlessness. He has a hell of a story to tell, and tells it.

The current reworker of the icons on *Ultimate Spider-Man*, Brian Michael Bendis, is high on everyone's favorite-writer list. A two-time Eisner Award winner and successful creator of his own titles — not to mention mastermind of a killer stint on *Daredevil* — Bendis brings a free-flowing

CHAPTER 1

style to *Ultimate Spider-Man,* where the action unfolds so rapidly yet so logically the comic seems to be transcribed from actual events as opposed to created from whole cloth. He's not afraid to mess with a few icons — Peter Parker has already revealed his secret identity to high-school sweetheart Mary Jane Watson, Aunt May's something of a looker, and Uncle Ben wears a ponytail — but the humanness and edge Stan Lee brought to the character are thankfully intact. *Ultimate Spider-Man* artist Mark Bagley feeds off Bendis' street-luge pacing and creates likeable, appealing main characters and supercharged villains — all rendered in a style reminiscent of recent Disney movies like *Treasure Planet* and *Atlantis* except for one small detail: Bagley was there first.

The continuity, the star writers and artists, the fantastic villains, and the gripping plots not only connected with readers when they first came out, but they continue to connect.

Figuring out why doesn't take a microscope, a mainframe or even an abacus. Spider-Man is totally what he purports to be: your friendly neighborhood Spider-Man. Friendly: easy to understand, easy to root for, easy to like, easy to read, easy to get hooked on. Neighborhood: hangin' in the same 'hood he's hung in for almost half a century, swinging with the same crowd. Spider-Man: accept no substitutes.

As if there could be such a thing.

Art by John Romita Jr.

CHAPTER 2

SPINS A WEB... ANY SIZE

Spider-Man on TV

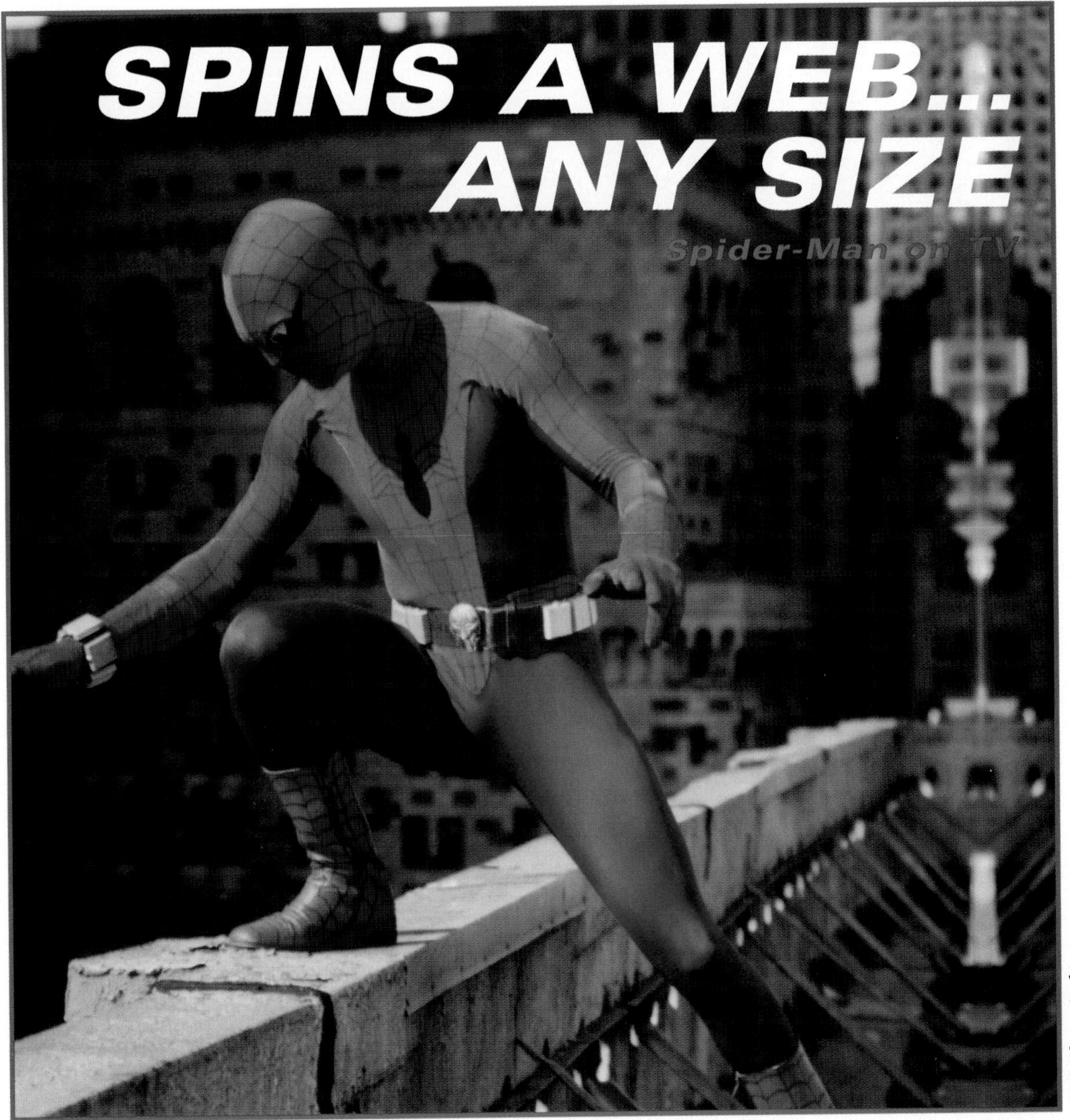

CBS Photo Archive

"Spider-Man. Spider-Man. Does whatever a spider can. Spins a web, any size. Catches thieves just like flies. Look out! Here comes the Spider-Man! Is he strong? Listen, bud. He's got radioactive blood. Can he swing, from a thread? Take a look overhead. Hey, there! There goes the Spider-Man! In the chill of night, at the scene of a crime. Like a streak of light, he arrives just in time! Spider-Man. Spider-Man. Friendly Neighborhood Spider-Man. Wealth and fame? He's ignored. Action is his reward. To him, life is a great big bang-up. Wherever there's a hang-up, you'll find the Spider-Man!"

You don't hear a hip jingle like that emanating from any comic book, which is okay. Spider-Man's had a great run in the comics, to the eternal delight of those who like their novels graphic. Everyone else's spider-sense has come from one of the many TV incarnations of Spider-Man, and the majority of these people have had that darn theme song run through their heads at the most inopportune times. During the big presentation. At their wedding. In the middle of a chem exam. During the Enron hearings. It's infectious, but that's not the half of it.

Spider-Man has done his time on the tube. Check your local listings for details, but he's probably going to be on your television some time today. That's because in all his small-screen incarnations, Spider-Man has been as true to his comic-book roots as a TV super hero is allowed to get without being cancelled immediately.

Spider-Man's TV career began in 1967 with a cartoon produced by Grantray, Laurence and Krantz Animation. This was the series that foisted the hideously catchy Spider-Man theme song on an unsuspecting Saturday-morning audience. Though the series ran only three seasons, its impact is still felt — in its look, in its style and particularly in its reverent attitude to its source material.

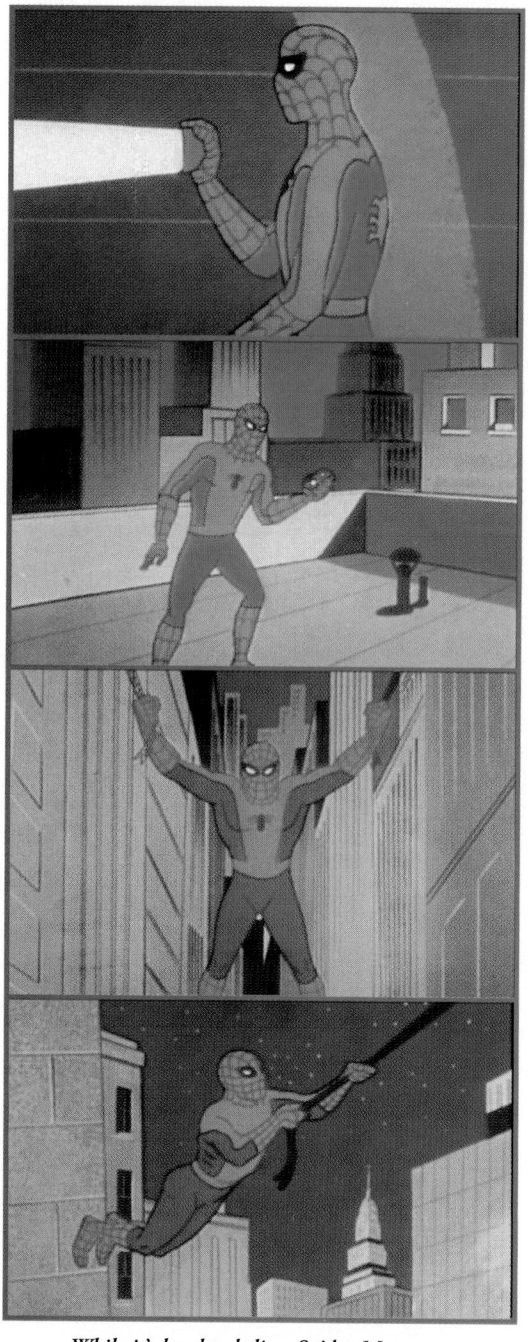

Courtesy of Buena Vista Home Entertainment, Inc.

While it's hard to believe Spider-Man *was state-of-the-art animation in the late '60s, a combination of tight plots, favorite villains and a timeless theme song keeps the original* Spider-Man *animated series fresh and vital.*

The '67 series was a cover band, copping licks and lines from the original comic books. The TV show took comic books and transformed them into cartoons without pausing for an instant to add sidekicks, make the cast multiethnic or bring on a bloodthirsty but ultimately misunderstood space creature. That says more about the quality of the original Spider-Man stories than Stan Lee could ever say — and he's said a lot.

For instance, the first appearance of the animated Lizard is a scene-for-scene recasting of *Amazing Spider-Man #6*. Mysterio's TV debut is identical to his appearance in *Amazing Spider-Man #13*. The Spider-Man origin show (which, surprisingly, was not the series' first episode) is a straight rehash of *Amazing Fantasy #15*. Even when the plots are not the same — as in the small-screen debuts of Doctor Octopus, Electro, the Rhino and the Vulture — the characters have the same motivations and appearances as their comic-book counterparts. The result is a cartoon series that for all its choppy, cheap, Hanna-Barbera-style animation is still fun to watch — and not in the same time-capsule way that contemporaries like *Josie and the Pussycats* are fun.

Spider-Man is hiply old-school, and here's why: No Marvel super hero — and no Silver Age super hero, for that matter — made a better first TV impression than Spider-Man, and no animated TV series was truer to its source material. Good thing, too, because the second time around for Spider-Man was definitely not the charm.

People who claim the '70s rock never lived in the '70s. The '70s did not rock. The '70s were squarer than George Clooney's jaw. The '70s were not an era when good taste was in vogue, and there are examples large (Tony Orlando and Dawn) and small (the peach-colored suit I wore to the prom). One of the nadirs of good taste in the '70s was the TV-super-hero bubble. Some bright network executive saw a few too many episodes of the old *Batman* series; critically overlooked the fact that the show never took itself seriously; and decided to camp up, tart up, deface and destroy a new batch of icons in a misguided attempt to duplicate the caped crusader's unlikely success.

CBS Photo Archive

Ain't It Cool News' Harry Knowles loves the short-lived Spider-Man live-action series because it's Spider-Man, and it's live action. Others find the oaken acting, weapons-grade writing and underwhelming special effects a little too much to swallow.

The results were too silly to be taken seriously and too serious to be considered comedy. They included bowlderizations of Wonder Woman and Buck Rogers; several made-for-TV super heroes (including the Greatest American Hero, a doofus high-school teacher turned doofus super hero); and a version of the Incredible Hulk that reduced the titular man-monster to a glorified, fugitive fetcher of kittens from trees.

This trend also included Spider-Man. A live-action, made-for-TV Spider-Man movie premiered on April 19, 1977 — about the time "You Light Up My Life" was rocketing up the music charts, which speaks volumes right there.

The program starred world-renowned actor Nicholas Hammond as Spider-Man. That's right: Nicholas *who?* Unfortunately for the success of *The Amazing Spider-Man*, Hammond wasn't capable of carrying a show the way Bill Bixby could with *The Incredible Hulk*. He was just a face, a haircut and a pair of legs that ran around L.A. backlot rooftops.

Hammond got the same sort of quality work from his supporting cast that the Marx Brothers got from Zeppo. Other shows have made it with a so-so supporting cast and a Krispy Kreme in the lead, but they usually had one thing the Spider-Man live-action TV flick didn't: a plot. Instead of following the animated series' lead and crashing the world's greatest library of comic-book plots for a storyline, the made-for-TV movie whipped up one out of whole cloth, with nary a Stan Lee one-liner in sight.

The TV movie starts out promisingly, with Peter Parker being bitten by a radioactive spider. He discovers his powers just fine, but then decides out of the blue to fight crime. Uncle Ben does not die so that Spider-Man might live. No great-power-requiring-great-responsibility jive here. "Responsibility" was not the watchword of the '70s.

The unmotivated crime-fighter's first foe is a blackmailer named Edward Byron who threatens to unleash ten brainwashed human bombs on New York if he's not paid $55 million. One of the bombs just happens to be Peter Parker.

Downtown Baghdad has fewer holes than this plot. First of all, New York has way more than ten human bombs on the street on a very good day. What's an extra ten going to matter? Second, why $55 million? $50 million, yes. $100 million, yes. $55 million must have the extra ten percent for his agent built in. And finally, the brainwasher's spell is broken when the antenna on the brainwashing device *falls off.* As a plot mechanism, this is only surpassed by the great evil person on the brink of total world domination deciding he doesn't want to be evil anymore, and turning himself in. It's so lame it wouldn't even show up in an Austin Powers movie. This was also the best plot the series was able to generate.

Encouraged by the slightly-better-than-lukewarm reception for the Spider-Man movie, CBS ordered a season's worth of episodes as a replacement series in spring 1978. As it turned out, that's all the network would need.

The episodes weren't very good. Going into

CHAPTER 2

CBS Photo Archive

detail isn't necessary. And besides, the titles say it all: "The Deadly Dust, Part 1," "The Deadly Dust, Part 2" (later packaged as a movie, *Spider-Man Strikes Back*, that was released in those parts of the world that consider Jerry Lewis a comic genius), "The Curse of Rava," "Night of the Clones," "Escort to Danger." You could write stories around titles like these that would have been Spider-Man-live-action-TV-series quality. Maybe you did. The bottom line: No Lizards, no Doc Ocks, no Kingpins and no reason to watch.

Spider-Man fans didn't have to wait very long for another reason to watch television. Within four years, another Spider-Man series was on the air, and it was a balm to the sores opened by the last show. *Spider-Man and His Amazing Friends* (also known as *The Incredible Hulk and the Amazing Spider-Man* in its third season) was produced by Marvel Productions and aired on NBC for 24 episodes starting Sept. 12, 1981.

For better or worse, it's sacred texts be damned when it comes to animated series. They really need to be judged on their merits as entertainment, and there the second animated take on Spider-Man delivers more pure enjoyment than an entire *American Idol* cast left to fend for itself in the Amazon jungle. The cartoon is fast-paced, nicely written, relatively well-animated compared to its contemporaries, fairly respectful of its source material and more than willing to rely on characters from the Spider-Man comic-book family tree.

Not that the animators were content to leave the source material completely alone. Several characters were added, including two ex-X-Men: Firestar, a mutant capable of producing tremendous heat, and Iceman, a mutant who can turn atmospheric moisture into ice. Also added were a niece of Norman Osborn's named Mona and a dog sidekick named Ms. Lion. Ms. Lion was not a mutant, though she was a dog in every sense of the word.

Shows were produced on a semi-haphazard basis. The first season featured 13 episodes, the second season added three new episodes plus narration by Stan Lee, and the final season added eight episodes. As often happens with animated series, past seasons' shows were added to the slate of shows for a new season, sometimes with their parts chopped up and sometimes not.

Show plots were a mix of comic-book elements and familiar animated-series clichés. It's not always a comfortable blend. For instance, the first episode has the Green Goblin attacking Spider-Man, Iceman and Firestar while the gang is attending a super-hero costume party. The action's good, the animation is slick, the voiceovers are right-on — but no amount of slam-bang action, slick animation or spot-on voiceovers can compensate for the super-hero-costume-party plot device. It's Archie. Actually, it's worse than Archie. It's Scooby-Doo. Actually, it's just '70s and '80s animation. It's the genre — and if you like the genre, you can certainly dig Spider-Man as a part of the genre.

Fortunately, not all the plots leave you wondering when a great dane with a soul patch is going to come whipping around the corner. The episode where Captain America, Shanna, the Sub-Mariner and Doctor Strange take on the Chameleon is pure comic-book action start to finish. The episode where Magneto tries to free the Brotherhood of Evil Mutants is more of the same. The re-examination of Spider-Man's origin in the second season is extremely well done, as is the episode reuniting Firestar and Iceman with the X-Men.

Incidentally, five versions of these cartoons have aired on American network television: the original 24-minute cartoons; reruns with Stan Lee narration tacked on; shorter versions without the Stan Lee narration that aired on 1988-89's *Marvel Action Universe*; episodes broadcast on the UPN network from 1998-99 with occasional Stan Lee narration; and versions that aired on the ABC Family Channel in 2002 with a couple minutes edited out and occasional Stan Lee narration.

You get a little bit of everything with this series — some comic-book-based storytelling, a few '80s animation archetypes, a little Godzilla here, a little troubled-teen saga there, a little Dr. Doom, a little Sandman, a little Doc Ock, a little Kingpin, a little Beetle. If you want straight comic-book plots, stick to the '67 series. If you want something more far-out, Spidey has you covered there, too.

By the '90s, there was more demand than ever for animation old and new. Burgeoning cable channels devoured animation as soon as it was produced. Among the chief animation-eaters was Fox, which needed shows for its Fox Kids block of programming. In addition to going the quick-and-dirty route of importing scads of new characters from Japan in the form of existing and long-running series like *Digimon* and *Pokemon*, Fox went in heavily for super heroes and authorized offshore production of a new series of Spider-Man cartoons.

The third Spider-Man animated series was produced by Saban Entertainment to atone for foisting the Mighty Morphin Power Rangers on an innocent world, debuted on Fox Kids in 1995 and encompassed 65 episodes over four seasons. *Spider-Man: The Animated Series* is an unusual mix of vintage themes familiar to Spider-Man comic-book legions (the transformation of Curt Connors into the Lizard, the Kingpin/Silvermane power struggle) and plots exclusive to the series, animated in a style less angular and detached than *Batman: The Animated Series*, but with much of that show's interplay between light and dark.

The series began with a teaser/pilot episode, "Night of the Lizard," that reprised *Amazing Spider-Man #6* yet again. (Why not? It's a great story.) From there, the series swiftly brought in Norman Osborn, Alistair Smythe, Mysterio, Doctor Octopus, the Kingpin, the Rhino and the Shocker. Despite the mix of old and new characters and storylines, everything fits together pretty well (think Hyundai, not Lexus), and the kids never seem to pay any attention to the man behind the curtain.

One of the best things about the Fox Kids series is the quality of the voiceovers. Voiceovers aren't acclaim magnets, but where would Looney Tunes be (where are Looney Tunes right now?) without Mel Blanc; where would the Simpsons be without Hank Azaria and friends; and where would Rocky and Bullwinkle be without June Foray, Hans Conried, Edward Everett Horton and the gang?

The Fox Kids Spider-Man series can't boast Mel Blanc, but it does feature the classic voices of Joe Campanella (as Curt Connors), Rue McClanahan (as Anastasia Hardy), Martin Landau (as the Scorpion), Efrem Zimbalist Jr. (as Doctor Octopus), Edward Mulhare (as Alistair Smythe), Brian Keith (as Uncle Ben), Roscoe Lee Browne (as the Kingpin), Eddie Albert (as the Old Vulture), John Philip Law (as the Cat) and whaddya know, Hank Azaria (as Eddie Brock).

The animation is top-notch, too. As recognition of that, the prime-time conclusion of the series'

Edgy yet classic, MTV's Spider-Man *hit the music-and-entertainment channel hard in July 2003.*

CHAPTER 2

third season, which featured the Chameleon taking on Nick Fury and Spider-Man, was nominated for an IMAGE Award — the Oscars of animation, awarded annually to cartoons that don't win Oscars in animation, if that makes any sense.

As with any animated series that runs a while and isn't *The Simpsons*, *Spider-Man: The Animated Series* lost some of its edge in its fourth season. The plots took Spider-Man farther from his vintage roots and more toward the storylines that did so much to drive Marvel into bankruptcy. Still, as *Spider-Man: The Animated Series* heads into perpetual reruns, the many years filled with good episodes mean viewers are never more than a couple days away from a great Spider-Man cartoon. Among the best: the "Alien Costume" triptych that introduces Venom (episodes seven through nine), the re-emergence of the Green Goblin (episode 31), the death-of-Gwen Stacy variant that has Mary Jane at the top of the Brooklyn Bridge (episode 41), and the four-part "Six Forgotten Warriors" storyline that brings Golden Age heroes Captain America and the Whizzer storming back to Spider-Man's side (episodes 54-57). The final episode, where Peter Parker thanks Stan Lee for creating him, is either the best of the lot or indescribably weird, depending on how deep you get into this stuff. Don't make it the first episode you watch.

It would be nice to escape on that note — but alas, Saban went to the well one more time and dragged up the stinking and short-lived *Spider-Man Unlimited* in 1999. The series put Spider-Man in the one place he should never be: an alternate universe on Counter-Earth — where theoretically, wall-goo can't cling (and really theoretically, there are no walls). Spider-Man and his pals spend 13 episodes fighting the Beastials of the High Evolutionary, and then it's done — and not a Beastial too soon.

The prospects are better for the MTV-produced *Spider-Man*, which hit the cable channel July 11, 2003. The voice cast is top-notch (Gina Gershon as Shikata, and how about Rob Zombie as Curt Connors?), the animation is a neat fusion of anime and CGI that lends many scenes a dreamlike quality, and MTV promises lots of time devoted to Peter Parker, where lots of time should be devoted.

If you've seen the movie, you should be right at home with the TV series. It starts where the movie left off. "The spirit of the series is picked straight out of the movie," writer/executive producer Morgan Gendel told *Wizard: The Comics Magazine*. "The combination of humor and seriousness, Peter's romantic dilemmas, and the dichotomy of being both Peter Parker and Spider-Man — we're going to explore those very same themes."

Spider-Man has spent hours of quality time on television, and millions of viewers have spent millions of hours with him. The TV Spider-Man, in all his incarnations, is some people's prime or sole Spider-Man. He occasionally gets a little off-course — but in the end, he's a real stand-up guy.

The unique blend of CGI and conventional animation in MTV's Spider-Man *series is a boon to ethereal characters like Electro.*

CHAPTER 3

THE ULTIMATE SWING

Spider-Man at the Movies

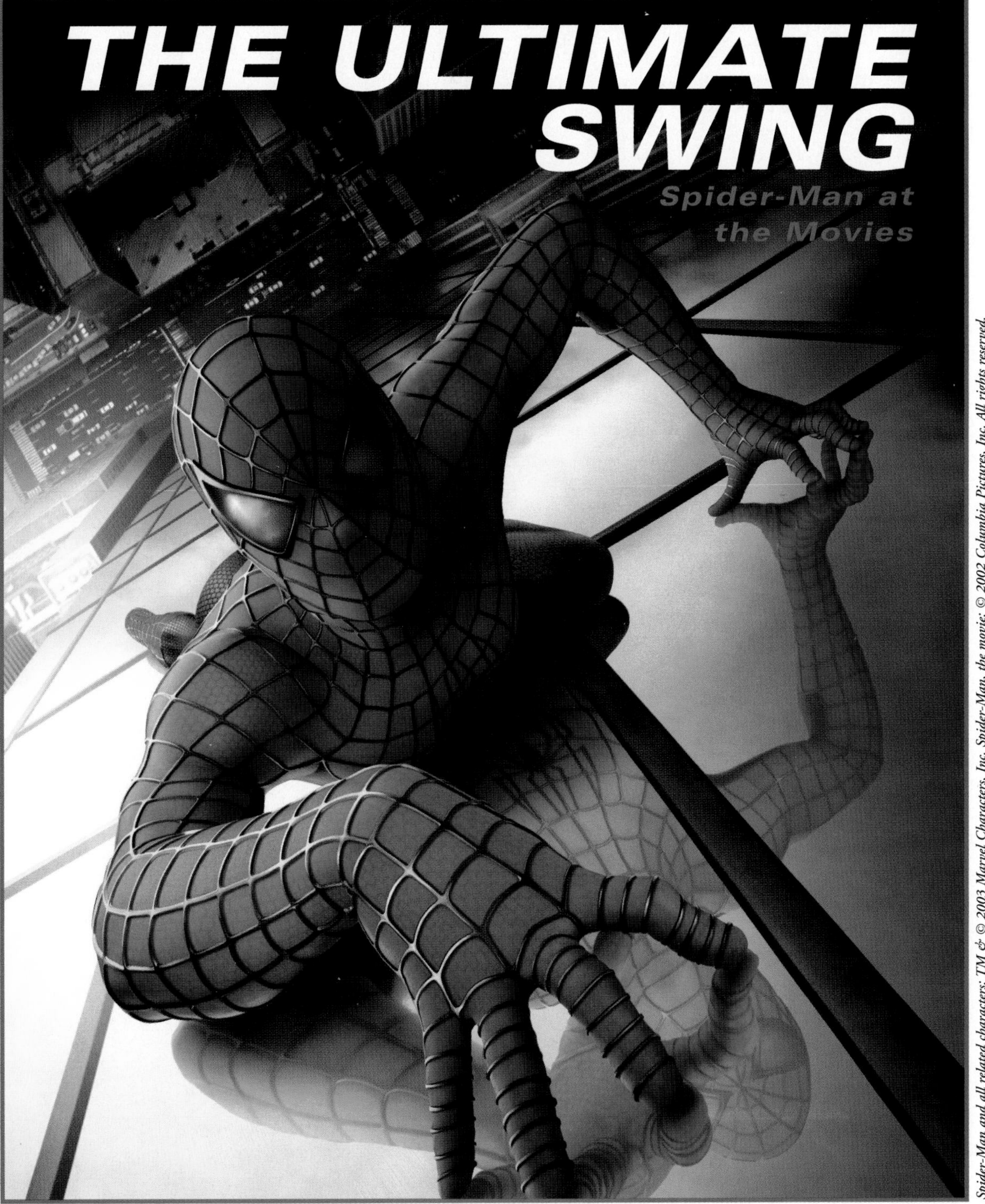

The fact that 2002's *Spider-Man* is great is less surprising than the fact that it took so incredibly long for a Spider-Man movie to get made.

Not counting the movie made from two episodes of the thankfully short-lived live-action TV show of the late '70s, Spider-Man was a big-screen ingénue until 2002. In the meantime, movies were made featuring Superman, Batman, Conan the Barbarian, Tarzan (at least three times), George of the Jungle, Rocky and Bullwinkle, Red Sonja, Josie and the Pussycats, 37,000 space aliens, 12 vampires, seven werewolves, a houseful of Greeks, and Howard the Duck — but that's Hollywood for you.

Saying Spider-Man was overdue is like saying the Boston Red Sox are overdue.

CHAPTER 3

Maybe Spidey was letting the other players play themselves out, because the run-up to the eventual web-flick moved at the same excruciating pace as a Celine Dion ballad. Rumors and reports of a Spider-Man movie had been swirling ever since the last Spider-Man quasi-movie went down over the English Channel. James Cameron, the budget-busting director who sunk the Titanic once and for all, had been attached to a Spider-Man project for a decade — even though the project's most real existence was in the pages of fan magazines. Serious reports of a Spider-Man movie moving past the project stage revved up in January 2000 — so there were more than two years of hype, rumors and hyped rumors before a single big-screen web was slung. That's not an outlandish time period by Hollywood standards, where some people are still waiting breathlessly for Orson Welles in *Citizen Kane II: Return to Rosebud* — but for ordinary people who would love nothing more than to see the greatest super hero ever do the Cinemascope Swing, it's a great big hunk of lifetime.

The life-and-death questions surrounding the movie as it was building from rumor to fact were, in the following order: Who would play Spider-Man? Who would play Mary Jane — or to be less specific, the love interest? Who would be the villain (not who would play the villain, but which villain or villains would Spider-Man face)? And who would direct?

The answer to Life-or-Death Question No. 1 started with Heath Ledger, passed through Wes Bentley and Freddie Prinze Jr., and ended with Tobey Maguire. The 28-year-old co-star of *Wonder Boys* was a dark horse going in, at least to the film-rumor press, but sealed his deal with an all-out screen test.

"I had to get dressed in a unitard thing," Maguire told the comics magazine *Wizard*. "I did an entire fight scene for them. By the middle of the scene, I had shed the top layer and tied it off at my waist. So I went topless and finished this kind of martial-arts fight scene. It was a good-looking screen test, and I think it finally clicked with them that I could play both parts."

Clicking with the comics crowd took a little more time. To true-blue comics fans, Spider-Man is the Role of Roles. It makes Hamlet, Prince of Denmark, look like the guy who cleans up after the elephant parade at the end of the Bullwinkle cartoons — and to cast anyone less than, oh, Sir Laurence Olivier, dead or not, is not giving the Webbed One his due. (And when you watch *Wuthering Heights*, you realize: Sir Laurence

The next Tracy and Hepburn? The next Bogie and Bacall? It's too soon to tell, but Tobey Maguire and Kirsten Dunst make one heck of an on-screen couple.

Faithful to the original and downright frightening, Willem Dafoe's Green Goblin was a bright spot in a movie full of highlights.

Olivier would have made one heck of a Spider-Man.) Casting Tobey Maguire was perceived as a slight, as grievous as the casting of Christopher Reeve as Superman, Michael Keaton as Batman and Eric Bana as Bruce Banner. The fact that those three turned out okay is irrelevant. Sooner or later, you cast a semi-unknown actor in an epochal role, and it's gonna bite you.

To allay fans' fears, the producers brought in a big hitter off the bench: Stan Lee filmed a cameo in the movie where he talks at length with Peter Parker. While the cameo wound up on the cutting-room floor for the theatrical release, that didn't dim Stan the Man's enthusiasm for the film.

"The movie will simply blow people away," Lee told *Wizard* before the picture's release. "Tobey Maguire comes across incredibly believably and totally likable. The romance between Peter and Mary Jane is handled superbly."

Once again, Smilin' Stan hit it on the head. (Maguire's take: "It was an honor to meet him. It was also so weird to meet one of the guys who created Spider-Man. I just wanted to make sure we weren't ruining his creation.") The friendly neighborhood Spider-Man is all that.

The casting of Kirsten Dunst went over quite a bit better for several reasons: She's a very good-looking woman, and she's not *the character.* She supports *the character.* No one ever bought a comic titled *The Really Good-Looking Mary Jane Watson*; heck, that's the business Marvel got out of to go into super-hero comics. While the fact that the love interest was Mary Jane and not Gwen Stacy or Betty Brant raised a few eyebrows — especially when it became apparent the movie was built around Spider-Man's origin, and MJ was not the primary object of his affection at that time in the original origin story in the original comics — once those eyebrows and the eyes beneath them got a shot of Kirsten Dunst as a redhead, all was well in Fanville.

As for the villain, the rumor mill churned out names like Electro, the Sandman, the Lizard and Doctor Octopus before settling on the Green Goblin. As the most colorful and cinematic of Spider-Man's villains, and also the one with the deepest ties to the most characters, the Goblin was the obvious choice — too obvious, perhaps. Maybe the thought was that anything that looked, moved and acted like the Green Goblin was going to be murder to put on the screen — and it was, to an extent. But as long as the computer-animation guys were making Spider-Man do back flips through the canyons of Manhattan, it didn't add much to the invoice to stick the Green Goblin in the picture, too.

Speaking of the computer-generated imagery, let's dispense with this right off: The CGI is this movie's weak point. Casting — excellent. Acting — top-notch. Direction and editing — great. Director Sam Raimi moves into the big leagues with this movie. Plot and script — very good. But sometimes, Spider-Man in action looks too much like a video-game character and not enough like Tobey Maguire doing a Harold Lloyd and personally dangling from the 21st-century equivalent of the minute hand on the courthouse clock. It's not that the CGI isn't slick and seamless and capable of inducing vertigo in Navy test pilots; it's that it is.

Criticisms aside, the thing that hits you three minutes into *Spider-Man* is that this movie is

CHAPTER 3

J.K. Simmons as Jonah Jameson: Straight outta The Front Page, *by way of Donald Sutherland.*

sweet. Not necessarily sweet in the quasi-hip sense — or sweet as in sickly sweet, blue-food sweet or Teletubbies sweet — but sweet as in *aw-shucks* sweet. That's a good thing. Ninety-eight percent of human beings relate well to aw-shucks sweet, though only 62 percent say they do. You could look it up.

The main sugarplum fairy in this particular Nutcracker is Peter Parker. Peter Parker's a nice kid — a bit of a nerd, but not a caricature nerd — very real and very likable. You never doubt for a minute that he's 17 and naïve, thanks to a superb portrayal by Maguire that earns him the 2002 Michael J. Fox Be Old/Act Young Achievement Award. You're rooting for Peter even before he becomes Spider-Man, which of course is the idea. You don't cringe when the spider bites him — as the moment on which Peter's life spins 180 degrees, it's very understated, especially by action-movie standards — and you laugh out loud, but sweetly, at the scene where Peter wakes up in the morning and discovers he doesn't need glasses, and look, ma, I've got muscles!

His Aunt May (Rosemary Harris) and Uncle Ben (Cliff Robertson) don't look like the Aunt May and Uncle Ben in the comics (any of the comics, from the origin issue to *Ultimate Spider-Man*), but nobody really looks like that — and except for Katherine Hepburn, the movies are kinda short on tall, skinny old ladies who can act.

Mary Jane Watson doesn't look exactly like she does in the comics either, but she makes up for any shortcomings by being three-dimensional — and Kirsten Dunst, to boot. She is the girl next door, literally and figuratively — and if she runs with a fast crowd and hangs with the jocks, well, girls-next-door sometimes do that. And besides, there's always the boy next door to come home to. Fellow named Parker. *She's* sweet, too — quasi-hip sweet, as well as aw-shucks sweet. "That Mary Jane is one sweet girl" has multiple meanings.

Norman Osborn makes an appearance early on — and while Willem Dafoe lacks the physical presence of the comic-book version of Norman Osborn, he personifies utter villainy so doggone well you don't mind the fact that he's not built like a linebacker. And as he proves early and often in the movie, he's built well enough to take a licking and keep on ticking.

A special treat is J. K. Simmons as J. Jonah Jameson. Simmons has the looks and acting style of a younger Donald Sutherland, and his rapid-fire dialogue is straight out of *The Front Page.* In a movie where so much is nearly perfect, Jameson, like the editor he is, crosses out the modifier. He *is* perfect.

The high-octane thrills and heart-pumping special effects are theoretically what people came to see when they traded their cash for a ticket to *Spider-Man* — but if that were truly the case, *Spider-Man* would have been no more popular than a slew of other high-action, tricky-tech movies. The reason *Spider-Man* was the highest-grossing movie of 2002 had nothing to do with special effects, thrills, spills, fights or tights. *Spider-Man* brought home $405 million of box office because it has a heart. It has soul. It uses dialogue for greater purposes than delivering semi-funny insults between megaton-grade punches. (Though it does its fair share of that. After all, the Spider-Man comics practically invented the technique.) It builds up relationships between characters we come to really care about, characters who actually charm us.

Put another way, Spider-Man is a great, popular movie because *it's a romantic comedy*. It's *Sleepless in Seattle, When Harry Met Sally, Pillow Talk.* With tons of mind-bending, web-swingin' action.

Want proof? Here you go: What's *Spider-Man*'s most memorable scene? Uncle Ben's death? Sorry. The cage match between the newly named Spider-Man and Bonesaw McGraw (played with tooth-spitting vim by Macho Man Randy Savage)?

Guess again. The ultimate showdown between Spider-Man and the Green Goblin that starts on the Queensboro Bridge but relocates to a ghostly Brownfield? Nope. How about Spidey and Mary Jane's upside-down kiss in the rain? Bingo. As all-time movie kisses go, this one's destined to be up there with Jimmy Stewart kissing Donna Reed in *It's a Wonderful Life* or Burt Lancaster and Deborah Kerr kissing with the tide in *From Here to Eternity.* When an action movie is most remembered for a kiss, that's not a bad thing — quite the contrary: It's a sign of great filmmaking. And if you want further proof, watch *North by Northwest* sometime, and see whether Cary Grant and Eva Marie Saint's last kiss doesn't stick with you a while.

"That was a challenging moment," Maguire told *Wizard*, referring to the kiss. "It was unfortunate because it was like five in the morning after working all night, and we were racing to beat the daylight. I was in a really uncomfortable harness upside down with rain pouring into my nose. I couldn't breathe. I had to literally spit on her as we were kissing. Poor girl."

The romance may charm viewers, but the ones who paid to see action are rewarded with a steady crescendo culminating in a fortissimo finish. Early on, action is used to push the plot relentlessly — as when Peter fights Flash Thompson, or in the hilarious scene where Peter tries to figure out web-shooting and swinging, and gets a face full of billboard for his efforts. Later, it supplies the pivotal moments: Spider-Man's encounter with the Green Goblin at World Unity Day, the Thanksgiving Day rescue of a child from a burning building that comes with an unexpected turkey twist, the attack on Aunt May, the finale. The scenes are quickly paced and neatly edited, and the kids love 'em.

Critical response to *Spider-Man* was overwhelmingly positive. Moviegoers got it, too, in part because they saw it more than any other movie in 2002. The film did a record $115 million in its opening weekend and finished at $405.7 million, putting it squarely on top of the charts for the year.

The overwhelming success of *Spider-Man* spawns the question of the inevitable sequel, which in Spidey's case is more inevitable than most. How could there not be a sequel? If *Inspector Gadget* merits a sequel, then any movie does. (Hold it; that didn't come out right...) If God allows four *House Party* movies without visiting a plague of frogs on Hollywood, then surely a second Spider-Man movie is okay. (Better.)

The *Spider-Man* sequel is set to hit theaters July 2, 2004. At this point, it has the big weekend all to itself, though that's subject to change without notice.

All the good stuff from the first movie is back

Shades of Norman Osborn: Willem Dafoe reportedly really got into his fight scenes with Tobey Maguire. Must be the suit.

CHAPTER 3

for an encore: Tobey Maguire as Peter Parker/Spider-Man, Kirsten Dunst as Mary Jane, Rosemary Harris as Aunt May — and most important, Sam Raimi behind the camera. Maguire and Dunst's undeniable chemistry aside, Raimi showed the first time around he's into the character so deep he knows without checking whether it's Old Spice or Right Guard. Everyone knows Raimi can handle the action, and he showed with the first movie he has a deft touch with the softer stuff.

The scriptwriting was kicked up a notch for the sequel when Pulitzer Prize-winning author Michael Chabon (*Wonder Boys, The Amazing Adventures of Kavalier & Clay*) was signed to do the penning. Chabon definitely knows his way around a relationship, so expect more deft dialogue and light romance between the web-swinging and fist-fighting.

The additions to the cast are doubly interesting. Not only are the actors interesting, but their characters shed some light on where the plot is headed. Topping the list is Alfred Molina (*Boogie Nights*) as Dr. Otto Octavius — a.k.a. Doctor Octopus, a.k.a. Doc Ock. Dylan Baker (*Happiness*) has been cast as Dr. Curt Connors — without mention of the Lizard. And finally, the casting of Daniel Gillies as John Jameson suggests this movie is headed in the direction of either the Man-Wolf storyline or the John Jameson-out-of-control storyline — either of which would make a great movie. (There are scores of Spider-Man storylines that would make great movies. The character's just so darn cinematic.)

Filming of exteriors for the sequel started in November 2002 in Chicago. Full-blown production kicked off April 12, 2003, in New York City, with Columbia University standing in for the fictitious Empire State University.

Just as in the comic books, an Asia-sized piece of *Spider-Man 2* is carried over whole from *Spider-Man*. Peter Parker doesn't look much different, and neither does Spider-Man. His hangouts don't morph from gothic doom to amusement-park neon the way a certain caped crusader's did from movie to movie. The same actors play the same key characters. The major changes from the first movie to the second are the gentle changes of real life — a new school, a new love interest, a few new faces popping up among the familiar. Spider-Man's firm footing in a 20-year-old's reality serves him well in the comics and does a bang-up job of making the transition from movie to sequel look as easy as walking from the kitchen to the living room.

Spider-Man doesn't appear to be a two-room flat, however. Maguire and Dunst are signed for one more sequel, though Raimi isn't. That looks like a formality, because *Spider-Man 2* has all the earmarks of the best action-picture sequels of the age: *X2: X-Men United, Superman II, Star Wars: The Empire Strikes Back, Star Trek II: The Wrath of Khan*. The ingredients are in place. All that's required is the right amount of mixing.

Insanity incarnate in a crunchy candy shell? The Green Goblin — and Willem Dafoe — fit the description.

CHAPTER 4

FROM MEGOS TO MINI-MATES

Just Toying Around, Spidey-Style

When Shakespeare wrote, "There are more things in heaven and earth, Horatio, than are dreamt of in your philosophy," he could have been talking about Spider-Man toys and collectibles. Dream of kid-friendly web-shooters with aerosol cans of web-fluid you can buy off the shelf at Target? Dream come true. Dream of a Spider-Man Web-Copter, from the long line of Aircraft For Super Heroes Who Need Aircraft Like They Need A Kneecap Growing Out Of Their Foreheads? It's right next to the web-fluid. Dream of a Spider-Man board game, where it's the flip of the spinner and not atomic energy filtered through spider spit that can send the Green Goblin careening to his doom? Gotcha covered.

Horatio's not the only one whose dreams can't begin to encompass the enormity of Spider-Man stuff in the universe. Who dares to dream of something as transcendent as a Spider-Man Day, a super-hero variant on the Midas theme where everything you touch has but one degree of separation from Spider-Man — yet such a day has been made possible by the thousands of Spider-Man products produced over the years.

You lift your head from your Spider-Man pillowcase as your Spider-Man alarm clock rings you awake, throw off your Spider-Man comforter, slip out of your Spider-Man sheets, yank open your Spider-Man curtains and head to the bathroom. After you slide down your Spider-Man pajamas, you jump into the shower, lather up with Spider-Man shampoo — boy, doesn't that get your spider-sense tingling, huh? — slip on your Spider-Man bath mitt and luxuriate in the experience of Spider-Man bath soap. After rinsing, you dry off with a Spider-Man bath towel, change into a clean pair of Spider-Man boxer shorts, squeeze some Spider-Man-approved Aim toothpaste onto your Spider-Man toothbrush, and you're good to go.

Dressing is easy. You pull on some jeans and a Spider-Man T-shirt, and lace up your Spider-Man tennis shoes. A Spider-Man cap cinches the look — whether you wear it backwards, forwards or sideways. From there, it's breakfast: either Spider-Man Pop-Tarts or Spider-Man cereal eaten from a Spider-Man bowl with a Spider-Man spoon, accompanied by juice from a Spider-Man glass. You're running late, so you toss last night's leftovers into your Spider-Man lunchbox and dash out the door.

After work, it's back home — where you throw the Spider-Man movie in the DVD player, slap the Spider-Man soundtrack on the CD player and go a couple rounds with Spider-Man for Xbox while noshing on Spider-Man snack crackers. Later, friends come to visit. You play Spider-Man Monopoly, Spider-Man HeroClix and Spider-Man Canasta until long after midnight — and then, after enjoying a lemon pop from your Spider-Man ice-pop maker, you settle back into your Spider-Man sheets, plug in your Spider-Man night light, grab your Spider-

CHAPTER 4

Man Pillow Time Pal, cuddle up with your Spider-Man latch-hook pillow, turn down the Spider-Man camp lantern and drift off to sleep.

Spider-Man is a 40-year-old licensing machine who does at least as well at bringing home the pork belly as that other famous 40-year-old licensing machine, Michael Jordan. The ingredients of the Spider-Man Day just scratch the surface of Spidey's stuff-filled world. The following 2,000 words are the Cliff's Notes to the overview of the introduction to the highlights of the general guide to Spider-Man toys, games, collectibles and bathroom items. Type www.spidermancollector.com in your browser window and buckle your seatbelt. You'll be catapulted into a red-and-blue dream world faster than the Millennium Falcon drag-racing in a Hardee's parking lot. But you've been warned.

Spider-Man stuff from the '60s and '70s reflects the way kids were in those decades. If you can't remember how kids were back then, too bad. Kids were *great.* And the music kicked.

To be a little more specific and less snide, kids in the '60s played with board games and cars and motorcycles and figures — not action figures, but figures. They supplied their own action. They flew paper kites and Styrofoam gliders, put together plastic model kits, peered through ViewMasters and stuck baseball cards in their bicycle spokes. Match this image against the Spider-Man toys and miscellany of those decades, and it's a pretty good fit, even down to the baseball cards.

Spider-Man's first appearance on a trading card — and one of the first appearances of Spider-Man on anything outside a comic book — came in the 1966 Marvel Super Heroes set produced by Donruss, one of the top non-sport cardmakers of the '60s.

Marvel Super Heroes cards are from the "funny-card" school, which in the '60s walked this way: Take all the jokes that couldn't make the cut in *Cracked*, dumb them down 85 percent, translate them into Farsi and back again, and then put them on trading cards. Less than a pint of milk nationwide was snorted through noses as a result of reading these cards.

The best news with the Marvel Super Heroes set is that it contains a whopping 11 Spider-Man cards out of a 66-card set. Two Spider-Man cards let you write your own captions — or, if you're conscious of your cards' condition, just *imagine* your own captions. The good news is that what are technically Spider-Man's rookie cards are *very* reasonably priced, lame flypaper jokes notwithstanding. A couple bucks will get

One of the rarest Spider-Man figures is the Spidey-suited version of all-around good guy Captain Action, who came with his own bottle of nitrous oxide to break up those really tense moments.

you a respectable example; full sets run around $100, but expect at least one of the write-your-own-caption cards to be written in. Buy the set, and upgrade the written-in cards if you're persnickety.

The follow-up Marvel set, the 1968 Topps Marvel Flyers, combined gliders with cards through the same sort of out-of-the-box thinking that produced the barium enema. Turn Spider-Man into an unpowered airplane? Sure! Why not? Great idea! Marvel Flyers took a super-hero body, whacked off the arms, mounted the body on the sides of a Styrofoam glider, put the arms on a wing assembly, and then sold the body sides and arm wings in a baseball-card-style pack. Kids inserted the wing-arms through a gash in the body, pointed the assembled glider nose-up into the wind and let fly, only to discover that a Marvel Flyer flies about as well as a chocolate-chip granola bar. Awesome Spider-Man image on the display box, though.

Unlike the Hulkcopter and the Thorboard, the Spidey Scooter's existence is partially justified by the fact that Peter Parker tools around on a motorbike. The depiction of speed on the box is a lie.

Compared to the current sound-chip-laden, action-packed, we-do-the-playing-so-you-don't-have-to generation of Spider-Man toys, the first wave of Spider-Man toys look like they were hewn by cave-dwellers. Items like a Marx-made license plate, a Marx tin train festooned with Marvel characters (if you handle one, bring along Band-Aids; that Tab-C-into-Slot-D intersection is a killer), a Spider-Man pennant, Spider-Man buttons and a Marx plastic figurine (one in a series of cheap plastic figurines showing Marvel super heroes) are startling in their primitiveness. It's almost impossible to believe these toys were the stuff dreams were made of less than four decades ago.

The few semi-sophisticated items from this era include the Milton Bradley Spider-Man board game, Marvel Superheroes ViewMasters and the Spider-Man Aurora plastic model kit. Unassembled Aurora kits are impossible to find, which should surprise absolutely no one. Once that smell of model cement and Testor's Royal Blue gets in your blood, you're hooked.

The Spider-Man ViewMasters from this era are called See-A-Show Stereo Viewers, but they're ViewMasters. You put the slides in the slot and look at them through the eyeholes. What in that description makes them something other than ViewMasters? They were the GameBoys of the '60s with less wanton slaughter and more scenes of the scenic Oregon coast.

Milton Bradley introduced the first Amazing Spider-Man game in 1967. Like most MB-Marvel board games made from the mid-'60s through the '80s, it features multiple Marvel super heroes and adheres to Weinstein's Theory of Playability: The playability of a Milton Bradley-made Marvel-super-hero game is inversely proportional to the number of Marvel super heroes shown on the box. The fact that the Spider-Man game's box features the Mighty Thor, the Fantastic Four and a line of other super heroes stretching into infinity should tell you something. And it ain't lying, either.

In the '70s, Spider-Man took these non-flying flyers, ViewMasters, unplayable games and pinback buttons, and forged them into a genuine licensing machine. Never mind that as a licensing machine in the '70s, Spider-Man was about as well-controlled as kudzu vine. It was a *machine*.

That helps explain why the '70s were the decade when "Spider-Man" was first associated with "health and beauty aids." This is not a natural association. Spider-Man's got to have some heavy natural musk going for him after a long night of swinging around Manhattan in a leotard. And bed-head's got nothing on web-head. Furthermore, the Green Goblin once drugged Spider-Man's toothpaste. Think you're going to want to pick up a Spidey SpinBrush after that?

On the other hand, the free-flowing growth of Spider-Man stuff also encouraged the development of the Spider-Man action figure.

CHAPTER 4

It'd be cool to say the development of the Spider-Man action figure was comparable to the Manhattan Project, but it was actually just an exporter named Mego that took a page from the Barbie book and dressed up made-in-Hong Kong Ken dolls to look like pop-culture heroes.

Megos were the first super-hero action figures, but don't attach too much significance to that fact. Megos are also among the worst action figures for two of the traditional components of action figures, "action" and "figures." Megos have movable arms and legs, but the number of realistic poses they can strike is somewhere between three and minus-seven. "Twisted ToyFare Theater," the brilliant feature in the action-figure magazine *ToyFare* that builds highly sick plots around posed-and-photographed Megos, would lead you to believe there are several poses, but in reality there are just four: standing, arms up; standing, arms down; sitting, arms up; and sitting, arms down. One arm up and one arm down doesn't count.

The first Megos appeared in stores in 1972 as part of the Official World's Greatest Super Heroes series. While these eight-inch figures featured hands lovingly referred to as "oven mitts," they did sport some awesome costumes, particularly Spider-Man. (Stands to reason: Mego also exported underwear to England, which tells you more than you need to know about what Brits wore under their trousers back then.) If costumes are your first priority when choosing an action figure, Megos are your figures.

The Official Spider-Man Super Streak was an early action figure … in a manner of speaking.

Mego went bankrupt in 1982 because it built its own plastics factory to make better-quality figures, which speaks volumes about the '80s. But that's another decade.

The '80s were a lost decade marked by 78 different Saturday-morning cartoons sharing one plot. They were a coming-of-age period for many comics. They were also the time when the licensed-merchandise megalith began to move from the Spider-Man toys that could have been Mickey Mouse toys or Gilligan's Island toys or Eldridge Cleaver toys with a swab of paint and some new decals, toward electronic toys, computers, clothes and "lifestyle items."

Spider-Man-themed toy cars said goodbye to their age of innocence in 1980 after a final flurry of activity from Corgi, Hot Wheels and Buddy Lee. It was like Wendy leaving the nursery; when Spider-Man cars came back a decade later, they were all grown up. They were collectibles, not toys. Megos were gone by '82 — and while the first smaller-size, fully articulated action figures were still several years off, there was no pressure to rush new figures to market because there wasn't a market. The toy scene of the '80s was dominated by dynamic new Saturday-morning properties. Spider-Man was your father's Oldsmobile with a pipe smoldering in the ashtray.

What did you do with an unhip, old-school property in the 1980s? Let progress take its course. In 1980, the Spider-Man Super 8 movie cartridge was the pinnacle of Spidey tech. In 1985, the first Spider-Man game for the Atari computer was released. By 1990, Spider-Man computer games were running on many of the most popular platforms.

If the course of Spider-Man stuff in the '80s lacked direction, the '90s were all about direction — and the direction was way up. Anything associated with comics was hoisted to the rafters like a championship banner, including X-O Manowar, Ultraforce, Hardware and Todd McFarlane. The challenge was to lift up as many things as possible as quickly as possible — and in an environment like that, Spider-Man dust ruffles make sense. Sort of.

In with all this heavy lifting were the

Corgi was one of Spidey's biggest boosters in the late '70s, though anyone without a pending death wish should probably steer clear of the Spidercopter.

essential components of the current Spidey-stuff scene. Today's ToyBiz and Diamond Select Spider-Man action figures, with their computer-scanned features and multiple points of articulation, are direct descendants of the ToyBiz Spider-Man action figures introduced in 1990. They're better — they look better and move better — but essentially, they're the same figure. You can't say that about Megos.

The first SkyBox Marvel Universe trading-card set also appeared in 1990 and defined the parameters for a decade's worth of trading cards of increasing complexity, style, beauty, scarcity and price. Trading cards featuring Spidey and his cohorts were a multimillion-dollar business in the '90s, and they furthered the causes of super heroes as icons and renderings of comic characters as art. Fine art, too: The Marvel Masterpieces sets — which feature paintings by Joe Jusko, Greg and Tim Hildebrandt, and others — are an unbeatable source of some breathtaking Spider-Man art. Spider-Man cards are experiencing a mini-renaissance thanks to some strong current efforts from Topps, so it won't be long until new collectors start checking out the older stuff and paying more for the privilege.

Spider-Man collectible game cards debuted in Fleer's Overpower Collectible Card Game (CCG) in 1995 — and while the cards didn't set any standards or define any parameters, Overpower was the first CCG to successfully incorporate existing super-hero characters into a CCG format. Compared to the CCG that started it all, Magic: The Gathering, Overpower's a lightweight. It didn't add sufficient complexity with each new expansion, and it gives super heroes too many powers. Still, as a set-'em-down-and-let-'em-whack game, Overpower suffices. It's also cheap, and it serves as a nice segue into the current decade.

Not that the decade was free of Darwin Award-caliber Spider-Man collectibles. One of 1999's pricier Spider-Man items was the $3,500 Spider-Man Gibson Les Paul guitar. This custom job does feature a spectacular Spider-Man graphic on the guitar top, but the problem with $3,500 custom guitars is they don't get played. And if you don't play a Spider-Man guitar, what have you got? A picture of Spider-Man with six wires running through his skull and a couple black boxes where his ears should be painted, on a weird-shaped hunk of wood.

The credo of the double-naughts is to not repeat the mistakes of the past — no Spider-Man windup toys or Play-Doh molds — while adding lines for the future. It takes responsibility for the Spider-Man Web O'Melon Belly Washer, but it's also responsible for spawning at least two new collectible categories: collectible miniature games and collectible figural art.

Chicago-based WizKids broke the collectible miniature game category with its Mage Knight game in 2000. After 18 months of phenomenal growth with Mage Knight, WizKids landed the license for what became Marvel HeroClix in 2002.

HeroClix figures are relatively small — hey, they're called "miniatures" — and have zero-count-'em-zero points of articulation if you don't count the movable pointers on their bases that tally up damage and show powers. As the figures move around the game environment, they encounter enemies and try to whack the boogers out of them — simulated booger-whacking, naturally, with multiple dice rolls per whack.

HeroClix is a geek game, but a good one, with enough strategy to keep gamers glued down for at least the duration of a Big Party Bag and a Mega Slam. Layers of scarcity, team powers and expansion sets keep veteran players engaged without totally freaking out newbies.

Spider-Man and his posse fare very well in the

CHAPTER 4

HeroClix environment — both in terms of buying and selling, and actual game play. Spidey's not the strongest, fastest, biggest or smartest super hero on the board, but he's the one most likely to still be standing when the smoke clears. But you knew that.

Figural art really took off with the introduction of a line of busts sculpted by Randy Bowen. There had been super-hero busts before — literally — but Bowen took the old busts, shrunk them by half, cranked up the implied action to 11 and priced them reasonably, at which time they absolutely refused to stay on the shelves. Mini-busts begat statues, which begat mini-statues — all good-looking, reasonably priced, somewhat limited stuff, collectibles that are worthy of the name. Bowen's current Marvel licenses no longer include busts and statues, but his mark's been made. The latest and greatest offerings from Diamond Select and Art Asylum have been made possible by a grant from Bowen Studios, and that grant is creating the market to start with.

When it comes to the making and selling of Spider-Man stuff, Spidey isn't just Spidey anymore. He's a franchise. McDonald's, Subway and your friendly neighborhood Spider-Man. And like all franchises, Spider-Man needs to be managed. Someone has to make the biscuits in the morning and clean out the grease trap at night. Spider-Man's been managed pretty tightly throughout the double-naughts except for a certain blip on the radar screen called the *Spider-Man* movie, named Best License of the Year for 2002 by the International Licensing Industry Merchandisers' Association. For companies wanting to make Spider-Man stuff, *Spider-Man* was like the liberation of Paris — and everyone wanted to kiss a tank driver.

So much stuff came out in association with *Spider-Man* you could practically have a Spider-Man Day with movie stuff alone. (Don't worry; we won't.) The interesting thing about the stuff is the range of prices. You could get a Spider-Man popcorn tub for free (exclusive of the cost of the popcorn and the movie ticket you had to buy to qualify for the popcorn), or you could spend $20,000 for a piece — a piece, mind you — of a Spider-Man suit worn in the movie.

Fortunately, cool knows no price point, and some of the coolest Spider-Man movie items are the most reasonably priced: Spider-Man and Green Goblin bobble-head dolls, the Spider-Man lava lamp, Spidey- and Goblin-shaped walkie-talkies, the Spider-Man Wacky Wall Climber, Spider-Man electronic gloves, Spider-Man Movie Swim Gear, the Spider-Man LEGO Action Studio and the Spider-Man Ceramic Cookie Jar, which holds more than two dozen of Aunt May's famous chocolate-chip cookies.

Speaking of LEGO, here's one last Spider-Man toy-slash-collectible for the present and future: Spider-Man Minimates. They're LEGO figures that aren't made by LEGO, do look like Spider-Man and his mates (Green Goblin, Carnage, Battle Spidey, Parker/Spidey), are cheap, and have incredible play value. (They even fit great with the Spider-Man LEGO Action Studio, but you didn't hear that from me.) Incredible play value *and* Spider-Man — it takes you back to square one, which is a very cool place to be. Especially if you're playing Spider-Man Monopoly.

The $3,500 Spider-Man Gibson Les Paul guitar and the Venom head are equally sick, but you can't play the intro to "Stairway to Heaven" on a Venom head.

SPIDER-MAN, A TO Z

His Friends, His Family, His Foes

Art by John Romita Jr.

ANNEX

Real Name: Alexander Ellis
First Appearance: *Amazing Spider-Man Annual* #26 (1993)
Hgt: 6'1"
Wt: 185 lbs.

After Alexander Ellis lost his leg in combat, he became the test subject for a prototype suit of body armor invented by Dr. Hillman Barto of Adarco. Using the exoskeleton, Alexander could regenerate his lost limb and create weapons from onboard computer schematics. Annex almost had his mind overwritten by that of fellow soldier Danny Dunson, the son of Adarco's president. Abner Dunson blamed Alexander for Danny's death in combat and had secretly arranged his acceptance into the research program so as to engineer the switch. Reversing the process with Spider-Man's help, Annex has since used his abilities for good.

POWERS/WEAPONS

- Bio-regenerative body armor
- Flight
- Creation of weapons and equipment from stored schematics

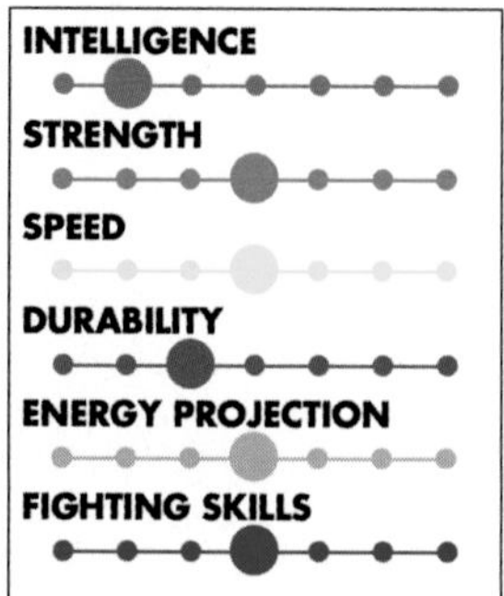

ANSWER

Real Name: Unrevealed
First Appearance: *Spectacular Spider-Man* #91 (1984)
Hgt: 6'0"
Wt: 170 lbs.

An agent of the Kingpin before acquiring superhuman powers, the Answer employed his exceptional intellect to solve difficult problems. Using the power of his mind and the equipment of Dr. Harlan Stillwell, the Answer gained the amazing capacity to develop any ability necessary to perform the same task. After easily humbling Spider-Man, the Answer sacrificed his life energies in a failed attempt to revive the Kingpin's comatose wife, Vanessa Fisk. He survived as inert energy, later regaining his mind and body. When the Answer joined forces with Doctor Octopus, he and the villain ended up at each other's throats. The Answer came up the loser, landing back in jail.

POWERS/WEAPONS

- Development of any ability required to resolve a given problem

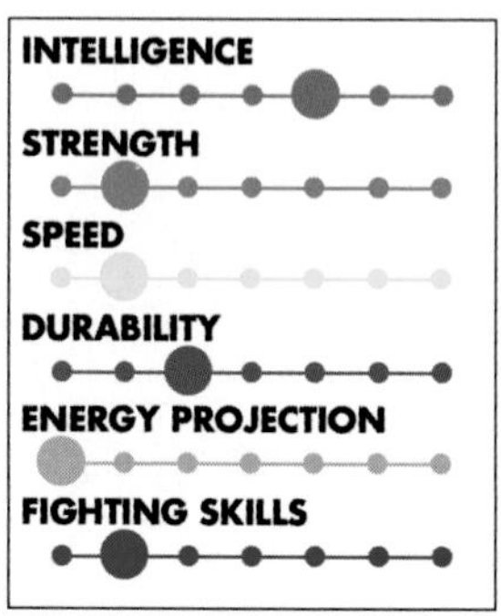

ARCADE

Real Name: Unrevealed
First Appearance: *Marvel Team-Up* #65 (1978)
Hgt: 5'6"
Wt: 140 lbs.

It is unclear how Arcade initially acquired his vast wealth; some reports say he killed his father for his oil millions. In any case, Arcade used his fortune to construct Murderworld, a deadly theme park designed to whimsically murder those he was paid to kill. Arcade's first victims were to be Spider-Man and Captain Britain. They survived, which greatly irritated the assassin-for-hire. Arcade was later retained by Norman Osborn (Green Goblin) to kill Phil Urich and return Osborn's Goblin equipment. He failed. Arcade subsequently subjected Spider-Man and the Black Cat to Murderworld, but ended up in prison for his pains. Arcade is chiefly an adversary of the X-Men.

POWERS/WEAPONS

- Brilliant inventor of lethal automated devices

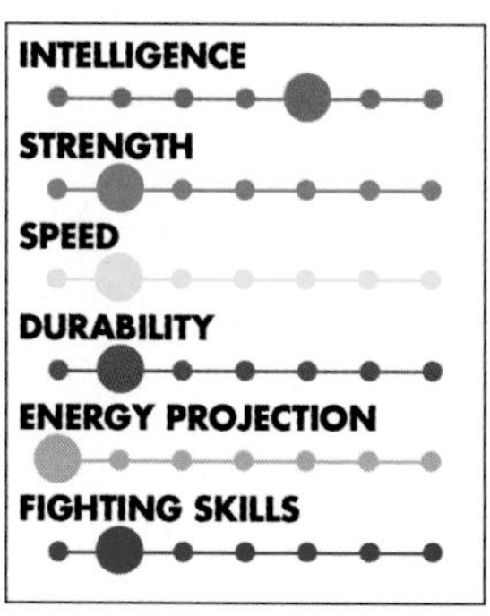

ARMADA

POWERS/WEAPONS

- Jet-propelled battle armor
- Small, flying, AI-endowed robots

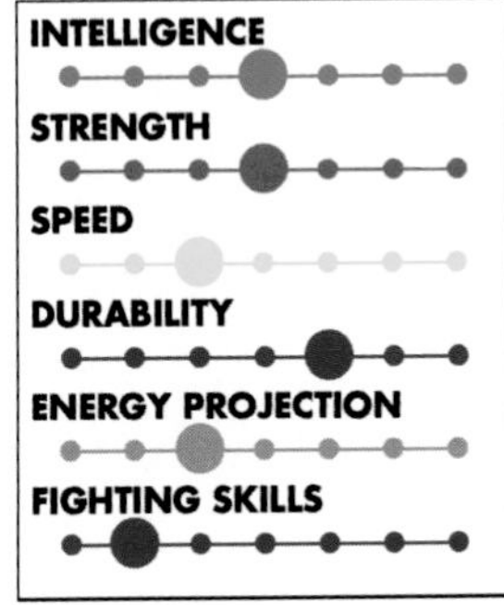

Real Name: Unrevealed
First Appearance: *Sensational Spider-Man #0* (1996)

Hgt: 6'2"
Wt: 195 lbs.

Armada is a high-tech mercenary whose battlesuit is highly adaptable, typically upgraded following each mission. Armada possesses a strong emotional attachment to his miniature flying robots, each of which bears a female name — such as Shirley, Tricia and Penelope. Mysterio initially hired Armada to steal an experimental computer chip created by Professor Ramirez. Armada fought alongside Mysterio in two subsequent battles — until Mysterio deliberately placed Armada's beloved robots in harm's way, causing the mercenary to furiously abandon his former ally.

ARRANGER

INTELLIGENCE
STRENGTH
SPEED
DURABILITY
ENERGY PROJECTION
FIGHTING SKILLS

Real Name: Oswald P. Silkworth
First Appearance: *Marvel Team-Up* #138 (1984)

Hgt: 5'9"
Wt: 190 lbs.

As a personal secretary of the Kingpin, Oswald Silkworth was tasked with the organization of the crime lord's Brooklyn extortion operation. To help him achieve this end, the Arranger hired the Enforcers as muscle. Though Spider-Man and the Sandman defeated his heavies, Silkworth survived and eventually became the Kingpin's head operations manager. In that role, he waged a highly unproductive war against the Lobo Brothers. The Kingpin did not forgive him that poor decision, and had him killed by the British assassins Knight and Fogg. Spider-Man failed to save Oswald's life, but did seek justice against his killers.

A'SAI

POWERS/WEAPONS

- Temporary access to the virtually unlimited power of the Galactus-Weapon

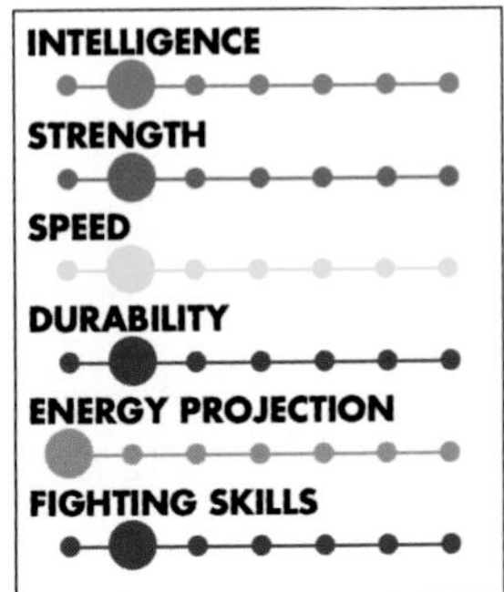

Real Name: A'Sai
First Appearance: *Web of Spider-Man* #34 (1988)

Hgt: 6'2"
Wt: 300 lbs.

Coming into possession of a weapon once belonging to the world-devourer Galactus, compulsive extraterrestrial gambler A'Sai accepted a wager from his friend, Grunz, and abducted Uatu the Watcher. Seeking even greater rewards, A'Sai staked the Galactus-Weapon against the Watcher's own technology. Their bet hinged on the results of an earthly football game — Spider-Man and some children vs. a team of larger boys. Correctly guessing the wall-crawler's inspiring leadership would win the day, Uatu won the bet and transformed A'Sai into a joker card in an Atlantic City casino.

ASHCAN

Real Name: Alex Woolcot
First Appearance: *Spectacular Spider-Man* #112 (1986)

Hgt: 5'2"
Wt: 105 lbs.

POWERS/WEAPONS

- Disintegration of most forms of matter

The young son of brilliant but abusive scientist Fritz Woolcot, Alex Woolcot unwittingly activated his father's incineration device and caused his own uncanny mutation. When his father next attempted to hit him, Alex instinctively used his new powers and turned him to ash — which was unknowingly vacuumed up by Alex's mother, Evelyn. As his abilities continued to escalate, Alex fled. He was pursued by police, the international law-enforcement agency S.H.I.E.L.D. and Spider-Man. Seemingly killed, Alex was in fact secretly relocated to live under S.H.I.E.L.D. protection. He later encountered and befriended the Hulk.

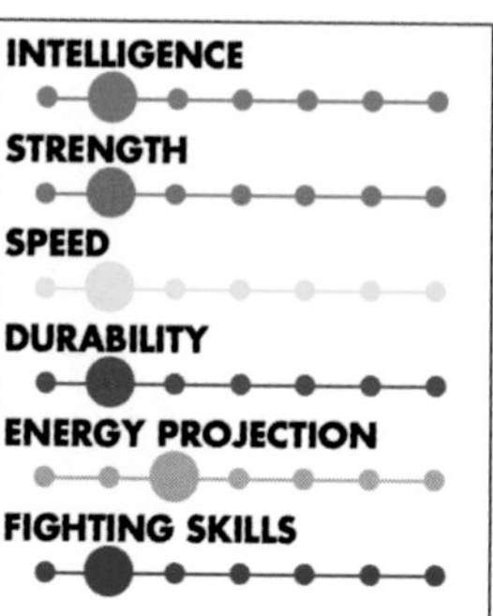

AURA & OVERRIDE

Real Name: Annie Herd (Aura) and Greg Herd (Override)
First Appearance: *Spectacular Scarlet Spider* #1 (1995)

Hgt: Aura: 5'9" / Override: 5'10"
Wt: Aura: 130 lbs. / Override: 170 lbs.

An engineer in cutting-edge network technologies, Greg Herd was hired by Dr. Carolyn Trainer, the second Doctor Octopus; he insisted his beloved wife also receive a position. When offered the chance to take a more active role, the two were easily swayed. Armed with powers and cybernetic costumes, Aura and Override battled the Scarlet Spider (Ben Reilly) with limited success and later pursued Spider-Man for the price on his head. In a melee involving police, armed gunmen and Spider-Man, Aura was critically wounded. Override later took part in the mystic Gathering of Five ceremony and became half of Shadrac.

POWERS/WEAPONS

- Force-field (Aura)
- Control of machinery and electronics (Override)
- Cybernetically enhanced strength (both)

AVANT GUARD

First Appearance: *Web of Spider-Man* #74 (1991)

The Perilous Painter possessed the power to manipulate reality as he desired, but lacked inspiration. Joining with Bora, a 7-foot-tall interpretive dancer who already exhibited mutant talents, and Spark, an unskilled performance artist, the Painter performed a ritual that empowered his allies. Bora's ability to generate freezing winds was enhanced; Spark could now release electrostatic bursts and assume a larger form, possessing superhuman strength. Together, they embarked on their magnum opus: the transformation of Manhattan into a frozen wasteland. Spider-Man and the Human Torch intervened, defeating Bora and Spark. Though the Painter possessed power enough to best the heroes, he instead opted for drama over victory. He transformed his two fellow "artists" into images on his canvas, and then exploded into a shower of cockroaches.

SALLY AVRIL

POWERS/WEAPONS

- Varsity gymnast

INTELLIGENCE

STRENGTH

SPEED

DURABILITY

ENERGY PROJECTION

FIGHTING SKILLS

Real Name: Sally Avril
First Appearance: *Amazing Fantasy* #15 (1962)

Hgt: 5'2"
Wt: 110 lbs.

Sally Avril was Midtown High School's star gymnast, but the brash teenager was constantly seeking new ways to shine. When Spider-Man began appearing around Midtown High, Sally enlisted the aid of her friend, Jason Ionello, and created the costumed identity of Bluebird. Sally's beginner's luck soon ran out, and Spider-Man saved her life — allowing her to take enough of a beating to persuade her to quit the game. Instead, Sally was inspired to become an action photographer, "just like Parker." But Jason was injured and Sally killed in an automobile accident when they ran a red light trying to photgraph the Black Knight.

BAMBI, CANDI & RANDI

Real Name: Barbara "Bambi" Modica, Candice "Candi" Muggins and Miranda "Randi" Couper
First Appearance: *Spectacular Spider-Man* #99 (1985)

Height: Bambi: 5'10" Candi: 5'6" / Randi: 5'7"
Weight: Bambi: 135 lbs.; Candi: 115 lbs. / Randi: 125 lbs.

Before marrying Mary Jane Watson, Peter Parker lived alone in a Chelsea apartment — across the hall from roommates Barbara "Bambi" Modica, Candice "Candi" Muggins and Miranda "Randi" Couper. The trio had dormed together since college at the University of Maryland. Candi's aunt and uncle, Mamie Muggins and Barney Muggins, were the building's landlords. Frequently using the roof to sunbathe, the three were often an obstacle when Spider-Man attempted to access his apartment via skylight. All were friendly, but Bambi — a single mother — occasionally flirted with the "cute guy" across the hall. Spider-Man once rescued Bambi from a burglar heartlessly posing as Santa Claus.

BASILISK

POWERS/WEAPONS

- Eye-beams
- Flight
- Superhuman durability

INTELLIGENCE

STRENGTH

SPEED

DURABILITY

ENERGY PROJECTION

FIGHTING SKILLS

Real Name: Basil Elks
First Appearance: *Marvel Team-Up* #16 (1973)

Hgt: 5'11"
Wt: 210 lbs.

A lowlife criminal, Basil Elks attempted to steal the mystic Alpha Stone gem. As Elks escaped, a guard fired at him and shattered the Alpha Stone. The gem's power was released, bonding with Elks and transforming him into the Basilisk. He then set after the Omega Stone to increase his powers — but was temporarily thwarted by Spider-Man, universal guardian Captain Marvel and Mister Fantastic of the Fantastic Four. After obtaining the Omega Stone, the Basilisk was flung into a volcano by Spider-Man and the Fantastic Four's Thing. Emerging years later to seek revenge, he was shot and killed by the Scourge of the Underworld.

AVENGERS

First Appearance:
Avengers #1 (1963)

While Spider-Man and the Avengers are in the same business, the structured crime-fighting approach of the government sanctioned team is at great odds with the web-slinger's far more unofficial and unorthodox methods. Spider-Man's initial meeting with the Avengers got off on the wrong foot when Earth's mightiest heroes somewhat naively decided to test his suitability for membership by arranging for him to capture the Hulk. When Spider-Man discovered that the man they were chasing was in fact a harmless scientist, the subsequent misunderstanding greatly soured the wall-crawler's opinion of the team; relationships were temporarily strained.

The matter was eventually resolved. Since then, Spider-Man has added his weight to the Avengers' roster on many missions. Eventually, Spider-Man applied to formally join the team, but the government rejected his application as a security risk. They later relented, and he became a full member for one mission — then a reserve Avenger for some months, before resigning. He realized his aims and means were just not compatible with those of the Avengers.

LANCE BANNON

Real Name: Lance Bannon
First Appearance: *Amazing Spider-Man* #208 (1985)

Hgt: 6'0"
Wt: 185 lbs.

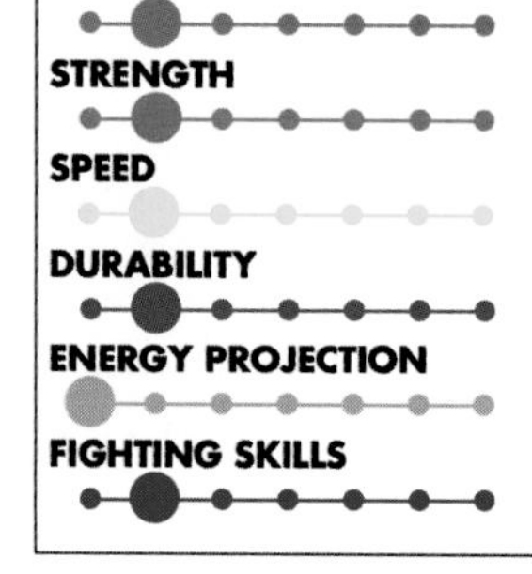

When Peter Parker left the Daily Bugle to join the Daily Globe as the newspaper's head photographer, he was shocked to discover he would share that title with a talented show-off named Lance Bannon. Competition was fierce between the two. When Peter went back to the Bugle, Lance followed — and their rivalry escalated.

Lance was hard-working, and often beat Peter to the punch. What's more, he was happy to please J. Jonah Jameson by taking photos that portrayed Spider-Man in a bad light. If anything, Lance worked too hard — and his girlfriend, Amy Powell, set out to use Peter to regain Lance's attention. She set Peter up, deliberately grabbing him for a kiss just as Mary Jane Watson walked through the door. This left Peter with some very awkward explaining to do.

Lance would not live long enough to marry Amy. Presumably, he knew too much for his own good, as the unidentified wearer of the F.A.C.A.D.E. combat armor murdered him. The mystery of his death was never solved. Angela Yin filled Lance's position at the Daily Bugle.

BATWING

POWERS/WEAPONS
- Flight
- Sonar
- Razor-sharp claws

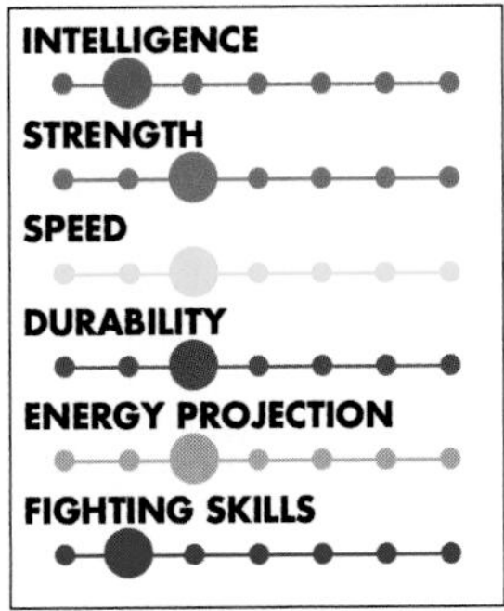

Real Name: Jimmy Santini
First Appearance: *Untold Tales of Spider-Man* #2 (1995)

Hgt: 4'2"
Wt: 100 lbs.

Trapped in the Carlsbad Caverns when his father died during an investigation into illegal dumping, Jimmy Santini was mutated by the chemicals in question. Alone and homeless in Manhattan, he was thought to be a monster. With the aid of Spider-Man, Jimmy was brought before Dr. Curt Connors (Lizard) — who attempted unsuccessfully to reverse the youngster's physical transformation. Jimmy resisted the changes, and it was not until he faced and overcame the psychological trauma of being rejected by his mother that he was finally able to revert to human form and return to his shattered family.

BEETLE

POWERS/WEAPONS
- Flight-enabled battlesuit
- Superhuman strength
- Electricity blasts
- Suction cups

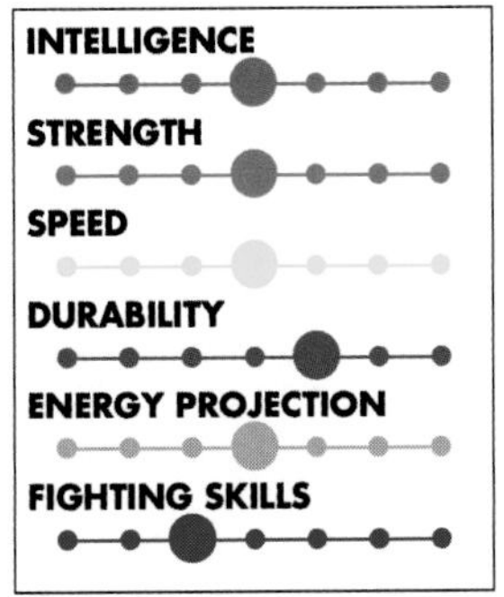

Real Name: Abner Jenkins
First Appearance: *Strange Tales* #123 (1964)

Hgt: 5'11"
Wt: 175 lbs.

Seeking fame, glory and profit, Abe Jenkins spent several years as the armored villain called the Beetle. Following a long and mostly unsuccessful career as a solo operative, he led the Sinister Syndicate. Jenkins proved no more successful in that role — thwarted at every turn by such heroes as the Human Torch, Silver Sable, Iron Man of the Avengers and Spider-Man. Known successively as MACH-1 through MACH-3, Jenkins later sought redemption as a member of the Thunderbolts, a team of villains-made-good. He went so far as to willingly allow himself to be imprisoned so he could rejoin society with a clean slate.

BELLADONNA

POWERS/WEAPONS
- Chemical weapons capable of causing unconsciousness and dissolving Spider-Man's webbing

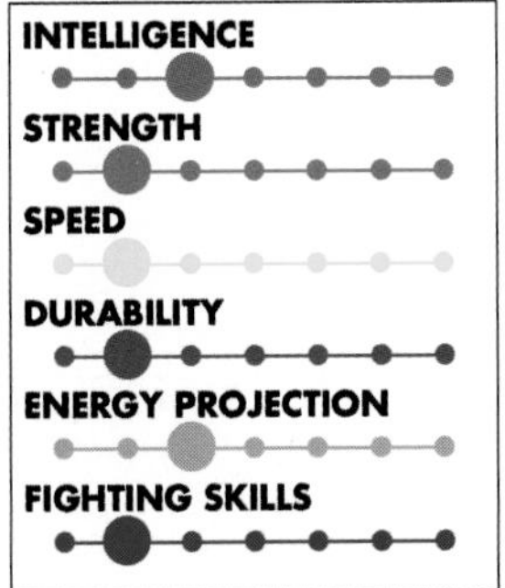

Real Name: Narda Ravanna
First Appearance: *Spectacular Spider-Man* #43 (1980)

Hgt: 5'5"
Wt: 120 lbs.

Narda Ravanna and her sister, Desiree Vaughn-Pope, ran a cosmetics firm in Europe until ruined when competitor Roderick Kingsley (Hobgoblin) led a smear campaign against them. Using knowledge from her work, Narda developed a number of chemical weapons and crossed the Atlantic to seek vengeance on Kingsley. In the United States, she employed the former Cat to steal the Prowler's costume and use it to assist her. Belladonna destroyed many of Kingsley's business holdings, assassinated his character and attempted to trick him into killing Spider-Man. The web-slinger uncovered her deceptions, exposed them and left her for the police.

BEYONDER

Real Name: Not Applicable
First Appearance: *Marvel Super Heroes Secret Wars* #1 (1984)
Hgt: 6'2"
Wt: 240 lbs.

POWERS/WEAPONS

• Omnipotence

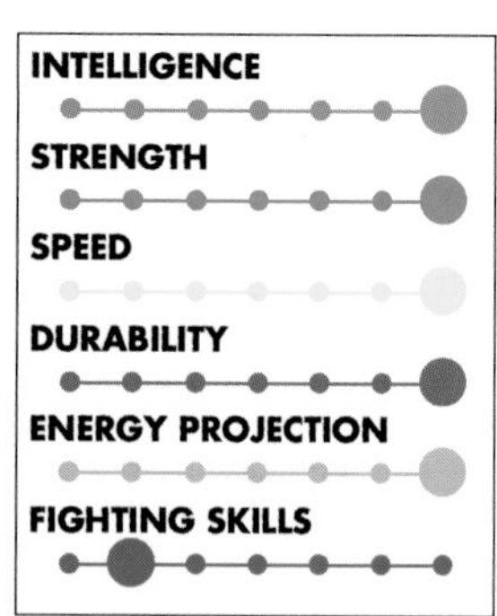

The Beyonder was an omnipotent being wishing to understand human desire. He first interacted with Earth's heroes when he transported them to another world to clash with their most formidable adversaries, during which time Spider-Man received his alien costume. Later, the Beyonder traveled to Earth, seeking out Spider-Man and others for guidance in mortal affairs. His transformation of a skyscraper into solid gold led to a moral dilemma for Spider-Man after he took a Gold Notepad as "payment" for his troubles. Eventually, the Beyonder learned he was part of an incomplete Cosmic Cube, a vast energy matrix responsive to the wills of sentient beings. He now exists as the powerful female entity Kosmos.

BIG WHEEL

Real Name: Jackson Weele
First Appearance: *Amazing Spider-Man* #182 (1978)
Hgt: 5'5"
Wt: 140 lbs.

POWERS/WEAPONS

• Thundering metal wheel with molybdenum steel treads
• Spinning outer shell, protecting rider from attack
• Mechanical arms

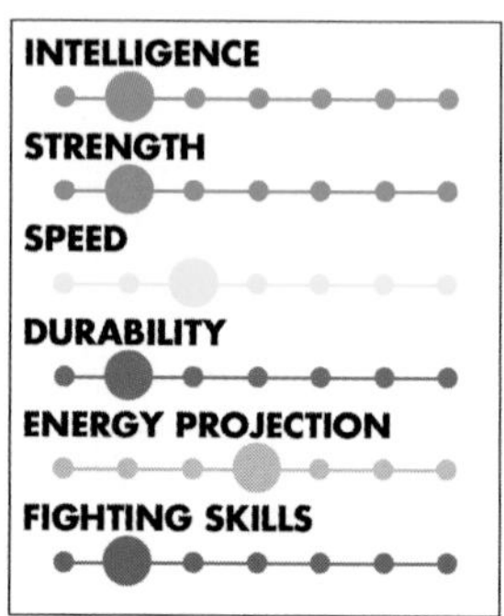

A crooked businessman, Jackson Weele hired Rocket Racer to steal the information that could expose his embezzling. The Racer blackmailed the "Big Wheel" instead, leaving Jackson angry and desperate. Jackson then approached the Tinkerer, who had created Rocket Racer's skateboard, asking him to manufacture a far more powerful device based on his own epithet. But Jackson was too hungry for vengeance to learn to control his new contraption. When Spider-Man rescued Rocket Racer from under the Wheel's crushing treads, Jackson could not prevent his thundering vehicle from crashing into the Hudson River. He survived his plunge and has since returned to action.

BLACK FOX

Real Name: Unrevealed
First Appearance: *Amazing Spider-Man* #255 (1984)
Hgt: 5'9"
Wt: 152 lbs.

POWERS/WEAPONS

• Capable, though aging, athlete
• Smoke grenades
• Burglary tools

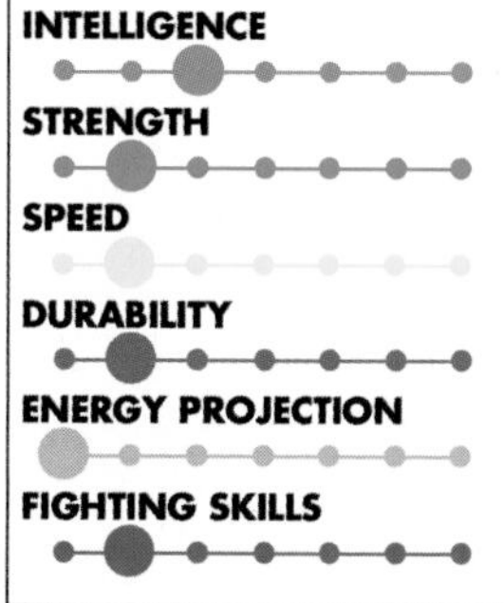

A gentleman criminal, the elderly Black Fox continues to steal from the wealthy — proving still to be a capable thief. He crossed paths with Spider-Man several times, but cunningly took advantage of the wall-crawler's naiveté to convince the hero to let him go free. After being tricked by the Fox one time too many, Spider-Man was no longer willing to believe his adversary's promises to turn over a new leaf and handed him over to the police. The Fox has also crossed paths with Silver Sable, Chance, the Red Ghost and Doctor Doom — in the latter case requiring Spider-Man's assistance to avoid Doom's deadly anger after stealing the Trask Diamond from the powerful dictator.

BLACK CAT

Felicia Hardy grew up as "daddy's little girl," idolizing her father. When Walter Hardy suddenly disappeared, Felicia's mother, Lydia, told her he had died in a plane crash; in reality, he had been incarcerated for his crimes as a notorious cat burglar. Upon discovering the truth about her father, Felicia became determined to follow in his footsteps — embarking on an intense training regimen of martial arts, acrobatics, safe-cracking and lock-picking. Adopting the masked identity of the Black Cat, Felicia's first mission was not to steal a valuable object, but to free her dying father in a daring prison break. She was aided by hired muscle Bruno Grainger and demolitions expert Dr. Boris Korpse. It was during this escape that she first encountered Spider-Man, easily evading the web-slinger with a series of carefully planned traps — as well as the use of her highly suggestive feminine wiles.

Following her father's death, Felicia used her skills to establish herself as New York's premier cat burglar. While Spider-Man attempted to capture the Black Cat a number of times, his efforts were continually thwarted by Felicia's elaborate games of cat and mouse. Although they operated on opposite sides of the law, Felicia had grown increasingly attracted to the heroic Spider-Man; she soon came to desire his heart above all other treasures. To ensnare Spider-Man in her romantic web, Felicia allowed herself to be caught by the crime-fighter and revealed her attraction to him. Spider-Man initially resisted the Black Cat's affections, but he could not hide his own feelings for the seductive beauty for long. After Felicia swore off her criminal activities, the Black Cat and Spider-Man became crime-fighting partners — as well as lovers.

While Spider-Man enjoyed his costumed relationship with Felicia, he also wanted to share his personal life with her. After bringing the Black Cat to his apartment, the web-slinger removed his mask — revealing his secret identity as Peter Parker. Felicia was shocked to learn the hero she

Continued...

Real Name:
Felicia Hardy

First Appearance:
Amazing Spider-Man #194 (1979)

Height:	5'10"
Weight:	120 lbs.
Eye Color:	Green
Hair Color:	Platinum blonde

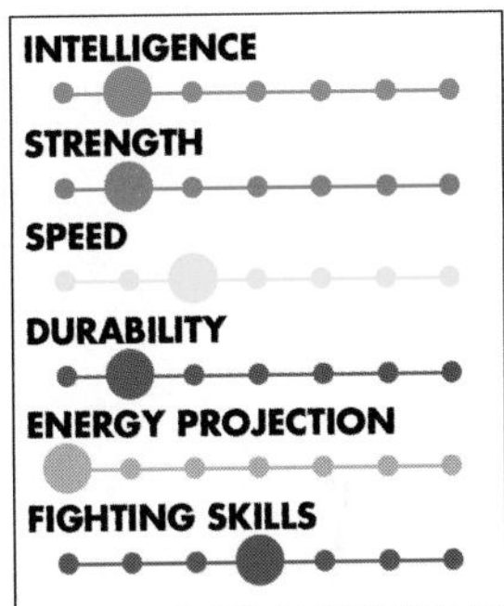

POWERS/ WEAPONS

- Balance-enhancing earrings
- Infrared contact lenses
- Projectile grappling hook
- Extendible electro-claws
- Master thief

Art by Terry Dodson

idolized was truly just an ordinary guy. Peter eventually realized Felicia was only interested in Spider-Man the super hero, not Peter Parker the man.

Although Felicia had employed artfully designed traps at pre-arranged locations to make others believe she possessed the ability to inflict bad luck, the Black Cat in reality had always relied only on her natural physical skills and training as a costumed adventurer. When she was nearly killed in a battle involving Doctor Octopus and the Owl, for which she was granted amnesty for her past crimes, Spider-Man abruptly ended their working partnership — wracked with guilt for having put her in harm's way with no powers of her own. Distraught, Felicia secretly accepted assistance from the Kingpin, who helped her attain genuine powers through scientific means in exchange for a debt. Armed with the ability to cause others to experience bad luck, Felicia soon returned to her former crime-fighting lifestyle.

Felicia's new powers came with the Kingpin's hidden, heavy price — bringing bad luck to those closest to her. Spider-Man, specifically, received a heavy dose of misfortune. Once he discovered this side effect, the hero enlisted Doctor Strange to strip the Black Cat of her powers without her knowledge, leaving her prey to a vicious beating during a dangerous heist. Bitter over her loss and feeling betrayed by Spider-Man, Felicia briefly struck up a relationship with Flash Thompson — mainly to irritate Peter. Flash ended their affair not long after, believing himself too far afield from Felicia's lifestyle of high stakes and high adventure.

Art by Terry Dodson

Felicia eventually accepted the harsh reality of her failed romantic relationship with Peter, and they reconciled their differences. When the Chameleon temporarily removed Spider-Man's powers, the Black Cat teamed with her old partner to help him regain his abilities.

Felicia now operates on the right side of the law as proprietor of the private-security firm Cat's Eye Investigations. She still dons her Black Cat costume whenever the need arises in the course of her work, most recently teaming with Spider-Man to take down a lethal drug dealer. To enhance her natural strength and training, the Black Cat currently employs a series of custom-made devices created by the Tinkerer to imitate the natural abilities of a cat — gadgets paid for with proceeds from her criminal career.

Although she and Peter are no longer romantically involved, Felicia remains quite fond of Spider-Man — seemingly no less so since he became a married man.

BLACK TARANTULA

POWERS/WEAPONS
- Greatly enhanced strength and agility
- Resistant to physical harm
- Can heal near-fatal injuries in himself and others

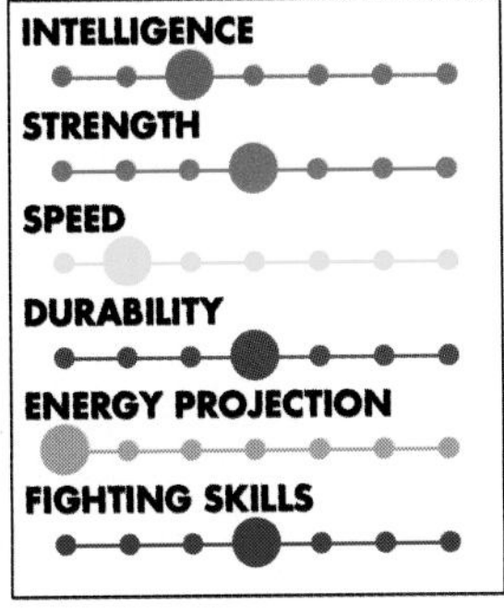

Real Name: Carlos LaMuerto
First Appearance: *Amazing Spider-Man* #419 (1997)

Hgt: 7'0"
Wt: 290 lbs.

For centuries, the powers and position of the Black Tarantula passed from father to first-born son in the Argentinian LaMuerto family. Carlos LaMuerto employed the powers of the Tarantula to extend his family's criminal empire — until his wife, Marina, fled with their son, Fabian. Carlos chased her to New York City and expanded his business there, starting a war with Don Fortunato and the Rose (Jacob Conover). Spider-Man never managed to defeat Carlos, but the Tarantula's sense of honor led him to spare the hero's life and eventually leave New York without his son. Most recently, he was seen working with Roxxon Oil to create super-powered soldiers.

BLACK WIDOW

POWERS/WEAPONS
- Olympic-level athlete and gymnast
- Master martial artist
- Multi-purpose wrist cartridges

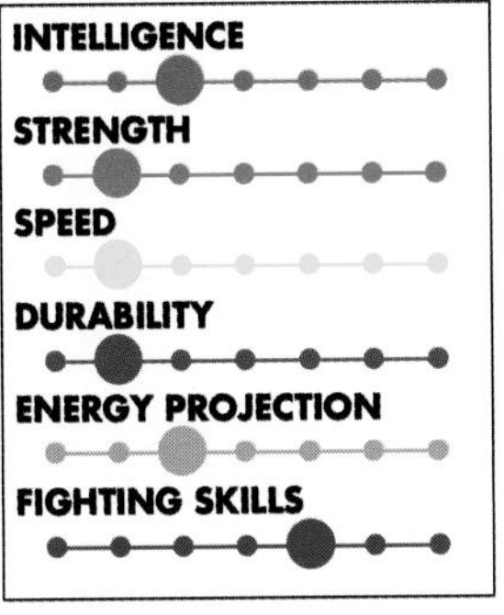

Real Name: Natasha Romanov
First Appearance: *Tales of Suspense* #52 (1964)

Hgt: 5'7"
Wt: 125 lbs.

When the Soviet super-spy called the Black Widow first saw Spider-Man, he was suffering from both the flu and a beating at the hands of the Kingpin. Observing him undetected, she set out to steal the secret of his powers — but soon learned that even weakened, Spider-Man was too powerful for her. Following the Widow's defection, Spider-Man helped Natasha regain her personality after it had been submerged under a sleeper persona during a mission gone awry. Along with S.H.I.E.L.D. and Shang-Chi, Spider-Man and the Widow completed the operation — halting a plot by the cunning and deadly Viper to crash the S.H.I.E.L.D. Helicarrier into the Capitol building in Washington, D.C.

BLADE

POWERS/WEAPONS
- Superhuman strength, senses and stamina
- Immunity to vampire bites
- Accelerated healing factor
- Master martial artist

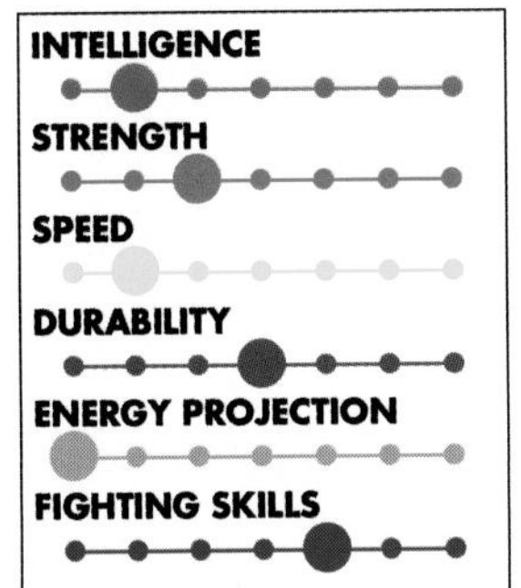

Real Name: Eric Brooks
First Appearance: *Tomb of Dracula* #10 (1973)

Hgt: 6'2"
Wt: 180 lbs.

Born to a woman feasted on by the vampire Deacon Frost, Blade found himself immune to their powers. Half human and half immortal, he has dedicated his life to ridding the world of vampires. Blade's vendetta against the undead has brought him into contact with Spider-Man on several occasions. While he has proven to be an exceptional ally, Blade's methods are reminiscent of those employed by the Punisher — often leaving the two heroes at loggerheads. Blade formerly teamed with the Nightstalkers and the Midnight Sons, but has more recently preferred to work alone.

BLAZE

Real Name: Ashley Crawford, Johnny Storm and Kirk Donahue
First Appearance: *Spectacular Spider-Man* #103 (1985)

Hgt: Various
Wt: Various

POWERS/WEAPONS
- Flame-throwing gun

Blaze is the villain that never was. Three bored Empire State University students — Ashley, Thomas and Barry — set out to prove themselves superior to Spider-Man. Identifying Spider-Man's ties with Peter Parker and J. Jonah Jameson, they created the fictional Blaze to threaten them. When a real Blaze appeared shooting blistering flames, Thomas was apparently badly burnt.

Terrified, the other two owned up to the plan. In reality, the scene had been staged to teach them a lesson. Thomas, uncomfortable with the whole affair, had confessed everything. Working with Spider-Man and the Human Torch, he helped turn the tables on his fellow students.

Blaze appeared for the second and final time during Peter's affair with the Black Cat. When Felicia Hardy's apartment was dramatically bombed, the trail led to Kirk Donahue, a small-time crook who had donned the old Blaze costume, purchased on the cheap off two unidentified ESU students. The Foreigner had hired Kirk to battle Spider-Man and the Black Cat. However, Kirk pushed his luck by trying to extort money from the heroes by torturing an innocent bystander. His plan went too far, and Kirk killed his hostage. The Foreigner then assassinated Kirk for exceeding his mission parameters, framing Spider-Man for the murder.

BOOMERANG

Real Name: Fred Myers
First Appearance: *Tales to Astonish* #81 (1966)

Hgt: 5'11"
Wt: 175 lbs.

POWERS/WEAPONS
- Expert thrower, especially of various trick boomerangs
- Skilled acrobat
- Competent fighter
- Jet boots

INTELLIGENCE
STRENGTH
SPEED
DURABILITY
ENERGY PROJECTION
FIGHTING SKILLS

Having emigrated from Australia to America at a young age, Fred Myers demonstrated a most unusual talent at baseball. Suspended from the major leagues under charges of accepting bribes, he returned to Australia, where he specialized in throwing the boomerang before returning to America to seek employment as an assassin-for-hire.

Spider-Man first encountered Myers' deadly boomerangs while helping S.H.I.E.L.D. director Nick Fury protect the Black Widow from Boomerang and the Silver Samurai. During a later rematch in San Diego, Boomerang had Spider-Man drugged and bound in chains on a boat packed with explosives, but made the classic mistake of underestimating the hero's extraordinary recuperative powers.

Just like his namesake, Boomerang seems to have a way of coming back. At times, he has sought revenge on Spider-Man, joining teams such as the Sinister Syndicate. Other times, he works as muscle-for-hire in the employ of criminals such as Hammerhead — who retained Boomerang's services in his search for the Lifeline Tablet, which bears the secret of eternal youth.

BETTY BRANT

When a young Peter Parker joined the Daily Bugle staff, the newspaper's fiery chief, J. Jonah Jameson, terrified him. But Peter's dislike of Jameson was tempered by his growing fascination with the boss' beautiful secretary, Betty Brant. Like Peter, Betty was a quiet type; she was also new to the Bugle, recently filling her ailing mother's position at the paper.

Real Name:
Elizabeth Brant

First Appearance:
Amazing Spider-Man #4 (1964)

Height: 5'7"
Weight: 125 lbs.
Eye Color: Brown
Hair Color: Brown

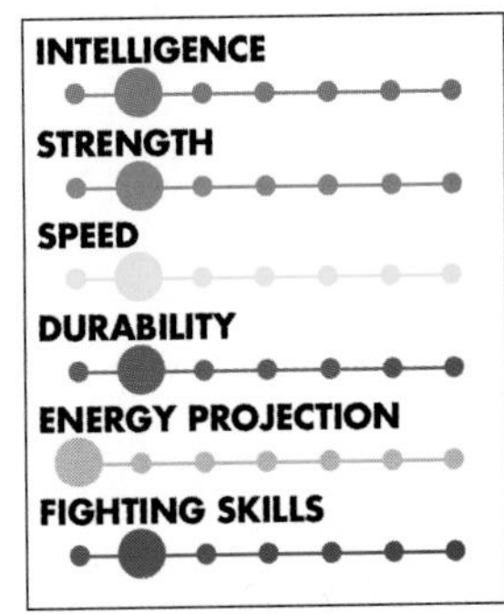

Betty returned Peter's romantic interest, impressed by his seemingly fearless work capturing photographs of Spider-Man. They enjoyed a few dates together, but their growing relationship was soon soured by tragedy. Betty's attorney brother, Bennett Brant, had become entangled in a nasty affair involving Doctor Octopus. When Doc Ock took Betty and Bennett hostage, Peter attempted to rescue the pair as Spider-Man. In the ensuing battle, Bennett was caught in the crossfire. Betty unfairly blamed Spider-Man for her brother's tragic death.

Seeking peace after Bennett's death, Betty ended her relationship with Peter and married Ned Leeds. Their union was not to last: Betty eventually entered into an affair with Flash Thompson and soon after separated from Ned. When the Hobgoblin was falsely identified as Flash and then Ned, the combined trauma drove Betty to the brink of madness.

After Ned's murder at the hands of the Foreigner's assassins, Betty fled to the sanctuary of the Cult of Love. Brainwashed, Betty was heroically rescued by Flash and freed from the cult's control — but her mind was still fragile. It was not until she faced Mister Fear that she was finally able to begin her mental recovery.

Her healing process was capped by a confrontation with Ned's ghost during a demonic invasion of Earth, leading to a great change in Betty. The woman who once rejected Peter for being too much of a thrill-seeker became a strong-willed, gun-toting investigative reporter. She single-handedly tracked down the Foreigner and fought his high-powered assassins to a standstill. She even discovered the true identity of the Hobgoblin and sent him to prison by recording his arrogant criminal confessions.

Betty and Flash have slowly rekindled their relationship, even as Flash battles alcoholism. Meanwhile, Betty's spirit remains strong, as one of the best investigative reporters on the Daily Bugle's staff.

Art by Steve Ditko

BRAINSTORM

Real Name: Jimmy, last name unrevealed
First Appearance: *Web of Spider-Man* #33 (1987)

Hgt: 6'10"
Wt: 300 lbs.

POWERS/WEAPONS
- Superhuman strength
- Projection of psychoses

In the Mad Dog Ward of a private mental hospital, Dr. Hope experimented on patients to create an assassin for the Kingpin. Forcing Jimmy to believe he was sleeping, the psychiatrist freed him to act out his rage without compunction. When Spider-Man was drugged and imprisoned in the ward, Hope sent Brainstorm to kill the wall-crawler; the attempt failed. Hope later mutated Jimmy further — accentuating the primitive reptilian part of his brain, and transforming him into a psionic and physical powerhouse. Sent to silence a reporter investigating the ward, Brainstorm was again defeated by Spider-Man — aided this time by former patient Captain Zero.

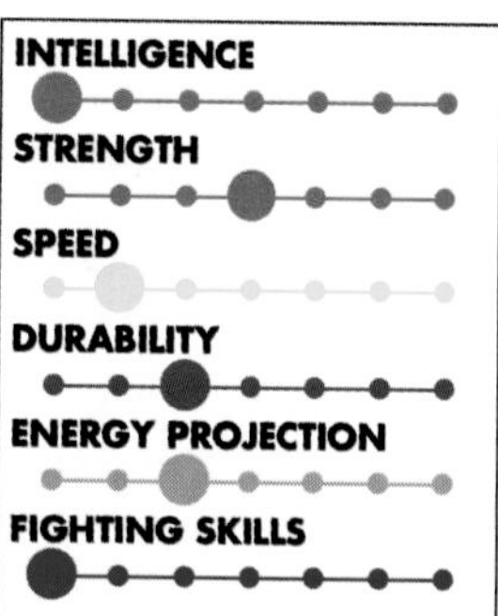

BRAND CORP.

First Appearance: *Amazing Adventures* #11 (1972)

A division of the Roxxon Oil conglomerate, the Brand Corporation has developed several superhumans for its employers — including the Griffin, Will O' the Wisp and the Killer Shrike. The Brand Corporation's larcenous dealings were made public through the efforts of Spider-Man and Will O' the Wisp, although Roxxon successfully denied any knowledge or involvement in these activities. Then-company president James Melvin was convicted, though the firm was re-launched under Herbert Landon.

BROTHER POWER

Real Name: Achmed Korba
First Appearance: *Spectacular Spider-Man* #4 (1977)

Hgt: 6'4"
Wt: 225 lbs.

POWERS/WEAPONS
- Superhuman strength
- Projection of energy blasts

A smuggler in Saigon, Achmed Korba observed the arrival of the Man-Beast and became his servant. The evolved wolf known as Man-Beast empowered Korba, but forced him to unite with a being of purity to use his powers. Korba chose Sha Shan to be his wife and partner in the Legion of Light, transforming her into Sister Sun. Moving to the United States, the cult spread its false message of love and light while secretly gathering an army under the control of the Man-Beast. Ultimately, Sha Shan turned against Achmed, and he burnt himself out in a futile effort to destroy her. The Man-Beast was defeated by the combined efforts of Spider-Man, Razorback and Flash Thompson.

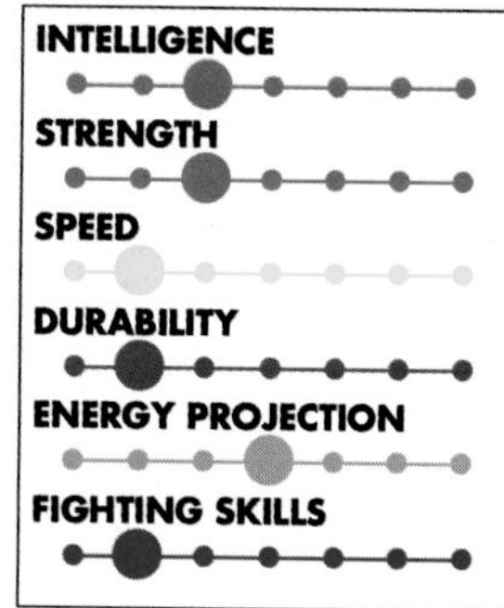

BURGLAR

As Spider-Man prepared to leave a Manhattan TV studio, gloating from his first foray into show business, a Burglar ran past him — chased by a police officer, who yelled at the wall-crawler to trip the crook before he could get to the elevator. The carefree Spider-Man refused; the Burglar escaped.

Days later, the Burglar attempted to rob the Parker home in Queens. When Ben Parker surprised him, the Burglar shot and killed him — then ran away. Learning his uncle had been murdered, Peter tracked the Burglar to the Acme Warehouse. There, Peter Parker discovered the murderer was the same criminal he had allowed to go free at the TV station. In that terrible second of awareness, Peter gained his lifetime mantra: With great power, there must also come great responsibility.

But there was nothing coincidental about the robbery attempt. The Burglar had once shared a cell with a notorious gangster, Dutch Malone, who would talk in his sleep about a treasure he had hidden in his home. After seeing a TV show on Malone's life, the Burglar went to the station to find out where the house was located. On that fateful day, he learned the Parkers owned the home in question.

Once released from prison, the Burglar rented the now-deserted Parker home and tore the house apart, looking to uncover what he could not years earlier. Finding nothing, he tracked down May Parker's nursing home and threatened its psychiatrist, Dr. Ludwig Rinehart. Rinehart faked Aunt May's death so the Burglar could interrogate her without interference from her nephew. The Burglar then attempted to kill Rinehart — who, it turned out, was Mysterio in disguise, running the nursing home for his own duplicitous ends.

When Spider-Man arrived, Mysterio defeated him and made off for Queens; the battered web-slinger pursued. When Mysterio realized the promised treasure was unlikely to surface, he fought Spider-Man once more — then departed, leaving the hero drugged. The Burglar, however, remained as tenacious as ever. He easily captured the feeble Peter, tied him up in the abandoned Acme Warehouse and confessed the entire plot. The Burglar left, only to return with a terrified Aunt May. In a last-ditch effort, a reinvigorated Spider-Man pulled off his mask — revealing himself to the Burglar as Peter Parker. Convinced Peter would kill him in retaliation for his uncle's murder, the Burglar suffered a fatal heart attack. As for the treasure — May and Ben had found the box behind the wallboards years ago; silverfish had eaten the contents.

Real Name:
Unrevealed

First Appearance:
Amazing Fantasy #15 (1962)

Height:	5'9"
Weight:	150 lbs.
Eye Color:	Blue
Hair Color:	Blond

INTELLIGENCE

STRENGTH

SPEED

DURABILITY

ENERGY PROJECTION

FIGHTING SKILLS

Art by Steve Ditko

BARNEY BUSHKIN

Real Name: Barney Bushkin
First Appearance: *Amazing Spider-Man* #27 (1965)

Hgt: 5'8"
Wt: 200 lbs.

INTELLIGENCE
STRENGTH
SPEED
DURABILITY
ENERGY PROJECTION
FIGHTING SKILLS

Barney Bushkin is photo editor of the Daily Globe, chief rival of the Daily Bugle. Bushkin shares J. Jonah Jameson's energy, but with more enthusiasm and less acerbic surliness. Early in his career, Peter Parker attempted to sell photos to the Globe; he was dissuaded by Bushkin's excessive curiosity concerning his relationship with Spider-Man. Bushkin later hired Peter for the Globe at the direction of the newspaper's publisher, K.J. Clayton, in an attempt to steal the Bugle's best staffers. After a few weeks working with the overbearing and curious Bushkin, Peter returned to the Bugle to bask once more in Jonah's sunny disposition.

JONATHAN CAESAR

Real Name: Jonathan Caesar
First Appearance: *Amazing Spider-Man* #304

Hgt: 5'6'
Wt: 180 lbs.

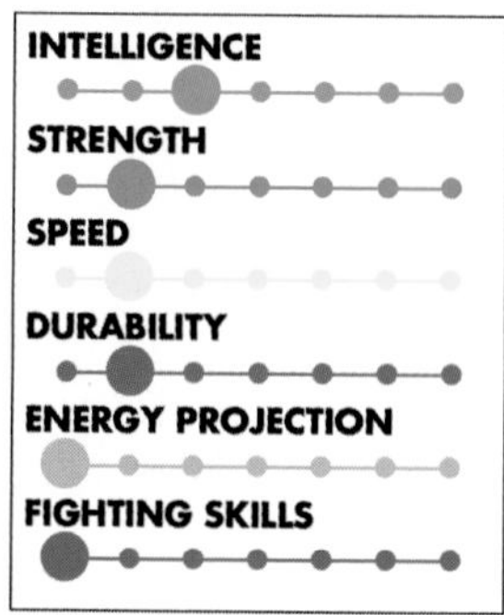

Jonathan Caesar was neighbor and landlord to Peter Parker and Mary Jane Watson in their spacious Manhattan loft. This was no coincidence: Caesar was infatuated with Mary Jane, a famous model. He abducted her, and hired Styx and Stone to discourage anyone who dared investigate — such as Spider-Man. However, MJ affected her own rescue, KO'ing Caesar with a lamp and stealing his gun. Caesar was imprisoned, but had MJ and Peter evicted in his absence. Upon his release, Caesar attempted to kill Mary Jane, but was himself murdered by Hal Goldman — another obsessive fan who sought to possess MJ himself.

CAGE

Real Name: Carl Lucas, a.k.a. Luke Cage
First Appearance: *Luke Cage, Hero for Hire* #1 (1972)

Hgt: 6'6"
Wt: 425 lbs.

Imprisoned on false charges, Carl Lucas was subjected to an unusual experiment that granted him bulletproof skin and superhuman strength. He later escaped, assuming the identity Luke Cage, and set out to use his newfound powers to help clear his name. Also adopting the alias Power Man, Cage became a hero-for-hire to pay the rent — but was always willing to help those in need, money or no. Although best known as the partner of Iron Fist, he has also assisted Spider-Man from time to time — even though J. Jonah Jameson initially hired Cage to capture the web-slinger.

POWERS/WEAPONS

- Superhuman strength
- Abnormally dense muscle and bone tissue
- Bulletproof skin

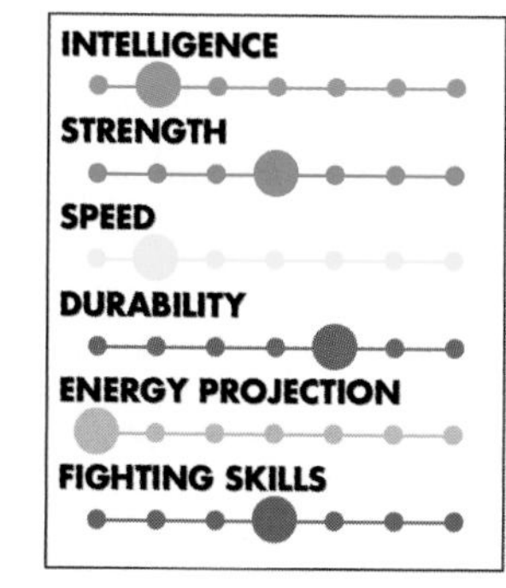

CALYPSO

POWERS/WEAPONS

- Witchcraft
- Potions, powders and spells
- Control of animals via Yorumba spirit drum
- Can revive the dead

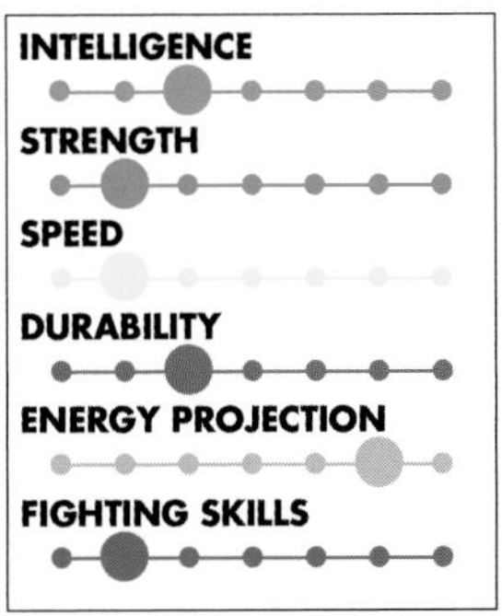

Real Name: Calypso Ezili
First Appearance: *Amazing Spider-Man* #209 (1980)

Hgt: 5'8"
Wt: 120 lbs.

Calypso grew up on a Caribbean island, surrounded by black magic. She met Kraven the Hunter after his first defeat by Spider-Man. As his lover, she manipulated his pride until he returned to battle Spider-Man, again unsuccessfully. Following Kraven's death, Calypso murdered her sister to acquire supernatural powers. She then dispatched the Lizard to seek revenge against Spider-Man, but was killed by the beast herself. Her spirit subsequently possessed Glory Grant and forced her to help perform a voodoo resurrection of her own body. Calypso later teamed with Alyosha Kravinoff, though he resisted her attempts to manipulate him and cold-bloodedly murdered her.

CAPTAIN AMERICA

POWERS/WEAPONS

- Peak-human athlete
- Expert combatant
- Unbreakable shield

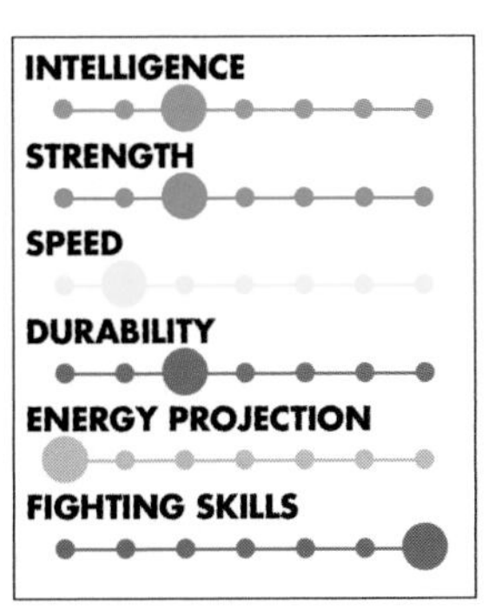

Real Name: Steve Rogers
First Appearance: *Captain America Comics* #1 (1941)

Hgt: 6'2"
Wt: 220 lbs.

Empowered by the military's experimental Super-Soldier Serum, sickly Steve Rogers became America's sentinel of liberty during World War II. Facing menaces such as the Red Skull, he was trapped in suspended animation near the war's end. Revived in the present, he continues his never-ending crusade against injustice. As leader of the Avengers and the country's pre-eminent super hero, Captain America has fought side by side with Spider-Man on numerous occasions. He even sponsored the wall-crawler's brief membership on the team. Captain America is one of the few heroes respected by almost all others.

CAPTAIN BRITAIN

POWERS/WEAPONS

- Superhuman strength
- Flight
- Force-field
- Enhanced senses
- Projection of energy blasts

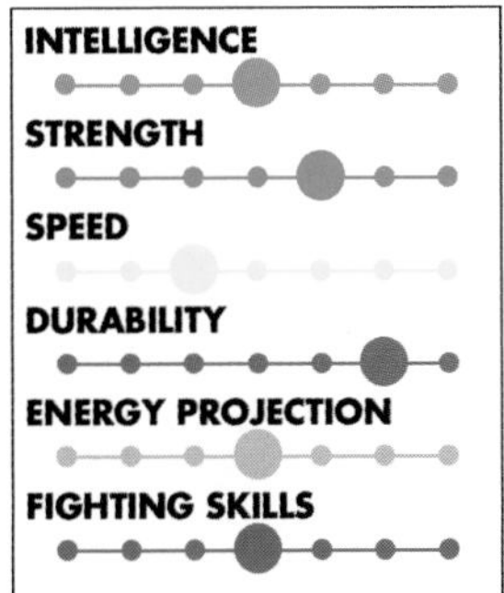

Real Name: Brian Braddock
First Appearance: *Captain Britain* #1 (1976)

Hgt: 6'6"
Wt: 257 lbs.

Brian Braddock was selected by the god-wizard Merlin to be Earth's representative in the reality-spanning Captain Britain Corps. Already an established hero in Britain, Brian first met Spider-Man during a student-exchange program when he roomed with Peter Parker. The two became fast friends while fighting Arcade. Captain Britain co-founded the super-team Excalibur, and he and Spider-Man have encountered one another occasionally since then. Brian has subsequently become ruler of Otherworld — a glorious kingdom positioned at the nexus of reality, where science and sorcery exist as one.

CARDIAC

Real Name: Elias Wirtham
First Appearance: *Amazing Spider-Man* #344 (1991)

Hgt: 6'5"
Wt: 300 lbs.

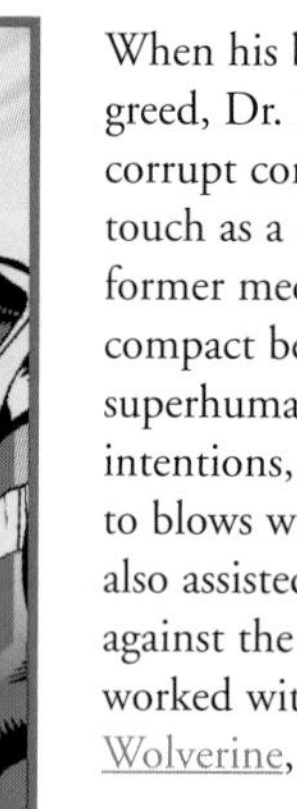

When his brother died due to a drug company's greed, Dr. Elias Wirtham set out to bring down corrupt corporations and others the law could not touch as a costumed vigilante. To that end, the former medical scientist replaced his heart with a compact beta-particle reactor — granting him superhuman strength. Despite Cardiac's noble intentions, his violent methods have brought him to blows with Spider-Man. However, the two have also assisted one another on occasion, notably against the Rhino and Boomerang. Cardiac has worked with and against Nightwatch and Wolverine, as well.

POWERS/WEAPONS

- Superhuman strength and durability
- Projection of beta-particle blasts from electrified staff

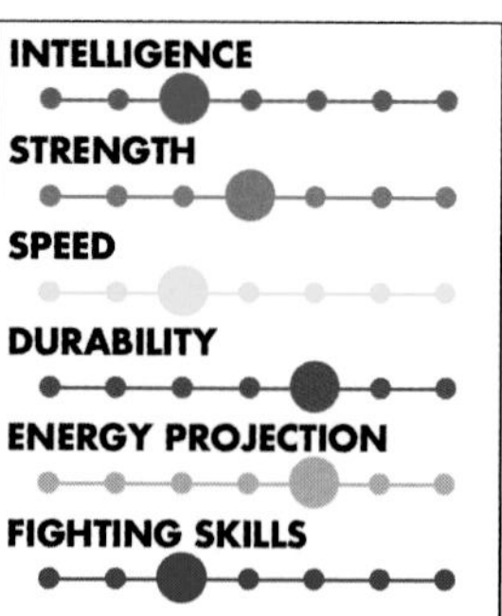

CARLYLE

Real Name: Unrevealed, Carlyle assumed to be alias
First Appearance: *Amazing Spider-Man* #43 (2002)

Hgt: 6'1"
Wt: 180 lbs.

Playing on Doctor Octopus' ego, Carlyle invited Otto Octavius to meet him at his corporate headquarters in California. He then trapped the villain and revealed his own nefarious plan: to unlock the secret of Doc Ock's mechanical arms, which he accomplished in short order. Leaving to put his newly constructed tentacles to the test, Carlyle abandoned Doc Ock to die. Octavius managed to escape, setting the scene for a final confrontation between the two. When Carlyle proved superior, Doc Ock and Spider-Man realized their only chance to defeat him was to join forces. Doctor Octopus then took advantage of Spider-Man's weariness to escape.

POWERS/WEAPONS

- Full-body armor
- Six extendable steel tentacles capable of firing powerful jolts of energy

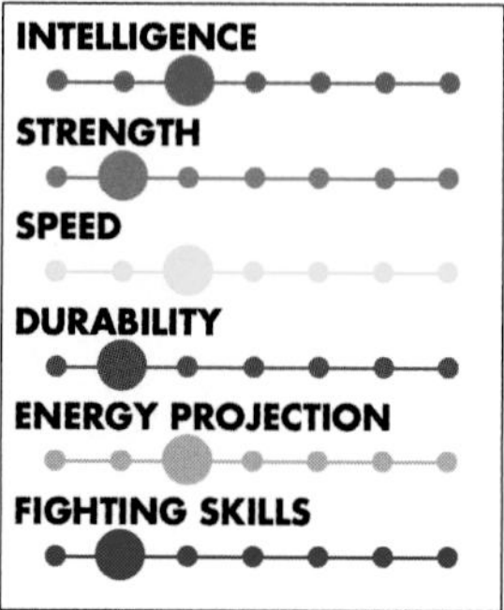

CARYN & BARKER

Real Name: Caryn Earle and Barker the Dog
First Appearance: *Peter Parker: Spider-Man* #30 (2001)

Hgt: Caryn: 5'6" / Barker: 2'2"
Wt: Caryn: 120 lbs. / Barker: 105 lbs.

Peter Parker is unlucky in many respects, but not when it comes to attractive neighbors. To wit: Mary Jane Watson, Glory Grant and Bambi, Candi and Randi. Peter's latest apartment is small and dingy, but the view from his fire-escape balcony looks across the alley to the apartment of Caryn Earle and her uncannily intelligent rottweiler, Barker. Caryn flirts shamelessly with Peter, hanging her lingerie out to dry in full view. She even crashed his apartment as he was toweling off from a bath. Peter and Caryn enjoyed one date together — but with the return of Mary Jane, their relationship seems almost certainly over before it truly began.

CARNAGE

Sentenced to eleven consecutive life terms for the slaughter of numerous innocents, psychopathic serial killer Cletus Kasady shared time with his new cellmate, Eddie Brock. Also known as Venom, Brock had become separated from his symbiotic other half, but the creature sought out Brock in his jail cell and bonded with its host once more. As Venom, the two easily smashed through the cell wall and vanished into the night, failing to notice the trace of alien biomass they left behind.

The symbiote that had possessed Brock — and at one time, Peter Parker — belonged to a less-violent caste of a bloodthirsty race of space-faring parasites. Not so its offspring. Quickly setting about to consume a host, the biomass melded with the murderous Kasady — and the deadly symbiotic duo calling itself Carnage emerged. Far more lethal than Venom, Carnage left jail to embark on a murderous spree, killing a graduate student at Empire State University who happened to be friends with Peter.

Learning of the recent escape of Brock's cellmate, Spider-Man identified Kasady as a former resident of St. Estes Home for Boys — an orphanage destroyed by arson. On a hunch, Peter returned to the ruined scene of that crime. There, Spider-Man battled Carnage — but the powerful entity easily defeated him and disappeared. Along with the Human Torch, Spider-Man traveled to the island on which he had sequestered Brock to inform him of Carnage's rampage.

Continued...

Real Name:
Cletus Kasady

First Appearance:
Amazing Spider-Man #344 (1991)

Height:	6'1"
Weight:	190 lbs.
Eye Color:	Green
Hair Color:	Red

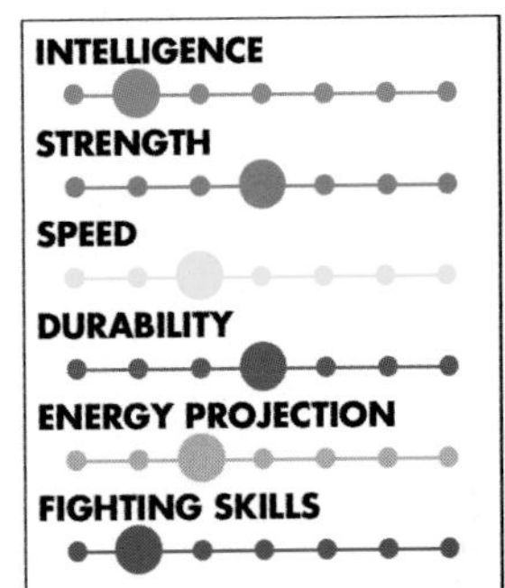

POWERS/ WEAPONS

- Symbiotically enhanced strength
- Generation of snares, swing lines and bladed weapons
- Dampening of Spider-Man's spider-sense

Art by Mark Bagley

CARNAGE

Identifying a golden opportunity, Brock agreed to help defeat Carnage — but only in return for his own freedom. Spider-Man had little choice but to consent. True to his word, Venom helped the two heroes incapacitate Carnage. Spider-Man could not live up to the agreement; with help from the Fantastic Four, he ambushed Venom and took him into custody.

Carnage was remanded to Ravencroft Institute. Resisting all treatment, his powers made him nearly impossible to contain; shortly thereafter, he escaped. On the lam from Ravencroft, Carnage teamed with fellow lunatics Shriek, Carrion, Demogoblin and Doppelganger. To battle this threat, a reluctant Venom again joined forces with Spider-Man. Aided by other heroes — including Deathlok, the Black Cat, Captain America and Iron Fist — they returned Kasady to Ravencroft. His incarceration did not last long. During a subsequent jailbreak, Kasady made it his mission to kill the only man who had ever befriended him, Billy Bentine — hoping to perpetuate his message of chaos and explode the conventions dictating that friendship should be repaid in kind. Spider-Man defeated Carnage only after Bentine tricked the creature into returning to human form, rendering Kasady vulnerable to a simple knockout punch.

With other Ravencroft escapes attempted and ultimately foiled, Kasady seemed to be reveling in the thrill of it all. But the symbiote had another trick up its own sleeve: Attempting the unexpected, it abandoned Kasady and overwhelmed John Jameson, chief of security at Ravencroft. Tracking down Spider-Man — Ben Reilly, at the time — the symbiote allowed the web-slinger to defeat its new host. With Jameson out of the picture, the creature overwhelmed Ben, creating the near-unbeatable Spider-Carnage. But Ben's willpower won out; he was able to contain the symbiote's murderous urges long enough to return it to Ravencroft, where it was subdued once more. The determined symbiote soon adopted another approach: It attempted to possess the space-faring Silver Surfer, creating Cosmic Carnage. Already familiar with the deadly race of symbiotes, the Surfer overcame the creature and encased it in a container of ethereal energy.

Art by Lee Weeks

The symbiote eventually escaped and returned to its host, only to be forcibly re-absorbed by Venom — leaving Kasady powerless. But just as the world began to believe Carnage was gone for good, Kasady escaped Ravencroft yet again — called into the other-dimensional Negative Zone by a distant voice. The voice belonged to another symbiote. Although not Kasady's original parasitic partner, this creature was every bit as deadly. Merged again with an entity more evil than himself, Kasady battled Spider-Man and Blastaar. Though recaptured, the deadly Carnage had found its way back into the world.

CARRION

Carrion's origins have long been shrouded in mystery, the truth twisted by many people. The Green Goblin, the Jackal and the High Evolutionary have all confessed to creating false evidence regarding Carrion. For some time, Carrion was believed to be an ordinary human mutated by an experimental virus. However, it has since become clear that Carrion's original claim is the truth: He is a clone of his creator — Dr. Miles Warren, a.k.a. the Jackal. Following a heated battle with Spider-Man, Warren disappeared — leaving his newly created clone in an accelerated-growth capsule. In Warren's absence, the malfunctioning device altered the clone into the superhuman Carrion.

Carrion possessed great physical power, plus a brilliant and cunning intellect. With Warren's memories driving him to seek Spider-Man's destruction, he coerced Randy Vale (Darter) to act as his reluctant human accomplice with death threats and the promise of power. While Carrion proved invulnerable to attacks by living beings, he fell prey to the amorphous creature known as the Spider-Amoeba, created by similar means as himself.

Although the original Carrion was destroyed, the Red Dust he wielded in his strange life proved to be just as dangerous in the wake of his death. The dust, renamed the Carrion Virus, infected an Empire State University graduate student named Malcolm McBride, transforming him into Carrion II. Following a heated battle with Spider-Man, Shriek sacrificed herself to cure McBride of the Carrion Virus, returning him to human form.

The most recent person to fall victim to the Carrion Virus was Dr. William Allen, a scientist infected while studying the Jackal's corpse. Carrion III created a Zombie Plague that left his victims subject to his commands. He was eventually defeated by Spider-Man and is now in government custody, where researchers are seeking a cure for the Carrion Virus once and for all.

Real Name:
Not Applicable

First Appearance:
Spectacular Spider-Man #25 (1978)

Height:	5'10"
Weight:	175 lbs.
Eye Color:	Yellow
Hair Color:	None

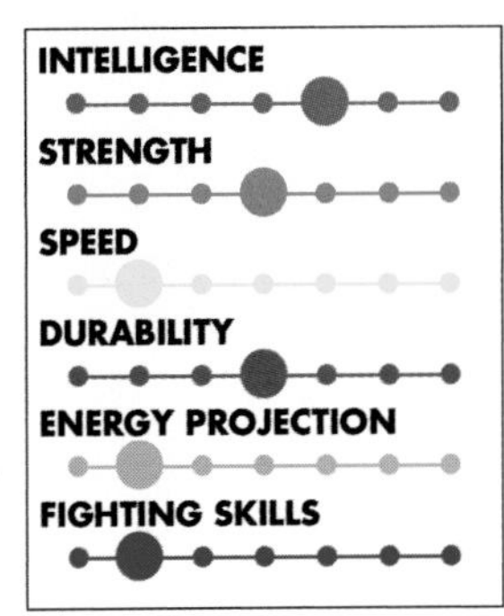

POWERS/ WEAPONS

- Can mentally repel living matter
- Levitation
- Destruction of living matter by touch
- Creation of Red Dust — which can render victims unconscious or susceptible to suggestion, or act as super-acid or flesh-eating bacteria

Art by Alex Saviuk

CAT

Real Name: Unrevealed
First Appearance: *Amazing Spider-Man* #30 (1965)

Hgt: 5'10"
Wt: 150 lbs.

This mysterious cat burglar made a name for himself by robbing the apartment of J. Jonah Jameson, who then posted a large reward for his capture. Spider-Man sought the bounty, but the Cat held his own until caught by police. Years later, the same man stole the Prowler's costume and worked for Belladonna. He led Spider-Man into Belladonna's trap, but she betrayed her ally and snared him along with the web-slinger. Spider-Man broke them both out, and the Cat nearly achieved vengeance on his employer — until Spider-Man sent them both to jail.

POWERS/WEAPONS

- Master of stealth
- Can scale walls

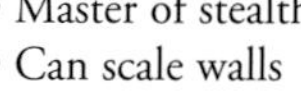

INTELLIGENCE
STRENGTH
SPEED
DURABILITY
ENERGY PROJECTION
FIGHTING SKILLS

CHANCE

Real Name: Nicholas Powell
First Appearance: *Web of Spider-Man* #15 (1986)

Hgt: 6'0"
Wt: 185 lbs.

A former professional gambler, Nicholas Powell is now Chance — a mercenary-for-hire who stakes his own fee against the success of his assignments. A compulsive risk-taker, Chance once offered an employee the option of a small payment or a choice between a pair of boxes — one containing a much larger sum of money; the other, a cobra. Chance's employers have included the Foreigner and the Life Foundation. His missions have brought him into conflict with Spider-Man, who nevertheless assisted Chance when the Life Foundation turned on him. Chance's compulsive gambling has often contributed to his downfall, as he will risk everything on a needless challenge.

POWERS/WEAPONS

- Flight-enabled battlesuit
- Wrist-blasters
- Active heads-up display radar system

INTELLIGENCE
STRENGTH
SPEED
DURABILITY
ENERGY PROJECTION
FIGHTING SKILLS

CHTYLOK

Real Name: Chtylok the Che-K'n Kau
First Appearance: *Sensational Spider-Man* #13 (1997)

Hgt: 25'
Wt: 8 tons

In the distant past, dwellers of the isolated, Antarctic jungle known as the Savage Land worshipped the immense, subterranean creature called Chtylok. When Roxxon Oil sought to exploit the Savage Land's resources, a steady flow of water poured into the jungle's underground tunnels and awakened Chtylok. The creature's resultant rage drew the attention of the Hulk. The two fought for several days — eventually emerging in the midst of a struggle between Spider-Man, Ka-Zar, Stegron and Roxxon. As the floodwaters drained into the hole created by the two behemoths, Chtylok ate Dr. Gerald Roth, the Roxxon agent responsible for the debacle.

POWERS/WEAPONS

- Immense strength
- Winged flight
- Razor-sharp beak and claws
- Rock-hard hooves
- Semi-prehensile tail

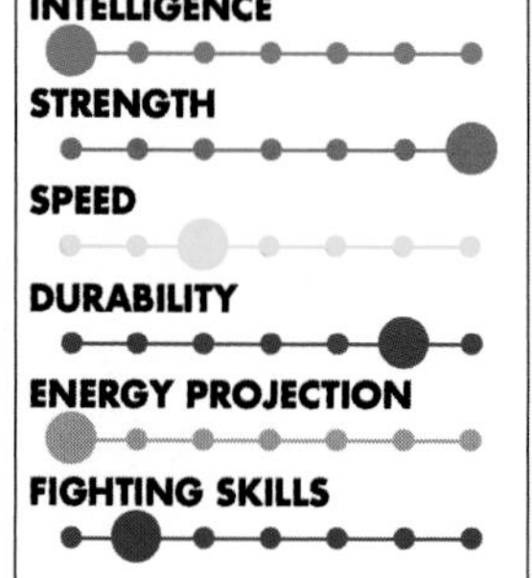

CHAMELEON

The Chameleon's cunning schemes have established him as one of Spider-Man's deadliest foes. The Chameleon generally prefers to avoid direct violence, instead relying on manipulation and deceit to achieve his goals. Particularly when opposed by Spider-Man, he has allied himself with more physically commanding figures, such as Hammerhead. Although he initially employed a variety of techniques to assume different identities, he later underwent a special process that altered his skin and flesh — allowing him to effortlessly change his body, clothing, face and voice.

Real Name:
Dmitri "Kravinoff" Smerdyakov
First Appearance:
Amazing Spider-Man #1 (1963)

Height:	Unrevealed
Weight:	Unrevealed
Eye Color:	Brown
Hair Color:	Unrevealed

The Chameleon first encountered Spider-Man during a Soviet plot to steal a set of secret U.S. military plans. Posing as Spider-Man in the daring robbery, the Chameleon was nearly able to frame the web-slinger for the crime — but the hero ultimately exposed his double's disguise. Following his deportation, the Chameleon quietly slipped back into New York and sought the aid of his childhood friend — Sergei Kravinoff, better known as Kraven the Hunter. Working together, the Chameleon and Kraven attempted to exact revenge on Spider-Man, but the wall-crawler defeated their joint attack.

Although the Chameleon and Kraven shared the same father and each frequently battled Spider-Man, Dmitri and Sergei exhibited starkly differing backgrounds and personalities. While Kraven was esteemed as the proud heir to the Kravinoff legacy, Dmitri was unknowingly the illegitimate offspring of his father's dalliance with a humble household servant. Throughout their shared childhood, Kraven frequently beat Dmitri and treated his half-brother as little more than a lowly subject. The Chameleon supressed the memory of this brutal treatment, remaining devoted to Kraven. This subservient relationship between the two would prove disastrous to the Chameleon's mental state many years later.

Continued...

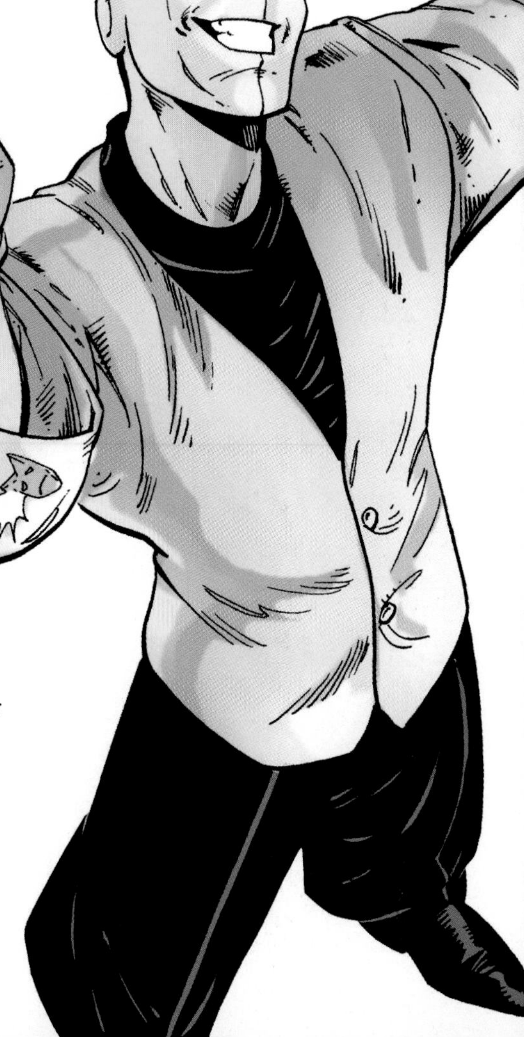

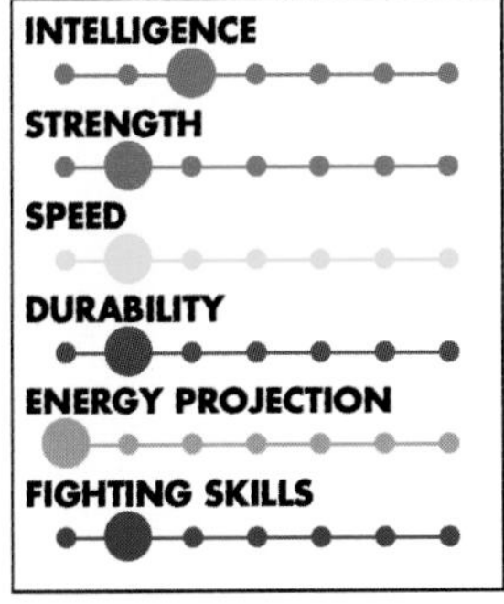

POWERS/ WEAPONS

- Can mimic any human or near-human shape
- Projection of almost any style of clothing
- Flawless reproduction of human voices, faces and mannerisms

Art by Luke Ross

CHAMELEON

The Chameleon has engaged in a variety of plots in his attempts to destroy Spider-Man, but Harry Osborn suggested Dmitri's greatest scheme during one of his spells as the Green Goblin. Osborn maliciously proposed that the Chameleon create lifelike androids to impersonate Peter Parker's long-dead parents. He promised that Peter would reveal his connection to Spider-Man once his "parents" won his trust, allowing the Chameleon to exact the vengeance on the web-slinger he had so desperately craved since his first defeat.

The Chameleon's robots were able to fool Peter for a time, until he discovered the cruel deception. Furious with the Chameleon for tampering with the memory of his late parents, Spider-Man tracked the villain to the deserted Kravinoff mansion — where Kraven had killed himself some time before. Facing a beserker Spider-Man, the Chameleon's suppressed memories were triggered by fear. Suddenly realizing what his "friend" had done to him, he collapsed in a catatonic state.

Art by Steve Ditko

Trapped in a seemingly perpetual state of madness, the Chameleon was imprisoned at Ravencroft Institute. Driven to a nearly psychotic thirst for vengeance by his insanity, the Chameleon boldly escaped Ravencroft and managed to capture, drug and unmask Spider-Man. After finally learning the hero's identity and realizing he was Kraven's half-brother, the Chameleon used sets, disguises and drugs to leave Peter believing himself to be Herbert Filmore Smith, a deluded writer locked in an insane asylum. The Chameleon, meanwhile, attempted to pass himself off as Peter Parker. Ultimately, Mary Jane Watson foiled the seemingly triumphant Chameleon's plans. Knowing her husband beyond any shadow of doubt, Mary Jane was able to see through even the Chameleon's advanced disguise and overpower him with a baseball bat.

While he has always lived a dangerous lifestyle, the Chameleon faced and survived two instances of virtually certain death. First, he was gunned down by Kraven's son, Alyosha Kravinoff, but recovered from near-fatal wounds. Then, in a moment of passing lucidity, the Chameleon arranged to meet Spider-Man atop the Brooklyn Bridge. To atone for his sins, Dmitri attempted to take his own life by leaping into the water — but he once again cheated death, washing up on shore still alive. He was returned to the confines of Ravencroft not long after.

Since permanently adopting his late half-brother's identity, the Chameleon seems also to have acquired many of Kraven's fighting techniques. Although he is now certifiably insane, he remains a dangerous and unstable threat to Spider-Man — especially if he retains his knowledge of the web-slinger's true identity under his haze of dementia.

CIRCUS OF CRIME

First Appearance:
Hulk #3 (1962)

Antoro, Blackwing, Clown, Fire-Eater, the Great Gambonnos, Human Cannonball, Iron Jack Baker, Livewire, Princess Python, the Professor, Rajah, the Ringmaster, Strong Man, Tarrax the Tamer, Teena the Fat Lady. Everybody loves the Greatest Show on Earth, but the Circus of Crime is a true sleeper. With the crowd rendered helpless by the hypnotic projector in the Ringmaster's hat, the Circus would strip them of their valuables. A post-hypnotic suggestion would send the audience home, convinced they had enjoyed a great show. But you can't please all the people all the time, and you never know when there's going to be a super hero in the audience — like Peter Parker and Matt Murdock, also known as Spider-Man and Daredevil.

The cast of the Circus of Crime changed over time, with leadership alternating between the Ringmaster and Clown (a.k.a. Funny Man). They briefly adopted the name Masters of Menace — but all to no avail. The judges were not amused, and the evil entertainers spent more time in prison than out of it. The Ringmaster, for one, finally listened to the critics and decided to go straight.

CLOAK & DAGGER

POWERS/WEAPONS

- Living portal to Dark Dimension (Cloak)
- Emits knives of living light (Dagger)

Real Name: Tyrone Johnson (Cloak)
Tandy Bowen (Dagger)

First Appearance: *Spectacular Spider-Man* #64 (1982)

Hgt: Cloak: 5'9"
Dagger: 5'5"

Wt: Cloak: 155 lbs.
Dagger: 115 lbs.

Runaways Tyrone Johnson and Tandy Bowen were kidnapped by agents of an experimental chemist working for the Maggia and used as guinea pigs to test a new addictive drug intended to replace heroin with a cheaper substitute. Tyrone and Tandy survived; however, the drug released unsuspected latent abilities, transforming them into Cloak and Dagger. Thereafter, they used their powers to track down and destroy those who traded in drugs.

Spider-Man's path crossed theirs as they took on the forces of Silvermane, who was desperate to capture Dagger and use her abundant life force to restore his body — then reduced to little more than a near-dead shell. Cloak and Dagger later joined Spider-Man to quash the mercenary arsonist Firebrand, battling to defend the residents of a downtown shelter for the homeless against a property developer with little respect for the law. Spider-Man subsequently sought their help to defeat a ragtag army of criminally insane beings assembled by Carnage. They teamed again to defeat Thule, leader of a neo-Nazi cult who was in fact an unwitting pawn of Mephisto. In defeat, Thule was consumed by his dark master.

COBRA

Real Name: Klaus Voorhees
First Appearance: *Journey into Mystery* #98 (1963)
Hgt: 5'10"
Wt: 160 lbs.

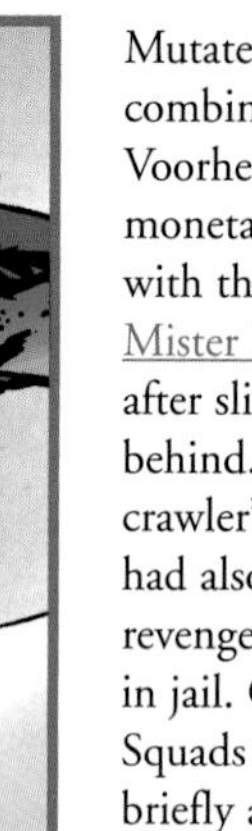

Mutated by the bite of an irradiated cobra combined with an experimental anti-toxin, Klaus Voorhees embarked on a life of crime purely for monetary gain. Early in his career, Cobra partnered with the bloodthirsty and superhumanly strong Mister Hyde. Cobra first fought Spider-Man shortly after slipping away from prison, leaving Hyde behind. But not long after, Cobra sought the wall-crawler's protection from a rampaging Hyde — who had also escaped from custody and was seeking revenge on his former partner for abandoning him in jail. Cobra was a member of one of the Serpent Squads and went on to lead the Serpent Society, briefly adopting the alias King Cobra.

POWERS/WEAPONS

- Frictionless costume
- Compression and contortion of body
- Superhuman speed
- Venom darts

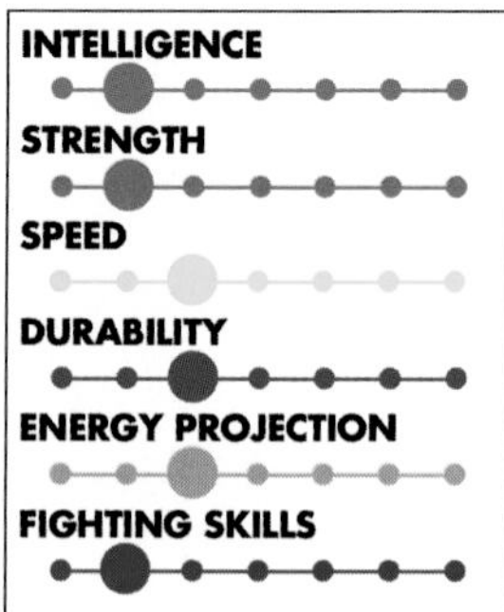

COMMANDA

Real Name: Lady Catherine D'Antan
First Appearance: *Untold Tales of Spider-Man* #9 (1996)
Hgt: 5'10"
Wt: 125 lbs.

Lady Catherine D'Antan had it all: brains, beauty and money. But she grew bored with her idle life and sought out greater challenges, becoming Europe's greatest jewel thief. In search of further adventure, she ventured abroad to New York City — where she encountered and escaped Spider-Man by keeping him off-guard with her feminine wiles. During their second meeting, the web-slinger was wise to her tricks; when she attempted to seduce him, Spider-Man stole her tiara — rendering her powerless. Commanda posed as an innocent victim by teleporting away her armor, framing Spider-Man as the would-be thief. She walked away scot-free with the protection of the local authorities.

POWERS/WEAPONS

- Battle armor
- Palm-mounted shock device
- Tiara-controlled force-field and robot drones
- Skilled jewel thief

INTELLIGENCE
STRENGTH
SPEED
DURABILITY
ENERGY PROJECTION
FIGHTING SKILLS

COMMUTER

Real Name: Ron, last name unrevealed
First Appearance: *Amazing Spider-Man* #267 (1985)
Hgt: 6'0"
Wt: 170 lbs.

A modern, middle-class criminal, the Commuter led a double life. During the day, he made his living as a thief in Manhattan. At 5 p.m., he would take the train back home to the suburbs. The Commuter eventually ran afoul of Spider-Man, but caught every lucky break imaginable and escaped back to the 'burbs. The web-slinger soon located the Commuter, but found himself very much out of his natural element. Unable to web-swing, Spider-Man was reduced to crime-fighting by taxicab. Struggling with the neighborhood watch, lonely housewives and rows of houses all the same, the hero ultimately caught up with the Commuter. But the wall-crawler had learned his lesson: City super heroes do not belong in the suburbs.

POWERS/WEAPONS

- Unnaturally good luck

INTELLIGENCE
STRENGTH
SPEED
DURABILITY
ENERGY PROJECTION
FIGHTING SKILLS

JACOB CONOVER

INTELLIGENCE
STRENGTH
SPEED
DURABILITY
ENERGY PROJECTION
FIGHTING SKILLS

Real Name: Jacob Conover
First Appearance: *Daredevil* #131 (1976)

Hgt: 5'7"
Wt: 155 lbs.

Three years before a radioactive spider bit Peter Parker, Jacob Conover — a street-level reporter for the Daily Bugle — saved the life of New York City crime lord Don Fortunato.

Years later, Conover found himself in financial difficulty and returned to Fortunato to cash in the debt of gratitude he was owed. He was paid in full. The mobster gave Conover the identity of the Rose and part of his territory to run.

Conover nonetheless retained his role at the Bugle — until the destruction surrounding the rampage of the sentient psionic entity Onslaught caused a round of layoffs, at which point Conover developed a hatred for J. Jonah Jameson and Joseph "Robbie" Robertson. He was re-hired when Norman Osborn (Green Goblin) took over the Bugle, but his hatred for his two former bosses remained.

When the Black Tarantula came to New York, Conover resisted with the help of Delilah and Electro. During the final battle between Spider-Man, the Black Tarantula, the Rose and Fortunato, Conover was unmasked and arrested.

COSMIC SPIDER-MAN

POWERS/WEAPONS

- Flight
- Near-infinite strength
- Alteration of molecular structures
- Invulnerability
- Blasts of cosmic energy
- Telescopic vision

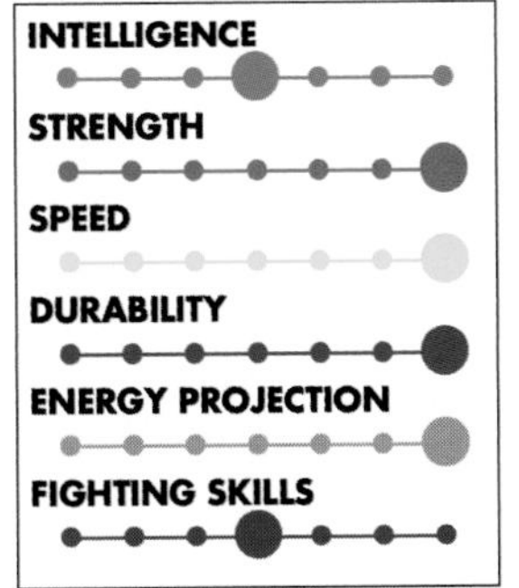

Real Name: Peter Benjamin Parker
First Appearance: *Spectacular Spider-Man* #158 (1989)

Hgt: 5'10"
Wt: 165 lbs.

In a carefully coordinated attack, the world's most powerful criminals, tired of defeat at the hands of their regular opponents, launched a series of surprise assaults on each other's foes. Consequently, Spider-Man was unexpectedly attacked by Graviton and soundly trounced, surviving only through good fortune and Graviton's carelessness.

The next day, while assisting Dr. Maxwell Lubisch's experiments into alternative energy sources, Peter Parker found himself inexplicably endowed with cosmic abilities — transforming him into the most powerful hero in the galaxy. Assailed by a series of villains, Spider-Man was the undisputed victor of each contest.

Ultimately, Spider-Man battled for the survival of mankind itself against the Tri-Sentinel — a massively powered robot created by the Asgardian trickster Loki. It was then revealed that Peter was in fact the holder of the Enigma Force, which transforms certain individuals into Captain Universe at the time of humanity's greatest need. Having defeated the Tri-Sentinel, Spider-Man lost his newfound powers.

CONUNDRUM

Real Name: Unrevealed
First Appearance: *Spectacular Spider-Man* #257 (1998)
Hgt: 5'10"
Wt: 170 lbs.

Conundrum kidnapped an ambassador's daughter, demanding a national treasure in return. Under the direction of Norman Osborn (Green Goblin), Mad Jack (Danny Berkhart) stole the sought-after item so Osborn could trade it for the girl and place the ambassador in his debt. During the exchange, Conundrum and Mad Jack fought Prodigy. Mad Jack escaped, but the girl and the treasure were saved. Conundrum was captured, remaining in jail to this day. Very little is known of his origins, although it appears both he and Mad Jack were trained by the original Mysterio (Quentin Beck). Almost certainly, all three employ similar techniques to perform their illusions.

POWERS/WEAPONS

- Special-effects expert
- Appears to employ hypnosis and/or hallucinogens

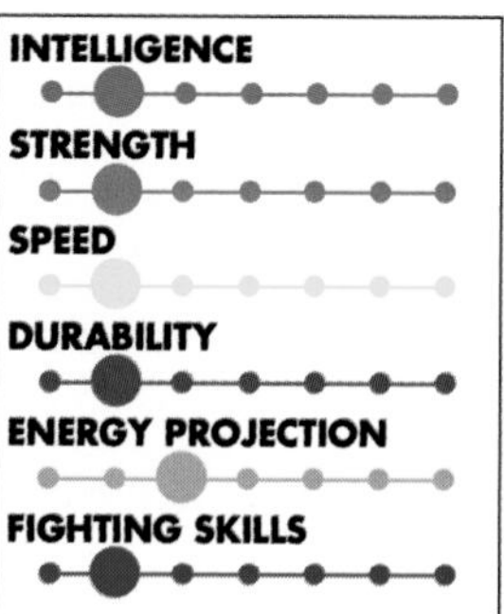

CORONA

Real Name: Dagny Forrester
First Appearance: *Spectacular Spider-Man* #176 (1991)
Hgt: 5'9"
Wt: 140 lbs.

Dagny Forrester was a scientist working in her brother's illicit laboratory. Experimenting on herself, she was transformed into Corona. Fluctuating between monstrous and super-powerful forms, Corona was manipulated by her brother, Cedric. He placed her under his control by implanting a pain-generating device in her head, but also managed to stabilize her transformations. Spider-Man tricked Cedric into ordering Corona to attack him in the lab, and the ensuing battle destroyed the machines that caused the pain feedback. Having regained her independence, Corona left her brother behind.

POWERS/WEAPONS

- Flight
- Personal energy field
- Heat blasts
- Matter control

INTELLIGENCE
STRENGTH
SPEED
DURABILITY
ENERGY PROJECTION
FIGHTING SKILLS

CRIME-MASTER

Real Name: Nick "Lucky" Lewis
First Appearance: *Amazing Spider-Man* #26 (1965)
Hgt: 5'9"
Wt: 150 lbs.

A masked criminal, the Crime-Master struck an uneasy alliance with the Green Goblin. The two agreed to exchange knowledge of their secret identities, but the Goblin led the Crime-Master to believe he was really J. Jonah Jameson, not Norman Osborn. The Goblin and the Crime-Master subsequently jockeyed for control of New York City's crime syndicates, with Spider-Man caught in the middle. The Crime-Master was ultimately slain by the police in a gunfight. Years later, his son became the new Crime-Master and attempted to pick up where his father had left off; he was also foiled by Spider-Man.

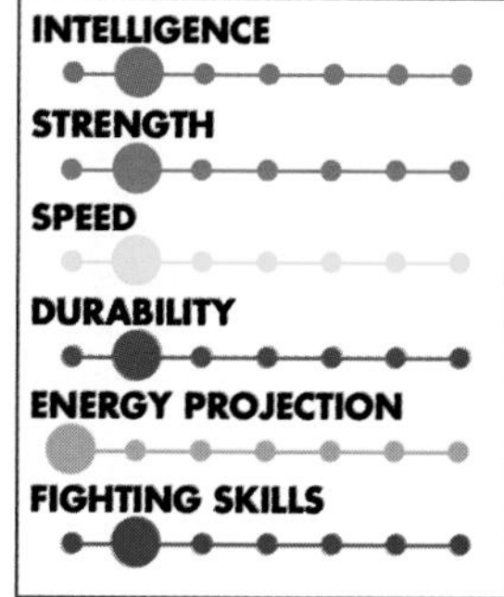

COSTUMES

CLASSIC RED AND BLUE

Spider-Man's original costume was a red-and-blue, screen-printed outfit with black web-lines and a black-spider motif on the chest.

ALIEN SYMBIOTE

Spider-Man's first black costume was actually an alien Symbiote that attempted to bond itself permanently to Peter Parker. Upon discovering his costume's true nature, Peter removed it with the aid of Reed Richards of the Fantastic Four. The alien costume later bonded with Eddie Brock, giving rise to Venom. The costume responded to Peter's mental commands to cover him at will and could generate organic webbing without the need for web-shooters.

CLASSIC BLACK

After removing the alien, Peter created a cloth version of the black costume he alternated with his regular red-and-blue threads. Following Venom's terrifying attack on Mary Jane Watson, Peter permanently retired his black costume at his wife's request.

ELECTRO-PROOF

In response to his numerous clashes with Electro, Spider-Man has developed an insulated costume in defense against the electrically charged villain. The original was a simple rubber outfit, but a modern version included additional padding and styling.

Continued...

COSTUMES

SPIDER-ARMOR

Peter required additional protection against the heavy-caliber firearms wielded by the combined might of the Blood Rose (Richard Fisk), Gauntlet and the New Enforcers. While virtually negating his agility, the costume did provide Spider-Man with increased resistance against gunfire. The armor was destroyed by acid in battle.

SPIDER-MAN REVISED

After Ben Reilly discarded his Scarlet Spider outfit and assumed the role of Spider-Man, he updated Peter's classic look with a revised red-and-blue costume. When Peter returned to the webs, he reinstated his traditional costume.

THE AMAZING BAG-MAN

In times of extraordinary crisis, Peter has been forced to swing into action sans his regular outfit. He has resorted to the use of an ordinary paper bag to conceal his identity.

BEHIND THE MASK

Peter usually wears his costume and belt beneath his regular clothes, with his mask and gloves tucked somewhere handy. The lenses in the mask are made of polarized, one-way reflective material — protecting Peter from glare and helping preserve his identity.

KATE CUSHING

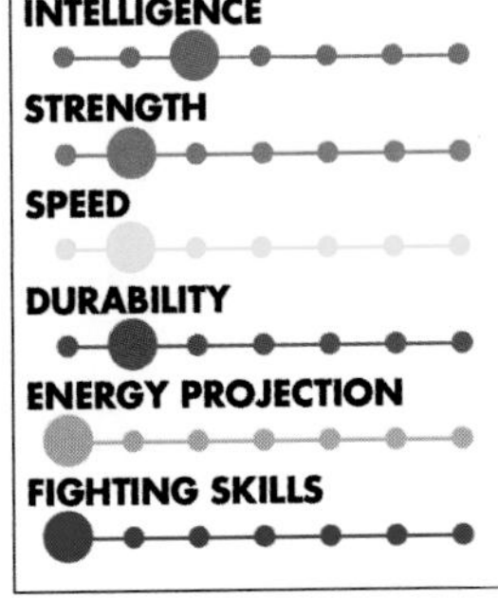

Real Name: Kathryn Cushing
First Appearance: *Web of Spider-Man* #5 (1985)

Hgt: 5'8"
Wt: 120 lbs.

As the former city editor of the Daily Bugle, Kathryn Cushing was a dedicated professional. Priding herself on her integrity and no-nonsense attitude, she was a regular and well-respected part of Peter Parker's life at the Bugle. Kate became involved with the investigation of the Students of Love, as she believed her sister had fallen victim to that cult. Thomas Fireheart (Puma) was attracted to Kate when he ran the Bugle, but their relationship did not develop further. After regaining control of the paper, J. Jonah Jameson fired Kate during budget cutbacks.

CYCLONE

POWERS/WEAPONS

- Generation of whirlwinds

Real Name: Unrevealed
First Appearance: *Amazing Spider-Man* #143 (1975)

Hgt: 5'11"
Wt: 195 lbs.

A Frenchman and former NATO engineer, Cyclone stole the wind-generating suit he had developed and embarked on a criminal career. He first fought Spider-Man after kidnapping J. Jonah Jameson, who was in Paris fleeing the consequences of his decision to fund Danny Berkhart as Mysterio II. Subsequently recruited for the Maggia by the Masked Marauder, Cyclone was defeated by Spider-Man and Moon Knight. He was later slain by the Scourge of the Underworld. Two new Cyclones have since emerged employing his technology. One assisted the Beetle against Silver Sable; the other was a member of the Masters of Evil.

INTELLIGENCE
STRENGTH
SPEED
DURABILITY
ENERGY PROJECTION
FIGHTING SKILLS

LEILA DAVIS

POWERS/WEAPONS

- Amplified strength, energy blasts, flight and other abilities via exoskeletons

Real Name: Leila Davis
First Appearance: *Deadly Foes of Spider-Man* #1 (1991)

Hgt: 5'6"
Wt: 115 lbs.

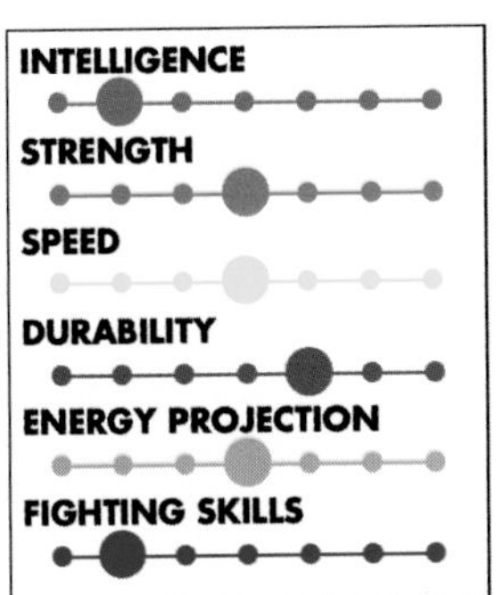

Widowed when the Scourge of the Underworld killed the Ringer (Strikeback), Leila Davis sought vengeance on the Beetle — who had previously humiliated her husband. Posing as the girlfriend of the Speed Demon, she infiltrated the Sinister Syndicate and nearly succeeded in killing the Beetle. Only Spider-Man's intervention prevented her from realizing her murderous vendetta. Leila next obtained a suit of battle armor; as Hardshell, she led a reorganized Syndicate in another failed plot against the Beetle. Leila later became a member of the U.S. government's Redeemers, seeking absolution for past crimes as the new Beetle — until crushed to death by Graviton.

DAILY BUGLE

First Appearance:
Fantastic Four #2 (1962)

Art by Tim Sale

When Peter Parker found himself in desperate need of money to keep himself and his aunt, May Parker, above the poverty line, he hatched the clever idea to photograph himself as Spider-Man and sell the resulting pictures to the Daily Bugle. With his obsessive hatred of the web-slinging hero, Bugle publisher J. Jonah Jameson was eager to get his hands on Parker's pics and use them to discredit Spider-Man in the public eye. While Peter has abandoned his freelance photography position at the Bugle a number of times throughout the years, he has always remained friendly with the staff of the newspaper — most notably reporters Ben Urich and Betty Brant, and editor-in-chief Joseph "Robbie" Robertson.

Jameson began his journalistic career as a reporter for the Bugle while still in high school and later purchased the newspaper. Under Jameson's control, the Bugle has remained New York City's leading paper, resulting in spin-off publications such as NOW and Woman magazines. More recently, the paper temporarily changed ownership — first to Thomas Fireheart (Puma) and later to Norman Osborn (Green Goblin), who used the Bugle to torment Peter. In both cases, it quickly returned to Jameson's control.

The Bugle's reputation has been harmed by its often sensationalist style, and by Jameson's use of the paper as his own personal platform — unfairly attacking Spider-Man as a menace to the city. However, after a public scandal revealed Jameson's involvement in the Scorpion's creation, JJJ scaled back his editorial role at the newspaper — leaving most of the day-to-day decisions to Robertson.

D.K.

POWERS/WEAPONS

- Superhuman strength
- Can decay objects and age people on contact

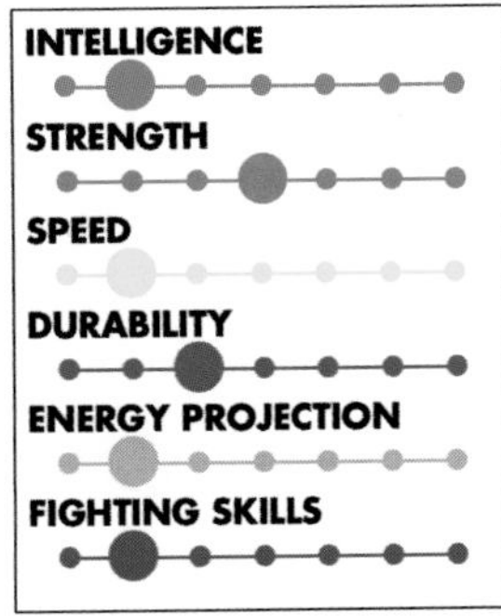

Real Name: David Kalen
First Appearance: *Spectacular Spider-Man* #230 (1996)

Hgt: Variable
Wt: Variable

David Kalen and his brother, Hank, were environmental consultants. While they were investigating illegal dumping performed by Sanders Chemical Corporation, an exploding barrel of chemical waste killed Hank and mutated David. As D.K., David encountered Spider-Man (Ben Reilly) in the process of bringing Sanders to justice. Ben talked David out of killing Sanders and suggested he seek help at the Ravencroft Institute. While in Ravencroft, D.K. became extremely depressed and killed two guards in a blind rage. Horrified at what he had done, he turned his powers inward and dissolved himself. The Vulture was nearby and came into contact with D.K.'s residue, rapidly re-aging into his elderly form.

DAILY GLOBE

First Appearance:
Fantastic Four #2 (1962)

The Daily Globe is the chief rival of the Daily Bugle. Abandoning the Bugle, Peter Parker worked briefly at the Globe. Although the tabloid's photo editor, Barney Bushkin, treated him well, Peter never felt comfortable at the Globe — which often devoted substantial ink to sleaze and sensationalism, even more so than the Bugle. It was at the Globe that Eddie Brock seemingly broke the Sin-Eater case, a story ultimately proven false by Spider-Man. Brock's hubris cost him his job and set him along the path to becoming Venom. The Globe later exposed Matt Murdock as Daredevil, leading him to sue the paper for libel in return.

DARK MAIRI

POWERS/WEAPONS

- Age-old wisdom
- Ability to summon Gaea, Mother Earth

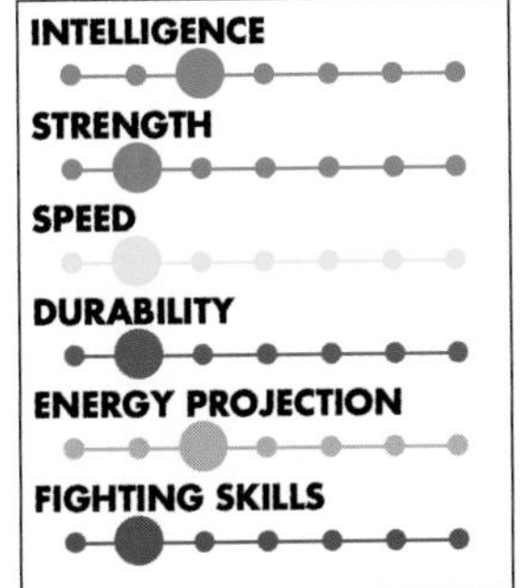

Real Name: Mairi, last name unrevealed
First Appearance: *Spider-Man: Spirits of the Earth* (1990)

Hgt: 5'8"
Wt: 90 lbs.

Dark Mairi of the Shore is the spiritual guardian of the Scottish village of Lochalsh. The Hellfire Club — an exclusive society of the world's wealthiest, most powerful individuals — joined Lochalsh's Lord Angus Munro to kill the elderly Lord Hugh Munro. They faked the presence of evil spirits to drive out the superstitious villagers, allowing them to use the remote location to develop a secret weapon. Mairi led a vacationing Spider-Man to the Hellfire Club's headquarters; when he was captured, she joined her life force with Mary Jane Watson and summoned Gaea to destroy the base. Mairi is now caretaker to young Hugh Munro, who will someday become lord of Lochalsh.

DAREDEVIL

Real Name:
Matthew Murdock
First Appearance:
Daredevil #1 (1964)

Height:	6'0"
Weight:	200 lbs.
Eye Color:	Blue
Hair Color:	Red

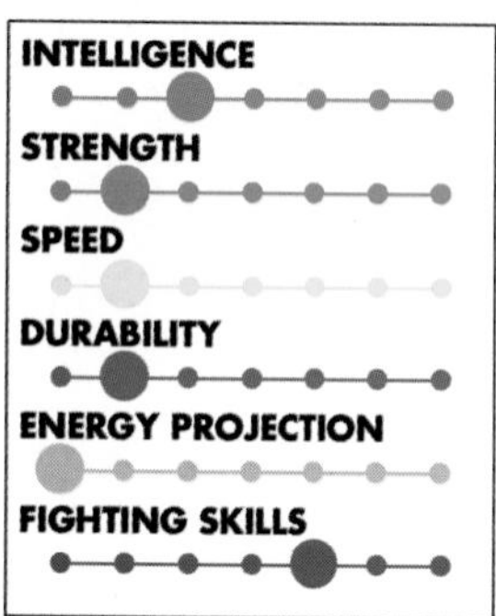

Like Spider-Man, Matt Murdock's heroic costumed identity was shaped first by chance, then by cruel tragedy. Matt's father, prizefighter "Battlin'" Jack Murdock, was a noble-hearted soul who instilled in his son a strong sense of integrity and selflessness, and the desire to help others less fortunate. As a teenager, Matt took his father's teachings to heart, bravely pushing an elderly man out of the path of an oncoming truck. Radioactive waste from the vehicle's payload splashed onto Matt's eyes, instantly blinding him. Matt was devastated by his loss, but soon realized the accident had enhanced his remaining senses.

Under the tutelage of the blind martial-arts master known only as Stick, Matt honed his senses to emerge an Olympic-level gymnast and formidable hand-to-hand combatant. When Matt's father was murdered in cold blood for refusing to throw a boxing match, Matt used his skills to track down the killers. After those responsible were brought to justice, Matt permanently adopted the costumed identity of Daredevil so he could bring the same deserved justice to others.

Daredevil and Spider-Man first teamed up to take down the Circus of Crime, but it was not until the serial killer known as the Sin-Eater struck that they truly formed their current deep bonds of trust and friendship. After the Sin-Eater brutally murdered Jean DeWolff, an enraged Peter Parker vowed vengeance. With the Sin-Eater's life at Spider-Man's mercy, Daredevil intervened — putting his own life on the line to prevent Peter from making a tragic mistake. Since that time, Daredevil and Spider-Man have shared knowledge of each other's secret identities. Daredevil remains one of Spider-Man's most trusted friends and confidantes, and a valuable ally in their mutual fight against crime and injustice.

Art by Joe Quesada

- Superhumanly acute senses of touch, smell, taste and hearing
- Radar-like "proximity sense"
- Expert martial artist and boxer
- Two billy clubs modified with retractable sling line

DAZZLER

POWERS/WEAPONS

- Transformation of sound into light energy

INTELLIGENCE
STRENGTH
SPEED
DURABILITY
ENERGY PROJECTION
FIGHTING SKILLS

Real Name: Alison Blaire
First Appearance: *X-Men* #130 (1980)

Hgt: 5'8"
Wt: 115 lbs.

Although her mutant powers first emerged in her teens, Alison Blaire has largely avoided the life of a super hero. Save for a brief tenure with the X-Men, she has instead focused on her singing career. Dazzler met Spider-Man twice early in her career, and helped him battle Lightmaster and Thermo, the Thermodynamic Man. Spider-Man was quite taken with Alison; he attended two of her concerts as Peter Parker, but their relationship never developed further. Dazzler's career was thrown into crisis when she was outed as a mutant; she even left Earth for a time to live with the extradimensional adventurer known as Longshot. Her career now seems to be back on track.

DEATH SQUAD

First Appearance: *Web of Spider-Man* #91 (1992)

The Foreigner established the Death Squad as his elite infiltration and assault team. Spider-Man first encountered Whisper, Pulse, Swift and Warfare while helping Betty Brant investigate the murder of her husband, Ned Leeds. Each member of the Death Squad possessed power-enhancing combat armor, and model-specific powers and weaponry — including Whisper's swords, throwing blades and silence zone; Pulse's sonic-pulse projector; Swift's enhanced reaction time and speed; and Warfare's high-caliber multi-function projectile weapon. Also, each was prepared to die for his master. If their operation were to be compromised, they would upload any valuable information acquired, and then self-destruct. In subsequent missions, a sequentially numbered replacement would appear — e.g., Pulse-4.

DEATHLOK

POWERS/WEAPONS

- Cyborg components
- Superhuman strength
- Computer-augmented reflexes and data resources
- Energy pistol

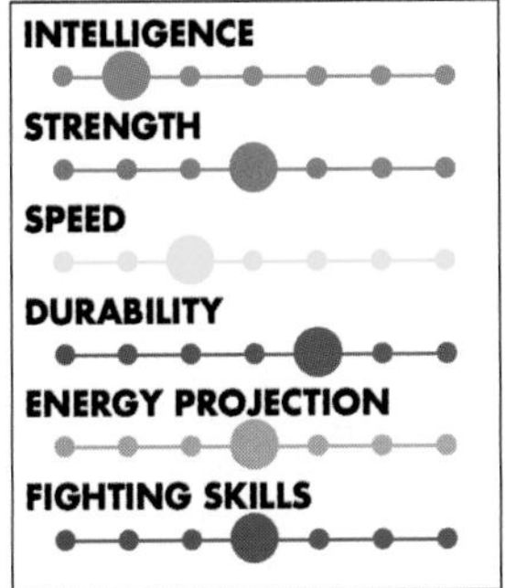

Real Name: Luther Manning
First Appearance: *Astonishing Tales* #25 (1974)

Hgt: 6'4"
Wt: 395 lbs.

Nearly killed in battle, soldier Luther Manning was rebuilt as the Deathlok cyborg in an alternate timeline in which Roxxon Oil's Nth Command wiped out Earth's heroes, initiating a war that ravaged the planet. Spider-Man briefly traveled to Deathlok's chaotic timeline via Doctor Doom's time machine. Deathlok has also journeyed to present-day Earth. After meeting Deathlok, Captain America prevented Roxxon's plot from occurring in our timeline. Luther's circuitry was the developmental basis for several other Deathloks on mainstream Earth — including the Michael Collins Deathlok, who Spider-Man also encountered.

DELILAH

Real Name:	Unrevealed	**Hgt:**	5'9"
First Appearance:	*Amazing Spider-Man* #414 (1996)	**Wt:**	125 lbs.

A highly skilled assassin, Delilah battled Spider-Man (Ben Reilly) while apparently attempting to kill Garon Lewis, ex-husband of the proprietor of Ben's favorite coffee shop. During a gang war, Delilah killed the Black Tarantula's henchman El Uno. Delilah and the Rose (Jacob Conover) then re-powered Electro and revived Doctor Octopus, but still failed to defeat Spider-Man. Ambushed, Delilah's neck was broken by the Black Tarantula — but he healed her as a warning to the Rose. Humiliated, Delilah sought revenge, aided by Ricochet. Together, they fought the Black Tarantula's operatives, Roughhouse and Bloodscream. Defeated, Delilah was imprisoned.

POWERS/WEAPONS

- Superhuman strength and agility
- Impervious to physical harm
- Proficient in the use of all weapons

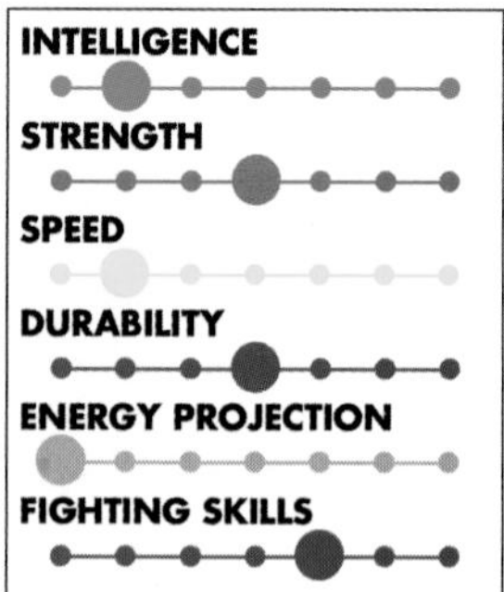

DEMOGOBLIN

Real Name:	Not Applicable	**Hgt:**	6'1"
First Appearance:	*Web of Spider-Man* #86 (1992)	**Wt:**	210 lbs.

When Jason Macendale bargained for power with the demon N'Astirh, he was tricked and possessed by another demon. The two struggled for possession of Macendale's body; their separation was as inevitable as it was painful. The exorcised demon became Demogoblin, determined to destroy all sinners — which, in his mind, meant all save children. This doctrine often brought Demogoblin into conflict with Spider-Man. During Demogoblin's final battle, Macendale damaged a church's structure. Demogoblin held a collapsing pillar while Spider-Man rescued a child beneath it. The pillar crushed Demogoblin to death.

POWERS/WEAPONS

- Demonic strength
- Mystical Goblin Glider
- Magically spawned Pumpkin Bombs
- Limited psychic abilities

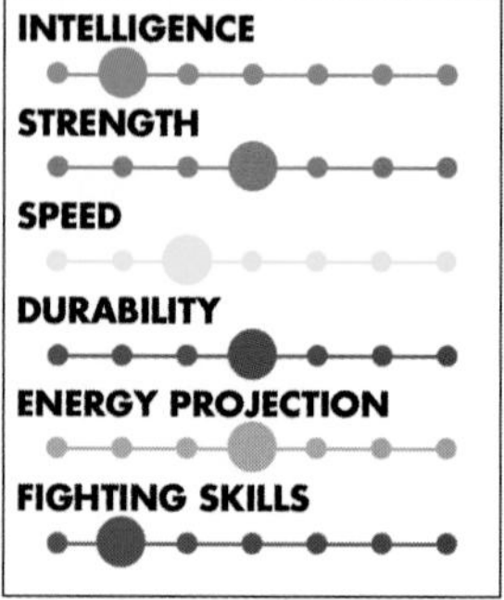

JEAN DeWOLFF

Real Name:	Jean DeWolff	**Hgt:**	5'8"
First Appearance:	*Marvel Team-Up* #48 (1976)	**Wt:**	135 lbs.

A tough police captain, Jean DeWolff first met Spider-Man while investigating a mad bomber. The trail led to her own father, Phillip DeWolff, who had transformed her brother, Brian, into the Wraith. With Spider-Man's aid, Jean eventually freed Brian from her father's control. Through the years, Jean often encountered Spider-Man during the course of her investigations. She grew attracted to him, although he never realized it. Jean's career and life ended when she was brutally murdered by the Sin-Eater — a deranged former lover, Stan Carter, who was ultimately captured by Spider-Man and Daredevil.

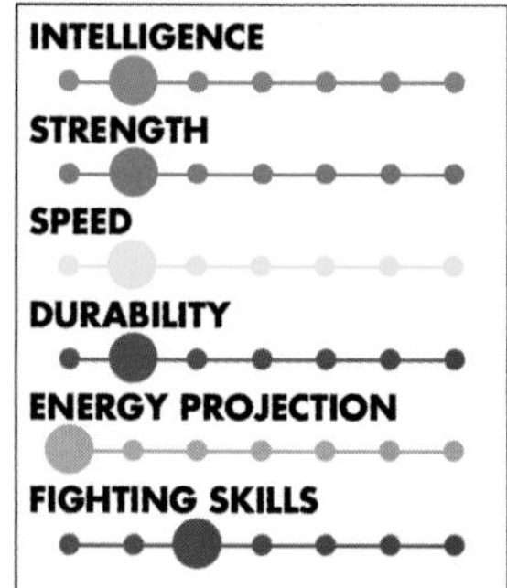

DISRUPTOR

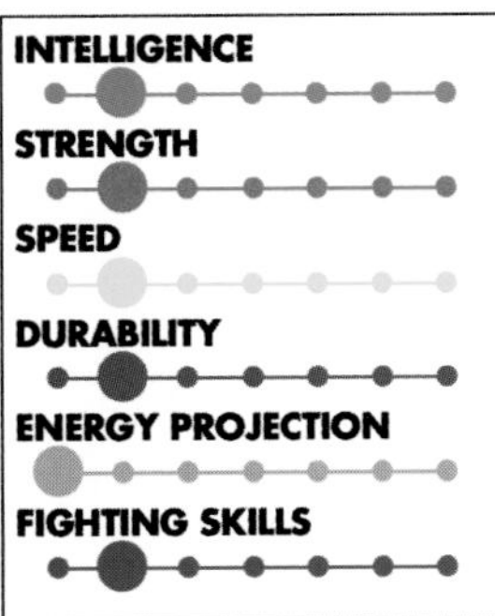

Real Name: Richard M. Raleigh
First Appearance: *Spectacular Spider-Man Magazine* #1 (1968)
Hgt: 5'10"
Wt: 165 lbs.

Richard Raleigh refused to let his sordid past stop him from running for mayor of New York City. Hiring scientist Dr. Thraxton to create the Smasher to serve as his agent, Raleigh used the man-monster to foster the illusion that the underworld was against him — boosting his chances of election. George Stacy suspected wrongdoing, despite J. Jonah Jameson's staunch support of Raleigh. When Raleigh learned of Stacy's suspicions, he sent the Smasher to kill him. Spider-Man saved Stacy, and then followed the Smasher back to Raleigh's townhouse. Raleigh used his pain-stimulating headband to punish the Smasher, but pushed the creature too far; it killed him with a single punch.

DOCTOR DOOM

POWERS/WEAPONS

- Extremely advanced, nigh-impregnable armor
- Force-field generator
- Range of built-in offensive weapons

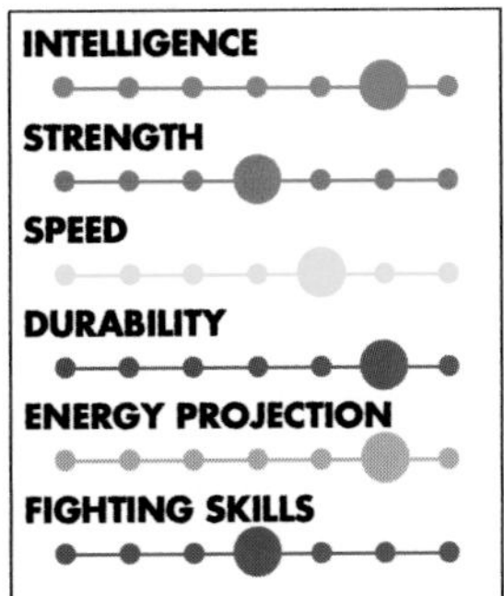

Real Name: Victor Von Doom
First Appearance: *Fantastic Four* #5 (1962)
Hgt: 6'2"
Wt: 225 lbs.

Twisted, disfigured scientist Victor Von Doom rules his homeland, the European nation of Latveria, with an iron fist — while swearing to one day bring about the demise of the Fantastic Four and his longtime rival, Mister Fantastic. When he first encountered Spider-Man, Doom attempted to convince the web-slinger to join forces with him — but the hero was not fooled. Despite the despot's often-wicked ambitions, Spider-Man has nevertheless teamed with Doom to combat the Dark Rider, the Arcane Order of the Night and other common foes.

DOCTOR STRANGE

POWERS/WEAPONS

- Master of the mystic arts
- Cloak of levitation
- Astral projection
- All-seeing Eye of Agamotto
- Various mystic artifacts

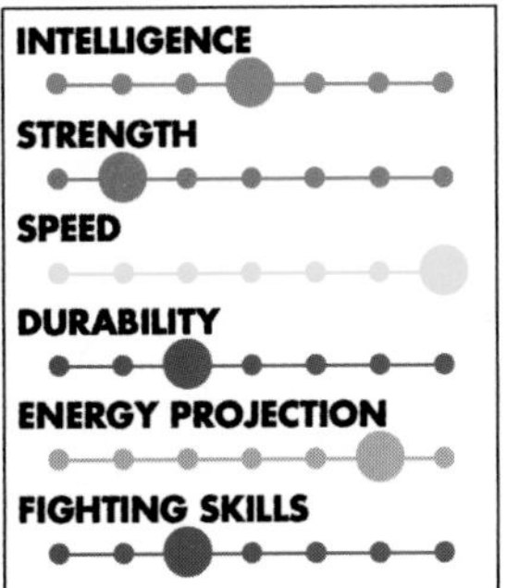

Real Name: Dr. Stephen Strange
First Appearance: *Strange Tales* #110 (1963)
Hgt: 6'2"
Wt: 180 lbs.

Selected by the all-powerful Ancient One to serve as Earth's Sorcerer Supreme, Dr. Stephen Strange left behind his ruined career as a surgeon to become the world's foremost master of the mystic arts. As fellow adventurers, Doctor Strange and Spider-Man have crossed paths a number of times — battling foes such as Xandu, Nightmare, the Technomancers and Dormammu. Doctor Strange has also recruited Spider-Man twice to serve as a member of the Secret Defenders. Most recently, Strange appeared to warn Spider-Man about the extra-dimensional spider-wasp Shathra.

DOCTOR OCTOPUS

Real Name:
Otto Octavius
First Appearance:
Amazing Spider-Man #3 (1963)

Height:	5'9"
Weight:	245 lbs.
Eye Color:	Brown
Hair Color:	Brown

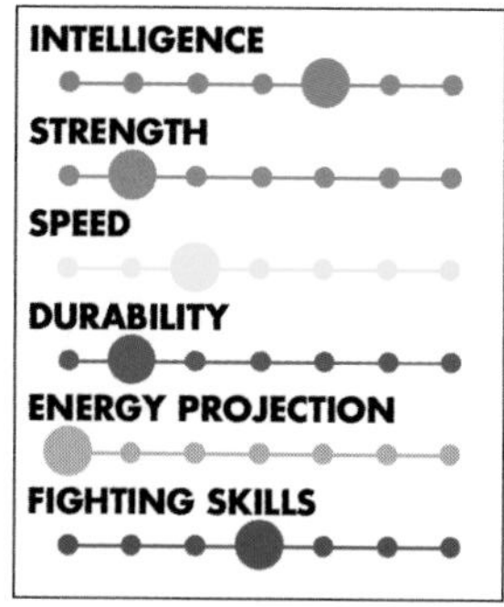

POWERS/WEAPONS

- Four telepathically controlled, super-strong steel tentacles attached to a harness encircling his lower chest and waist
- Brilliant engineer and inventor
- Extraordinary intelligence and concentration, enabling him to perform multiple complex actions simultaneously with his tentacles

Art by Steve Skroce

The son of an overbearing mother and a bullying father, Otto Octavius grew up to become a reclusive but brilliant atomic researcher. To help manipulate radioactive substances from a safe distance, Otto constructed a chest harness controlling four mechanical, tentacle-like arms — earning himself the nickname Doctor Octopus. In a freak laboratory accident, volatile liquids exploded — bombarding the scientist with radiation. The substances left him capable of mentally controlling the arms, but the accident also caused irreversible brain damage — transforming the respected scientist into a megalomaniacal criminal. Waking in a hospital, Otto knew this newfound strength — combined with his awesome intellect — could render him supremely powerful. Holding the medical staff hostage, he easily defeated Spider-Man in their first meeting. Doc Ock then took control of a leading nuclear research facility and again squared off with the wall-crawler, who this time defeated him with one punch to the jaw.

After serving time, Doc Ock attempted to raise funds by springing gangster Blackie Gaxton from prison — assisted by Gaxton's lawyer, Bennett Brant. Spider-Man foiled the scheme, but could not save Bennett from being shot in front of his sister, Betty Brant. Octopus then assembled the first Sinister Six to combat Spider-Man. He plotted to take Betty hostage, knowing Spider-Man had previously rescued her and would likely do so again. May Parker, visiting Betty at the time, was also captured. Otto treated May kindly, and she remained blissfully unaware she had been kidnapped by the charming villain.

Following Spider-Man's defeat of the Sinister Six, Ock assembled another group of criminal underlings and established an undersea base. Calling himself the Master Planner, he embarked on a series of thefts of experimental substances — seeking to further expand his mastery of the atomic sciences. His goal: to develop a radiation ray with which he could rule the world. But his path was fated to entwine with Spider-Man's: When May fell sick, Peter provided her with a blood transfusion — not realizing the radioactivity in his plasma would kill her. The only substance capable of saving her was the experimental ISO-36. Peter managed to obtain enough money to fund the operation, but the Master Planner's forces hijacked the shipment for their own deadly research. Spider-Man tracked the Master Planner to his underwater hideout and confronted his foe, revealed to be Doc Ock. After the base was destroyed, Doctor Octopus escaped once more. Spider-Man recovered the ISO-36 and saved Aunt May's life with the aid of Dr. Curt Connors (Lizard).

Doctor Octopus' next scheme involved the theft of a projector that could disable any device. After two failed attempts, Otto finally succeeded on his third. Turning the Nullifier against Spider-Man, he caused the wall-crawler to lose his memory and persuaded him they were allies. He then enlisted Spider-Man's help to steal the remaining components for the device. Though the hero had not regained his memory, his instinctive spider-sense persuaded him not to trust Doc Ock, and he defeated him once more. Now imprisoned, with his arms confiscated, Otto demonstrated that the range of his psionic control over the limbs had increased to a far greater distance than previously believed. The arms freed him from captivity; in the ensuing battle between Doc Ock and Spider-Man, George Stacy was killed while protecting an innocent child.

Free again, Doctor Octopus seized upon the Kingpin's absence to gather his forces and launch an all-out gang war against Hammerhead's thugs. But Spider-Man's involvement quickly resulted in Otto's return to prison. While incarcerated, Doctor Octopus learned May Parker had inherited a small Canadian island containing a commercial nuclear reactor. On his release, he set out to woo and marry May. But Hammerhead interrupted the wedding, and the ensuing chase and brawl led to the destruction of the reactor.

Continued...

DOCTOR OCTOPUS

When Doc Ock went to war with the Owl, Spider-Man and the Black Cat attempted to intervene. Devastated that the confrontation had left the Black Cat near death, a cold-hearted Peter said farewell to his friends before entering what he believed to be his final showdown with Doctor Octopus. Spider-Man's victory was remorseless, and Doc Ock developed a morbid fear of his arachnid foe. Imprisoned in a mental institution, Otto struggled with his overwhelming phobia of Spider-Man. Knowing he could not face his foe directly, Ock's next plan involved the use of biological weapons to kill the entire population of New York. Spider-Man was forced to fake a humiliating defeat lest the city be destroyed, restoring Otto's self-confidence.

Still, Otto had clearly changed. As a young scientist, he had fallen in love with a fellow researcher, Mary Alice Burke — but his demanding mother jealously sabotaged the relationship. Learning Mary Alice was dying from AIDS, Otto began a desperate search for a cure — stealing research materials to do so. His attempts failed, Mary Alice died, and the villain meekly surrendered to Spider-Man. A world-weary Otto nonetheless escaped from prison. At the time, Spider-Man was dying from a chemical virus. Hoping to one day kill the hero himself, Doc Ock captured and unmasked his foe. Analyzing the virus, Otto offered him a cure. Daring to trust his enemy, Peter accepted the mixture and was healed.

But having found his own salvation in this act, Doctor Octopus did not live to enjoy it. Intending to protect Peter by killing his enemies, Kaine murdered Doc Ock by snapping his neck. But Dr. Carolyn Trainer, Otto's young assistant, had been working with him in the area of solid holographic projection and mind-to-computer communication. Prior to Peter's unmasking, she had created a backup brain-imprint of Doc Ock. With Otto's passing, the backup of his mind became a software projection known as the Master Programmer, and Carolyn used his tentacles to become the second Doctor Octopus. Meanwhile, the Rose (Jacob Conover) employed a cult, the True Believers, to magically resurrect Doctor Octopus as an empty-minded servant. Aas soon as he was raised, Carolyn uploaded the Master Programmer persona into Octavius' brain. She returned his tentacles to him, and they fled.

With his memories restored from a past snapshot, Otto has forgotten he once knew Spider-Man's true identity. He remains very much the deadly and manipulative criminal genius he was in his heyday.

Art by John Romita Jr.

DOPPELGANGER

POWERS/WEAPONS

- Superhuman strength and speed equal to Spider-Man's
- Wall-climbing claws
- Razor-sharp webbing

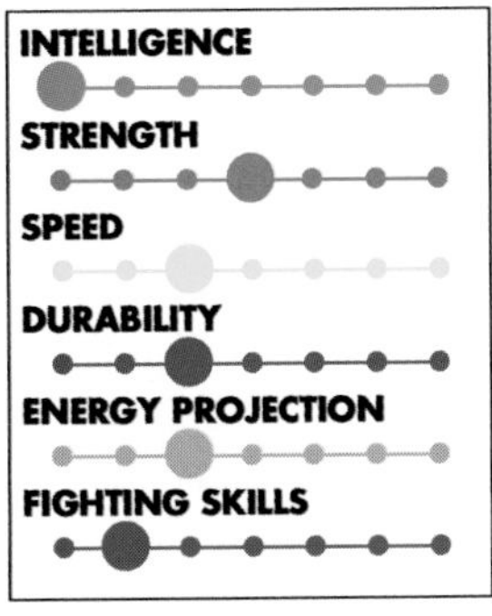

Real Name: Not Applicable
First Appearance: *Infinity War* #1 (1992)

Hgt: 6'5"
Wt: 230 lbs.

During a cosmic conflict, Magus — an evil, future version of Adam Warlock — spawned twisted doubles of Earth's heroes. Spider-Man's Doppelganger was a feral, multi-limbed monstrosity. In his seminal battle against Spider-Man, the Hobgoblin (Jason Macendale) and Demogoblin, Doppelganger was believed killed. But Demogoblin secretly revived him. Preserved by his psychic link with Demogoblin, Doppelganger remained as the latter's servant. Separated from Demogoblin, Doppelganger encountered Carnage and Shriek. Doppelganger bonded with Shriek and attacked Carnage when he tried to kill her, and was slain in her place.

DORMAMMU

POWERS/WEAPONS

- Composed of magical energy
- Possesses vast mystical powers

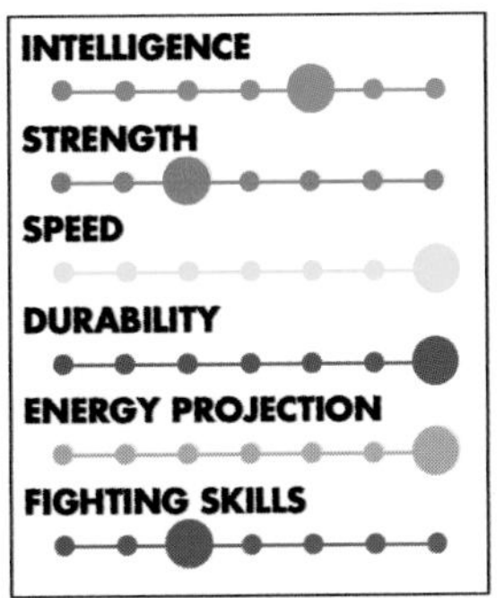

Real Name: Dormammu
First Appearance: *Strange Tales* #126 (1964)

Hgt: 6'1"
Wt: Unknown

The Dreaded One originated as one of the extra-dimensional energy beings known as the Faltine. He and his sister, Umar, were banished after destroying their progenitor, Sinifer. They went on to take over the composite realm known as the Dark Dimension, though Dormammu and Umar have frequently struggled for supremacy. Dormammu seeks to conquer Earth and pull it into his Dark Dimension, but is usually thwarted by Doctor Strange. Spider-Man has been attacked by Dormammu's agents, such as Baron Mordo, though he has yet to encounter the mighty being himself.

DRAGON MAN

POWERS/WEAPONS

- Superhuman strength and durability
- Flight
- Fire-breathing

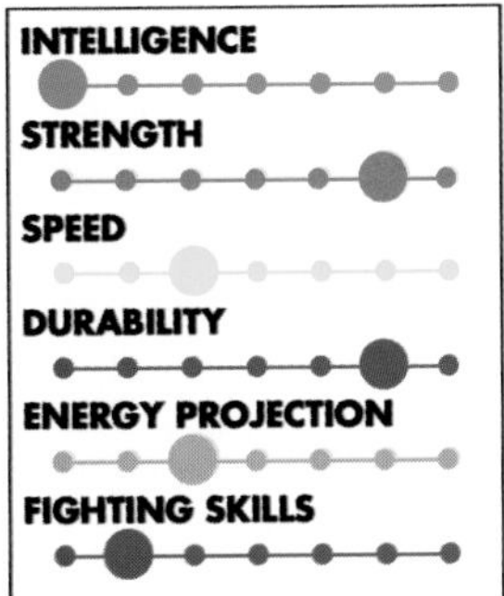

Real Name: Not Applicable
First Appearance: *Fantastic Four* #35 (1965)

Hgt: 15'4"
Wt: 3.2 tons

Constructed by Professor Gregson Gilbert and brought to life by the alchemist Diablo, this powerful yet childlike android has fought the Fantastic Four on several occasions at the behest of its masters, but is not truly evil. At one time, the Wizard sent it against Cosmic Spider-Man, but the super-charged web-slinger had little difficulty vanquishing it. Sans his cosmic powers, Spider-Man had a much tougher time against Dragon Man when it served first as a member of the short-lived New Enforcers and later as a pawn of Dr. Jonas Harrow.

DROM

Real Name: Drom
First Appearance: *Marvel Team-Up* #31 (1975)

Hgt: 5'8"
Wt: 150 lbs.

At birth, a time-space misfire switched the infant Drom with himself as an elderly man — causing him to live his life backwards. He grew increasingly younger over the course of 45 years, able only to slow his descent by absorbing energy from others and through the use of a special mirror. Drom attempted to siphon life energies from Spider-Man, but was thwarted by Iron Fist. When the two heroes destroyed Drom's mirror, he rapidly de-aged past infancy — disappearing to nothing. Before long, Drom's backwards existence vanished also, and the two heroes forgot they had even met him.

POWERS/WEAPONS

- Ages backwards
- Chronal gun capable of decaying objects and aging living beings

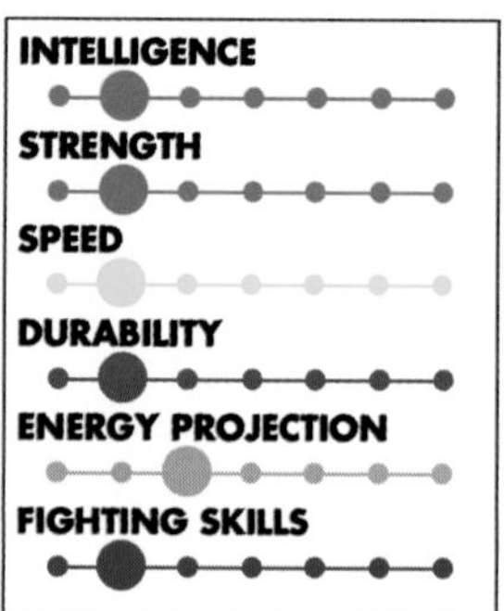

DUSK

Real Name: Peter Benjamin Parker
First Appearance: *Peter Parker: Spider-Man* #90 (1998)

Hgt: 5'10"
Wt: 165 lbs.

One of the four identities Peter Parker assumed during a brief identity crisis was that of the dark and mysterious Dusk, donning an alien costume he obtained aiding a rebellion in the anti-matter universe known as the Negative Zone. By altering his appearance, he aimed to avoid a million-dollar bounty on Spider-Man's head for an unjust murder charge. Dusk teamed with Arthur Stacy to clear the web-slinger's name by pretending to befriend the Trapster, who in turn was being manipulated by Norman Osborn (Green Goblin). The Trapster admitted in court to framing Spider-Man for the murder of Joey Z. Cassie St. Commons of the Slingers later assumed the role of Dusk.

POWERS/WEAPONS

- All the abilities of Spider-Man
- Invisibility in shadows

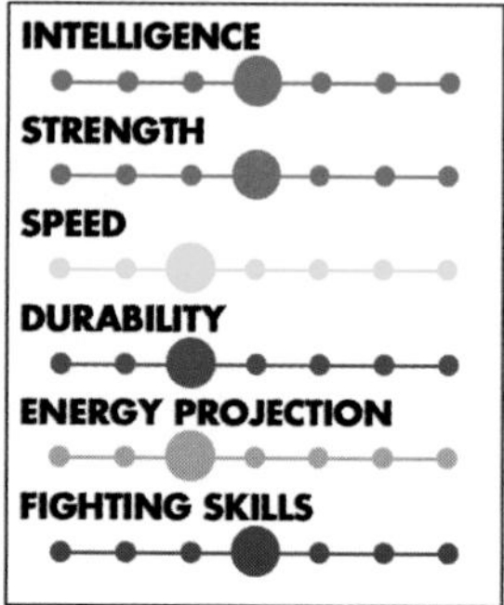

KEN ELLIS

Real Name: Ken Ellis
First Appearance: *Web of Spider-Man* #118 (1994)

Hgt: 5'10"
Wt: 165 lbs.

Ken Ellis is an investigative reporter for the Daily Bugle. Willing to put his life and livelihood on the line to secure a scoop, Ellis has survived several perilously close encounters with Spider-Man and his deadly foes. Ellis' driving ambition has been to replace Ben Urich as the Bugle's leading reporter. Ellis doggedly pursued Ben Reilly and was responsible for dubbing him the Scarlet Spider. He also once came close to exposing Peter Parker as Spider-Man, but was thrown off the trail by Joseph "Robbie" Robertson's deceptive intervention.

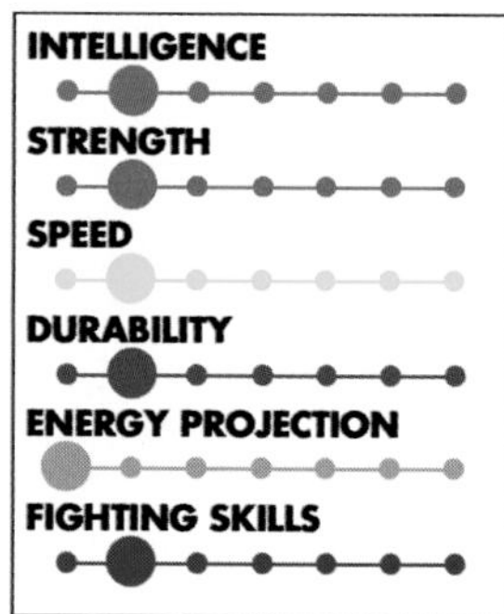

ELECTRO

Max Dillon was a good linesman, but selfish and friendless when not on the job. One day, while he was repairing a downed power line, an unexpected thunderstorm rolled in. Hit by a lightning strike, Dillon foolishly grabbed the power line. The two shocks cancelled each other out; instead of leaving Dillon dead, they granted him extraordinary powers. Upon discovering he possessed the ability to generate, store and project electrical charges, the arrogant Dillon sought a more lucrative profession: crime. Donning a colorful costume, Dillon chose J. Jonah Jameson as his first victim, successfully looting Jameson's safe in front of the newspaperman's very eyes.

Real Name:
Maxwell Dillon
First Appearance:
Amazing Spider-Man #9 (1964)

Height:	5'11"
Weight:	165 lbs.
Eye Color:	Blue
Hair Color:	Reddish-Brown

An enraged Jameson made the bold claim that Electro was simply Spider-Man in disguise. Spider-Man could hardly resist that challenge, and he set out to fight Electro to prove they were not the same man. Totally unprepared for Electro's attack, Spider-Man was nearly killed when he received a jolt of electricity just from touching the villain. He realized he could defeat Electro only by outsmarting him; spotting a nearby fire-hose, Spider-Man short-circuited his enemy. Seeking revenge, Electro joined the original Sinister Six, but the web-slinger defeated the villian by deactivating his power source. Grounding himself with a steel cable, Spider-Man was able to close in for the knockout punch.

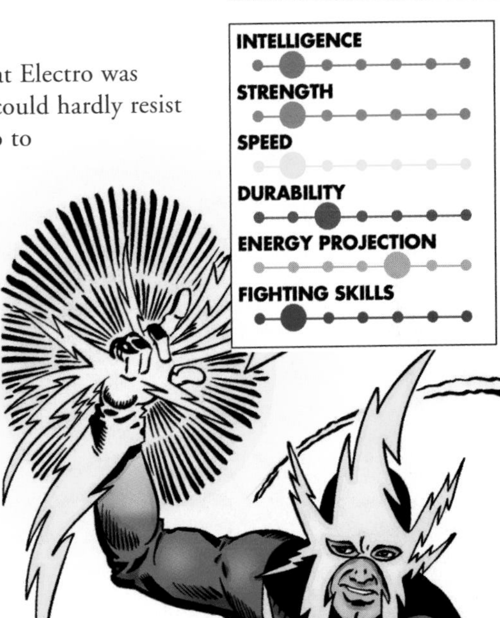

Electro also came into conflict with Daredevil early in his career. He later teamed with the Blizzard to battle Daredevil and Spider-Man together. Ever the team player, Electro joined the Frightful Four in an attack on the Fantastic Four. Following several failed reunions of the Sinister Six, Electro suffered a crisis of confidence. Attempting to go straight, he ended up as a freak show act in a Coney Island

Continued...

Art by Steve Ditko

POWERS/WEAPONS

- Generation of up to 1,000,000 volts of electricity
- Projection of electric lightning bolts, up to lethal force
- Flight via Earth's magnetic-force lines
- Override and control of simple electrical devices
- Emission of a static charge that disrupts Spider-Man's wall-crawling ability
- Overload of victims' synapses, causing excruciating pain

ELECTRO

carnival. Unable to bear the crowd's laughter, Electro cracked. In a spectacular bid to overcome his self-doubt, he stood on the roof of the Top of New York Hotel and gradually absorbed all the power in Manhattan. Spider-Man arrived, and Electro easily blasted him off the edge of the building. But even Electro has his limits: With his head throbbing near to the bursting point, he attempted to discharge the excess electricity, but found he had overloaded his abilities. In that moment, his self-doubt came flooding back. Returning to the scene, Spider-Man reassured the confused Dillon. Treating Electro as an equal, Spider-Man convinced him his problems were purely psychological. The hero's pep talk worked, and Electro gradually returned the charge to the blacked-out city. In an unexpected mea culpa, the grateful Electro thanked Spider-Man profusely and went willingly to serve his jail sentence.

Fearing the murderous Kaine would come for him, Electro escaped and joined the Sinister Seven in self-defense. Afterwards, Electro struggled with his own self-worth — residual damage done to him in childhood after having been abandoned by his violent father and smothered by his overbearing mother. Realizing he had reached a crossroads, and remembering his moment of ultimate power atop the Top of New York Hotel, Electro prepared to take one more gamble in his quest for self-esteem. He allowed the Rose (Jacob Conover) and Delilah to strap him into a super-charged electric chair. The gamble paid off; Electro's powers were enhanced tenfold. In return, Dillon had promised to aid the Rose and Delilah in their gangland ambitions. But his drive for vengeance against Spider-Man — and indeed, the whole of Manhattan — took precedence. He created a plan to set off a chain reaction among the New York power stations that would destroy most of the city. Even equipped with an insulated costume, Spider-Man barely managed to defeat him.

Electro remains an ever-present threat — but normally faces defeat despite powers that make him, effectively, a force of nature. It is only Electro's profound lack of judgment that allows him to be beaten by less-powerful yet more prudent foes like Spider-Man.

Art by Steve Ditko

— EMPIRE STATE UNIVERSITY

Art by Mark Bagley

First Appearance:
Amazing Spider-Man #31 (1965)

When Peter Parker graduated from Midtown High School, he left some classmates behind, but soon encountered a brand-new group of students on campus at Empire State University. His relationship with fellow freshmen Harry Osborn and Gwen Stacy got off to a rocky start, as his constant distraction with the hospitalization of his aunt, May Parker, and costumed life as Spider-Man were misconstrued as snobbery. Once that misunderstanding was explained, Gwen, Harry, Peter and even his former high-school nemesis, Flash Thompson, became fast friends — frequently hanging out together at the Coffee Bean between classes. Though not a student herself, Mary Jane Watson would often join the quartet for fun times.

On campus, Peter's studies were rarely without distraction. He was forced to confront a student riot, as well as less-conventional complications caused by his professors: Dr. Curt Connors, who struggled with his transformations into the Lizard, and Dr. Miles Warren, whose dark obsessions gave rise to his maniacal Jackal persona. ESU was also a popular location for displaying valuable artifacts — such as the Lifeline Tablet, an exhibition that led to a full-scale firefight between the Kingpin and Silvermane. The university was also home to Dr. Ashley Kafka, until she was assigned to Ravencroft Institute.

As a post-graduate student, Peter's collegiate life proved no less eventful. In fact, the goings-on at ESU only grew stranger. Fellow students included Hector Ayala, also known as the White Tiger, and Chip Martin, the Schizoid Man. Former vice chancellor Dr. Edward Lansky became the Lightmaster, and even former professor Buck Mitty adopted the somewhat less frightening identity of Humbug.

Although Peter never finished his post-graduate studies, he did attempt to return, unsuccessfully, at least once. His lecturer, Dr. Maxwell Lubisch, unleashed a strange interdimensional energy that triggered Peter's transformation into the fantastically powerful Cosmic Spider-Man. Spider-Man also took on the mutant hate-group known as the Friends of Humanity and came to the aid of Professor Evan Swann, who was being blackmailed by the Tinkerer.

Some may claim it was just a twist of fate that attracted such trouble during Peter's time at Empire State University — but that theory seems unlikely, as Mary Jane found a much more peaceful environment when she returned to ESU to obtain her undergraduate degree.

ENFORCERS

First Appearance:
Amazing Spider-Man #10 (1964)

When Spider-Man first faced off against the Enforcers, he was ill-prepared for this trio of hired muscle under the command of the Big Man (Frederick Foswell). As individuals, Spider-Man could easily defeat any of the Enforcers. But when the lightning footwork and Judo skills of Fancy Dan (Daniel Brito) combined with the rope-throwing talents of Montana (Jackson W. Brice) and the brute strength of Ox (originally Raymond Bloch, later replaced by his twin brother, Ronald), this threesome formed a flawless team that sent Spider-Man reeling. Only with the aid of the NYPD, and later the Human Torch, Spider-Man was able to prevail.

Following a brief alliance with the Sandman, the Enforcers went on sabbatical for some time. They were lured back into action by the second Big Man — revealed to be Frederick Foswell's daughter, Janice Foswell — in her war against the Crime-Master. Teaming with the Human Torch, Spider-Man successfully trounced the lot of them.

Art by Steve Ditko

Deciding that if three members could nearly beat Spider-Man, then five could surely finish the job, the Enforcers added the lithe-limbed talents of Sylvester "Snake" Marston and the weight-wielding fists of Willard "Hammer" Harrison. The quintet set out to squash Spider-Man once and for all. What they could never have anticipated was the timely intervention of the formerly villainous Sandman, who had turned over a new leaf and came to Spider-Man's side in the midst of battle.

The new lineup lasted one more job, an ill-fated murder contract against Daredevil, before returning to their original lineup. Perhaps tired of the uncertainties of freelance work in New York's criminal syndicates, the founding Enforcers accepted semi-permanent positions in the employ of the Kingpin. They remained with the Kingpin until Wilson Fisk was ousted from power in an underworld coup, once again returning the trio to their original distinction as muscle-for-hire. The name New Enforcers was later adopted by another unrelated group of super-villains-for-hire, which also did not last long.

EZEKIEL

Real Name:
Ezekiel Sims
First Appearance:
Amazing Spider-Man #30 (2001)

Height:	6'0"
Weight:	180 lbs.
Eye Color:	Blue
Hair Color:	Gray

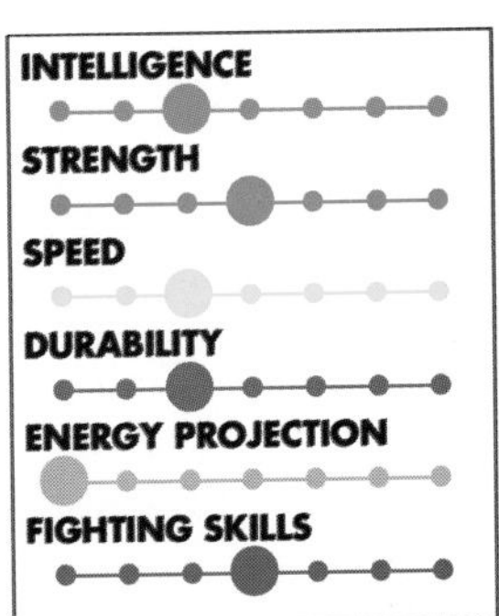

The enigmatic Ezekiel appeared seemingly out of nowhere, bearing an intimate knowledge of Peter Parker's powers and history. Ezekiel seems to possess similar abilities, obtained in an arcane Central American ritual. Notably, Ezekiel has employed his talents toward different ends, having built a powerful business empire with international reach.

Not surprisingly, Peter was curious to discover Ezekiel's intentions — but the older man remained quite dodgy, choosing instead to taunt Spider-Man with perplexing questions: Was it more than happenstance that a radioactive spider had bitten Peter, moments before dying? What is Peter's relationship with spiders? Just how deep does the spider part of Peter's nature run? Perhaps there is far more to being a man-spider than a costume and a pair of metal chemical-shooters? Ezekiel certainly hinted so, but confirmed nothing — indicating he wished simply to use his knowledge and resources to aid Peter, as Peter had aided others.

When Morlun set out to feed off the totemistic bond joining Spider-Man to the arachnid with which he identifies, Ezekiel offered Peter a way to hide from the creature's unusual senses. Peter refused, believing it was his responsibility to halt Morlun's rampage. Not until Spider-Man's doom appeared certain did Ezekiel step in to help bring the creature down.

Ezekiel then disappeared for some time, until Spider-Man — while in the Astral Plane — accidentally attracted the attention of Shathra, the embodiment of the spider-wasp totem, a spider's natural enemy. Ezekiel rescued Spider-Man, who was greatly outclassed by this cruel opponent and near death, promptly spiriting him away to Africa.

There, Ezekiel told Peter the story of the original Spider-Man — the first in an ongoing line of which Peter is the latest champion. Ezekiel revealed that a holy man in Ghana had studied the ways of the spider and ascended to the Astral Plane as some sort of spider-god. He hinted it was this being that had caused the events that led Peter to receive his spider-powers.

POWERS/WEAPONS

- Heightened agility, reflexes, strength, endurance and equilibrium
- Ability to cling to and climb vertical surfaces
- Presumably some form of "spider-sense," alerting him to danger

Art by John Romita Jr.

EQUINOX

Real Name: Terrence Sorenson
First Appearance: *Marvel Team-Up* #23 (1974)

Hgt: 6'0"
Wt: 200 lbs.

POWERS/WEAPONS

- Superhuman strength
- Generation of flames and ice

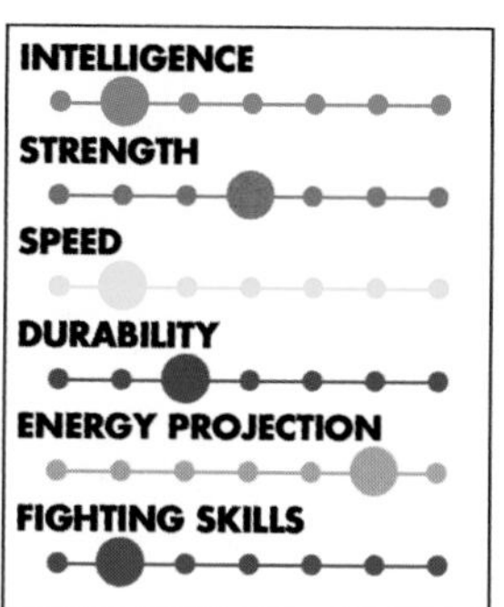

Mutated by an explosion in the thermodynamics laboratory of his alcoholic father, Terrence Sorenson acquired great power — but was pushed to the brink of insanity. Searching for a cure, Terry found himself fighting Spider-Man, Iceman of the X-Men and the Human Torch. Spider-Man eventually helped neutralize his powers. Terry resumed a normal life — though his powers did gradually resurface, now under his control. Terry's young daughter, Janet, later began to demonstrate similar powers — causing explosions around their Harlem apartment. Terry became desperate to stop her, even to the point of physical violence. The Falcon, the Avengers' high-flying hero of the people, helped guide him toward other avenues to help Janet.

EVIL VERSIONS

First Appearance:
Amazing Spider-Man #367 (1992)

Bloodspider, Deathshield and Jagged Bow were three trainees of the Taskmaster outfitted and specially instructed so as to mimic — respectively — the webs and strength of Spider-Man, the shield and fighting skills of Captain America, and the arrows and archery of the Avengers' Hawkeye. When Spider-Man and Solo stormed one of the Taskmaster's estates, the Taskmaster let his students have a go at the two real, live super heroes. The web-slinger and Solo captured all three following a short struggle, but the students made certain their teacher escaped.

F.A.C.A.D.E.

Real Name: Unrevealed
First Appearance: *Web of Spider-Man* #113 (1994)

Hgt: 7'4"
Wt: 900 lbs.

POWERS/WEAPONS

- Non-concussive paralytic arcs
- Bio-integrated systems
- Groundbreaking techno-organics

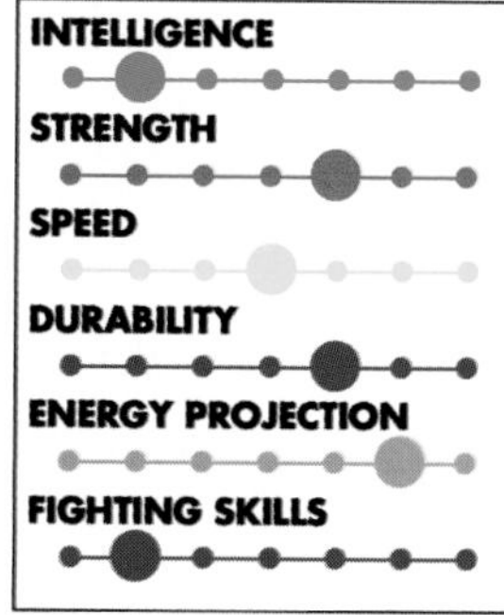

The Full Acclimation Combat And Defense Explo-skeleton (F.A.C.A.D.E.) body armor was a groundbreaking prototype manufactured by Morelle Pharmaceuticals under the auspices of Dr. Thomas Haney. The suit was stolen during its first celebrity-studded showing, and its inventor was accidentally killed in the process. Daily Bugle photographer Lance Bannon took a picture identifying the culprit, but was murdered by the armor-wearing criminal before he could reveal the villain's identity. Spider-Man battled F.A.C.A.D.E. and destroyed the armor — but the man inside escaped, and his true identity was never determined.

FANTASTIC FOUR

First Appearance: *Fantastic Four* #1 (1961)

Spider-Man and the Fantastic Four, the world's first family of superhuman explorers, share a long history, dating back to the web-slinger's early career. In his own inimitable style, Spider-Man forced his way into the Fantastic Four's heavily guarded headquarters, fought the adventurers to a standstill and bluntly asked for a job — which, unfortunately, they could not offer him.

Each of the four formed a unique relationship with Spider-Man. Mr. Fantastic admired Peter Parker's natural scientific genius, Invisible Girl secretly thought him rather cute, and the Thing respected anybody who could survive a scrap with him. As for the Human Torch, the two competitive young men eventually became the best of friends after an awkward start.

Through the years, Spider-Man has fought beside the Fantastic Four on countless occasions. With the original members temporarily out of action, Spider-Man, the Hulk, Wolverine and Ghost Rider II formed the New Fantastic Four; they opposed De'Lila. Doctor Strange later reunited the group to found his Secret Defenders.

FIRELORD

POWERS/WEAPONS

- Cosmic strength
- Manipulation of stellar fire
- Virtually impervious to harm

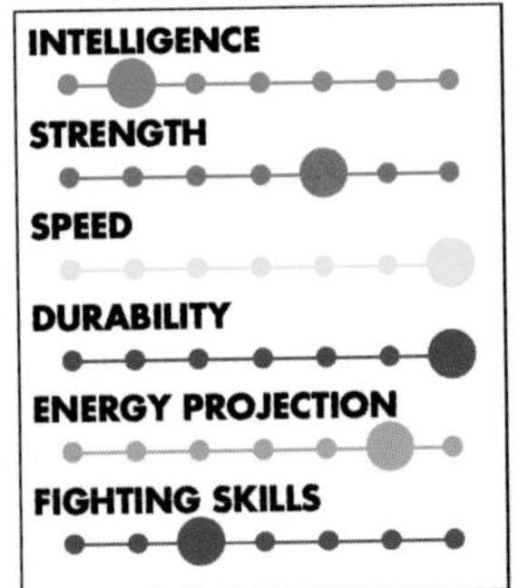

Real Name: Pyreus Kril
First Appearance: *Thor* #225 (1974)

Hgt: 6'4"
Wt: 220 lbs.

Firelord may be the most powerful foe Spider-Man has ever defeated. While traversing space at near light-speed, the former herald of the world-devouring Galactus stopped on Earth for rest and contemplation. He quickly ran afoul of a New York mob made jittery by a government-initiated stream of anti-mutant propaganda. A passing Spider-Man was alerted to the conflict, and a battle ensued. Frightfully aware he was greatly outclassed, Spider-Man fought on — through explosions and collapsing city blocks. When the Avengers arrived, they were stunned to discover a battered, half-crazed Spider-Man had proved victorious against an opponent with the power to destroy a planet.

FEMME FATALES

First Appearance: *Amazing Spider-Man* #340 (1990)

Bloodlust and Whiplash first fought Spider-Man as members of the Band of Baddies. The Femme Fatales, whose roster also included Knockout and Mindblast, initially appeared as agents of the Chameleon during a plot that briefly robbed Spider-Man of his powers. The web-slinger regained his abilities with help from the Black Cat, but the villains escaped capture. The Femme Fatales were a formidable crew — with powers and weapons ranging from Bloodlust's feral fury and razor-sharp claws to Knockout's superhuman strength, and from Mindblast's telekinesis to Whiplash's glove-mounted whips. The Femmes later joined the Femizons and were among the massive super-villain crowd at the Advanced Idea Mechanics Weapon Expo. Whiplash was also seen working independently as part of an extortion plot foiled by Heroes for Hire.

VANESSA FISK

Real Name: Vanessa Fisk
First Appearance: *Amazing Spider-Man* #70 (1969)

Hgt: 5'8"
Wt: 125 lbs.

INTELLIGENCE
STRENGTH
SPEED
DURABILITY
ENERGY PROJECTION
FIGHTING SKILLS

Vanessa Fisk staunchly opposed the criminal career of her husband, New York City's notorious Kingpin. She once made him retire, but was kidnapped and nearly killed in a plot to force his comeback. Vanessa survived, but lost her memory. Daredevil subsequently found and returned her to the Kingpin in exchange for his agreement to pull his backing from a crooked political candidate. Vanessa moved to Europe following a lengthy recovery, but returned when the Kingpin was nearly killed during an uprising of his underbosses. She led the swift and final punishment of all involved, personally executing her own son, Richard Fisk. Vanessa then divided up the Kingpin's former empire and again left America.

FLY

Real Name: Richard Deacon
First Appearance: *Amazing Spider-Man Annual* #10 (1976)

Hgt: 5'11"
Wt: 200 lbs.

Richard Deacon was shot fleeing police following an unsuccessful kidnapping attempt. Stumbling into the laboratory of Dr. Harlan Stillwell, Deacon coerced Stillwell to transform him into a superhuman being and hence save his life. Using equipment funded by J. Jonah Jameson, Stillwell imprinted the genetic coding of a common fly onto Deacon. As the Fly, Deacon killed Stillwell and used his newfound powers — including superhuman strength, speed and endurance — to further his criminal ambitions. He was defeated by Spider-Man. After escaping from a mental institution years later, Deacon was assassinated by the Scourge of the Underworld.

POWERS/WEAPONS

- Flight
- 360-degree vision
- Can cling to any surface
- Creation of powerful winds and shock waves via wings

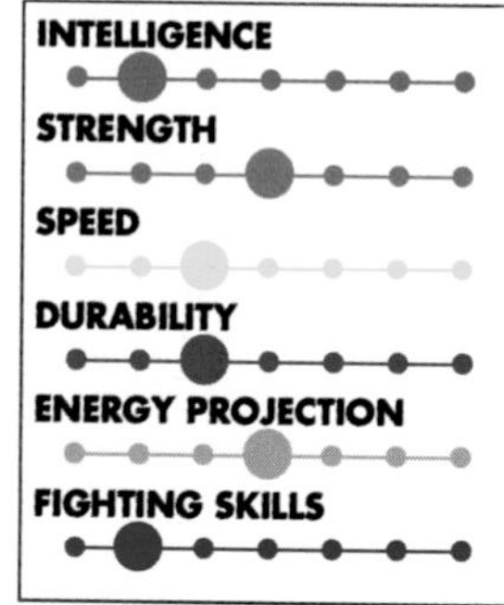

RICHARD FISK

As a young man, Richard Fisk attended the most prestigious schools in the Swiss Alps; his family's immense wealth was funded by his father's activities as New York City's notorious Kingpin. When Richard grew older, he swore to bring Wilson Fisk down. Adopting the identity of the Schemer, Richard pitted his own gang against the Kingpin's forces. In a climactic confrontation with his father, Richard revealed his identity, shocking the Kingpin into a catatonic state. Repentant, Richard briefly joined Hydra, using the organization's resources to return his father's mental faculties.

Years later, Richard returned to New York as the Rose, a masked and cultured crime lord, increasingly defying the Kingpin's empire. When the Kingpin abandoned New York, a gang war exploded in which Jack O'Lantern (Jason Macendale) and the Hobgoblin became Richard's key allies against the Arranger and Hammerhead. As the battle raged out of control, the police persuaded the Kingpin to return and restore peace. Richard, meanwhile, faced his own crisis when he was cornered by a rookie cop, whom he fatally shot. With blood on his hands, Richard realized that in attempting to bring down his father, he had perhaps become him. He then openly joined the Kingpin, abandoning the Rose identity.

Richard eventually overcame his grief and worked out a new plan with his friend, Alfredo Morelli (Gauntlet). With plastic surgery, Alfredo assumed Richard's identity. Using his combat training, Morelli would climb the ranks of the Kingpin's organization and topple the empire from within. But when Daredevil and Hydra forced Wilson Fisk from power, Morelli refused to abandon the power he had gained posing as Richard. Richard assumed the identity of the Blood Rose to dislodge him. Richard then entered the federal Witness Protection Program and disappeared from New York's criminal realm. When the Kingpin regained his grip on the city's underworld, however, Richard could not resist returning to New York.

Now a broken, alcoholic drifter, Richard was no longer the brilliant tactician he once had been. When a reckless, ambitious lieutenant named Mr. Silke organized an underworld coup against the Kingpin, Richard was persuaded to play a crucial role in the murderous plot. After the Kingpin was nearly stabbed to death, Richard was confronted by his mother, Vanessa Fisk. Forced to choose between her crooked husband and her treacherous son, Vanessa shot Richard dead.

Real Name:
Richard Fisk
First Appearance:
Amazing Spider-Man #83 (1964)

Height:	5'10"
Weight:	185 lbs.
Eye Color:	Blue
Hair Color:	Blond

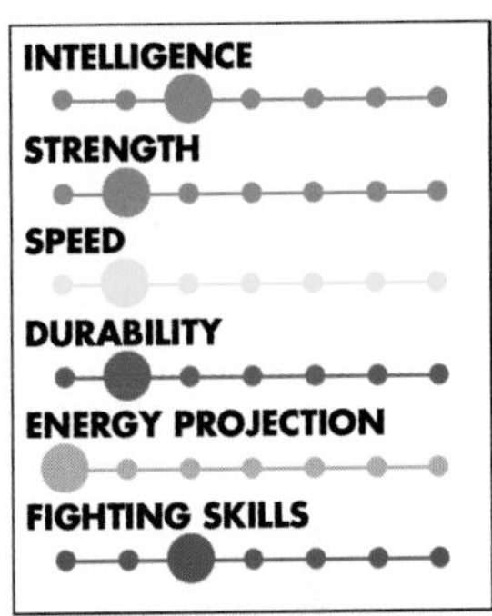

POWERS/ WEAPONS

- Impenetrable suit, resistant to gunfire and even Spider-Man's webbing
- Skilled in the use of various firearms

Art by Alex Maleev

FOOLKILLER

Real Name: Greg Salinger
First Appearance: *Omega the Unknown* #8 (1977)

Hgt: 6'0"
Wt: 197 lbs.

POWERS/WEAPONS

- Disintegration gun

His mind unhinged during military service, Greg Salinger was jailed for disorderly conduct. In prison, he learned of the original Foolkiller, Ross G. Everbest, who crusaded to rid the world of those with no poetry in their souls. Released, the inspired Salinger stole Everbest's paraphernalia from the authorities and became the new Foolkiller. Defeated by the Defenders, Salinger later enrolled at Empire State University, where he befriended Peter Parker — who eventually learned his identity and was forced to bring him in as Spider-Man when Salinger began another killing spree. Remanded to a mental institution, Salinger was falsely suspected as the Scourge of the Underworld and later inspired a successor, Kurt Gerhardt.

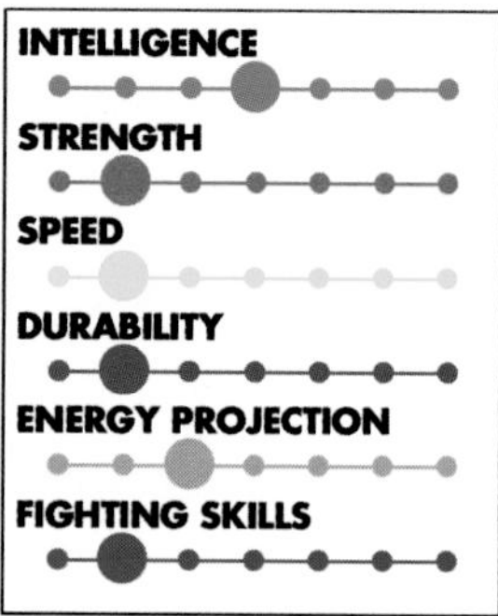

FOREST HILLS

First Appearance: *Amazing Fantasy* #15 (1962)

When out-of-towners think of New York City, images of skyscrapers, bright lights and fast-paced living often come to mind. But across the East River in the borough of Queens lies Forest Hills, a residential community complete with tree-lined streets and single-family homes. This is where Peter Parker was raised. Though only a subway ride from the city, Forest Hills offered the Parkers a haven of serenity and calm. Although violent crime in this part of Queens is less of a concern than in the heart of the Big Apple, it was here that Peter's beloved uncle, Ben Parker, was murdered in his own home — forever altering the direction of his nephew's life and inspiring the creation of Spider-Man.

DON FORTUNATO

Real Name: Fortunato, first name unrevealed
First Appearance: *Spider-Man* #70 (1996)

Hgt: 5'6"
Wt: 145 lbs.

POWERS/WEAPONS

- Army of armed criminals
- Access to Hydra resources
- Pet wolf

Years ago, the Kingpin killed Don Rigoletto to cement his leadership of New York City's criminal underworld. Don Fortunato was also targeted, but Jacob Conover saved his life. When Daredevil exposed the Kingpin, Fortunato claimed the throne with the help of Hydra — and the terrorist organization's armored Killdroids — subduing Hammerhead, Tombstone and other rivals. In addition to a feud with his son, Jimmy-6, Fortunato's most worrisome foe was the Black Tarantula. Fortunato was severely injured when the Kingpin made his return to power. His current status is unknown, and his son has led the family since his disappearance.

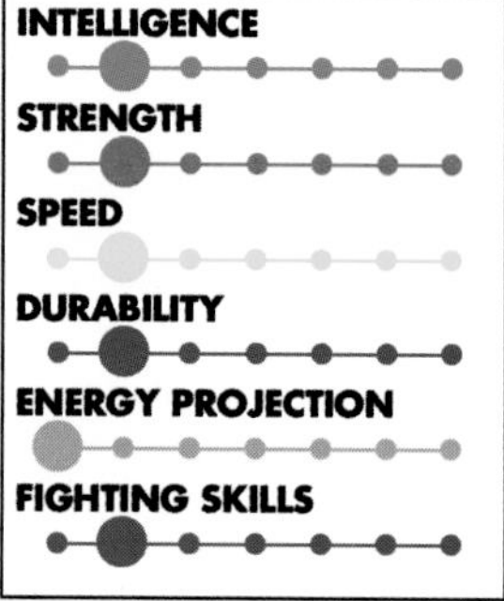

FOREIGNER

Real Name: Rafael Basil Sabitini
First Appearance: *Web of Spider-Man* #15 (1986)

Hgt: 6'2"
Wt: 240 lbs.

POWERS/WEAPONS

- Ability to cause temporary blackouts, creating the illusion of teleportation
- One-off acts of superhuman strength
- Master of disguise

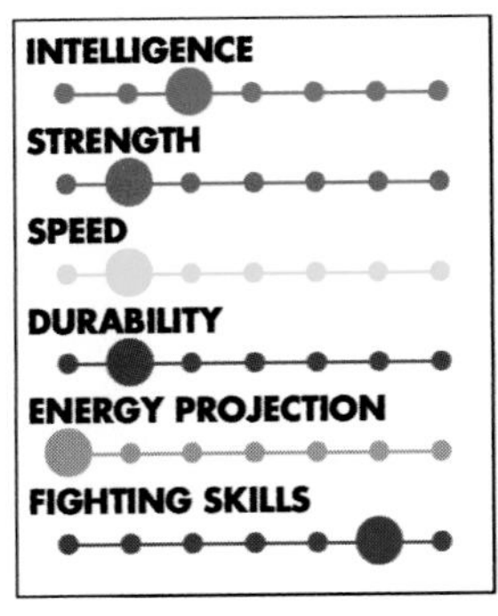

While the Foreigner was a highly mysterious figure, his mission was simple enough: He would arrange crimes for those who would pay. Murder and theft on any scale were no problem, as long as the budget was adequate.

Though deadly, he could also be charming. The former husband of Silver Sable, the Foreigner persuaded the Black Cat to work for him for some time — taking advantage of her fury at being rejected by Spider-Man.

In his Machiavellian enterprises, he frequently ran afoul of Spider-Man, although he was not the kind to fight when there was profit to be made by other means. Most of his actions were taken indirectly — by agents such as Sabretooth, Blaze and a look-alike puppet replacing the NYPD's Lt. Kris Keating, whom he had killed. Later, he employed the armored force of his own Death Squad. The Foreigner was responsible for arranging the assassination of Ned Leeds, whom he believed at the time to be the Hobgoblin. He was paid to carry out the act by Jack O'Lantern (Jason Macendale), who was afraid to face the Hobgoblin in open combat.

FREDERICK FOSWELL

Real Name: Frederick Foswell
First Appearance: *Amazing Spider-Man* #10 (1964)

Hgt: 5'5"
Wt: 157 lbs.

INTELLIGENCE
STRENGTH
SPEED
DURABILITY
ENERGY PROJECTION
FIGHTING SKILLS

Frederick Foswell was a short, slight, timid journalist for the Daily Bugle. Bucking his public persona, he used his reporter's skills and contacts to join with the Enforcers and unite the mobs of New York. He adopted the identity of the Big Man, wearing built-up shoes and a padded jacket to disguise his identity — until his secret was revealed through Spider-Man's intervention.

Upon his return from prison, Foswell was rehired by J. Jonah Jameson — and returned to the streets, disguised as a low-life named Patch. Foswell deduced the Crime-Master's identity and tipped off the police. He aided Spider-Man and the authorities in other cases, and became the Daily Bugle's best reporter. As Patch, Foswell was one of the first to discover Spider-Man's secret identity. He was certainly the first to fall for a now-familiar trick: a fake conversation between Peter Parker and Spider-Man, punctuated by the departure of a web-slinging web-dummy.

In his final appearances, Foswell reverted to his old ways. He became the right-hand man to the Kingpin — but when the crime lord's men attempted to kill Jameson, Foswell could not let any harm come to the man who had trusted him. Protecting Jameson, Foswell was gunned down by the Kingpin's men. His daughter, Janice Foswell, later played the role of the Big Man, and also died doing so.

DOMINIC FORTUNE

Real Name: Duvid Fortunov
First Appearance: *Marvel Preview* #2 (1975)
Hgt: 6'3"
Wt: 195 lbs.

A famous adventurer during the 1930s, Duvid Fortunov was a candidate to become the U.S. government's Super-Soldier, Captain America, but was passed over for anti-Semitic reasons. In the modern era, the elderly Dominic Fortune came out of retirement to battle Turner D. Century alongside Spider-Man. Since then, Fortune has occasionally assisted the web-slinger — including a notable bout with the Shocker. After years of searching, he also was reunited with his long-lost lover, Sabbath Raven, with help from Spider-Man and Silver Sable.

POWERS/WEAPONS

- Skilled athlete
- Master marksman

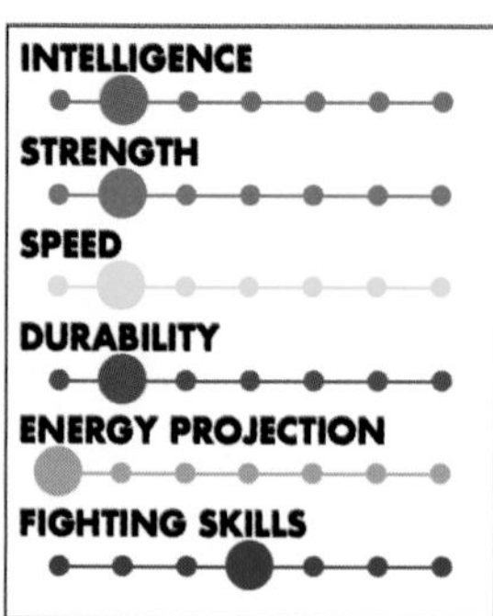

FRIGHTFUL FOUR

First Appearance: *Fantastic Four* #36 (1965)

Principally foes of the Fantastic Four, the Frightful Four have also clashed with Spider-Man. High turnover through the years has resulted in several recruitment drives. On one occasion, the Frightful Four even attempted to draft a brain-washed Spider-Man. During another drive, Electro briefly joined the team — whereupon he and the Frightful Four attempted to trap the Fantastic Four by using Spider-Man as bait. Despite a high dropout rate, the Wizard, the Sandman and the Trapster have remained the team's core members. Temporary members have included Brute, the Constrictor, Deadpool, Dreadknight, Hydro-Man, Klaw, Llyra, the Man-Bull, Medusa, a Punisher robot, the Red Ghost, the She-Thing, the Taskmaster, Thundra and Titania.

FROG-MAN

Real Name: Eugene Paul Colorito Patilio
First Appearance: *Marvel Team-Up* #121 (1982)
Hgt: 5'8"
Wt: 185 lbs.

When less-than-super-villain Leap-Frog retired, his teenage son co-opted one of his costumes to fight crime — with little success. Eugene Patilio offered unskilled and unconstructive assistance to Spider-Man and the Human Torch vs. the Speed Demon, hindered the web-slinger's efforts to overcome the White Rabbit, and accidentally aided and abetted Thunderball's escape. Later, Frog-Man was briefly a member of the short-lived super-hero group known as the Misfits. When he accidentally managed to help Spider-Man, who had been double-teamed by the White Rabbit and the Walrus, Eugene's father finally approved of his son's crime-fighting career.

POWERS/WEAPONS

- Electronic leaping springs
- Internal computer-guidance system
- Strength-enhancing exoskeleton

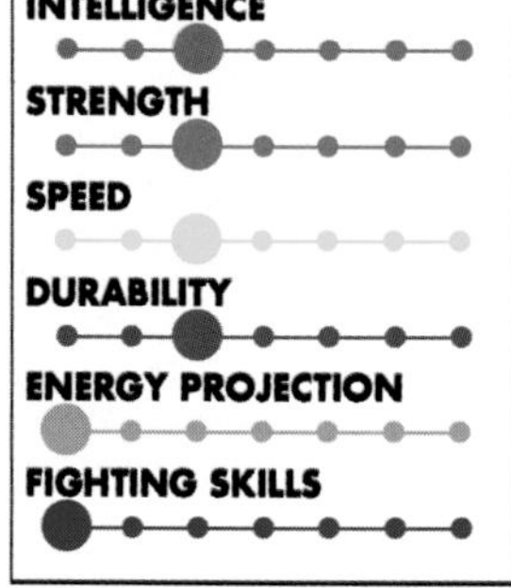

NICK FURY

POWERS/WEAPONS
- Paratrooper, Ranger, Green Beret, Black Beret, demolitions expert and vehicle specialist
- Expert combatant

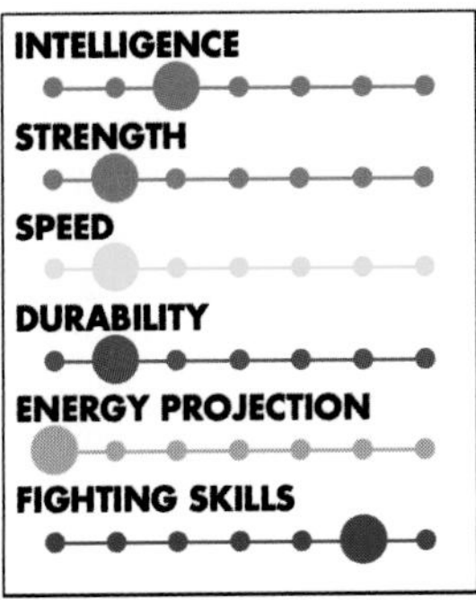

Real Name: Colonel Nicholas Joseph Fury
First Appearance: *Sgt. Fury and His Howling Commandos* #1 (1963)

Hgt: 6'1"
Wt: 225 lbs.

The Strategic Hazard Intervention/Espionage Logistics Directorate is a super-spy agency tasked with safeguarding the free world from global menaces such as Hydra and the scientific conglomerate Advanced Idea Mechanics. Led by Colonel Nick Fury, S.H.I.E.L.D. has been both a staunch ally of the super-hero community and among its worst enemies. The tough-talking, hard-as-nails Fury is the elder statesman of the spy game, having revolutionized the art of espionage. Having helped Spider-Man overcome such foes as the Viper and Doctor Octopus, Fury is aware of the hero's double identity.

FUSION

POWERS/WEAPONS
- Control of others' perceptions
- Immune to Spider-Man's spider-sense
- Power-enhancing wand

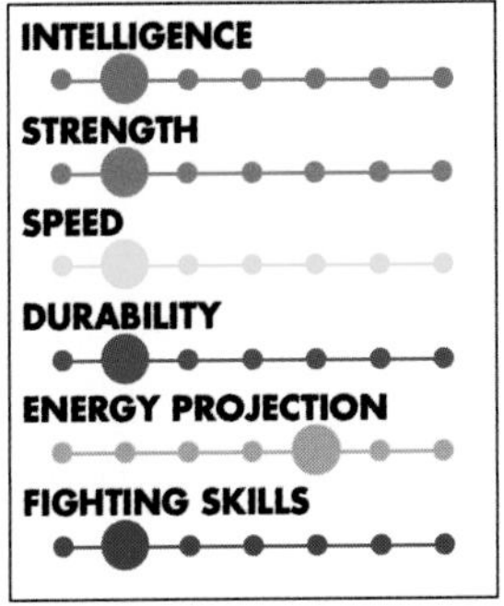

Real Name: Markley, first name unrevealed
First Appearance: *Peter Parker: Spider-Man* #30 (2001)

Hgt: 6'0"
Wt: 190 lbs.

Fusion's young son, Jeremy, died attempting to emulate his hero, Spider-Man. Blaming the web-slinger, Markley sought to exact vengeance. Employing his own innate abilities, Fusion caused Spider-Man to perceive him as possessing the powers of several heroes and villains. Believing his own neck to be broken, Spider-Man nonetheless deciphered the nature of Fusion's abilities and overcame his adversary. Fusion later forced Doctor Octopus to work on his behalf, only to discover Doc Ock had been faking submission to better achieve his own aims. Ending his charade, Ock beat Fusion nearly to death.

FUSION (TWIN TERROR)

POWERS/WEAPONS
- Superhuman strength
- Near-impervious to harm
- Energy absorption
- Decomposition of chemical constructs

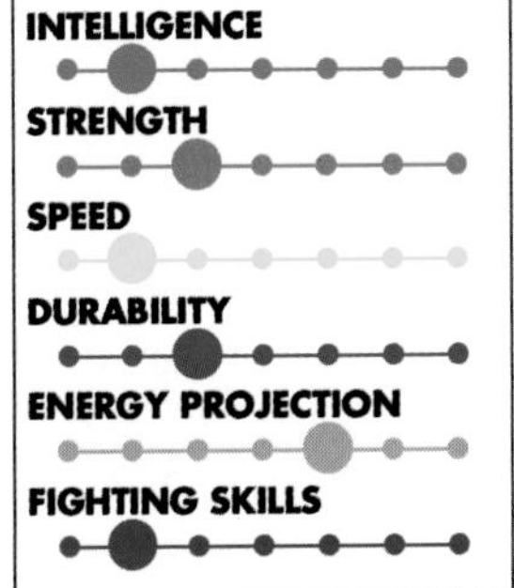

Real Name: Hubert and Pinky Fusser
First Appearance: *Amazing Spider-Man* #208 (1980)

Hgt: 4'
Wt: 80 lbs.

Twins with dwarfism, Hubert the nuclear physicist and Pinky the janitor merged into a single being following a particle-accelerator experiment gone awry. Hubert's enjoyment of their new-found power conflicted with Pinky's disgust over their forced conjoinment. Hubert's mind controlled the twins' merged form, guiding its rampages. With Spider-Man's help, Pinky was able to split them apart. Hubert and Pinky somehow wound up on the laboratory world of the Stranger, along with a number of other terrestrial superhumans. They were liberated by the Avengers' Quasar and eventually returned home.

GAUNTLET

Real Name: Alfredo Morelli
First Appearance: *Amazing Spider-Man* #282 (1986)
Hgt: 6'0"
Wt: 180 lbs.

POWERS/WEAPONS
- Skilled fighter
- Power-enhancing gauntlet

Alfredo Morelli was an old friend and ally of the Kingpin's son, Richard Fisk. Skilled in the use and creation of technology, he helped Richard amass an empire of his own. Their plan later called for Alfredo to imitate Richard, become the new Kingpin and dismantle the latter's empire. After gaining control of Wilson Fisk's territory, Alfredo did not wish to abandon his newfound power — bringing him into conflict with Richard, who defeated his former friend. Alfredo subsequently stole one of Nightwatch's power gloves and became the super-villain Gauntlet; he was later imprisoned for his crimes.

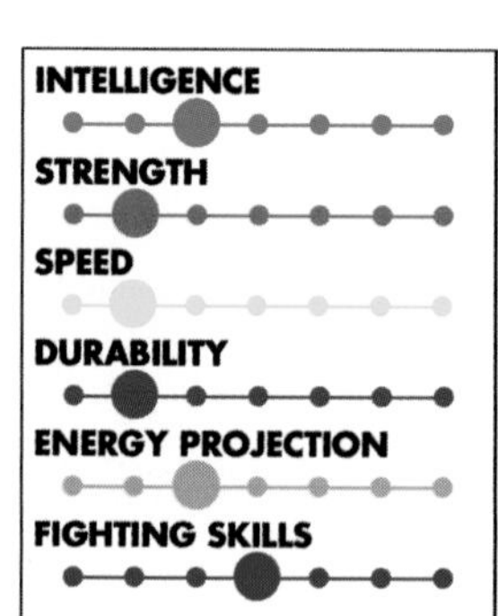

BLACKIE GAXTON

Real Name: "Blackie" Gaxton, first name unknown
First Appearance: *Amazing Spider-Man* #11 (1964)
Hgt: 6'0"
Wt: 210 lbs.

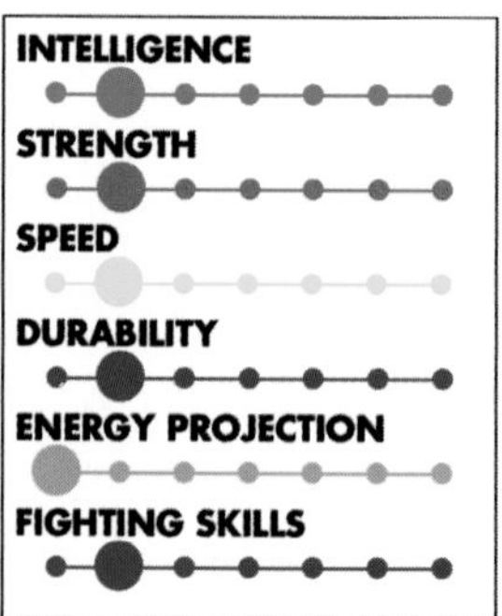

A small-time criminal, "Blackie" Gaxton nonetheless accumulated a large gambling debt from Bennett Brant and kept the lawyer firmly in his pocket. When imprisoned, Gaxton forced Bennett to arrange for Doctor Octopus to break him out. Spider-Man tracked down the two criminals and succeeded in returning Gaxton to jail, but Bennett was caught in the crossfire and killed. The horror of seeing her brother die traumatized Betty Brant, and she could no longer bear the thought or sight of Spider-Man. This was the first step toward the breakup of the budding romance between Betty and Peter Parker.

GIBBON

Real Name: Martin Blank
First Appearance: *Amazing Spider-Man* #110 (1972)
Hgt: 6'5"
Wt: 250 lbs.

POWERS/WEAPONS
- Above-average strength, agility and speed
- Fighting style akin to that of a Gibbon
- Natural kinship with animals

Circus acrobat Martin Blank sought to become Spider-Man's crime-fighting partner. Rejected, he fell in with Kraven the Hunter. Kraven enhanced his protégé's powers using an herb broth and sent him to fight Spider-Man, but the Gibbon was defeated. Attempting to prove his worth, he faced the web-slinger again. But when the Beetle attacked Spider-Man, Martin decided to aid the hero. The Gibbon later joined the Spider-Man Revenge Squad (Legion of Losers), but he and the Grizzly experienced a change of heart and helped Spider-Man defeat Kangaroo II and the Spot.

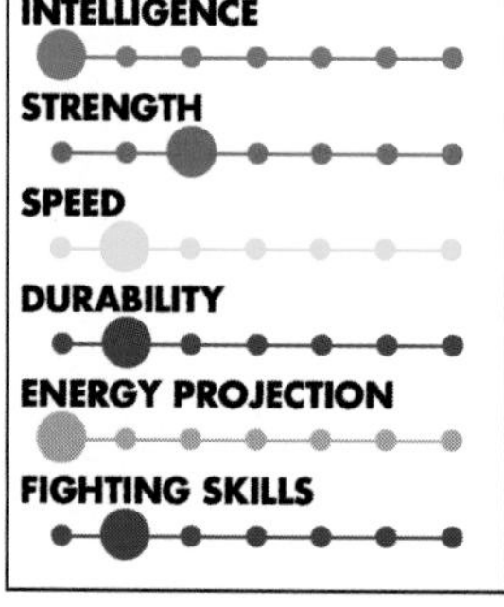

GLORY GRANT

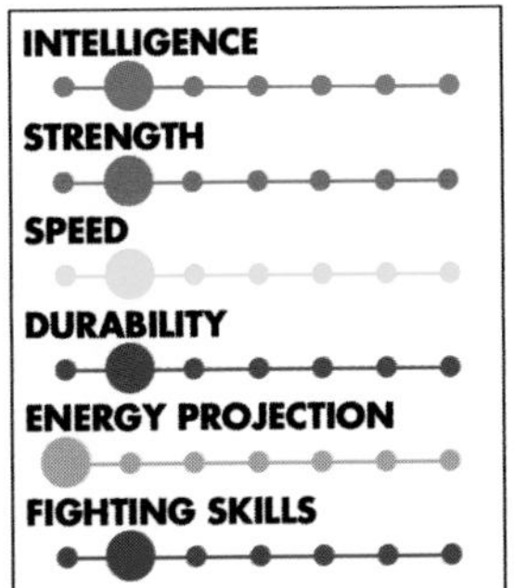

Real Name: Gloria Grant
First Appearance: *Amazing Spider-Man* #140 (1985)

Hgt: 5'8"
Wt: 120 lbs.

When Liz Allan (Liz Osborn) took Peter Parker apartment hunting on the Lower West Side, he ended up moving in across the hall from the glamorous Glory Grant.

After Betty Brant left the Daily Bugle to marry Ned Leeds, J. Jonah Jameson unsurprisingly struggled to find a replacement for his personal secretary who could handle his difficult ways. Following a number of failures, Peter suggested Glory try out for the job; she proved herself more than capable.

During the gang war between the Lobo Brothers and the Kingpin, Glory fell in love with Eduardo Lobo. As Eduardo and Spider-Man struggled in battle, Glory fired a gun into the fray — killing Eduardo. Spider-Man's thanks proved short-lived when a tearful Glory revealed she had in fact been aiming at him. Ever since, Glory has harbored a simmering hatred for the wall-crawler — although she is a staunch friend of Peter Parker.

Glory narrowly avoided being permanently possessed by the soul of Calypso when she was rescued by Spider-Man and Shotgun. Perhaps now, her loathing for him has eased. Of late, she has been dating Randy Robertson.

GREAT GAME

First Appearance: *Amazing Scarlet Spider* #2 (1995)

In the Great Game, super-powered individuals fight for points, levels, wealth, glory — and often their very lives. Funded by extraordinarily wealthy sponsors such as James Johnsmeyer, and refereed by the elegant Henri, battles take place worldwide.

Original players included Joystick, the Rhino, El Toro Negro, Muse and Polestar. Unwilling combatants are often forced to participate, and so it was that Ben Reilly and Phil Urich found themselves as unprepared contestants in an all-out battle for survival.

Soon added to the scorecard were Rocket Racer, the Prowler, Jack O'Lantern II and Nightwatch — with Chance and Cardiac walking the sidelines in search of profit and revenge. The resulting rumble cost the lives of Nightwatch and Polestar; the Prowler was left crippled.

When it was discovered that Johnsmeyer was mixing sports and high-finance — using rogue game players to assassinate CEOs of companies ripe for takeover — his fellow sponsors realized more than human life was at stake. They realized they could lose their companies — and their profits. And the game was over.

GREEN GOBLIN

Real Name:
Norman Osborn

First Appearance:
Amazing Spider-Man #14 (1964)

Height:	5'11"
Weight:	185 lbs.
Eye Color:	Blue
Hair Color:	Reddish-brown

INTELLIGENCE

STRENGTH

SPEED

DURABILITY

ENERGY PROJECTION

FIGHTING SKILLS

POWERS/WEAPONS

- Superhuman strength and speed
- Accelerated healing factor
- Armored costume
- Goblin Glider
- Projection of electric sparks from gloves
- Pumpkin Bombs
- Hallucinogenic, ghost-like grenades
- Razor-sharp, flying bats

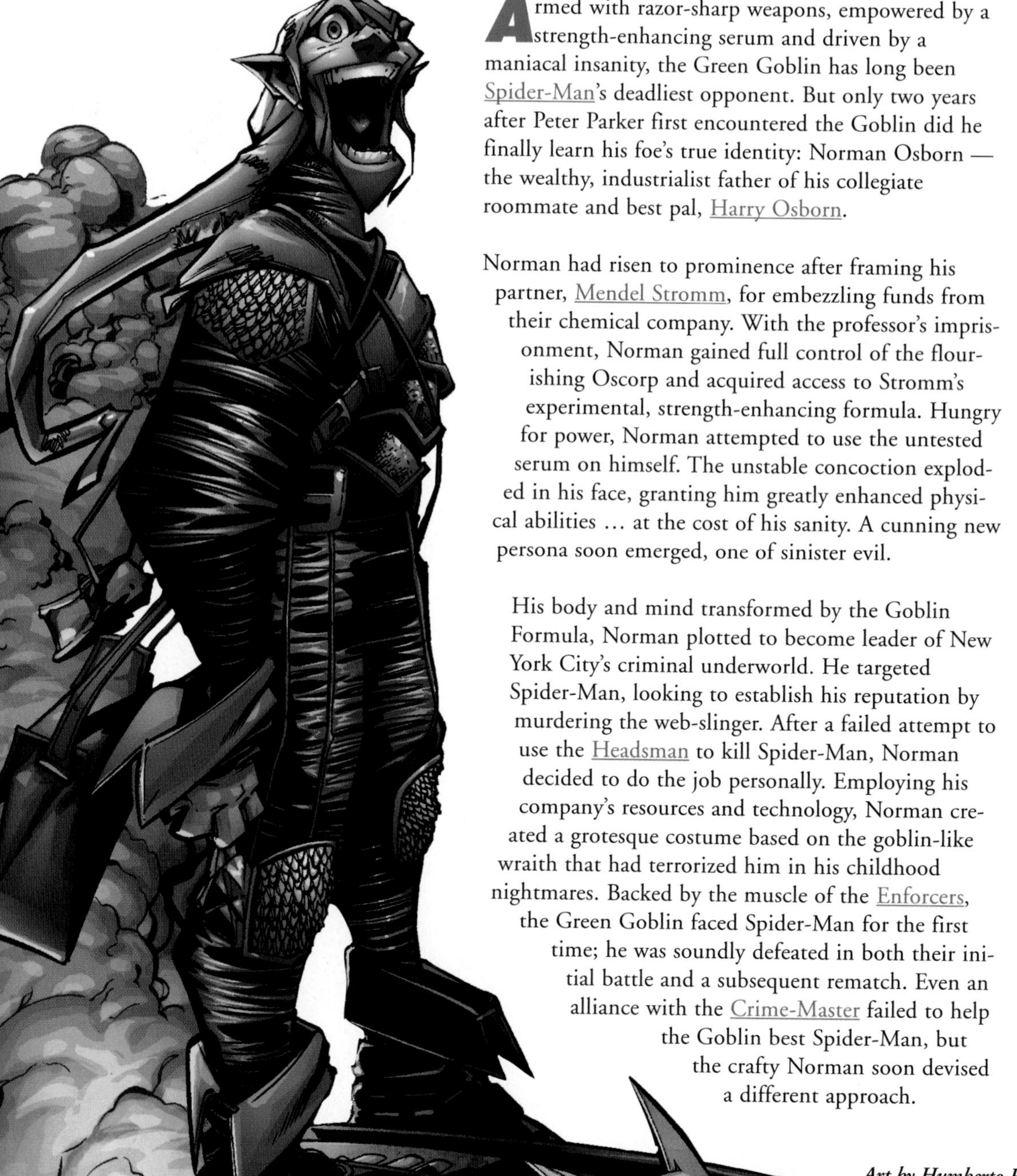

Armed with razor-sharp weapons, empowered by a strength-enhancing serum and driven by a maniacal insanity, the Green Goblin has long been Spider-Man's deadliest opponent. But only two years after Peter Parker first encountered the Goblin did he finally learn his foe's true identity: Norman Osborn — the wealthy, industrialist father of his collegiate roommate and best pal, Harry Osborn.

Norman had risen to prominence after framing his partner, Mendel Stromm, for embezzling funds from their chemical company. With the professor's imprisonment, Norman gained full control of the flourishing Oscorp and acquired access to Stromm's experimental, strength-enhancing formula. Hungry for power, Norman attempted to use the untested serum on himself. The unstable concoction exploded in his face, granting him greatly enhanced physical abilities ... at the cost of his sanity. A cunning new persona soon emerged, one of sinister evil.

His body and mind transformed by the Goblin Formula, Norman plotted to become leader of New York City's criminal underworld. He targeted Spider-Man, looking to establish his reputation by murdering the web-slinger. After a failed attempt to use the Headsman to kill Spider-Man, Norman decided to do the job personally. Employing his company's resources and technology, Norman created a grotesque costume based on the goblin-like wraith that had terrorized him in his childhood nightmares. Backed by the muscle of the Enforcers, the Green Goblin faced Spider-Man for the first time; he was soundly defeated in both their initial battle and a subsequent rematch. Even an alliance with the Crime-Master failed to help the Goblin best Spider-Man, but the crafty Norman soon devised a different approach.

Art by Humberto Ramos

After concocting a compound that weakened the web-slinger's spider-sense, the Goblin followed him undetected. When Spider-Man assumed his civilian identity, Norman swiftly attacked. Easily overpowering a surprised Peter, the Goblin abducted him and took him back to a secret hideout. There, the Goblin taunted Peter, his mind intoxicated with overwhelming arrogance. While the Goblin indulged in boastful speeches, Peter was able to escape his bindings. During the ensuing battle, Norman was electrocuted with a shock powerful enough to jolt his mind into partial amnesia. With all memories of the Goblin and Peter's true identity seemingly wiped from Norman's mind, Spider-Man decided to protect his friend Harry from the knowledge of his father's maniacal alter ego. To that end, Peter stripped Norman of the Goblin costume and hid the villain's true identity from the authorities.

Art by John Romita Jr.

Against Peter's hopes, Norman's amnesia proved to be as unstable as his sanity. When exposed to stress or images of the Goblin, his madness and memories would return — dominated by an aggressive hatred of Spider-Man. In their subsequent battles, Peter was able to use his knowledge of Norman's unbalanced mind to shock the villain back into brief sanity — but the episodes grew more frequent, and the Goblin's methods became increasingly insidious.

Art by Tim Sale

Knowing Peter's true identity, the Goblin hatched a scheme to attack Spider-Man through the people he loved. The Goblin kidnapped Peter's girlfriend, Gwen Stacy, and brought her to the Brooklyn Bridge. When Spider-Man attempted to rescue her, the Goblin hurled the girl off the bridge. While Spider-Man was able to catch Gwen with a well-placed web-line, the sudden stop snapped her neck. In frenzied grief, Spider-Man fought the Goblin as never before. The hero nearly beat the Goblin to death, but held back his final blow. Bloody, beaten and feigning surrender, the Goblin attempted to spear Spider-Man with the razor-sharp tip of his remote-controlled glider. Warned by his spider-sense, the hero was able to leap away at the last second — leaving the Goblin fatally impaled, the victim of his own final ruse.

Unknown to Spider-Man, Harry had secretly witnessed their final battle. Harry removed the Goblin's costume when Spider-Man departed, preserving his father's identity even after his seeming death. Believing Spider-Man was to blame for Norman's demise, Harry vowed revenge on the web-slinger; soon after, he took up the mantle of his father's criminal identity.

Continued...

GREEN GOBLIN

Though it was long believed he had been fatally wounded, Norman's death was not what it seemed. The chemicals that granted him enhanced strength and altered his sanity also gifted him with a superhuman healing ability. His impaled chest mended while Norman lay in the morgue, and the clever villain covered his escape by swapping his body with that of a murdered drifter. Returning to his hideout, Norman arrived in time to observe Harry vow vengeance on Spider-Man and don the Goblin costume. Passing the legacy of the Green Goblin to his son, Norman slipped away unnoticed to Europe.

In Europe, Norman joined a secret society known as the Scriers and soon took control of the shadowy cabal. His hatred of Peter still raging as strong as ever, Norman hatched a plan to surreptitiously use the Scriers to psychologically destroy the web-slinger. He dispatched a Scrier to America to aid one of Peter's professors, Dr. Miles Warren (Jackal), in his quest to create clones of both Gwen and Peter. With the Scrier's help, Warren successfully produced a clone of Peter and arranged for him to battle his double at Shea Stadium. Believing his clone had been fatally injured during their fight, Spider-Man cast the lifeless body into a smokestack. However, the clone was still alive; when he regained consciousness, he assumed the identity of Ben Reilly and lived as a drifter for five years.

Art by John Romita Jr.

After Harry fatally succumbed to the toxic effects of an updated Goblin Formula, Norman returned to the United States. It was at this time that both the Jackal and Ben also resurfaced in Peter's life. Shocked to face his clone after so many years, Peter fell prey to Norman's manipulations — believing he was the clone, and Ben the original. It was Norman's intention to devastate Peter with the false revelation. In fact, the news had the opposite effect: After passing the responsibilities of Spider-Man to Ben, Peter eagerly embraced the idea of a quiet civilian life with his wife, Mary Jane Watson, and moved to Portland. Infuriated by Peter's happiness, Norman was forced to abandon his psychological attacks and finally reveal himself.

The Goblin attacked Ben and Peter in a grand battle, destroying Spider-Man's long-held hope that his greatest foe was dead and buried. During the fight, Ben was killed protecting Peter. When his corpse rapidly disintegrated, it proved Ben had been the clone all along. Peter narrowly escaped death himself, tormented by the fact that he was facing a Green Goblin more driven than ever.

As the Goblin returned to public view, so did Norman. With a carefully contrived story, he resumed his role as a wealthy public figure — regaining control of his industrial empire from his daughter-in-law, Liz Osborn. With his financial control of Oscorp and subsidiary Multivex restored, Norman launched a hostile takeover of the Daily Bugle — using the paper to damage Spider-Man's reputation. Norman's growing lust

Art by Humberto Ramos

for power led to his participation in an ancient ritual called the Gathering of Five — in which each undertaker would randomly receive a gift of power, knowledge, immortality, madness or death. Hoping for power, he instead drew madness. Norman was defeated by Spider-Man after a mighty battle that destroyed the Daily Bugle building.

With the aid of his faithful Sciers, Norman escaped the destruction of the Bugle; the use of medicated patches restored some semblance of his sanity. While Norman recovered, J. Jonah Jameson was able to wrest control of the Bugle from his clutches. Shortly thereafter, Norman came to the realization that Peter was truly the son he had always wanted — studious, inventive, strong-willed and industrious — in contrast to the late Harry, who had always wilted under the pressures of life. Rather than kill his hated enemy, Norman now set out to mold Peter in his own image, an heir to the Goblin legacy. He initiated a mad plan to corrupt Peter and fill him with hatred, pushing him past the point of no return. But Norman had clearly misjudged Peter. No matter how many drugs he employed, the hero's will was too strong for Norman to sway. The time for such tricks was long past.

Relentless in pursuit of retribution, Norman decided to stake everything he had built on one final throw of the dice. Attacking Peter's friends and family, Norman first pressed Flash Thompson into an arranged drunken-driving accident, leaving him in a coma. Then the Goblin forced Spider-Man into battle, threatening to kill every person Peter loved — Mary Jane; his aunt, May Parker; even Norman's own grandson, Norman Osborn Jr. During their heated fight, Peter admitted to Norman that he should hate the Goblin for killing Gwen — but by giving in to that bitterness, he would forever blacken the memory of the first girl he ever loved. Although Norman soon fell to Peter's mercy, Spider-Man refused to give in to his anger and walked away from the fight. Shocked by the strength of Peter's unbreakable spirit, Norman seemed to arrive at the realization that Spider-Man would no longer be willing to continue this deadly cycle of violence. The Green Goblin cannot battle a Spider-Man who refuses to fight. Perhaps finally, after so many years, Norman has accepted the futility of his actions. What that ultimately means for these two men, only time can tell.

GOLDBUG

Real Name: Unrevealed
First Appearance: *Luke Cage, Power Man* #41 (1977)
Hgt: 5'9"
Wt: 170 lbs.

A minor menace with a grand obsession for gold, Goldbug's criminal quest has become a sickness — literally. Following a battle with Spider-Man, Goldbug contracted radiation poisoning from the irradiated gold he was attempting to steal. Spider-Man was not the first or last hero to contend with Goldbug. Before encountering the web-slinger, Goldbug clashed with Cage and the Hulk, among others. In his most recent scheme, he attempted to steal the sunken gold building created by the Beyonder, but was thwarted by Namor, the Atlantean Sub-Mariner.

POWERS/WEAPONS

- Golden exoskeleton
- Gun capable of coating others in gold
- Hovercraft

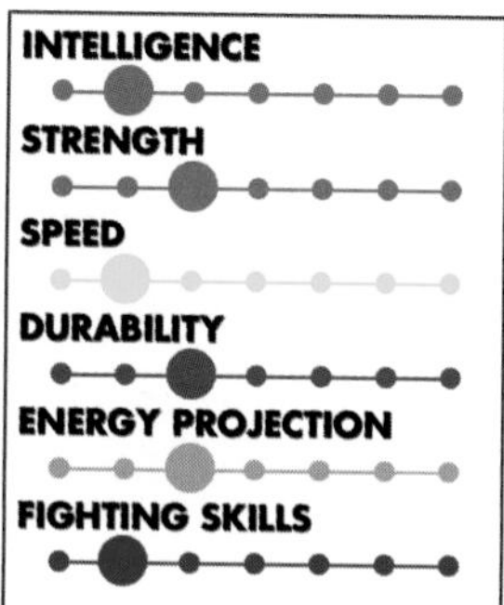

GRAVITON

Real Name: Franklin Hall
First Appearance: *Avengers* #158 (1977)
Hgt: 6'1"
Wt: 200 lbs.

Following a freak laboratory accident, scientist Frank Hall found himself able to control gravity. As Graviton, he tangled with the Avengers repeatedly. Hired to kill Spider-Man, he faced the wall-crawler three times. First, he destroyed the Daily Bugle and nearly killed Spider-Man. Next, he was soundly defeated by Cosmic Spider-Man. Finally, he had his eyes webbed over by his adversary. Later, with enhanced abilities and a steadier purpose, he decided to reshape the planet in his own image — literally. Stopped by the Thunderbolts, he apparently sacrificed his life to prevent the extra-dimensional P'tah from using his powers to invade Earth.

POWERS/WEAPONS

- Complete control over gravity
- Projection of force-bolts

INTELLIGENCE
STRENGTH
SPEED
DURABILITY
ENERGY PROJECTION
FIGHTING SKILLS

GRIZZLY

Real Name: Maxwell Markham
First Appearance: *Amazing Spider-Man* #139 (1974)
Hgt: 6'9"
Wt: 290 lbs.

Professional wrestler Maxwell Markham's violent tendencies brought him to the attention of J. Jonah Jameson, whose public crusade resulted in the Grizzly's expulsion from the sport. Equipped with an exoskeleton by the Jackal, Markham first fought Spider-Man when the wall-crawler prevented him from attacking Jameson. After years of failure, the Grizzly organized the Spider-Man Revenge Squad (Legion of Losers). But he and the Gibbon experienced a change of heart, helping Spider-Man defeat their teammates. The Grizzly fought crime for a time, but returned to the wrong side of the law when he grew disenchanted with civilian life.

POWERS/WEAPONS

- Superhuman strength

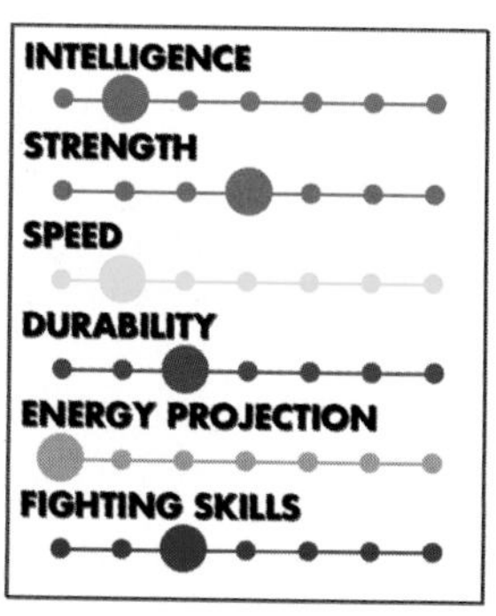

HAMMERHEAD

Hammerhead began his career as a Maggia hitman; after a brutal defeat in which Hammerhead's head was shattered, Dr. Jonas Harrow discovered him in an alley and replaced his broken skull with a metal substitute. The last thing Hammerhead saw before being knocked out was a movie poster for a film set in the 1920s. Awakening from his surgery, Hammerhead developed an infatuation with '20s gangster style — adopting the clothing and weapons of that era. Meanwhile, the brain damage he suffered left him violently unstable, with no memory of his former life.

Real Name:
Unrevealed
First Appearance:
Amazing Spider-Man #113 (1972)

Height:	5'10"
Weight:	195 lbs.
Eye Color:	Blue
Hair Color:	Black

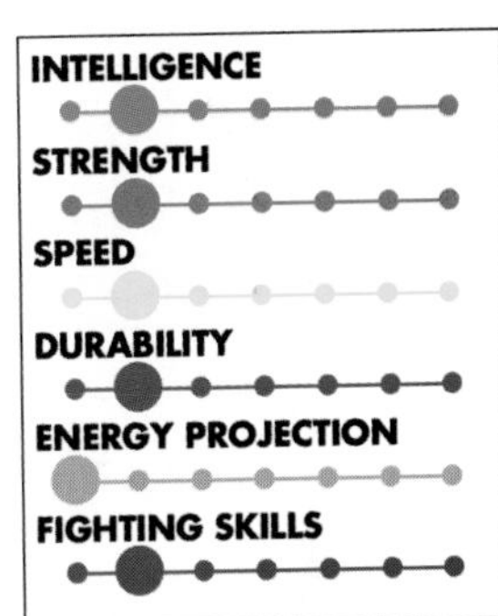

When the Kingpin's withdrawal left a power vacuum in the city, gang war erupted between Hammerhead's goons and Doctor Octopus' minions. Spider-Man intervened and helped the police capture Doc Ock, but Hammerhead escaped. He went on to reject work from the Jackal — choosing instead to fight a released Doctor Octopus over May Parker, who had inherited a Canadian nuclear processing facility. The conflict ended in a nuclear explosion, with both men presumed dead. In fact, Doc Ock had managed to escape the blast. Hammerhead, somehow, simply phased out of reality. But not for long. The ghost-like Hammerhead returned to trouble his old foe, who attempted to dispel his spectral sparring partner with a particle accelerator. Having the opposite effect, the device returned Hammerhead to his full corporal self.

POWERS/ WEAPONS

- Steel-alloy skull
- Proficient in the use of machine guns and other heavy weapons

Whereas gang lords such as the Kingpin, Don Fortunato and Silvermane are primarily focused on profit — viewing violence as nothing more than a means to an end — Hammerhead and his goons are almost overzealous in their pursuit of carnage. But one act would force Hammerhead to re-evaluate his commitment to mayhem. When the Lifeline Tablet resurfaced, holding the promise of eternal youth, Hammerhead led the chase — but not for himself. He sought the formula to save his sister, who was dying of cancer. Hammerhead consumed the resulting potion and was briefly granted cosmic awareness, along with the ability to alter the universe at his whim. Unable to maintain control, he reverted to normal before he could focus his newfound power to save his sister, with whom he had recently been reunited. His sister's life was spared thanks to a second potion concocted by Spider-Man, and Hammerhead was led away to prison — satisfied, perhaps for the first time in his life, with the manner in which events had unfolded. Eventually, Hammerhead escaped incarceration to once more menace society.

Art by Mark Buckingham

DR. BART HAMILTON

Real Name: Dr. Barton Hamilton
First Appearance: *Amazing Spider-Man* #167 (1977)
Hgt: 6'0"
Wt: 195 lbs.

A psychiatrist assigned to work with Harry Osborn, Dr. Bart Hamilton learned from him all the secrets of the Green Goblin. He used this knowledge to cast himself as the new Green Goblin, hoping to command the underworld as the crime lord the original had dreamed of becoming. As the Goblin, Hamilton fought Silvermane, Harry and Spider-Man. Ultimately, Hamilton met his end when he was caught in the blast of a bomb he had planted to kill Harry and Spider-Man.

POWERS/WEAPONS

- Goblin Glider, Pumpkin Bombs and other paraphernalia belonging to the Green Goblin

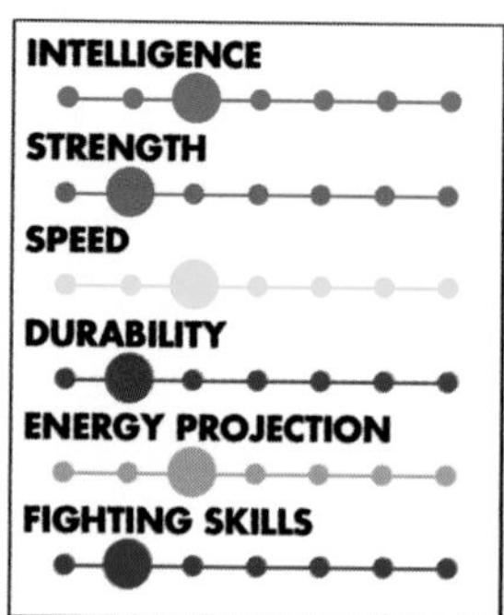

TIM HARRISON

Real Name: Timothy Harrison
First Appearance: *Amazing Spider-Man* #248 (1984)
Hgt: 4'6"
Wt: 55 lbs.

There has been perhaps no greater fan of Spider-Man than 9-year-old Tim Harrison, dubbed "The Kid Who Collects Spider-Man" in a Daily Bugle article written by Jacob Conover. The wall-crawler himself visited Tim one night and was thoroughly impressed by his massive collection of news clippings and unique memorabilia. Spider-Man explained how his powers and web-shooters work, and Tim had the time of his young life. Before he left, Spider-Man even agreed to reveal his secret identity. The hero had made Tim's dreams come true. Tim had leukemia, with only a few weeks left to live.

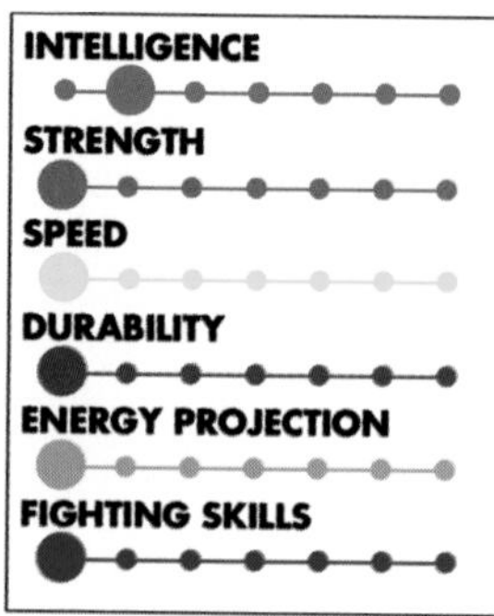

DR. JONAS HARROW

Real Name: Dr. Jonas Harrow
First Appearance: *Amazing Spider-Man* #114 (1972)
Hgt: 6'1"
Wt: 200 lbs.

Dr. Jonas Harrow's scientific genius helped empower many of Spider-Man's foes. His unconventional surgery gave rise to Hammerhead and granted the Kangaroo superhuman powers. When neither demonstrated the least bit of gratitude, Harrow implanted control devices in his next super-villain, Will O' the Wisp. Spider-Man persuaded the Wisp to resist, and Harrow discorporated his creation. He later drove J. Jonah Jameson temporarily insane, leading to Harrow's first direct confrontation with the wall-crawler. Harrow has since empowered Megawatt, briefly controlled Dragon Man and been suspected as the Hobgoblin.

POWERS/WEAPONS

- Scientific genius
- Expert in genetics, cybernetics, mechanics and surgery

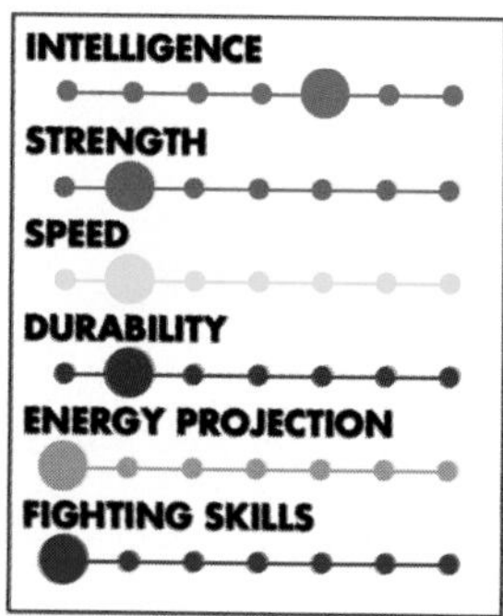

HERO KILLERS

First Appearance:
Amazing Spider-Man Annual #26 (1992)

Resurrected under unknown circumstances, the once-mighty Sphinx found himself virtually powerless. To gain sufficient strength to recreate his own power source, the Ka Stone, the Sphinx allied himself with a number of criminal corporations — including Hammer Industries, the Life Foundation and Roxxon Oil. The Sphinx and his partners dispatched agents — such as the Beetle, Boomerang, the Dreadnoughts, Hydro-Man, the Rhino, Blacklash, Bombshell, the Constrictor, Discus, Stiletto and the Speed Demon — to capture a number of superhumans, with the intent of killing them and studying their abilities. However, the Sphinx's own agenda — to drain their power into himself — superceded his alliance. Spider-Man and the New Warriors opposed him. Speedball reversed the Sphinx's power drain, overloading and defeating him.

HOPE HIBBERT

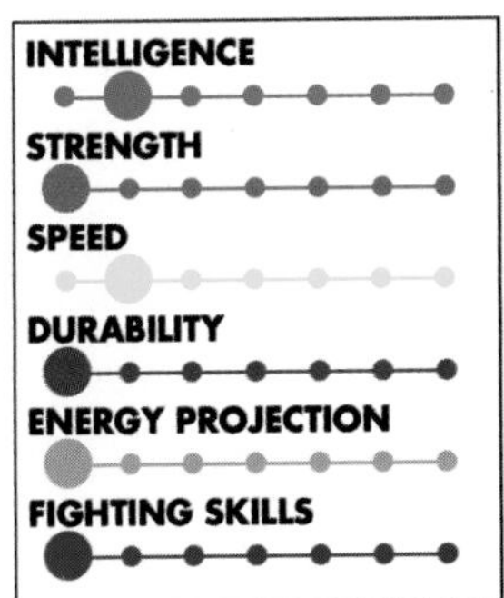

Real Name: Hope Hibbert
First Appearance: *Sensational Spider-Man* #18 (1997)

Hgt: 4'4"
Wt: 65 lbs.

Hope is the 9-year-old daughter of Ellen Hibbert — a policewoman who moved into Anna Watson's home in Forest Hills, next door to May Parker. A sweet, sensitive deaf girl, Hope seemed unusually troubled. When she made Spider-Man's web-shooting hand gesture to Peter Parker, he assumed she had somehow discovered his secret identity. Hope finally admitted she was frightened, having seen Spider-Man leave the Parker house. The wall-crawler's spider-sense hadn't warned him, because he was supernaturally mesmerized. The hero later rescued Hope from the Rhino, calming her fears with the sign for "friend."

HITMAN

POWERS/WEAPONS

- Master marksman and combatant
- Skilled in the use of various military weapons

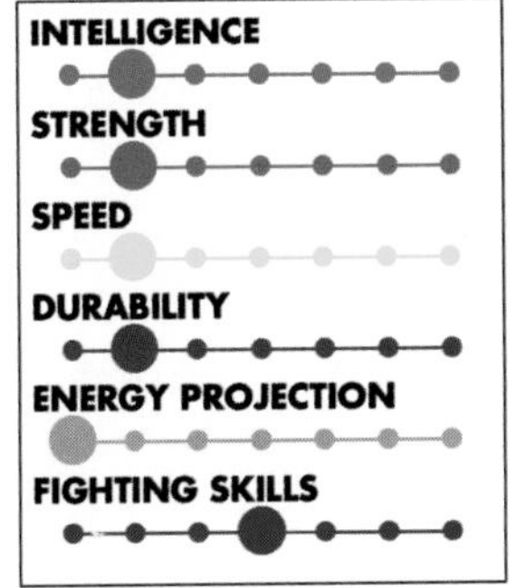

Real Name: Burt Kenyon
First Appearance: *Spectacular Spider-Man* #4 (1977)

Hgt: 6'1"
Wt: 210 lbs.

Burt Kenyon rescued Frank Castle during a military operation, telling the future Punisher he owed him a life. As a mercenary assassin, Kenyon was hired by Bossman Morgan to kill the Vulture — but Spider-Man thwarted his efforts. Retained by the radical terrorist organization known as the People's Liberation Front to terminate J. Jonah Jameson, the Hitman was again defeated by Spider-Man — this time in tandem with the Punisher. Forced to save either Spider-Man or the Hitman from falling to their death, the Punisher chose Spider-Man. Kenyon smiled as he fell, wrlying observing, "I told you you owed me a life, soldier, but I never said it had to be mine."

HOBGOBLIN

Real Name:
Roderick Kingsley
First Appearance:
Spectacular Spider-Man #43 (1980)

Height:	5'11"
Weight:	185 lbs.
Eye Color:	Blue
Hair Color:	Gray

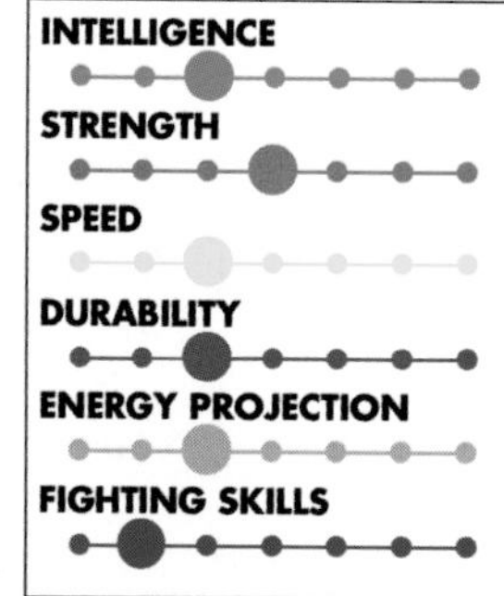

POWERS/ WEAPONS

- Superhuman strength
- Vertical-thrust Goblin Glider
- Jack O'Lantern bombs
- Razor-edged bat wings
- Electro-shock gloves

Art by John Romita Jr.

Roderick Kingsley began his career as a fashion designer, but harbored ambitions far greater. A ruthless and aggressive businessman, Kingsley was willing to work both sides of the law to parlay his talents into a financial empire. From the outset, Kingsley eliminated his competition either by stealing their ideas or ruining their reputations with brutal smear campaigns. After falling victim to Kingsley's underhanded machinations, designer Narda Ravanna sought vengeance in the guise of Belladonna. Her assault on Kingsley would have killed the designer if not for the timely intervention of Spider-Man. Although Kingsley suffered only broken ribs in the attack, the incident left him with a serious case of wounded pride. Swearing to protect himself from the threat of a future attack, Kingsley became increasingly obsessed with finding a way to enhance his strength and physical power.

Not long after, Spider-Man unwittingly became the catalyst for Kingsley's transformation into one of New York City's most feared criminals. In pursuit of a gang of thieves, Spider-Man was able to nab three, but lost the fourth in New York's maze-like sewer system. During the chase, the crook accidentally discovered a hidden cache of the Green Goblin's weapons and costumes. Knowing of Kingsley's quest for physical power, the criminal sold him the Goblin's long-abandoned arsenal. Kingsley eagerly purchased the weaponry. As the Hobgoblin, Kingsley carved out a piece of the New York underworld. His criminal activities soon brought him into conflict with Spider-Man, and the Hobgoblin was forced to face the hero in battle. Lacking the Green Goblin's original strength-enhancing formula, the Hobgoblin was overpowered by the web-slinger and barely escaped capture.

After tracking down the remainder of Norman Osborn's diaries, Kingsley was able to acquire the Goblin Formula. Using a common street tough named Lefty Donovan as his unwitting guinea pig, Kingsley refined the chemical mixture to remove the portion that had cursed the Green Goblin with insanity. Although Kingsley was now almost Spider-Man's equal in terms of strength, the web-slinger still was able to overcome the Hobgoblin in their next battle; the villain nearly drowned making his escape. Shaken by his brush with death, Kingsley set out to manipulate matters from behind the scenes. By brainwashing Ned Leeds into donning the Hobgoblin costume and acting as his pawn, Kingsley could continue his criminal pursuits while avoiding the increasing danger of physical confrontations with Spider-Man. Under Kingsley's direction, Leeds participated in a brutal gang war that nearly destroyed New York City. When Leeds became increasingly uncontrollable, Kingsley leaked word to the Foreigner that Leeds was the Hobgoblin. Leeds was murdered by the criminal's assassins soon after. With the Hobgoblin's career seemingly ended, Kingsley retired to Europe.

Jason Macendale, formerly known as Jack O'Lantern, later assumed the Hobgoblin's identity. Macendale's impersonation at first amused Kingsley — but when Macendale claimed in court that contrary to public perception, he was not the only Hobgoblin, Kingsley felt threatened and returned to New York to kill him. He quickly murdered the pretender and became the Hobgoblin once more. Despite Kingsley's efforts to conceal his identity, determined sleuthing by Betty Brant uncovered the truth and cleared her late husband Ned Leeds' name. With Spider-Man's help, Kingsley was imprisoned. Not long after Kingsley's defeat, Norman Osborn publicly re-emerged in an unexpected return from the dead. Kingsley subsequently leaked word he possessed the one surviving journal proving Osborn was the original Green Goblin. Seeking to eliminate a potential witness, Osborn broke Kingsley out of jail — only to discover the journal was merely a ruse to elicit his help in the prison break. After a brief battle between the men ended in a draw, Kingsley fled to the sanctuary of the Caribbean.

Art by Brett Breeding

CRUSHER HOGAN

Real Name: Joseph "Crusher" Hogan
First Appearance: *Amazing Fantasy* #15 (1962)

Hgt: 5'10"
Wt: 210 lbs.

INTELLIGENCE
STRENGTH
SPEED
DURABILITY
ENERGY PROJECTION
FIGHTING SKILLS

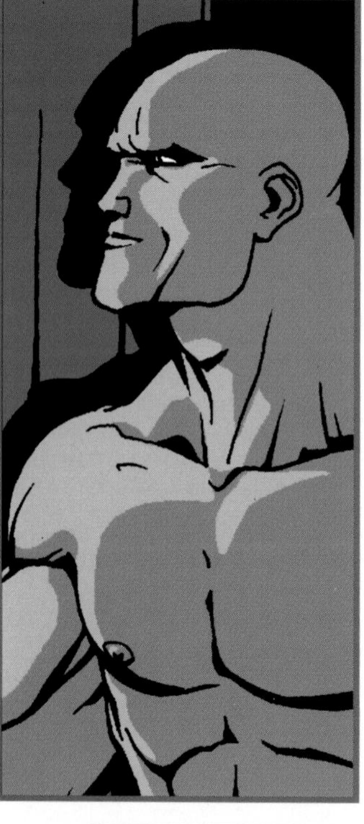

Crusher Hogan played a well-known role in Spider-Man's origin. When Peter Parker set out to test his newfound powers, he took up the challenge to last three minutes in the ring with the muscle-bound professional wrestler — whom he easily and spectacularly defeated.

The flip side of that tale is a better-kept secret. Joseph Hogan held a deep love of his chosen sport and a great loyalty to his league, which was in desperate financial straits. Unknown to young Peter, Hogan had borrowed the prize money from the mob — trusting nobody could beat him in the ring. He never counted on a nobody named the Amazing Spider-Man.

Defeated by Spider-Man, and no doubt mercilessly beaten by mob goons, Crusher was a broken man — relegated to sweeping up a third-rate gym run by the evil Madam Fang and her brutal enforcer Man-Slaughter. When he defied Madam Fang, Crusher was saved from near-certain death at Man-Slaughter's hands by a fortuitously passing Spider-Man. It was just dumb luck — but from that day forth, nobody doubted those stories Crusher loved to tell about the days when he helped train a young hero named Spider-Man.

HULK

Real Name: Dr. Robert Bruce Banner
First Appearance: *Hulk* #1 (1962)

Hgt: 7'0"
Wt: 1040 lbs.

POWERS/WEAPONS

- Near-limitless strength
- Impervious skin
- Immunity to disease
- Can leap great distances

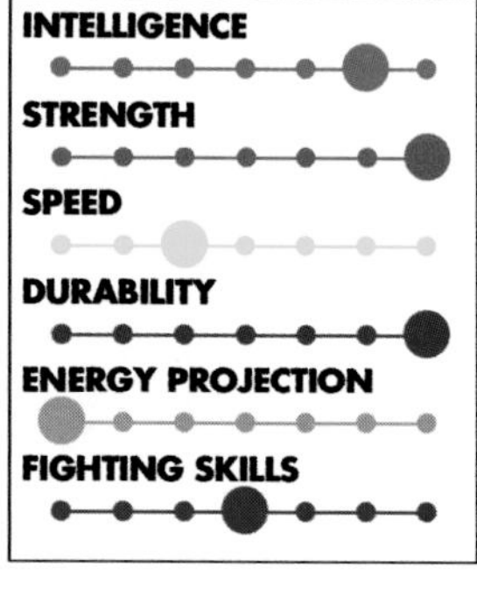

Curiously, Spider-Man's initial encounter with the most powerful man-like creature ever to walk the Earth coincided with the first appearance of another deadly green menace, the Green Goblin.

Early in his career, while fleeing both the Goblin and the Enforcers, Spider-Man sought refuge in a cave that was also home to a far-from-amused Hulk. Spider-Man was fortunate to get out with his skin intact — a narrow escape that set the pattern for many subsequent encounters during the following years. In almost every meeting, Spider-Man would find himself the unwilling sparring partner of a foe who greatly outclassed him in terms of raw strength. In all those battles, Spider-Man would consider a draw to be a great victory.

The most notable exception came when Spider-Man, as the super-powered Cosmic Spider-Man, struck the Hulk so hard as to send him into orbit — where eventually it seemed he would revert to Banner and meet with certain death. Admittedly surprised to discover his newfound cosmic strength and skills, Spider-Man then rescued the Hulk.

HUMAN TORCH

The contrast between Johnny Storm and Peter Parker could hardly be greater. As the Human Torch, Storm is a member of the famed Fantastic Four, celebrated and admired worldwide for their efforts fighting cosmic-level dangers and exploring the boundaries of human knowledge. As Spider-Man, Peter is feared, hated and publicly branded a menace by the Daily Bugle.

Real Name:
Jonathan Storm
First Appearance:
Fantastic Four #1 (1961)

Height:	5'10"
Weight:	170 lbs.
Eye Color:	Blue
Hair Color:	Blond

In his first battle against Doctor Octopus, Spider-Man was easily defeated. Humiliated, Peter considered giving up his costumed identity — until he attended a special assembly at Midtown High School with Johnny Storm as the guest speaker. In his talk to the school, Storm told the students to never give up. Peter realized that even for the fabled Fantastic Four, victory does not always come easily. With renewed confidence, Spider-Man defeated Doctor Octopus and tracked down the Human Torch to thank the confused firebrand for his unwitting good advice. With the ice between the two heroes melted, they formed a frequent partnership, battling any menace that put their shared city in danger. Together, the pair has defeated such foes as the Beetle, Mysterio, the Super-Skrull and the Sandman.

Art by Skottie Young

As the youngest member of the Fantastic Four, Johnny Storm resents his role as the "immature kid" of the group — but with Spider-Man, the Human Torch enjoys a friendship of mutual respect with a hero of comparable age.

The Human Torch is so confident in Spider-Man's noble heart he has refused knowledge of the web-slinger's secret identity, even when freely offered by Peter. Whenever Spider-Man is in need of his fiery friend, a web-signal is enough to summon Johnny to their usual meeting spot — aptly chosen to be the Statue of Liberty's torch.

INTELLIGENCE
STRENGTH
SPEED
DURABILITY
ENERGY PROJECTION
FIGHTING SKILLS

POWERS/ WEAPONS

- Projection and manipulation of flame in a broad range of temperatures and shapes
- Flight

HORNET

Real Name: Peter Benjamin Parker
First Appearance: *Sensational Spider-Man* #27 (1998)

Hgt: 5'10"
Wt: 165 lbs.

Peter Parker assumed the identity of the Hornet to escape a price on Spider-Man's head. When the Looter attempted to steal the reward from Norman Osborn (Green Goblin), taking Flash Thompson hostage, the Hornet saved the day. Ironically, Norman offered the Hornet a job and the reward, which the hero donated to charity. When the Hornet told the media the city no longer had to worry about Spider-Man, the Vulture misinterpreted his remark and attacked him for killing his sworn enemy. The Vulture recognized Spider-Man's fighting style and exposed the Hornet's secret. Eddie McDonough of the Slingers later adopted the costume.

POWERS/WEAPONS

- All the abilities of Spider-Man
- Battle armor
- Jet-pack created by Hobie Brown (Prowler)
- Web-stingers

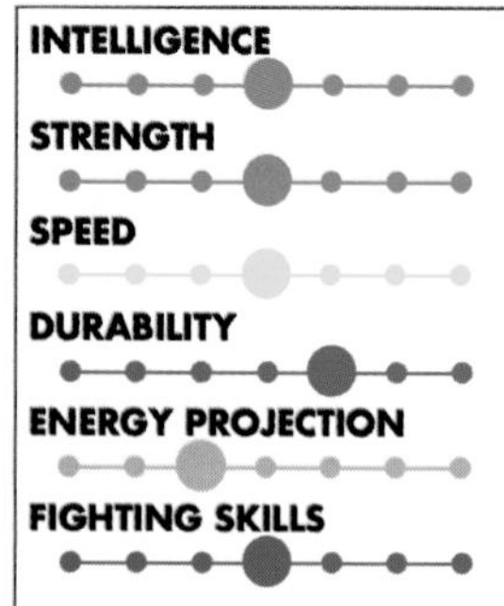

HOWARD THE DUCK

Real Name: Howard
First Appearance: *Adventures into Fear* #19 (1973)

Hgt: 2'7"
Wt: 40 lbs.

A native of the realm of Duckworld, Howard was deposited on Earth during a shift of the Cosmic Axis. Trapped in a world he never made, Howard has withstood a bizarre rogues gallery, a series of bodily transformations and even a meeting with God. He first encountered Spider-Man while rescuing his soon-to-be-girlfriend, Beverly Switzler, from the clutches of cosmic accountant Pro-Rata. The web-slinger and the web-footed waddler have since joined forces against Status Quo, the Circus of Crime and the homicidal Elf with a Gun. Howard's arch-foes include Doctor Bong — journalist, mad scientist and Bev's ex-husband — and the mentally unstable Kidney Lady.

POWERS/WEAPONS

- Biting sarcasm
- Master of Quak-Fu

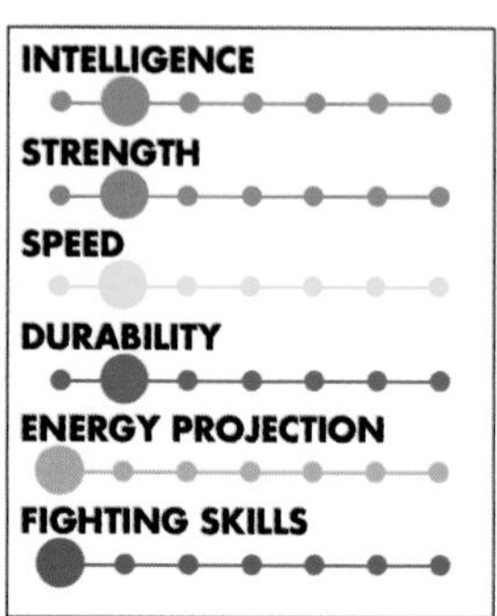

HUMBUG

Real Name: Buck Mitty
First Appearance: *Web of Spider-Man* #19 (1986)

Hgt: 5'6"
Wt: 130 lbs.

A senior entomology professor at Empire State University, Buck Mitty set out to harness the awesome power of insect noises to achieve his desired ends after his funding was cut. Humbug possessed enough power to succeed, but lacked a knack for victory. Spider-Man defeated him easily twice — first by exposing his weapons to their own power, and then by threatening to kill a jar full of roaches, prompting Humbug's surrender. Mitty became enough of a pest that a coworker at the university hired the wisecracking mercenary Deadpool to kill him. Deadpool accomplished his mission by dousing Humbug with honey and setting a swarm of fire ants on him.

POWERS/WEAPONS

- Projection of sonic blasts via amplified insect noises

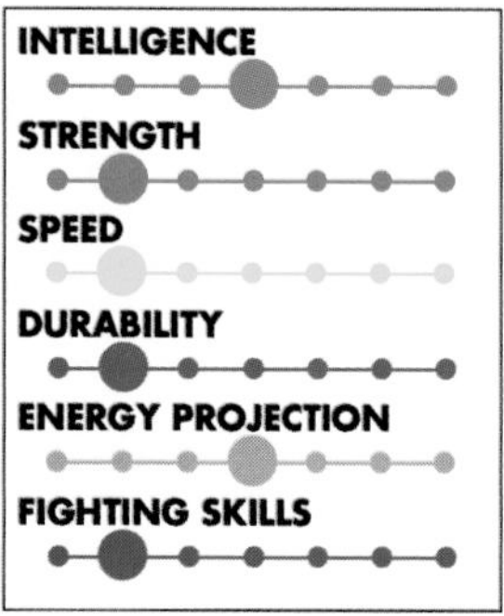

HYDRO-MAN

Morris Bench was working as a ship's laborer when he was knocked into the sea during the testing of a new underwater generator in an unusual deep-sea volcanic zone. The generator's energies combined with the gasses dissolved in the water, touching off an unexplained reaction that altered Bench's physical form into a liquid state. The psychologically destabilizing effect of his transformation combined with Bench's existing volatile personality completely alienated him from society, creating his Hydro-Man persona. At the time of the accident, Spider-Man was present on the ship resolving a dispute with Namor, the Atlantean Sub-Mariner. Hydro-Man blindly lashed out at the hero, believing the web-slinger responsible for his transformation. Spider-Man managed to defeat his liquefied opponent by carrying the fight to the city's rooftops, where the baking-hot sun evaporated his foe.

After Hydro-Man reincorporated his molecules, he became involved in a bitter rivalry with the Sandman for the affection of a local lady of the night, Sadie Frickett. Their competition for Sadie erupted into a full-blown brawl; in the ensuing battle, the villains' two forms combined into a near-invincible mud monster. After Spider-Man's unsuccessful fight with the Mud-Thing, the NYPD used a special gas to dehydrate the creature and imprison its frozen form.

Some time after the Sandman and Hydro-Man successfully separated their respective forms, Hydro-Man joined the Sinister Syndicate in an effort to exact vengeance on Spider-Man. With the Syndicate's repeated defeats and subsequent breakup, Bench has become increasingly paranoid and irrational. He seems to have lost all sense of judgement, focusing solely on the destruction of Spider-Man to the exclusion of all other interests.

Hydro-Man is an archetypical super-villain — plenty of potential, but continually let down by his own lack of direction and a tendency to get caught up in vengeance rather than profit. The combination of these traits renders him vulnerable to exploitation by others. In his most recent outing, he and the Shocker were fired by their regular employer, Hammer Industries. While the Shocker was keen to perform one more heist that would provide them with enough cash to settle down in luxury forever, Hydro-Man could not focus on anything other than vengeance. When Spider-Man arrived, Hydro-Man's blind thirst for a meaningless victory over the wall-crawler saw both villains defeated.

INTELLIGENCE (2 of 7)
STRENGTH (2 of 7)
SPEED (2 of 7)
DURABILITY (6 of 7)
ENERGY PROJECTION (4 of 7)
FIGHTING SKILLS (2 of 7)

Real Name:
Morris Bench
First Appearance:
Amazing Spider-Man #212 (1981)

Height:	6'2"
Weight:	265 lbs.
Eye Color:	Brown
Hair Color:	Brown

POWERS/ WEAPONS

- Composed of pigmented water; can freely alter form
- Projection of powerful jets of water
- Immune to physical attack

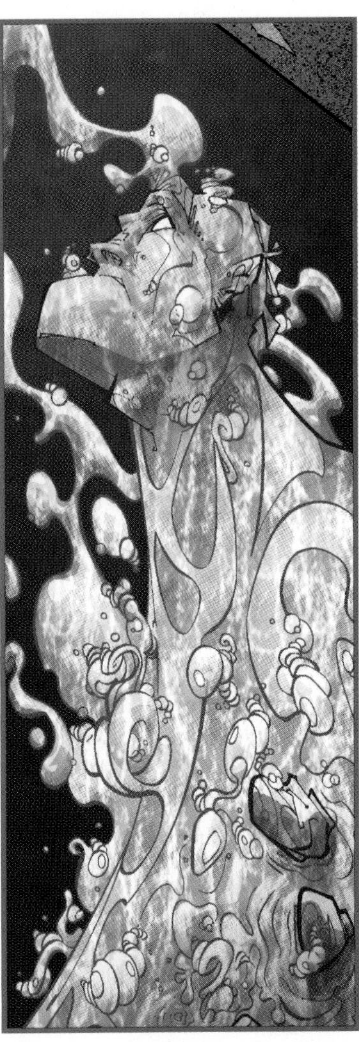

Art by Francisco Herrera

HYDRA

First Appearance: *Strange Tales* #135 (1965)

A terrorist organization founded by Nazi war criminals such as Baron Wolfgang von Strucker, Hydra has been a source of villainy for more than half a century. Splinter cells include the scientific conglomerate Advanced Idea Mechanics. Although Hydra's chief adversary has been the super-spy agency S.H.I.E.L.D., its operatives have also encountered Spider-Man — most notably during their war against New York City's gangsters. Hydra later participated in the fall of the Kingpin, decimating Fisk Towers with machine-gun fire from a squadron of helicopters. Hydra was involved with both incarnations of S.H.O.C., and also ran afoul of Spider-Man and Morbius while working with Crown (a.k.a. Hunger).

HYPNO-HUSTLER

Real Name: Unrevealed
First Appearance: *Spectacular Spider-Man* #24 (1978)

Hgt: 5'11"
Wt: 180 lbs.

Attempting to unwind, Peter Parker visited a nightclub with some friends. Hypno-Hustler and the Mercy Killers were the evening's featured entertainers. Using high-tech gimmicks such as hypnotic goggles and a mesmerizing sound system, the band sought to hypnotize the crowd and make off with their valuables. Peter was able to resist long enough to change into his Spider-Man costume and put an end to Hypno-Hustler's act. The Hustler must have continued his criminal ways; years later, he was revealed to be a prisoner in the Cage, a specialized prison for super-villains.

POWERS/WEAPONS

- Technological induction of mass hypnosis
- Gas and retractable blades in boots

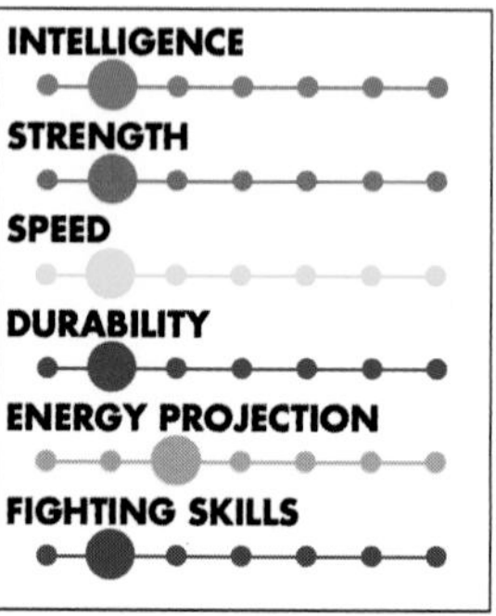

IGUANA

Real Name: Not Applicable
First Appearance: *Spectacular Spider-Man* #32 (1979)

Hgt: 6'4"
Wt: 520 lbs.

Through an experiment gone awry, Dr. Curt Connors mutated an ordinary iguana into a creature possessing the powers and memories of the Lizard, his own alter ego, plus the ability to mesmerize others at a glance. After fighting Spider-Man and the Lizard, the Iguana put aside his hatred for Connors long enough to strike an uneasy alliance against the hero. Using the device that had transformed the Iguana and the Lizard against them, the web-slinger defeated the reptilian duo. Conners was restored, while the power-overloaded Iguana apparently vanished in a burst of energy. But in the shadows, a small iguana was seen crawling away.

POWERS/WEAPONS

- Superhuman strength, speed and durability
- Regenerative abilities
- Prehensile tail and claws
- Hypnosis

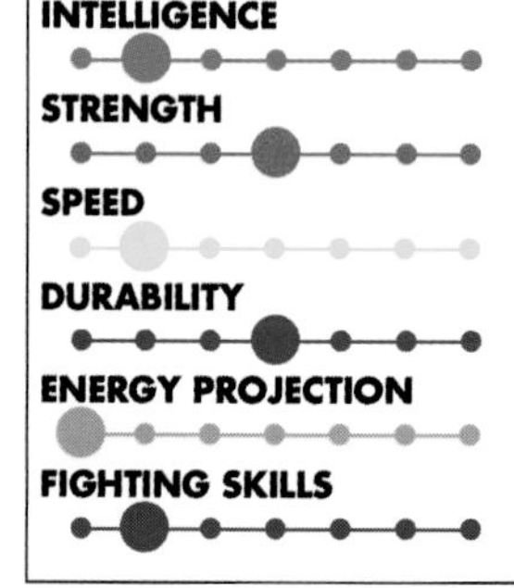

JASON IONELLO

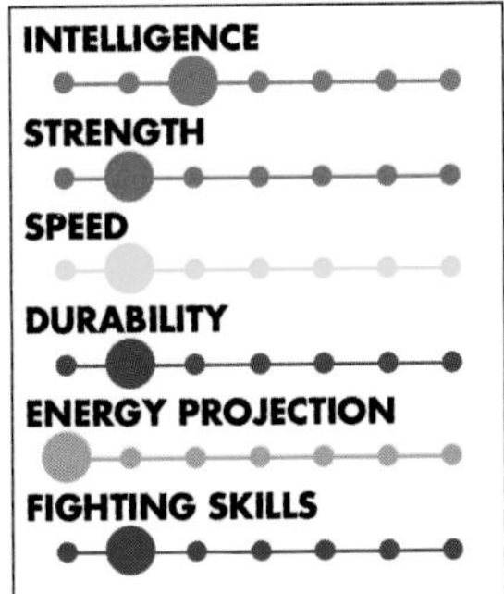

Real Name: Jason Ionello
First Appearance: *Untold Tales of Spider-Man* #1 (1995)

Hgt: 5'8"
Wt: 140 lbs.

Jason Ionello was best friend to Sally Avril, who briefly fought crime as Bluebird. When Sally was inspired by Peter Parker and set out to become a crime photographer, Jason served as her driver. Urged on by Sally, Jason ran a red light in pursuit of a story, straight into the path of an oncoming bus. Sally was killed. Though Jason survived, he was wracked with grief and sought someone — anyone — to blame. Using a fake Spider-Man costume, he attempted to ruin the web-slinger's reputation. Flash Thompson tracked down the imposter, and helped Jason start to come to terms with his guilt and loss.

CISSY IRONWOOD

INTELLIGENCE
STRENGTH
SPEED
DURABILITY
ENERGY PROJECTION
FIGHTING SKILLS

Real Name: Priscilla Ironwood
First Appearance: *Marvel Team-Up* #80 (1979)

Hgt: 5'6"
Wt: 120 lbs.

At one point in his bachelor life, Peter Parker briefly dated Cissy Ironwood while Mary Jane Watson was away from New York for the summer. On one of their earliest dates, a werewolf who proved to be Doctor Strange attacked Cissy. Along with her father, Professor Daniel Ironwood, she was later briefly kidnapped by Colonel Alexi Mikhailovitch Vazhin and the Soviet Super-Soldiers. Abandoning her on-again, off-again relationship with Peter, Cissy eventually moved west; she has not seen him in years.

JASON JEROME

INTELLIGENCE
STRENGTH
SPEED
DURABILITY
ENERGY PROJECTION
FIGHTING SKILLS

Real Name: Jason Jerome
First Appearance: *Spectacular Spider-Man* #166 (1990)

Hgt: 6'0"
Wt: 180 lbs.

A former co-star of Mary Jane Watson on the soap opera Secret Hospital, Jason Jerome later chanced into MJ at the airport. Jerome was returning from London's West End theater scene, while Peter Parker was heading to London to bring Knight and Fogg to justice for murdering the Arranger. A smooth-talking sleazeball, Jerome turned his manipulating charm on Peter's wife. Confused and lonely, Mary Jane nearly fell for his lines. She came to her senses before it was too late. Inviting Jerome to her apartment, Mary Jane flicked on the lights to reveal a room she had decorated with photos of her and Peter. She then kicked the humiliated Jerome out of her life for good.

JACKAL

Real Name:
Dr. Miles Warren
First Appearance:
Amazing Spider-Man #31 (1965)

Height:	5'10"
Weight:	175 lbs.
Eye Color:	Green
Hair Color:	Gray

INTELLIGENCE
STRENGTH
SPEED
DURABILITY
ENERGY PROJECTION
FIGHTING SKILLS

On Peter Parker's first day at Empire State University, little could he know that his unassuming biochemistry professor, Dr. Miles Warren, would become one of his most cunning foes. With Gwen Stacy among his students, Warren could not help but fall in love with the stunning beauty. After Stacy's death at the hands of Norman Osborn (Green Goblin), an increasingly obsessed Warren blamed Spider-Man for her fatal fall. He soon set upon a mad plan to both resurrect her and destroy the web-slinger.

At ESU, Warren used tissue samples taken from Peter and Gwen to create a set of clones in a process he had developed years before in the High Evolutionary's fabled city of Wundagore. When his assistant, Anthony Serba, discovered the professor's experiments, an enraged Warren strangled him. The shock of this violent act drove Warren to create an alternate, evil persona he dubbed the Jackal.

Through his continual observation of Peter, Warren discovered his student's secret identity — setting the young man's clone against the original in a heated confrontation. The battle seemingly ended with the death of both the Jackal and the original Spider-Man clone — but in reality, both survived.

Art by Sal Buscema

The Jackal returned years later, possessing superhuman strength and bearing a mutated physical appearance mimicking his original costume. Still obsessed with revenge on the wall-crawler, the Jackal lured both Peter and the original Spider-Man clone — who had adopted the name Ben Reilly — into a complex trap of deceit and half-truths. Manipulated by Osborn, even the Jackal believed that Peter, rather than Ben, was the clone — a delusion that drove Peter to temporarily abandon his Spider-Man identity. After Peter and Ben discovered the truth behind the Jackal's schemes, they confronted the villain at the Daily Bugle — initiating a battle that ended with the Jackal's final, unmistakable death.

POWERS/ WEAPONS

- Exceptional expertise in the field of cloning
- Superhuman strength
- Razor-sharp, poison-tipped claws
- Gas bombs

J. JONAH JAMESON

Real Name:
J. Jonah Jameson
First Appearance:
Amazing Spider-Man #1 (1963)

Height:	5'11"
Weight:	210 lbs.
Eye Color:	Blue
Hair Color:	Gray

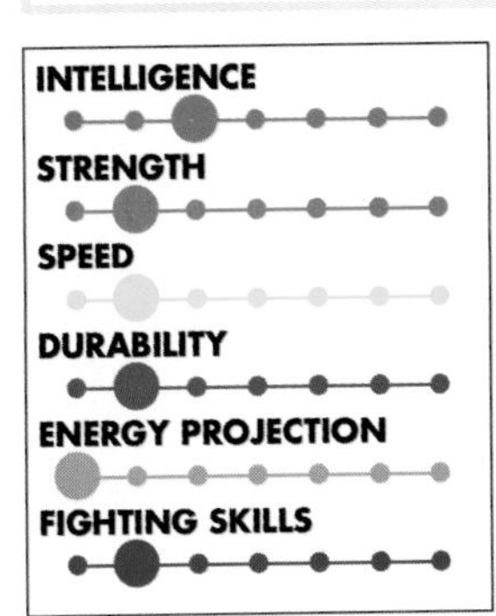

Jonah Jameson began his journalistic career as a part-time reporter while still in high school, working for a number of newspapers. While investigating for the New York Herald Journal Express, he unearthed a story that would help cement his career. An informant told him of the endemic corruption within the local police division, led by Sgt. Sam Kenner. When Kenner killed the informant in front of his very eyes, Jonah knew fear for the first time in his life. After his editor ordered him to drop the story, the owner of the competing Daily Bugle, William Walter Goodman, approached Jonah and encouraged him to pursue it — despite the clear risks. Jonah did so; for his tenacity, he took a savage beating at the hands of the police and witnessed the murder of his young assistant, killed by a bomb meant for him. Undeterred, he tricked a recorded confession out of Kenner and confirmed his reputation as a gutsy journalist who placed the search for truth above his own personal safety.

Jonah stayed with the Bugle and served a significant stretch overseas as a roving war correspondent. When the Bugle floundered financially, he made a timely buy-out offer funded by loans and a large inheritance. As it stands today, Jonah's company, Jameson Publications, owns the paper outright. As publisher of the Bugle, Jonah is the driving force behind the paper. Though he reinvigorated the tabloid, transforming it into a lucrative business, as an employer he remains a heartless tyrant who pays little heed to the opinions of others — except his editor-in-chief, Joseph "Robbie" Robertson.

A well-known public figure, Jonah is frequently invited to high-profile functions. Though he actively participates in social events for charity, his wealth and outspoken nature have often cast him as the target of theft, blackmail and outright physical attack.

Continued...

Art by Joe Madureira

J. JONAH JAMESON

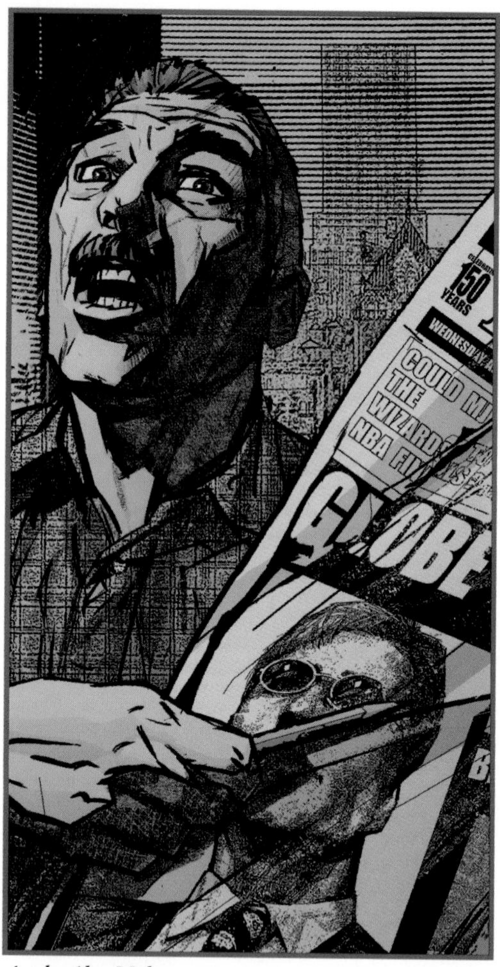

Art by Alex Maleev

Jonah's relationship with Spider-Man is longstanding and remarkable for its equally longstanding loathsomeness. Publicly, Jonah has used every editorial and journalistic resource at his disposal to bring the wall-crawler into disrepute. He has also privately funded a number of attempts to destroy Spider-Man — paying Dr. Farley Stillwell to transform Mac Gargan into the Scorpion, funding Spencer Smythe in his efforts to create Spider-Slayers and hiring Dr. Marla Madison to do the same. Jonah also provided resources for Dr. Harlan Stillwell, Farley's brother, to create the Fly.

The reasons behind Jonah's loathing for Spider-Man are complex and deep-rooted. Though he holds great respect for public defenders of law and order — including police officers, firefighters and members of the armed services — he scorns vigilantes, particularly those who would seek to hide their identities.

Jameson despises the way the public-at-large considers Spider-Man, and others like him, to be heroes. To Jonah, the true heroes are those men and women without powers who still put their lives on the line for their country — such as his own son, John Jameson, a former astronaut. But perhaps the truth is somewhat darker: Jonah has been heard to say that truly, nobody is a hero.

Certainly, as a child, his father gave him no reason to believe in heroes. In spite of his protective mother's entreaties, the overbearing David Jameson used threats and violence in his attempts to ensure that Jonah would grow up as strong and determined as he was. After a strange fashion, the war veteran's strategy worked. Jonah became a pig-headed, volatile bully — tempered only by his strong social conscience.

Jonah's first wife, Joan, died while he was working overseas. This affected him deeply, and it was some time before he entered into another relationship. Jonah met his second wife, Marla, when he hired her to build a next-generation Spider-Slayer that would rid New York City once and for all of "that wall-crawling freak." Instead, Jonah was the one trapped by Marla's affection, and they married not long afterwards — despite a predicament involving Marla's kidnapping by the Scorpion. Fortunately, as countless times before, Spider-Man came to the aid of his flat-topped, mustachioed, cigar-chomping nemesis and freed the bride from the Scorpion's clutches.

Spider-Man, rarely affected by Jonah's hatred, has saved his detractor's life and property from villainous attack on literally dozens of occasions. But Jonah is not the type to sacrifice his principles merely because of clear and unequivocal evidence to the contrary. Whenever Spider-Man has rescued Jonah from gangland mobsters, Spider-Slayers, Scorpions or countless other evils, Jonah's perpetual response has been, "Doubtless that no-good web-slinger is in cahoots with the bad guys anyhow!" It's good to know some things never change.

JOHN JAMESON

As a career test pilot and astronaut, John Jameson was ironically presented by his father, J. Jonah Jameson as "the kind of hero that people should be honoring, not dangerous vigilantes like that criminal wall-crawler!" Jonah ignored the fact that John was once saved by Spider-Man, who performed a miraculous in-flight replacement of his space capsule's control module. One of Jameson's early trips saw him temporarily affected by strength-enhancing space spores — which also clouded his mind, leading him to attack Spider-Man. On a subsequent secret lunar mission, John discovered a ruby-like gemstone he felt compelled to take for his own. The gemstone proved to be an alien artifact that attached itself to John's throat, and on nights of the full moon transformed him into the uncontrollable Man-Wolf.

As the Man-Wolf, John stalked his father and his then-fiancée, Kristine Saunders. Spider-Man intervened in the Man-Wolf's nocturnal activities and ripped the gemstone from the creature's throat. John reverted to human form, seemingly cured. Later, Morbius reattached the gemstone to John as part of a plan to cure himself of his vampiric illness — a scheme also thwarted by Spider-Man. Thereafter, John would transform into the Man-Wolf whenever the moon was above the horizon. His power decreased as the moon waned, and his self-control would return.

On the run and considered AWOL, John fought Kraven the Hunter and the Hate-Monger before finally surrendering to the authorities. Unaware of his condition, the government offered to drop charges if he would investigate a communications blackout on an orbiting space station. John agreed and discovered the station had been seized by warriors from the extra-dimensional Other Realm, the origin of his gemstone.

Traveling to the Other Realm, Jameson retained his personality and intelligence as the Man-Wolf. He learned his gemstone was called the Godstone, created centuries ago by a dying lupine star god to pass his powers on to his successor. The Man-Wolf defeated the tyrant Arisen Tyrk and returned to Earth, where he was again subject to the whims of the moon. After departing once more to safeguard the Other Realm in its time of need, John came home to allow Spider-Man and Dr. Curt Connors (Lizard) to administer a biomagnetic treatment that caused his body to reject the stone. After recovering in a sanatorium, John served for a time as Captain America's pilot before acting as a freelance monster-hunter. Named security chief at Ravencroft Institute, he was later replaced by gamma-irradiated psychiatrist Doc Samson.

Real Name:
John Jameson
First Appearance:
Amazing Spider-Man #1 (1963)

Height: 6'2" (6'6" as Man-Wolf)
Weight: 200 lbs. (350 lbs. as Man-Wolf)
Eye Color: Brown (red as Man-Wolf)
Hair Color: Reddish-brown (white as Man-Wolf)

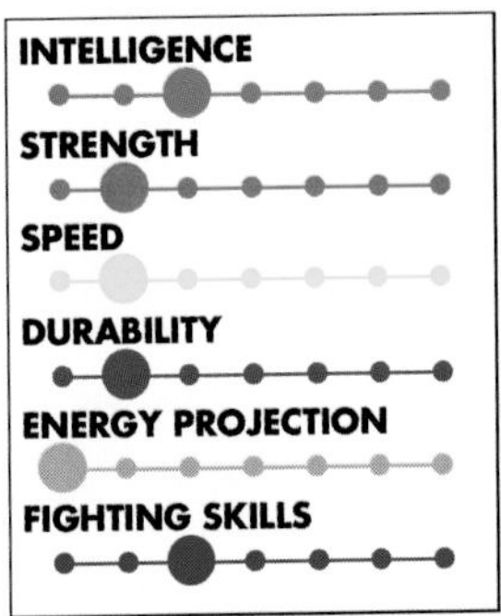

POWERS/ WEAPONS

- Superhuman strength and stamina (as Man-Wolf)
- Razor-sharp claws (as Man-Wolf)
- Test pilot and security expert

Art by Dean Haspiel & John Romita

JIGSAW

Real Name: Billy Russo
First Appearance: *Amazing Spider-Man* #162 (1976)

Hgt: 6'2"
Wt: 250 lbs.

Thrown through a plate-glass window by the Punisher, the man who would become Jigsaw had his face permanently disfigured. Seeking vengeance, Jigsaw led the Punisher into a trap by framing him for a series of assassinations. But Jigsaw also attracted the attention of Spider-Man and Nightcrawler, and could not contend with all three. Fearful of Spider-Man, Jigsaw was reluctantly goaded by his gang into robbing the guests on a midnight harbor cruise. Unfortunately for him, he picked a ship hosting Peter Parker and his friends. Spider-Man appeared and tracked the fleeing Jigsaw to his hideout, where the terrified villain surrendered.

POWERS/WEAPONS

- Criminal strategist
- Skilled in the use of various firearms

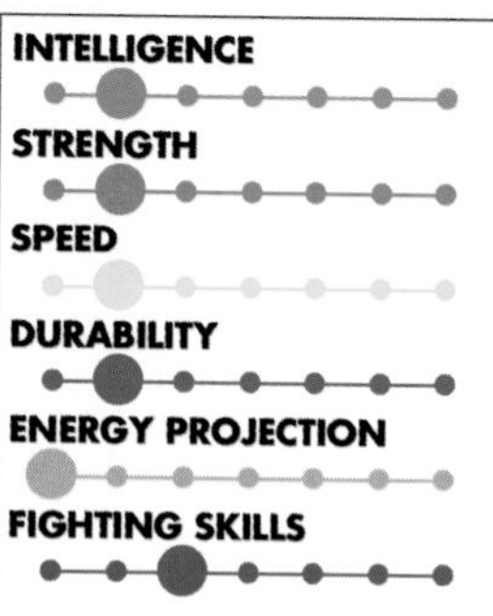

JIMMY-6

Real Name: Giacomo Fortunato
First Appearance: *Spider-Man* #70 (1996)

Hgt: 6'8"
Wt: 360 lbs.

Giacomo Fortunato is the son of Don Fortunato, underworld crime lord. A giant of a man, Jimmy's rebellious nature saw him ejected from his father's empire. With a gangland price on his head, Jimmy-6 was rescued by Ben Reilly; he briefly became Ben's roommate. Jimmy returned to his father to warn him of an impending attack, but earned his wrath once more when he intervened to save Spider-Man and Daredevil from certain death at Fortunato's hands. Jimmy assumed control of his father's criminal operations after agents of the Kingpin seriously wounded Fortunato.

POWERS/WEAPONS

- Powerful, well-armed fighter

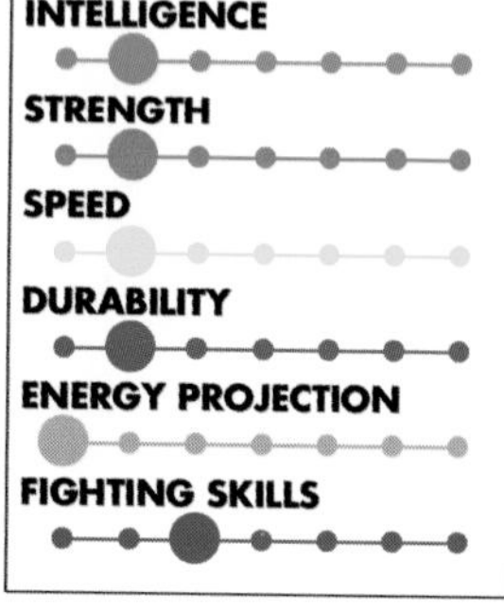

JUGGERNAUT

Real Name: Cain Marko
First Appearance: *X-Men* #12 (1965)

Hgt: 6'10"
Wt: 900 lbs.

The estranged stepbrother of Professor Charles Xavier, mutant mentor to the X-Men, the supernaturally empowered Cain Marko has made his unstoppable might known to every corner of the Marvel Universe — including Spider-Man's. In their first encounter, Spider-Man was helpless to stop the Juggernaut from almost killing Madame Web. Regrouping, the web-slinger ingeniously defeated the much more powerful villain by immobilizing him in cement. Although the two have clashed since, the Juggernaut has fought alongside Spider-Man against the Exemplars. Cain is currently attempting to reform, having taken up residence at his stepbrother's Xavier Institute.

POWERS/WEAPONS

- Supernatural strength
- Invulnerability
- Personal force-field
- Telepathy-blocking helmet

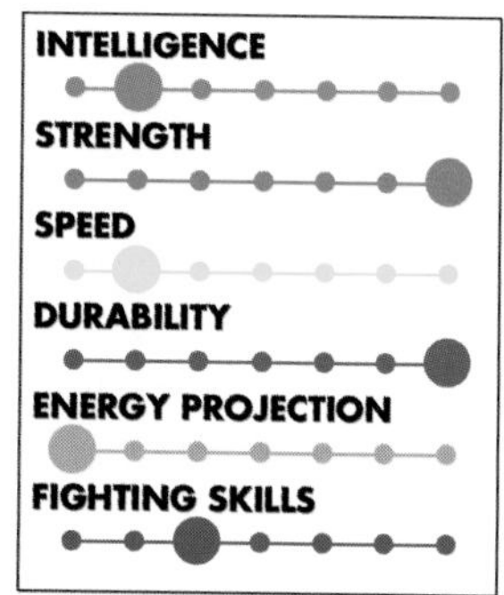

KAINE

POWERS/WEAPONS

- Enhanced spider-powers
- Spider-sense allows random visions of future events
- Projection of scars into flesh
- Razor-sharp claws

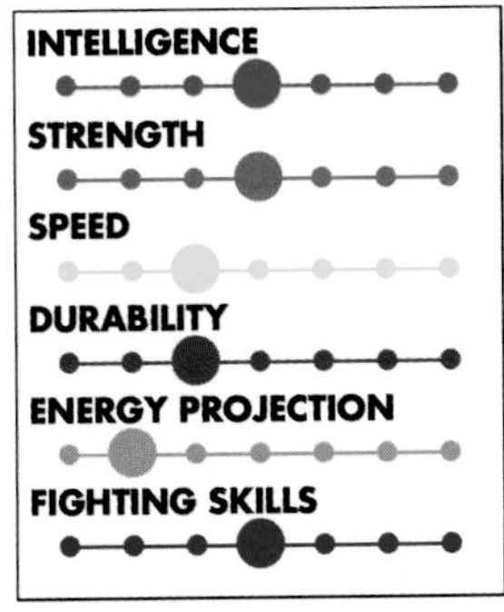

Real Name: Not Applicable
First Appearance: *Web of Spider-Man* #119 (1994)

Hgt: 6'4"
Wt: 250 lbs.

Before he successfully cloned Peter Parker to create Ben Reilly, the Jackal produced a flawed clone named Kaine. After Kaine parted ways with the Jackal, the collapse of his cellular structure accelerated — leaving him stronger than ever, but greatly deformed. As his body was ruined, Kaine's hatred grew — hatred for the world, but most of all hatred for Ben Reilly, whom both Kaine and the Jackal believed to be the original Spider-Man. The meddling of Norman Osborn (Green Goblin) fostered this misinformed notion.

Kaine followed Ben to Manhattan, attempting to protect Peter — whom he believed was the clone. Kaine wanted Peter to have a chance at the perfect life he himself was forever denied. When Peter was accused of a long-past murder Kaine in fact committed, Kaine confessed and went to prison, in order that Peter would go free. Kaine escaped soon after. He tracked down Ben and easily defeated him — but in a moment of redemption, Kaine could not bring himself to kill his opponent. Showing himself to be indeed made of the same stuff as Peter Parker, Kaine accepted true responsibility for his actions and allowed himself to be taken back into custody to pay for his crimes. Kaine was last seen attacking Osborn's Scriers, attempting to avenge Reilly's death.

KANGAROO

POWERS/WEAPONS

- Enhanced strength and resistance to pain
- Can leap great distances

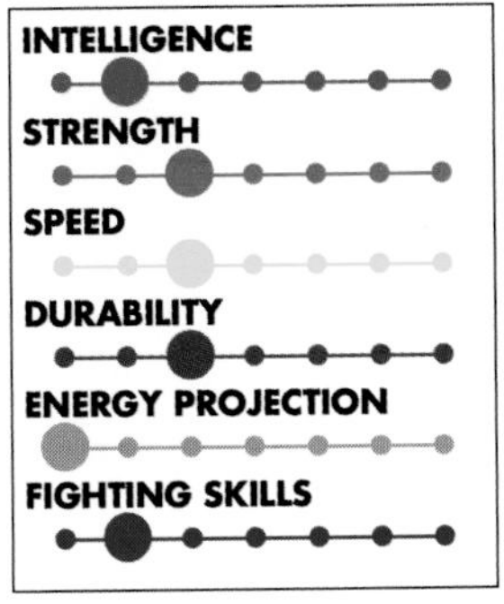

Real Name: Frank Oliver
First Appearance: *Amazing Spider-Man* #81 (1970)

Hgt: 6'3"
Wt: 235 lbs.

A native of Australia, Frank Oliver was fascinated with kangaroos. Through practice, diet and determination, he achieved the ability to jump and box as well as his much-admired marsupial role models. Turning his new skills at first to boxing in his homeland, he was forced to flee after he killed a man in the ring. Reaching America, he was apprehended by U.S. law-enforcement agents, but managed to escape custody. Living as a fugitive, he soon encountered Spider-Man, only to be defeated by the hero.

After that defeat, Oliver met Dr. Jonas Harrow, who provided him with enhanced powers for his own means. Oliver's native stupidity and stubbornness resulted in his demise shortly thereafter, when he ignored Spider-Man's warnings about the dangers of concentrated gamma rays while attempting to steal a special radioactive isotope.

Living as a fugitive, Oliver held up an armored car — unwittingly stealing a vial of deadly experimental bacteria. Spider-Man struggled to recover the lethal sample before Oliver could accidentally unleash a plague upon Manhattan. The wall-crawler successfully overpowered the Kangaroo and recovered the vial, but was unable to bring the villain to justice. Later, an American named Brian Hibbs adopted Oliver's mantle as Kangaroo II.

JURY

First Appearance: *Venom: Lethal Protector* #2 (1993)

Clad in flight-enabled combat armor, the Jury was organized to take out Venom. The villain had killed the son of the team's founder, Orwell Taylor. Failing, the members of the Jury next targeted Spider-Man, whom they believed to be responsible for Venom's creation. Following several encounters with the wall-crawler, the Jury abandoned its founder — choosing instead to pursue its own path. Since then, the Jury has executed Tarantula II, battled the New Warriors and allied with the government-sanctioned operative code-named U.S.Agent — fighting at his side both with and against the Thunderbolts, villains-turned-heroes. Ladies and gentlemen of the Jury have included Bomblast, Firearm, Ramshot, Screech, Sentry and Wysper.

DR. ASHLEY KAFKA

Real Name: Dr. Ashley Kafka
First Appearance: *Spectacular Spider-Man* #178 (1991)

Hgt: 5'6"
Wt: 140 lbs.

INTELLIGENCE
STRENGTH
SPEED
DURABILITY
ENERGY PROJECTION
FIGHTING SKILLS

Dr. Ashley Kafka's troubled childhood inspired her to study psychology, which brought her to Empire State University. There, she helped Spider-Man deal with a devastating psychological attack unleashed by the Green Goblin (Harry Osborn). She also helped heal Vermin, though she was denied the chance to treat Harry. Appointed director of Ravencroft Institute, Kafka saw her passionate attempts fail to cure inmates such as Carnage, Carrion II (Malcolm McBride), Shriek and the Chameleon. When the Chameleon took advantage of Kafka's trust and escaped, she and security chief John Jameson both were fired — replaced by gamma-irradiated psychiatrist Doc Samson. Ashley and John began dating soon after.

KANGAROO II

Real Name: Brian Hibbs
First Appearance: *Cage* #13 (1993)

Hgt: 7'7"
Wt: 377 lbs.

POWERS/WEAPONS

- Enhanced strength and leaping ability

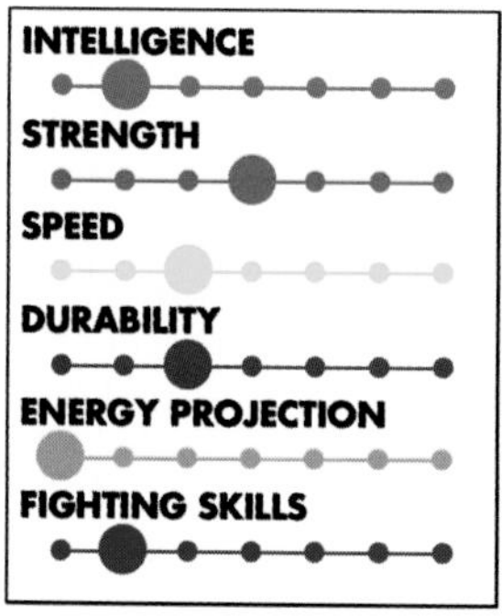

Brian Hibbs sought to emulate the original Kangaroo, Frank Oliver. To that end, he trained for the role while working for the corrupt Corporation in the American Midwest. Believing he was ready to face Spider-Man, Hibbs attacked the hero. The wall-crawler dropped him with a single punch. Even bolstered by battle armor or as a member of the Legion of Losers, Hibbs' struggles lasted scant seconds. To prove himself worthy of the name Kangaroo, he sought scientific enhancement — which left him bigger, dumber and sporting an exaggerated Australian accent. Remanded to the Cage, a specialized prison for super-villains, Hibbs was shafted as a result of his feud with Tombstone.

NICK KATZENBERG

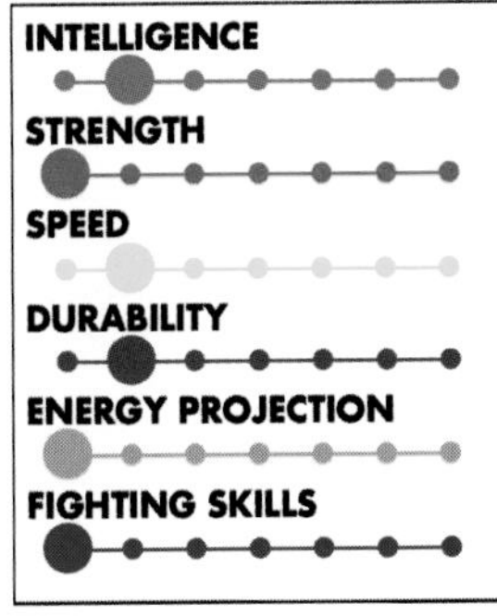

Real Name: Nicholas Katzenberg
First Appearance: *Web of Spider-Man* #50 (1989)

Hgt: 5'10"
Wt: 220 lbs.

A paparazzi sleazeball, Nick Katzenberg became J. Jonah Jameson's favorite photog after taking pictures portraying Spider-Man as a thief. He fell from favor after documenting the arrest of Joseph "Robbie" Robertson. Katzenberg subsequently attempted to prove Peter Parker was faking some of his Spider-Man photos by dressing as the web-slinger himself. After his pictures of a mob meeting drew the wrong kind of attention from the criminal fraternity, Katzenberg dropped out of sight. He was later revealed to be dying from lung cancer. Peter took Mary Jane Watson to visit him in the hospital, convincing her to quit smoking. Katzenberg died a few months later.

KA-ZAR

POWERS/WEAPONS

- Natural athletic, hunting, foraging, survival, and combative abilities that have been honed to the peak of human perfection

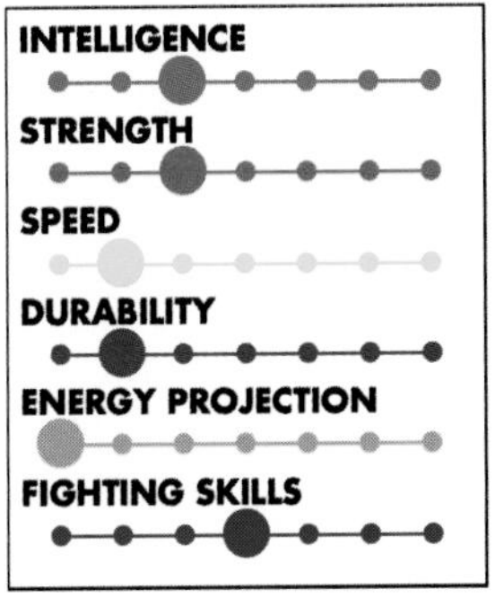

Real Name: Kevin Plunder
First Appearance: *X-Men* #10 (1965)

Hgt: 6'2"
Wt: 215 lbs.

The jungle lord of the forgotten Antarctic realm known as the Savage Land, where dinosaurs still live, Kevin Plunder has met and assisted Spider-Man on several occasions — along with Shanna, his wife, and Zabu, the last survivor of a species of saber-toothed tiger. Together, they have faced foes such as Kraven the Hunter, Stegron, Chtylok and the artificially engineered Savage Land Mutates. On one occasion, Ka-Zar was shot and seemingly killed in New York City. In grief, Shanna turned to her new friend, Peter Parker. The two almost became lovers, but Peter could see that her mind was filled only with images of her husband.

KILLER SHRIKE

POWERS/WEAPONS

- Enhanced strength
- Flight
- Energy blasters

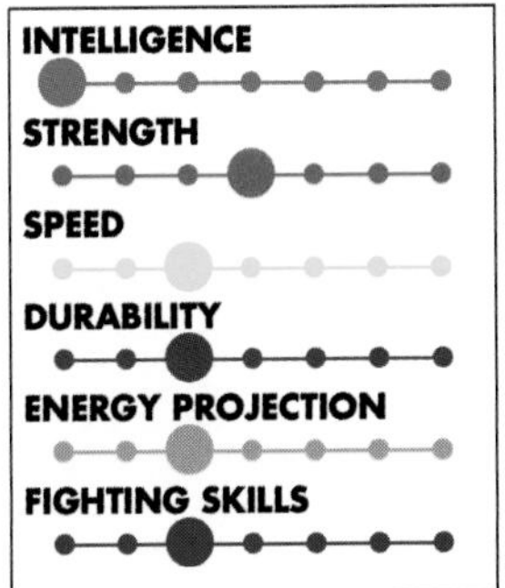

Real Name: Simon Maddicks
First Appearance: *Rampaging Hulk* #1 (1977)

Hgt: 6'5"
Wt: 250 lbs.

A former soldier, Simon Maddicks was outfitted as the Killer Shrike by the Brand Corporation. He first found employment with the enigmatic Conspiracy, meeting defeat at the hands of the legendary adventurer Ulysses Bloodstone. The Conspiracy's Modular Man recovered the comatose Maddicks from a hospital and revived him, but the two were overpowered and outsmarted by Spider-Man and the X-Men's Beast. Working as a mercenary or on his own, the Killer Shrike has fought Spider-Man on several other occasions — as well as Captain America, Moon Knight, the She-Hulk, the assassin Elektra, the Hulk, and even fellow criminals such as the Locksmith and the Tinkerer.

KINGPIN

Real Name:
Wilson Fisk
First Appearance:
Amazing Spider-Man #50 (1967)

Height: 6'7"
Weight: 450 lbs.
Eye Color: Blue
Hair Color: Bald

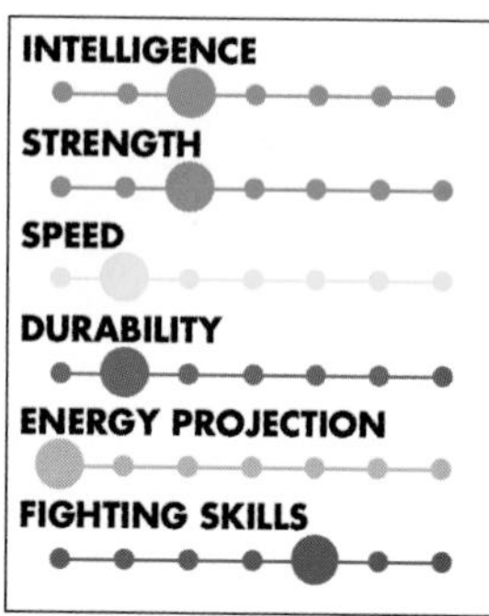

Although Wilson Fisk maintains a careful facade as a legitimate businessman, it is a poorly kept secret he is the most powerful crime lord in the Tri-State area. A criminal genius, Fisk is a massive man — his bulky frame comprised entirely of pure muscle and power. When a young and disillusioned Peter Parker abandoned his responsibilities as Spider-Man, the Kingpin seized the opportunity to unite the gangs of New York under his command. Upon Spider-Man's return, the Kingpin nearly eliminated the web-slinger and crusading editorialist J. Jonah Jameson. At the last moment, Fisk's plans were foiled by the intervention of his own lieutenant, Frederick Foswell.

Fisk has taken great pains to avoid any possible slur on his character. Even when he broke his own rule and personally ventured onto the grounds of Empire State University to steal the Lifeline Tablet, he was never convicted, thanks to lack of evidence — or more likely, one of the judges he kept on his payroll. The Kingpin's involvement runs deep in all aspects of the New York underworld. His criminal, financial and political ambitions bring him into frequent conflict with Daredevil, Spider-Man, the Punisher and S.H.I.E.L.D. The Kingpin himself habitually employs assistants and assassins such as the Arranger and Jack O'Lantern.

The Kingpin's activities have always been tempered by his devotion to his wife, Vanessa Fisk, who once went so far as to force him to choose between the destruction of Spider-Man and his love for her — a love tempered by the disruptive influence of their son, Richard Fisk, who has plagued him both as the Schemer and the Rose. While brutal, the Kingpin is undoubtedly a stabilizing force in the New York crime scene. On several occasions, he has withdrawn from the East Coast. Each time, his departure has left a power vacuum, causing greater violence than ever before — so much so that on one occasion, the police aided and abetted his return to prominence.

POWERS/ WEAPONS

- Skilled hand-to-hand combatant
- Unusual agility for a man his size
- Criminal genius

Art by Alex Maleev

KRAVEN THE HUNTER

Real Name:
Sergei Kravinoff
First Appearance:
Amazing Spider-Man #15 (1967)

Height:	6'3"
Weight:	240 lbs.
Eye Color:	Brown
Hair Color:	Black

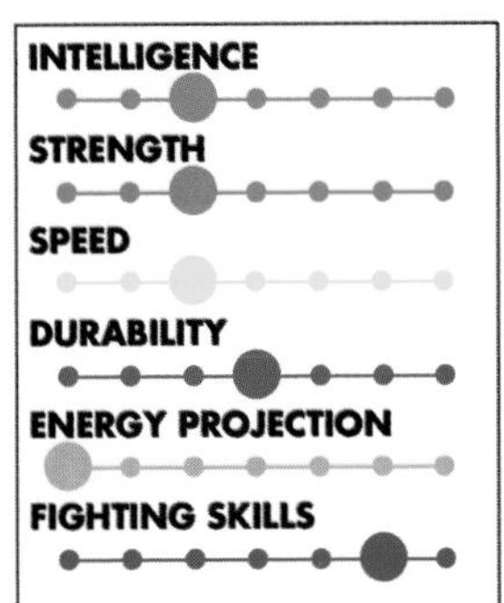

Born into a stagnant Russian aristocracy, Kraven became one of the world's greatest hunters to fulfill his sense of lost nobility. But he soon grew bored with the hunt of common game. When Kraven's half-brother, Dimitri Kravinoff (Chameleon), asked Sergei to come to America and help him seek revenge on Spider-Man, the Hunter knew he had finally found prey worthy of his skills.

Kraven came to Manhattan armed with traps, nets, and a range of drugs and mystical strength-enhancing potions sourced from the darkest jungles of Africa. These elixirs granted him the strength and speed of a savage beast, enough to make him more than a match for Spider-Man. Miscalculating their foe, Kraven and the Chameleon were defeated by Spider-Man; both were deported. Now Kraven was forced to fight not only for pride, but also for his very honor.

Alone and as a member of the first Sinister Six, Kraven again faced defeat at Spider-Man's hands. When the Green Goblin offered to pay him to destroy the hero, Kraven was so confident as to demand half his fee in advance — but he failed once more.

The two mortal enemies would not meet again until Spider-Man stumbled upon Kraven in the Savage Land, a time-lost Antarctic refuge. Spider-Man crushed Kraven, setting the stage for a rematch in New York when Kraven drugged the Gibbon and forced him to attack the hero. Once again, Kraven walked away a loser. Though Kraven had proven his supremacy over all the beasts of the land, Spider-Man continued to elude him.

After making elaborate preparations and imbibing numerous potions, Kraven managed to shoot Spider-Man with a powerfully drugged dart. He then buried his adversary alive and boldly took his place. Donning Spider-Man's black costume, Kraven hunted and defeated Vermin, something Spider-Man was previously unable to accomplish without outside assistance. When Spider-Man eventually clawed out from his living grave and attacked Kraven, he met no resistance. Having proven he was his foe's superior in every way, Kraven at last experienced some twisted measure of peace. Satisfied he had finally found true happiness, he took his own his life.

POWERS/ WEAPONS

- Hunter of unparalleled prowess
- Enhanced strength
- Skilled in the use of countless weapons, as well as various poisons and drugs

Art by John Romita Jr.

ALYOSHA KRAVINOFF

Real Name: Alyosha Kravinoff
First Appearance: *Spectacular Spider-Man* #243 (1997)

Hgt: 6'3"
Wt: 220 lbs.

Alyosha Kravinoff is the son of Sergei Kravinoff, known as Kraven the Hunter. When Sergei committed suicide, Alyosha became obsessed with his father's life. Seeking to recover Kraven's brutal and feral reputation, Alyosha attacked Spider-Man — then inexplicably entered into a truce with his opponent. Alyosha subsequently murdered Calypso, his father's mistress; attacked the Fantastic Four; and briefly joined the Sinister Six. More recently, however, Aloysha has appeared as an urbane sophisticate with the best of intentions. The world can only guess which is the real Alyosha Kravinoff. His current girlfriend, Timber Hughes, is an aspiring actress.

POWERS/WEAPONS

- All the abilities of Kraven the Hunter
- Communication with and mind-control over animals
- Trained pet wolf, Nickel

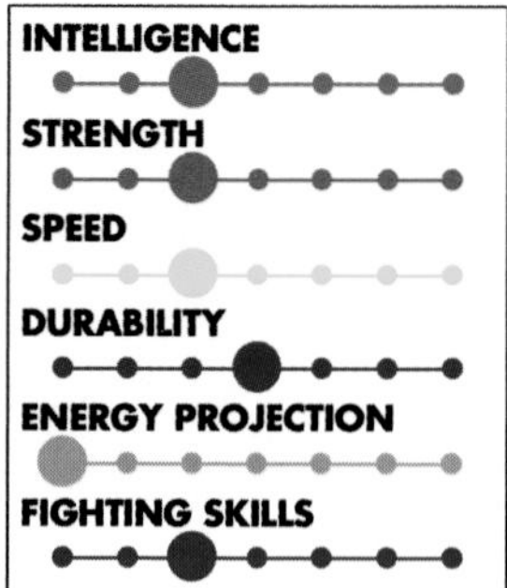

VLADIMIR KRAVINOFF

Real Name: Vladimir Kravinoff
First Appearance: *Peter Parker: Spider-Man* #47 (1994)

Hgt: 6'4"
Wt: 240 lbs.

Son of Sergei Kravinoff (Kraven the Hunter) and brother to Alyosha Kravinoff, Vladimir Kravinoff (a.k.a. the Grim Hunter) trained under his father — and his father's household staff — in Russia. Following Kraven's death, Vladimir fell in with the Hobgoblin (Jason Macendale). They came to America and both reaped the benefits of Kraven's power-enhancing elixir. Seeking to follow his father's path, the overconfident Vladimir battled Spider-Man, but was defeated and imprisoned. He bribed his way free and attacked the Scarlet Spider (Ben Reilly) before once more pursuing Peter Parker. Protecting Peter, Kaine easily overpowered and killed Vladimir.

POWERS/WEAPONS

- All the abilities of Kraven the Hunter
- Electrified glove

INTELLIGENCE
STRENGTH
SPEED
DURABILITY
ENERGY PROJECTION
FIGHTING SKILLS

LEAP-FROG

Real Name: Vincent Colorito Patilio
First Appearance: *Daredevil* #25 (1967)

Hgt: 5'9"
Wt: 170 lbs.

An unsuccessful and frustrated inventor, Vincent Patilio designed the Leap-Frog costume and embarked on an ill-fated criminal career. Foiled by Daredevil, the Avengers' Iron Man and the Defenders, he served his sentence and returned to a life of unemployment — only to watch his wife die of cancer. Vincent's son, Eugene (Frog-Man), later became a hero using his father's costume. But it was sans frog suit that Vincent himself made good, when he recorded the White Rabbit's confession and earned a hefty reward. Sometimes erroneously referred to as Frog-Man, Vincent has retired — though his Leap-Frog identity was stolen and used to attack Daredevil.

POWERS/WEAPONS

- Electronic leaping springs
- Internal computer-guidance system
- Strength-enhancing exoskeleton

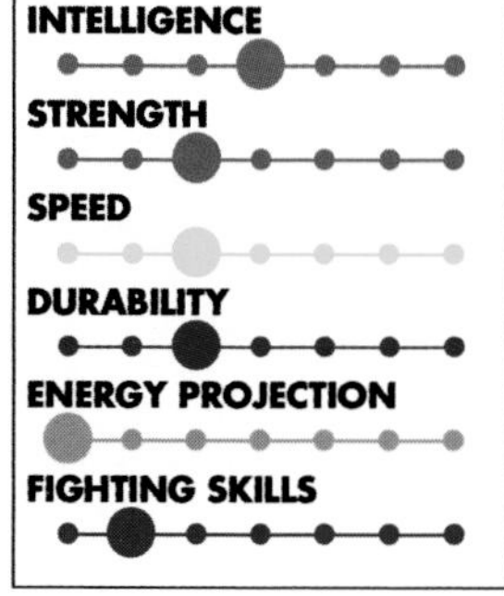

NED LEEDS

As a reporter for the Daily Bugle, Ned Leeds was overseas when Peter Parker first fell for receptionist Betty Brant. When Ned returned, he resumed the challenge for Betty's affections — and forced her to choose between him, the reliable reporter, and the newly hired, thrill-seeking photographer. Eventually, Ned won out, and the two became engaged. After Ned was promoted to city editor, they married.

Despite being confined to a desk as an editor, Ned remained a reporter at heart. When he stumbled across a battle between Spider-Man and the Hobgoblin, he watched the hero emerge victorious and the unmasked villian flee the scene. Ned followed the criminal to his hideout, but the Hobgoblin captured him. Instead of killing Ned, the Hobgoblin brainwashed him and used him to gather information. Eventually, the Hobgoblin gave Ned equipment and a costume, and used him as a stand-in for trivial or dangerous assignments. While brainwashed, Ned approached Richard Fisk for information concerning his father, the Kingpin. This act furthered the Hobgoblin's agenda, and he instructed Ned to cooperate with Richard and work to dethrone the Kingpin. The ongoing mental manipulation took its toll on Ned, and his personal and professional relationships suffered. Ned became aggressive and unstable, and drove Betty into the arms of Flash Thompson. Ned's behavior as the Hobgoblin's flunky became more erratic, as well: He sold out Richard to the Kingpin, undermining the true Hobgoblin's goals.

Clearly, the Hobgoblin could no longer rely on Ned. He leaked word to the criminal underworld that Ned was the Hobgoblin, and that he would soon be traveling to Berlin. Jack O'Lantern (Jason Macendale), who bore his own grudge against the Hobgoblin, hired the Foreigner to kill Ned so he could assume the mantle for himself. Ned was assassinated by the Foreigner's agents while in his German hotel room. An enraged Spider-Man sought to bring Ned's killers to justice, but to no avail.

Real Name:
Edward "Ned" Leeds

First Appearance:
Amazing Spider-Man #18 (1964)

Height:	5'11"
Weight:	205 lbs.
Eye Color:	Blue
Hair Color:	Brown

POWERS/ WEAPONS

- Could assume the Hobgoblin's abilities and equipment while brainwashed

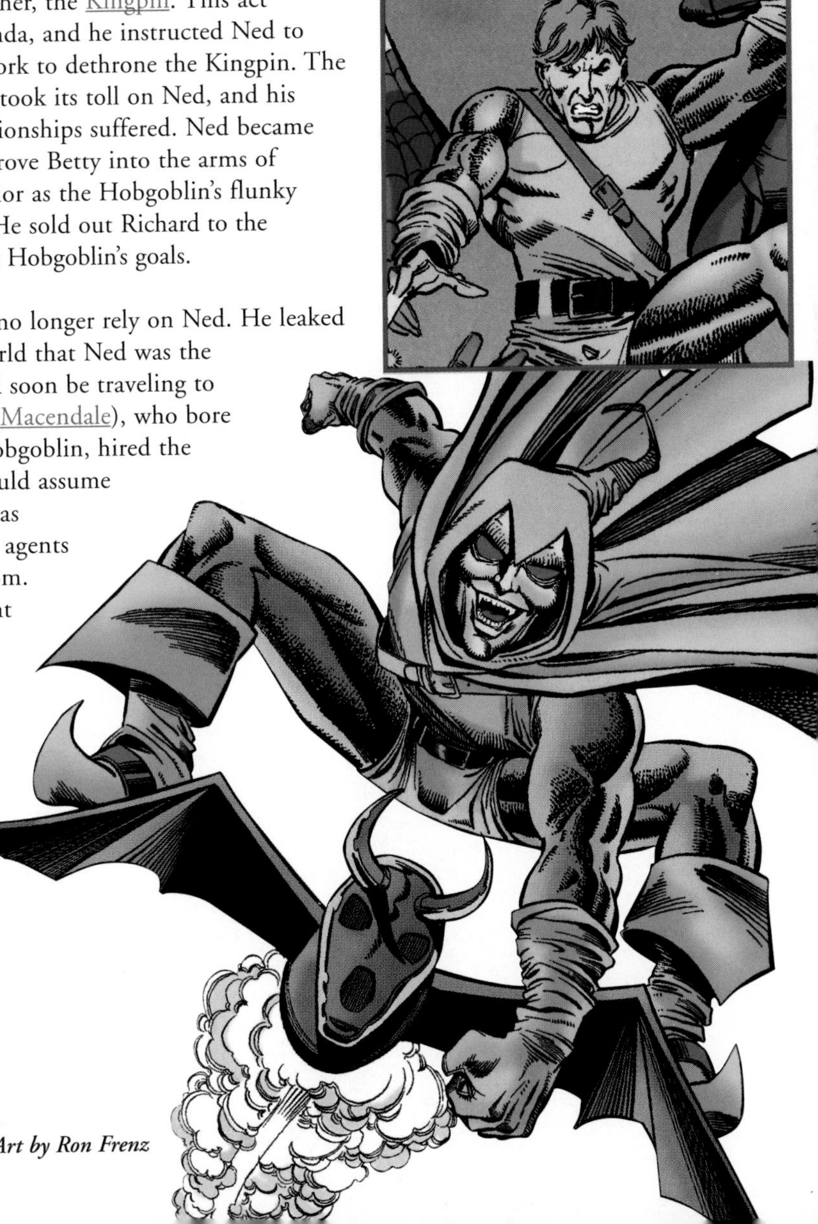

INTELLIGENCE

STRENGTH

SPEED

DURABILITY

ENERGY PROJECTION

FIGHTING SKILLS

Art by Ron Frenz

LEGION OF LOSERS

First Appearance:
Spectacular Spider-Man #245 (1997)

Still stinging from his latest defeat, the Grizzly approached like-minded, second-rate super-villains the Gibbon, the Spot and Kangaroo II to form the Spider-Man Revenge Squad — better known as the Legion of Losers. But when the Spot and the Kangaroo set out to rob a bank, the Grizzly and the Gibbon realized that while they desired revenge, crime was not their ultimate aim. Spider-Man faked defeat, allowing the Grizzly and the Gibbon time to return the stolen money. The Spot and the Kangaroo disagreed, but were defeated by the two fledgling do-gooders. The Grizzly and the Gibbon briefly joined forces as a vigilante duo, but the Grizzly has since returned to a life of crime.

LIFE FOUNDATION

First Appearance: *Spectacular Spider-Man* #143 (1988)

An organization of survivalists backed by vast corporate resources, the Life Foundation set out to create luxurious living compounds to which the ultra-wealthy could flee in the event of a nuclear war or long-term national collapse. Its leaders included Carlton Drake, Roland Treece and Mr. Pullman. To protect its first compound, Sanctus Maximus, the Life Foundation hired Chance to steal a cache of experimental weaponry, but then double-crossed him. Spider-Man rescued Chance and destroyed the facility. Again opposed by the web-slinger, the organization later reactivated the Tri-Sentinel to work as its agent. The Life Foundation next established the Arachnis Project, attempting to mutate humans to withstand any disaster. Drake's mutation into *Homo arachnis*, a giant man-spider, enabled him to survive the project's destruction in an enormous explosion — though he exhausted his powers and returned to normal in the process.

LIGHTMASTER

Real Name: Edward Lansky
First Appearance: *Spectacular Spider-Man* #3 (1977)

Hgt: 5'11"
Wt: 175 lbs.

POWERS/WEAPONS

- Flight
- Solid light blasts

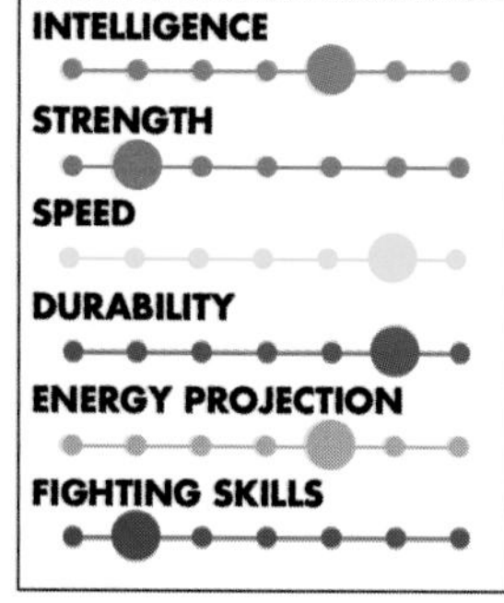

Donning a battlesuit of his own design, Dr. Edward Lansky has clashed with Spider-Man repeatedly. Initially, he was an ally of Kraven the Hunter and the Tarantula. After Spider-Man defeated him by running an electrical current through his armor, Lansky discovered he had been transformed into living energy and banished to a dimension of pure light. Spider-Man prevented him from siphoning Dazzler's powers to regain human form, but Lansky later harnessed the energy of Quasar's bands as a means of returning to normal. Not satisfied, he gained even greater power from the scientific research facility Genetech, but was defeated by Cloak and Dagger.

LIZARD

Real Name:
Dr. Curtis Connors
First Appearance:
Amazing Spider-Man #6 (1963)

Height: 5'11"
(6'8" as the Lizard)
Weight: 175 lbs.
(550 lbs. as the Lizard)
Eye Color: Blue
Hair Color: Brown

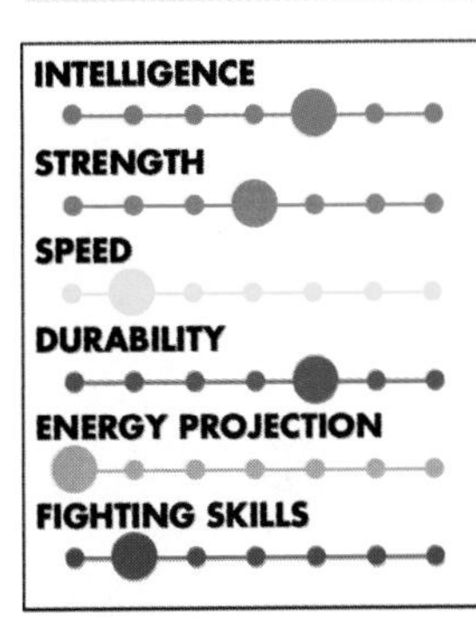

POWERS/ WEAPONS

- Brilliant biological scientist and herpetologist
- Expert in mutative medicine
- Superhuman strength and speed
- Armored skin
- Powerful tail
- Can scale sheer surfaces

Dr. Curt Connors was a gifted surgeon and biologist who went to war when his country called. He served as a battlefield medic until his arm was wounded in an explosion and was ultimately amputated. His surgical career brought to an abrupt end, Curt returned to his Florida laboratory. Inspired by a reptile's ability to regenerate lost limbs, he pursued a revolutionary study of reptilian molecular biology and DNA manipulation to replicate the process in humans. Curt then drank his untested formula; within seconds, his lost arm miraculously regenerated.

Although the serum worked as predicted, it was more powerful than Curt had expected. The chemical mix transformed him into a human lizard. Overwhelmed by his new reptilian nature, he fled into the dense Florida swamps. From his jungle sanctuary, the Lizard built an army of cold-blooded creatures — aiming to destroy humankind. Rumors of a "giant lizard" soon spread, drawing the attention of New York's Daily Bugle. Viewing the creature as a public menace, J. Jonah Jameson brazenly challenged Spider-Man to face the Lizard. As a photographer for the Bugle, Peter Parker traveled to Florida. Tracking down Curt's wife, Martha, and young son, Billy, Spider-Man learned the truth. Using Curt's lab notes and equipment, as well as his own scientific knowledge, he was able to concoct an antidote. Battling the Lizard to a standstill, Spider-Man forced the creature to swallow the solution and revert to human form — minus his newly regenerated arm. Spider-Man's aid earned him Curt's undying gratitude, as well as the enmity of his reptilian alter ego.

Curt would soon have the opportunity to repay the favor. When Peter gave his ailing aunt, May Parker, a transfusion, his radioactive blood put her in deadly peril. With doctors powerless, a desperate Spider-Man brought his friend a sample of May's blood. Curt helped the hero develop a formula to save May's life.

Continued...

Art by Tim Sale

LIZARD

However, Curt remained unaware of Spider-Man's secret identity. Shortly thereafter, Curt and Spider-Man again worked jointly to create a solution that would soften the Rhino's hide. Unfortunately, the chemicals in that solution caused Curt to revert to reptilian form once more. Knowing a cold-blooded creature cannot regulate its internal temperature, Spider-Man trapped the Lizard in a refrigerated train carriage.

For a while, Curt split his time between Florida and New York. A research grant at Empire State University established him for a time in Manhattan, where Peter worked as his teaching assistant. Yet Curt could not escape the Lizard's shadow. More and more frequently, extreme stress or exposure to chemicals would transform him into the horrific creature. Unable to deal with the toll of her husband's relapses, Martha left him and took their son with her. This emotional event triggered another transformation, and Calypso used her voodoo powers to usurp control of the Lizard's mind in pursuit of her own deadly vendetta against Spider-Man. Following Calypso's defeat, Curt embarked on a search for a permanent cure to his condition. To that end, he created a modified version of his original regeneration formula. This new serum was injected into a severed fragment of the Lizard's tail, with disastrous effects. The tail grew into a completely new Lizard, devoid of any shred of humanity. Curt was forced to trigger his transformation to protect his wife and son.

Art by Todd McFarlane

Following her husband's brave sacrifice, Martha returned to Curt. With his missing arm miraculously restored by Hammerhead, a happy ending for the Connors family seemed assured. However, the cellular structure of Curt's new arm proved unstable, and it soon became useless. A short time later, Martha and Billy were diagnosed with cancer, a result of pollution from an industrial lab near the Connors' Florida home. The combined efforts of Curt, his reptilian alter ego and Spider-Man were enough to persuade a Monnano Corporation employee to expose the company's misdeeds — but it was too late. Martha's cancer was inoperable, and Curt's long-suffering wife died. Though Billy was cured, Curt must now deal with life as a single father — trying to raise his son under the ever-present specter of the Lizard.

LOOTER

POWERS/WEAPONS

- Chemically enhanced strength
- One-man hot-air balloon
- Blinding dazzle-gun
- Various borrowed weapons

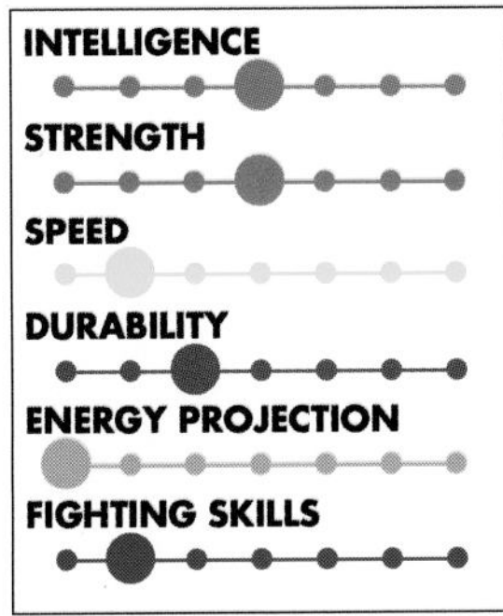

Real Name:	Norton G. Fester	**Hgt:**	5'9"
First Appearance:	*Amazing Spider-Man* #36 (1966)	**Wt:**	150 lbs.

Norton G. Fester was a crackpot scientist and part-time nut whose theory of microscopic life forms in meteorites was ignored by his peers. When a field trip uncovered a freshly fallen meteorite, he chiseled it open — releasing a gas that left him with superhuman strength.

Turning his back on academia, he resorted to super-powered theft — for money, and to obtain further meteorites that could contain more gas to replace his fading powers. In his search, he was unfortunate enough to select a museum at which Peter Parker and Gwen Stacy were separately pursuing erudition. Peter fled, leaving Gwen to assume he was a coward — but Spider-Man soon arrived. The Looter proved victorious, but was defeated shortly thereafter.

For a brief period, the Looter operated as Meteor Man. Nothing if not persistent, he once managed to use the meteoric gas to grow to giant size. Desperate, he borrowed equipment from the Ringer (Strikeback), the Trapster, the Mauler, the Shocker — even Stilt-Man. Still, he could not defeat his nemesis. Perhaps the Looter was pleased during his most recent outing to be defeated for a change by the Hornet. Little did he know, the Hornet was Spider-Man in disguise.

NATHAN LUBENSKY

INTELLIGENCE

STRENGTH

SPEED

DURABILITY

ENERGY PROJECTION

FIGHTING SKILLS

Real Name:	Nathan R. Lubensky	**Hgt:**	5'8"
First Appearance:	*Spectacular Spider-Man* #47 (1980)	**Wt:**	140 lbs.

May Parker met wheelchair-bound Nathan Lubensky while recovering from a heart attack at the Restwell Nursing Home. A former Vaudeville entertainer, Nathan proved to be so charming that when May left the hospital to set up a boarding house, she invited him to join her. He and May soon became engaged.

When a gang of thugs took hostage the occupants of May's boarding house, Spider-Man came to their rescue. This was not enough for Nathan; he knowingly opened a blind, allowing one of the NYPD marksmen outside to see the partial outline of the webbed-up gang leader and shoot him dead. May could not forgive Nathan, and she terminated their engagement.

Subsequently, Nathan was also revealed to have a serious gambling addiction. Having blown his savings, and in debt to the criminal underworld, he stole money from May in desperation — and lost that also. Hoping to repay her, he cashed in his life insurance and wagered it on the successful assassination of billionaire Richard Trask at the hands of the Vulture and Chance.

When the hit went down at the launching of Trask's new super-yacht, Spider-Man managed to defeat Chance and rescue Trask, but could not prevent the Vulture from seeking a hostage in the crowd. When the villain randomly chose May, Nathan intervened and was taken instead — suffering a fatal heart attack.

LIVING BRAIN

Real Name: Not Applicable
First Appearance: *Amazing Spider-Man* #8 (1964)
Hgt: 6'6"
Wt: 800 lbs.

The Living Brain was the greatest artificial intelligence of its time. During a demonstration by Mr. Petty of I.C.M. to Peter Parker's class at Midtown High School, it was set to the task of determining Spider-Man's secret identity. But before the machine could reveal the answer, the machine's two supervising technicians attempted to steal it. Instead, they caused the device to malfunction and embark on a frenzied rampage. After Spider-Man deactivated the Living Brain, production was discontinued. Steve Petty, the inventor's son, reactivated the device years later and dispatched it to punish a gang of bullies. This time, Spider-Man short-circuited it.

POWERS/WEAPONS

- Superhuman strength, speed and reflexes
- State-of-the-science artificial intelligence

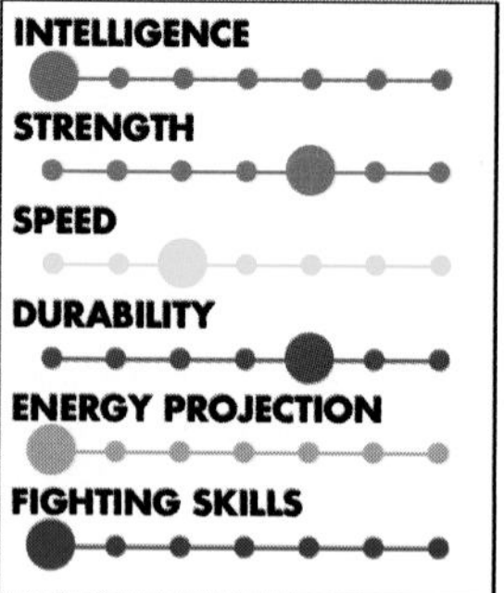

LOBO BROTHERS

Real Name: Carlos and Eduardo Lobo
First Appearance: *Spectacular Spider-Man* #143 (1988)
Hgt: 6'0"
Wt: 200 lbs.

Upon realizing their innate ability to transform into wolf-like creatures, Mexican street kids Carlos and Eduardo Lobo steadily clawed their way to the top of the South Texas underworld. Their success spurred an attack from the Arranger, the Kingpin's lieutenant. Seeking revenge, the brothers traveled to New York City and painted the streets red with the blood of the Kingpin's henchmen. Their spree culminated in a dramatic shoot-out involving the Kingpin, Hammerhead, the Chameleon, Spider-Man and Glory Grant. Aiming for Spider-Man, Glory shot Eduardo dead; the web-slinger himself KO'd Carlos, who was then captured by police.

POWERS/WEAPONS

- Wolf-like creatures, with the power to transform during the full moon

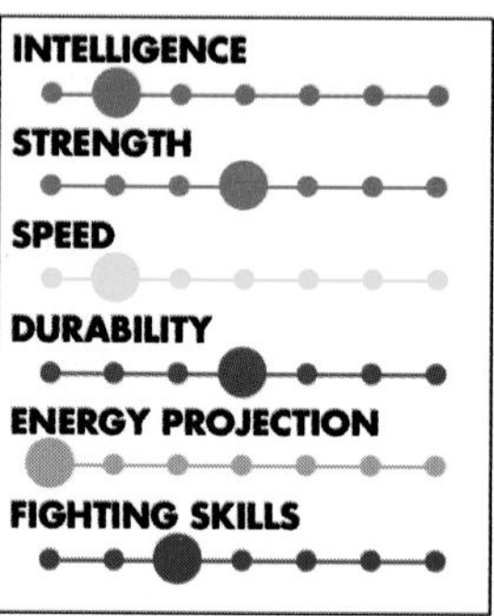

MAN-MOUNTAIN MARKO

Real Name: Michael Marko
First Appearance: *Amazing Spider-Man* #73 (1969)
Hgt: 6'11"
Wt: 270 lbs.

An enforcer for the Maggia, Man-Mountain Marko first clashed with Spider-Man during Silvermane's quest to acquire the Lifeline Tablet, which holds the promise of eternal youth. The Shocker was believed to possess the artifact, and Marko fought Spider-Man while interrogating the villain's girlfriend. Working for both the Maggia and the criminal mastermind known as Nightshade, as well as on his own, Marko has encountered Spider-Man, Daredevil, Cage, Iron Fist and private investigator Jessica Jones. He was later involved in a second struggle to obtain the Lifeline Tablet.

POWERS/WEAPONS

- Superhuman strength and resistance to injury

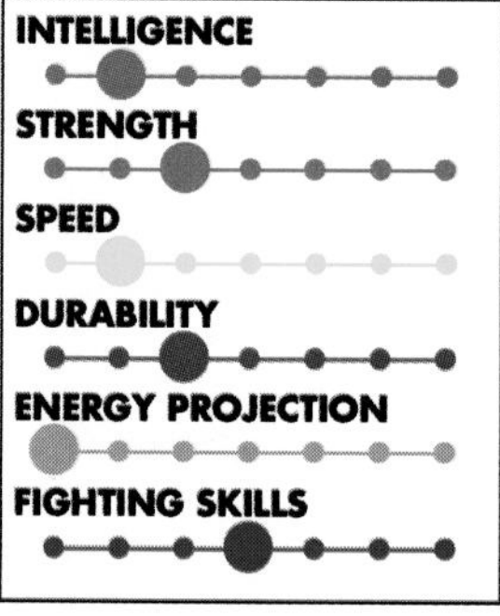

JASON MACENDALE

Real Name: Jason Phillip Macendale
First Appearance: *Machine Man* #19 (1981)

Hgt: 6'1"
Wt: 210 lbs.

POWERS/WEAPONS

- Expert armed and unarmed combatant
- Enhanced strength
- Cybernetically enhanced body
- Hobgoblin paraphernalia

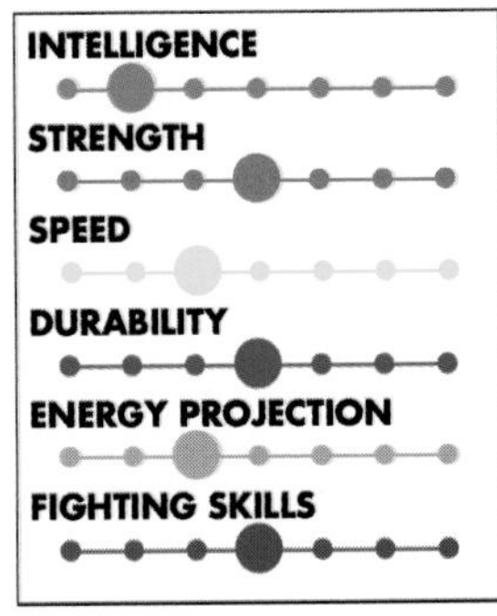

A former Marine and CIA agent, Jason Macendale's methods were too violent for even that bloodstained business. Kicked out of the agency, he began a new life as an international mercenary with a sideline in crime. As Jack O' Lantern, he encountered Spider-Man, then became an enforcer for the Kingpin. When the Rose (Richard Fisk) and the Kingpin formed an uneasy alliance, Macendale and the more powerful Hobgoblin were forced to cooperate. Filled with envy, Macendale set out to acquire the Hobgoblin's superior weapons and equipment, and paid the Foreigner to assassinate the villain.

After Macendale adopted the persona of the Hobgoblin, he underwent several transformations. During a demonic invasion, he sold his soul and became himself part-demon. His demonic half subsequently separated to become the Demogoblin. His strength enhanced by the potions of Vladimir Kravinoff, Macendale also paid to have his body cybernetically upgraded — but was captured regardless. It was later revealed that Ned Leeds, the man murdered by the Foreigner, was not the real Hobgoblin. When Roderick Kingsley returned to claim his place as the true Hobgoblin, he easily overpowered and killed Macendale in his prison cell.

MAD JACK

Real Name: Daniel Berkhart and Maguire Beck
First Appearance: *Spectacular Spider-Man* #241 (1996)

Hgt: Berkhart: 5'10" / Beck: 5'5"
Wt: Berkhart: 160 lbs. / Beck: 115 lbs.

POWERS/WEAPONS

- Jet glider
- Special-effects expert
- Exceptional hypnotist
- Master of hallucinogenic chemicals
- Skilled roboticist

Mad Jack was actually two people: Danny Berkhart, who had formerly borrowed Mysterio's identity, and Maguire Beck, cousin of the original Mysterio. They wore the costume in turns, sometimes even employing an android for the riskiest assignments. Berkhart and Beck worked in tandem, maintaining full-time radio contact. The third member of their team was in fact a cat, with whom they would speak as if it could understand them.

Mad Jack first appeared immediately following the return of Norman Osborn (Green Goblin). Osborn employed Jack to force J. Jonah Jameson to sell him the Daily Bugle. Berkhart, seeking vengeance against Jameson for an earlier betrayal, carried out this task with pleasure. Spider-Man's intervention saved Jameson's life, but the Bugle was already lost. Later, Berkhart and Conundrum fought Prodigy. Prodigy captured Conundrum, while Mad Jack faked his own death to escape. Following the suicide of Quentin Beck, Berkhart assumed the role of Mysterio permanently, while Maguire became the sole Mad Jack. Mysterio II and Jack teamed up to gain simultaneous revenge on Spider-Man, Jameson, Daredevil and Joe Smith. They were defeated, and Maguire went to jail. The mysterious cat, however, escaped with Berkhart.

MANHATTAN

1. Mary Jane Watson's first apartment
2. Bedford Towers
3. Matt Murdock's apartment
4. Peter Parker's former apartment
5. S.H.I.E.L.D. secret HQ
6. Tinkerer's workshop
7. Doctor Strange's sanctum
8. Harry Osborn's former loft
9. Ben Reilly's apartment
10. Yancy Street
11. Peter Parker's current apartment
12. Peter Parker & Randy Robertson's apartment
13. Peter Parker & Harry Osborn's college apartment
14 Coffee Bean
15. Empire State Universtiy
16. Daily Grind
17. Nick Fury's apartment
18. Daily Bugle
19. Fisk Towers
20. Marvel Comics office
21. Curt Connors' apartment
22. S.H.I.E.L.D. public HQ
23. Heroes for Hire office
24. Madame Web's apartment
25. Baxter Building
26. Mary Jane Watson & Peter Parker's luxury apartment
27. Latverian Embassy
28. Law Offices of Nelson & Murdock
29. Hellfire Club Mansion
30. Norman Osborn's penthouse
31. Avengers Embassy
32. J. Jonah Jameson's penthouse
33. Symkarian Embassy
34. Wakandan Embassy
35. Daily Globe
36. Luke Cage's apartment
37. Master Planner's undersea base

A. World Trade Center site
B. City Hall
C. Empire State Building
D. Times Square
E. Grand Central Station
F. United Nations
G. Metropolitan Museum of Art

Multivex, 140th St.
36
Harlem
Upper West Side
1
Hudson River
2
Central Park
G
Upper East Side
Harlem River
Wards Island
34
33
31
3
32
30
Hell's Kitchen
28
29
26
24
27
25
D
35
Roosevelt Island
Midtown
23
E
4
20
22
19
Chelsea
C
21
5
Queensboro Bridge
F
18
6
East Side
East River
QUEENS
h Village
Forest Hills, Queens
16
17
37
14
15
8
East Village
13
OsCorp, Eastern L.I.
12
11
Lower East Side
10
Williamsburg Bridge
Manhattan Bridge
OKLYN

MADAME WEB

Real Name: Cassandra Webb
First Appearance: *Amazing Spider-Man* #210 (1980)

Hgt: 5'7"
Wt: 115 lbs.

POWERS/WEAPONS

- Perception of aspects of the future
- Can perform psychic surgery
- Limited mind reading

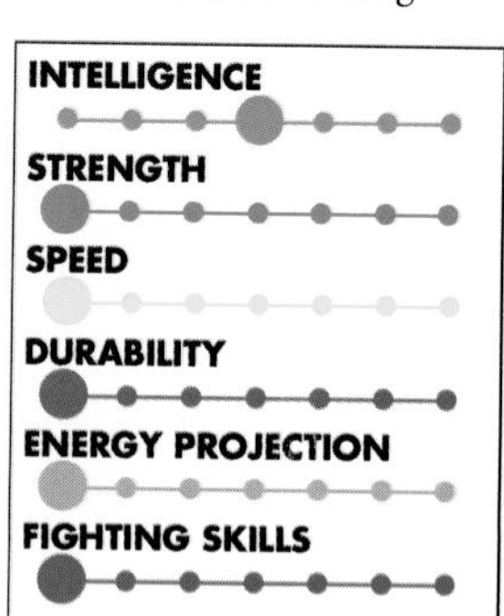

When Deborah Whitman showed Peter Parker an advertisement for the psychic Madame Web, he dismissed her as a fraud. But after a hostile takeover of the Daily Globe left Spider-Man with Madame Web as his only lead, he paid her a visit. Through her psychic powers, she revealed both the identity of the criminals and the identity of Peter Parker as Spider-Man.

Months later, threatened by the Juggernaut, Madame Web called on Spider-Man for aid. Despite Spider-Man's efforts, the Juggernaut succeeded in reaching Madame Web; in lifting her up, he removed her from the elaborate life-support system that was keeping her alive. The Juggernaut departed, leaving Madame Web near death.

Years passed, and Madame Web, seemingly recovered, was contacted by Norman Osborn (Green Goblin) to take part in the arcane Gathering of Five. During the ceremony, Madame Web was granted the gift of immortality. Rejuvenated, she joined forces with Jessica Drew and Julia Carpenter (Spider-Woman and Spider-Woman II), and Mattie Franklin (Spider-Woman III). Together, they defeated Cassandra's granddaughter, Charlotte Witter (Spider-Woman IV).

MIDTOWN HIGH SCHOOL

First Appearance: *Amazing Fantasy* #15 (1962)

Peter Parker was a student at Midtown High School in Queens, New York, when he first acquired his Spider-Man powers — but he was far from popular. Shy and bespectacled, Peter was an academic success, but a social dropout. Somehow, he survived each day under the watchful eye of Principal Davis and his sarcastic science teacher, Mr. Warren. First among Peter's tormenters was Flash Thompson, the school football star. Flash's girlfriend was Liz Allan (Liz Osborn). Initially as cruel as the rest, Liz later developed an interest in the new, more confident — and unknown to her, spider-powered — Peter. Flash and Peter both attended Empire State University after graduation and became friends, while Liz abandoned her studies.

At Midtown, Peter was friends with Brian "Tiny" McKeever, a muscular but academically challenged student. Tiny left home and abandoned high school after being battered by his father. He later returned, with Spider-Man's encouragement and Peter's tutorage. Other important figures in Peter's life were Sally Avril and her friend, Jason Ionello — who attempted to emulate Spider-Man and budding action photographer Peter, to Avril's peril.

Coming full circle, Peter has returned to Midtown High as a part-time science teacher.

MAN-THING

POWERS/WEAPONS

- Superhuman strength
- Resistant to conventional injury
- Acid touch
- Empath

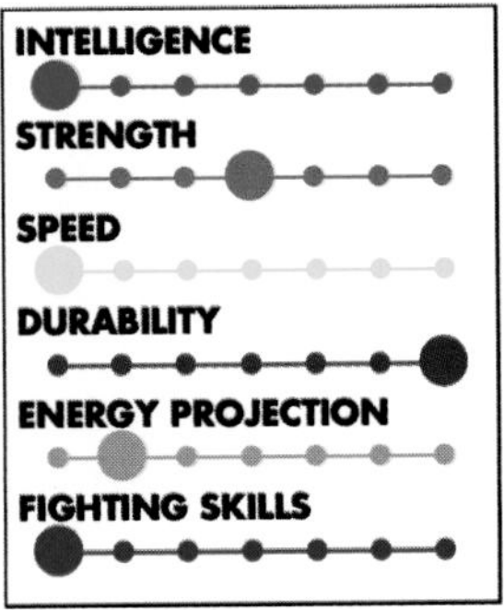

Real Name: Theodore Sallis
First Appearance: *Savage Tales* #1 (1971)

Hgt: 7'0"
Wt: 500 lbs.

The near-mindless, shambling guardian of the Nexus of Realities in the Florida Everglades, the Man-Thing was once scientist Ted Sallis. Attempting to re-create the legendary Super-Soldier Serum that had empowered Captain America, Sallis merged with the muck and mire of the swamp. Drawn by powerful emotions, the Man-Thing destroys those who bring evil into his realm. Whatsoever knows fear burns at the touch of the Man-Thing. Spider-Man helped the Man-Thing drive out the demon D'Spayre and defeat the original, mystical Scrier. The web-slinger fought Man-Thing once, when sorcerer Ian Fate controlled the bog beast.

JOY MERCADO

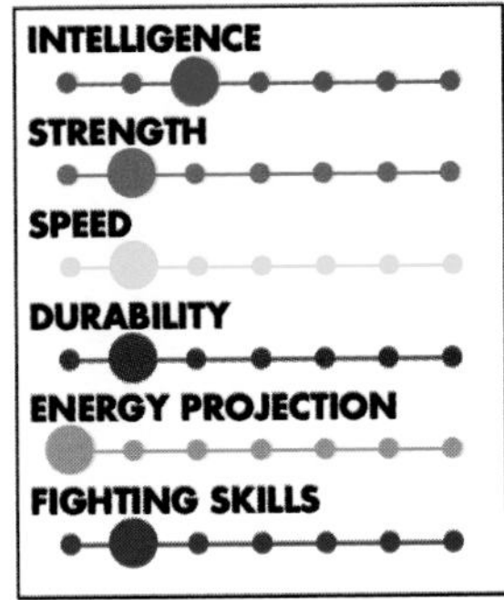

Real Name: Joy Mercado
First Appearance: *Moon Knight* #33 (1983)

Hgt: 5'10"
Wt: 135 lbs.

Confident, intelligent, ambitious and street-smart, Joy Mercado has what it takes to be one of the city's top reporters — first for NOW magazine and today for the Daily Bugle. Though glamorous, Joy is not above getting her nails dirty to chase a story. She first met Peter Parker investigating the enigmatic man called Ace. They have since partnered countless times for the Bugle on stories involving terrorism, demon attacks, werewolves and super-villains. On one occasion, Peter and Joy were kidnapped, caught in the middle of violence and turmoil in Belfast, Northern Ireland. Though Joy has been flirtatious with Peter, they remain just friends.

MINDWORM

POWERS/WEAPONS

- Can control and feed off the psychic energy of the weak-minded
- Superior athlete

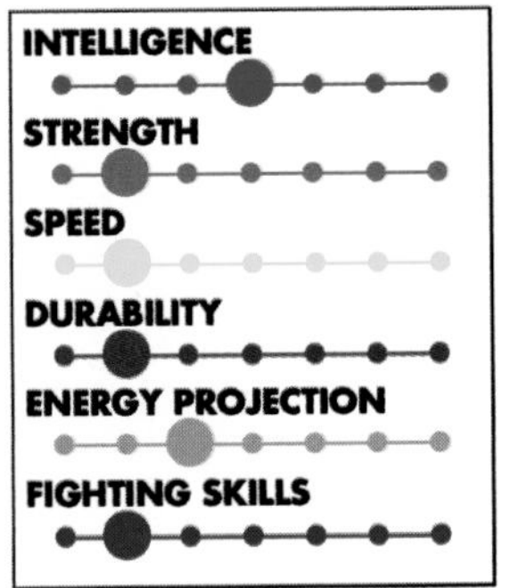

Real Name: William Turner
First Appearance: *Amazing Spider-Man* #138 (1974)

Hgt: 6'1"
Wt: 210 lbs.

Born deformed, William Turner's mutant powers surfaced early. He killed his parents, and then set about controlling the other orphans who mocked his appearance. As an adult, he made his home in an abandoned building in Queens — feeding off the emotions of those around him. Turner recognized Peter Parker's abnormal mental-energy signature as a threat and sent the local residents to attack him — but Spider-Man clapped Mindworm's ears, temporarily nullifying his powers. The web-slinger later helped Turner overcome his inner demons and rejoin humanity. Seemingly, Mindworm's turnaround did not last; he is currently in prison.

MIRAGE

Real Name: Desmond Charne
First Appearance: *Amazing Spider-Man* #156 (1976)
Hgt: 5'11"
Wt: 195 lbs.

Desmond Charne always wanted to be a super-villain. Studying optics and laser technology, he created the special suit that granted him his powers. Charne then embarked on a series of bold daylight robberies, targeting weddings and society events. One such wedding was that of Betty Brant and Ned Leeds, with Peter Parker attending as friend and photographer. Peter defeated Mirage as Spider-Man by dropping a huge chandelier on him. Mirage later attempted to kidnap the Thing of the Fantastic Four, but was defeated by Daredevil. Mirage finally met his end when the Scourge of the Underworld shot him dead at the Bar with No Name.

POWERS/WEAPONS

- Creation of illusionary self-duplicates

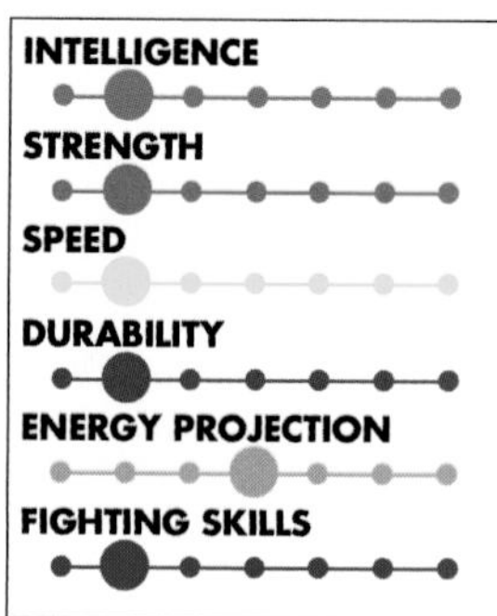

MISTER BROWNSTONE

Real Name: Garrison Klum
First Appearance: *Spider-Man/Black Cat* #1 (2003)
Hgt: 5'9"
Wt: 200 lbs.

Few realize Garrison Klum — well-known, affluent philanthropist — obtained his wealth in the guise of Mister Brownstone, a drug supplier to the rich and famous who discreetly teleports his product directly into the bloodstream of his clients. After accidentally overdosing Tricia Lane, a friend of the Black Cat, Brownstone went on to kill actor Hunter Todd, who had witnessed the entire episode, to keep the young man from talking. Before being brought to justice by the Black Cat and Spider-Man, Brownstone also managed to murder the entire Ortega family drug cartel for business reasons.

POWERS/WEAPONS

- Low-level teleportation

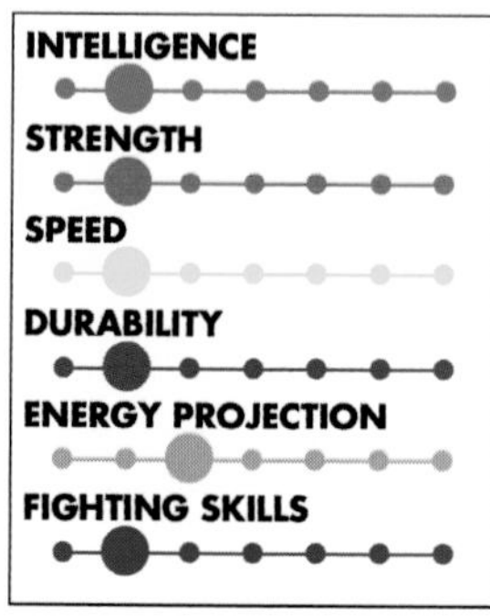

MISTER HYDE

Real Name: Calvin Zabo
First Appearance: *Journey into Mystery* #99 (1963)
Hgt: 6'5"
Wt: 420 lbs.

Like his literary namesake, Dr. Calvin Zabo periodically transforms into the bestial Mister Hyde with the aid of a chemically based formula of his own concoction. Of little cunning, Hyde depended on his lithe and clever ally the Cobra for a long period. When the Cobra ended their partnership by abandoning Zabo in prison, he became Hyde's enemy. Spider-Man came between the former allies twice — saving the Cobra from Hyde, and himself from both. Hyde — who has also faced Captain America, Asgardian thunder god Thor and countless others — is now a less-competent but still dangerous drug addict.

POWERS/WEAPONS

- Superhuman strength and durability

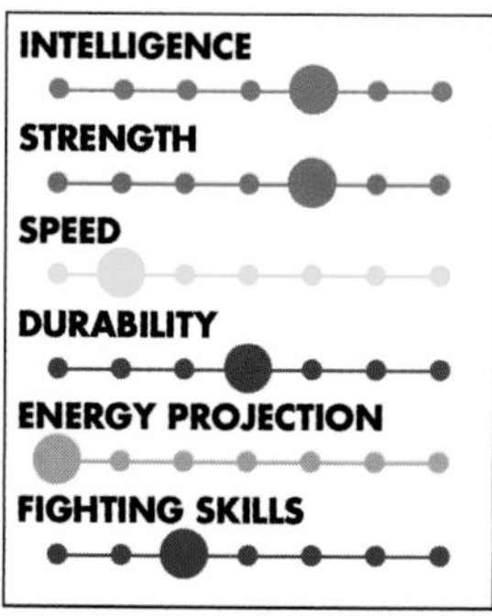

MORBIUS

Nobel Prize-winning chemist Dr. Michael Morbius became his own patient when he discovered that he was dying of a unique blood disease. The only way he could cure himself involved a combination of vampire bats and electric-shock therapy. Although his attempt to rid himself of his wasting disease proved successful, the cure also transformed him into a living vampire. Now unable to bear sunlight and plagued by an overwhelming lust for fresh human blood, Morbius struggled between self-hatred for the monster he had become and his will to live.

Real Name:
Dr. Michael Morbius
First Appearance:
Amazing Spider-Man #101 (1971)

Height:	5'10"
Weight:	170 lbs.
Eye Color:	Blue
Hair Color:	Black

Still coming to grips with his new form, Morbius encountered Dr. Curt Connors and Spider-Man as they sought to reverse a process that left Spider-Man with six arms. Connors, as the Lizard, entered into a furious battle with Morbius in which the vampire was defeated. His defeat allowed Connors to formulate a cure for Spider-Man's disturbing excess of limbs using a serum incorporating enzymes from Morbius' unusual blood.

In time, Morbius began living off the blood of the homeless and other, not-so-innocent street-dwellers. The terrifying nature of his condition made it nearly impossible for him to seek help from his former colleagues, as he discovered when he sought aid from his friend Professor Jorgenson — a visit that ended with a battle between Morbius, Spider-Man and the X-Men.

After a subsequent confrontation that saw him join forces with the Man-Wolf (John Jameson) to fight Spider-Man, Morbius took to traveling. When he returned, a lightning strike cured him of his vampiric disease during an encounter with Spider-Man — but the effects did not last. Reverting to form, but with greater control over his hunger than before, he joined forces for a time with the team of supernatural adventurers known as the Midnight Sons.

Art by John Romita Jr.

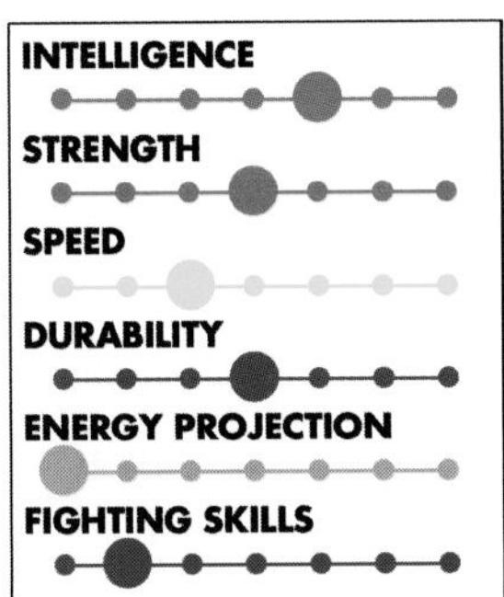

POWERS/ WEAPONS

- Enhanced strength
- Ability to float on air currents
- Regeneration from physical wounds

MOLTEN MAN

Real Name: Mark Raxton
First Appearance: *Amazing Spider-Man* #28 (1965)

Hgt: 6'5"
Wt: 550 lbs.

Mark Raxton, Liz Osborn's stepbrother, was a lab assistant to Spencer Smythe. Accidentally coated with an experimental chemical, Raxton found himself transformed into the Molten Man. Confused and violent, he clashed with Spider-Man. After she graduated from high school, Liz cared for Raxton until his body erupted into flame — increasing both his power and his rage. He later regained control and reverted to his golden metal-covered form, and Liz's husband, Harry Osborn, offered him an honest job. Raxton aided Spider-Man on several occasions, but Norman Osborn (Green Goblin) brainwashed him to kill Alison Mongrain.

POWERS/WEAPONS

- Super-strength and durability
- Generation of fire and flame

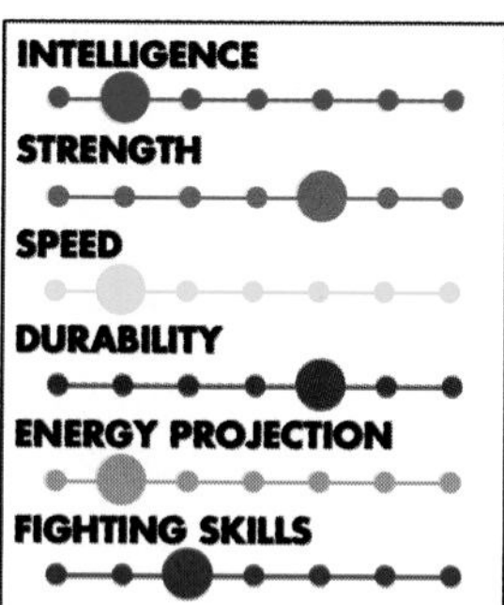

MOON KNIGHT

Real Name: Marc Spector
First Appearance: *Werewolf by Night* #32 (1975)

Hgt: 6'2"
Wt: 225 lbs.

The course of Marc Spector's life changed forever when he was slain by a brutal fellow mercenary, Roald Bushman. Thanks apparently to the divine intervention of Konshu, Egyptian god of the moon, Spector rose again. Abandoning his former existence, he devoted himself and his wealth to fighting crime in the guise of the Moon Knight. He fought alongside Spider-Man on numerous occasions — against such foes as the terrorist organization known as the Secret Empire, Cyclone, the Rat Pack and the will-sapping Purple Man. Later, Moon Knight joined forces with Daredevil, the Black Widow and others to further his war on crime.

POWERS/WEAPONS

- Enhanced strength, speed and agility in moonlight
- Scarab darts
- Grappling hook
- Moon-Copter

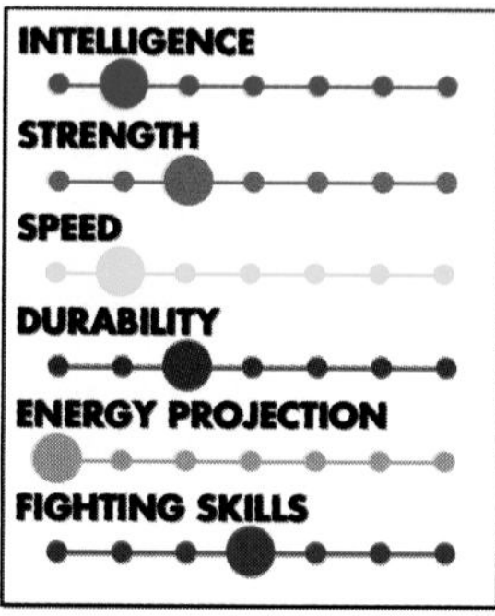

MORLUN

Real Name: Morlun
First Appearance: *Amazing Spider-Man* #30 (2001)

Hgt: 6'2"
Wt: 175 lbs.

According to Ezekiel, Spider-Man's abilities are totemistic in nature. One of many beings that subsist by consuming those with such powers, Morlun has roamed Earth for millennia — living off the life forces of others. Aided by his unwilling human assistant, Dex, Morlun played a deadly game of cat and mouse with Spider-Man — unwittingly allowing his foe sufficient time to prepare for their final battle. Discovering Morlun's need for pure food, Spider-Man poisoned his own blood with radiation. Morlun was weakened when he attempted to consume the hero, and Dex shot him dead as retribution for years of slavery at his master's hand.

POWERS/WEAPONS

- Superhuman strength, reflexes and speed
- Absorbs a victim's life force on touch

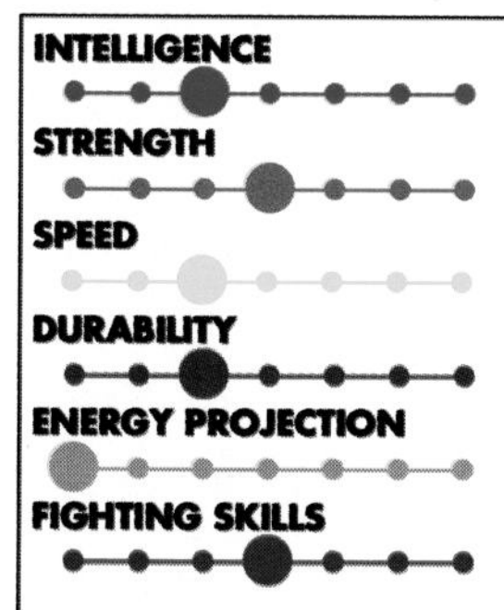

MYSTERIO

Quentin Beck began his career as a Hollywood stuntman. Branching into special effects, he proved himself unusually talented. But Beck grew tried of his backstage role; he wanted something more. A friend jokingly told him that if he wanted to make a name for himself, he should consider "offing" one of the new costumed heroes coming out of the woodwork. Beck took the idea to heart and began to study the then-fledgling Spider-Man. As part of his scheme, Beck entered into a partnership with the Tinkerer to steal industrial and military plans. The two men pooled their genius and developed alien disguises to mask the true nature of their crime. Though Spider-Man foiled the plot, the disguises worked like a charm. After further planning and study of his foe, Beck attacked Spider-Man as Mysterio, master of illusion, and was promptly defeated. Mysterio then accepted Doctor Octopus' invitation to join the original Sinister Six.

Though he continued to battle Spider-Man, Mysterio made little headway in conquering his enemy. While imprisoned, Mysterio was diagnosed with an inoperable brain tumor and terminal lung cancer — both caused by the products Beck had employed for years in his life of crime. With one year to live, and deemed sane and no longer a danger to society, Mysterio was granted a get-out-of-jail-free card. With no time left to waste, he began planning his final revenge — but not against longtime enemy Spider-Man, who had temporarily been replaced by Ben Reilly.

Mysterio chose another longtime foe, Daredevil, as a stand-in for his final scene. Purchasing information about Daredevil's identity from the Kingpin, Mysterio crafted a complex plan to drive the blind lawyer mad. He hired Bullseye to kill Daredevil's lover, Karen Page, then destroyed Foggy Nelson's relationship with Liz Osborn and almost forced Daredevil to murder an innocent baby. In the climax to his life story, Mysterio intended to have Daredevil kill him — but he severely underestimated his foe. Even on the brink of madness, Daredevil refused to take Mysterio's life. Utterly defeated yet ever the showman, Mysterio apparently committed suicide in front of the hero.

Real Name:
Quentin Beck a.k.a.
Dr. Ludwig Rinehart

First Appearance:
Amazing Spider-Man #13 (1964)

Height:	5'11"
Weight:	175 lbs.
Eye Color:	Blue
Hair Color:	Black

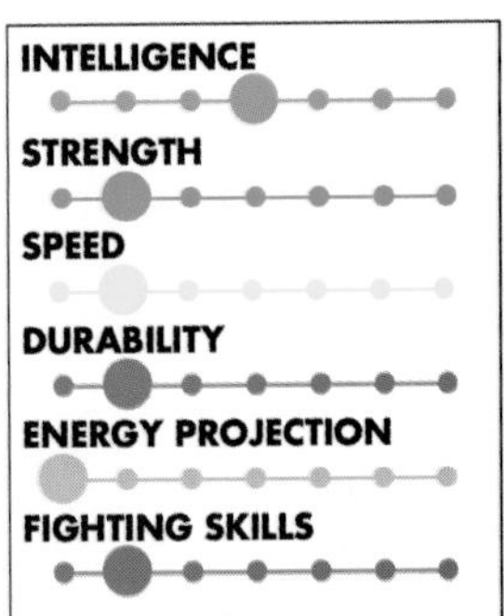

POWERS/ WEAPONS

- Accomplished magician and hypnotist
- Skilled amateur chemist
- Holographic projectors
- Hallucinogenic gasses
- Spider-sense dampeners

Art by Joe Quesada

MUD-THING

Real Name: Morrie Bench and William Baker
First Appearance: *Amazing Spider-Man* #217 (1981)
Hgt: 12-25'
Wt: 5-15 tons

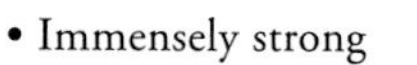

POWERS/WEAPONS

- Immensely strong
- Resistant to injury
- Can absorb mass and grow in size

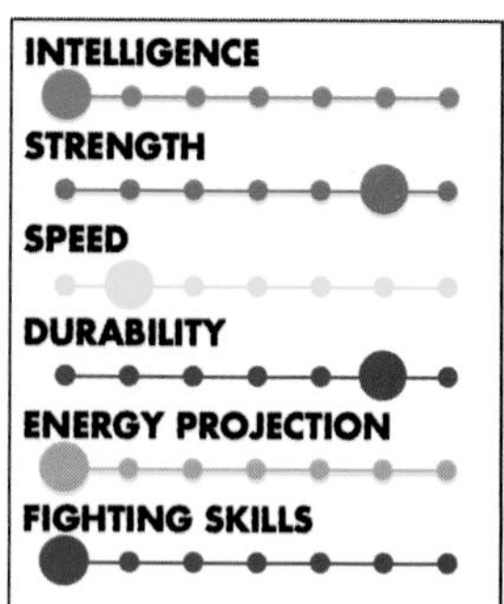

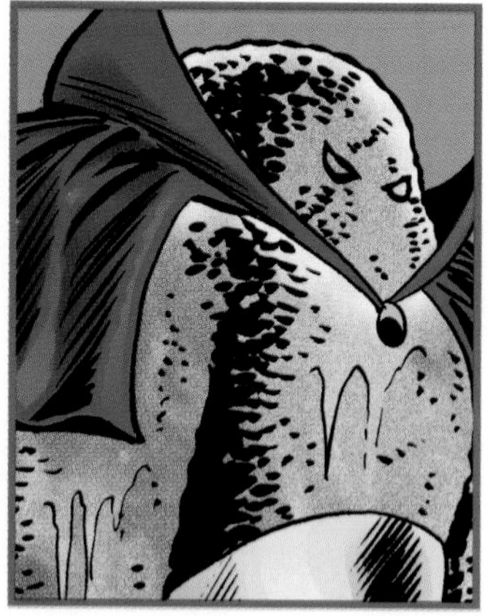

When the Sandman and Hydro-Man both attempted to charm a barfly named Sadie Frickett, Spider-Man's untimely arrival saw them smash into one another. Their collision resulted in the creation of the monstrous, rampaging Mud-Thing. Soothed by Sadie's presence, the now-tame Mud-Thing was paraded in front of paying crowds by an unscrupulous promoter, Travis Rave. When Sadie fell for the promoter, the jealous monster grabbed her and headed for a tall building. Police helicopters arrived and sprayed the beast with desiccant, and the Sandman and Hydro-Man eventually split apart and went their separate ways.

MURDEROUS MIMES

First Appearance:
Peter Parker: Spider-Man #21 (2000)

A classic case of street performers gone bad: Spider-Man thwarted this gang of miscreant mimes at every turn. With unspoken agreement, they launched a major campaign to forever silence the web-slinger under the guidance of their charismatic General. Staging a fake mugging, they tricked Spider-Man into an alleyway where their tank lay in ambush. But the hero turned the tables and lured them into a nearby factory. With his webbing, he constructed and trapped them in a Plexiglas prison. Arrested, they took advantage of their right to remain silent.

MYSTERIO II

Real Name: Daniel Berkhart
First Appearance: *Amazing Spider-Man* #141 (1975)
Hgt: 5'10"
Wt: 160 lbs.

POWERS/WEAPONS

- Special-effects expert
- Hypnotist and master of hallucinogenic chemicals
- Skilled roboticist

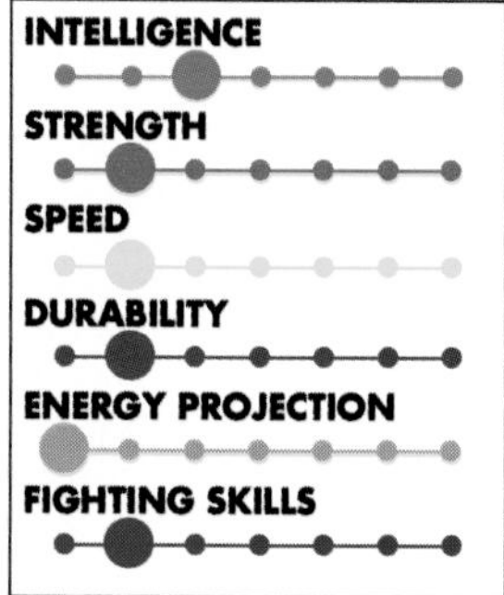

Imprisoned for his early crimes, the original Mysterio, Quentin Beck, faked his own death to escape. J. Jonah Jameson subsequently hired Danny Berkhart, Beck's friend and student, to adopt Mysterio's identity and fool Spider-Man into believing he was Beck's ghost. When Berkhart was defeated and jailed, Jameson abandoned him to his fate. Following Beck's dramatic suicide, Berkhart reclaimed the fishbowl; joined a newly formed Sinister Six; and teamed with Beck's niece, Maguire (Mad Jack), to torment Jameson, Spider-Man and Daredevil. Their plan failed, but Berkhart escaped — taking with him Mad Jack's mysterious cat, also named Maguire.

NEW WARRIORS

First Appearance: *Thor* #411 (1989)

Founded by the vigilante Night Thrasher, the New Warriors began their joint career by defeating the deadly threat of Terrax, a former herald of the world-devouring Galactus. The New Warriors have worked with Spider-Man on several occasions. Together, the Warriors and the web-slinger have faced the subversive Secret Empire, the shadow-casting Darkling, the Metahumes and the Hostiles; participated in cosmic wars and crusades; and rescued their own Speedball from the Sphinx and his Hero Killers. The New Warriors' membership has also included Firestar, Marvel Boy/Justice, Namorita/Kymaera, Nova, Silhouette, Rage, Hindsight Lad, Dagger, Darkhawk, PowerPax/PowerHouse, Turbo, Timeslip, Helix, Bolt, Aegis and even the Scarlet Spider (Ben Reilly).

NIGHTCRAWLER

POWERS/WEAPONS

- Teleportation
- Prehensile tail
- Limited invisibility
- Accomplished acrobat and aerialist

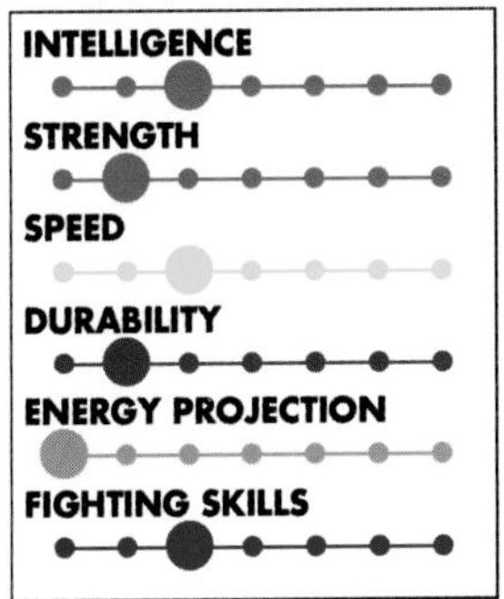

Real Name: Kurt Wagner
First Appearance: *Giant-Size X-Men* #1 (1975)
Hgt: 5'9"
Wt: 161 lbs.

A longtime member of the X-Men, the swash-buckling Kurt Wagner possesses superhuman agility, clings to walls, and fights evil in a world that fears and hates him. Though he has much in common with Spider-Man, Nightcrawler did not initially get along with the web-slinger. Mistaking one another for the enemy, the two tussled while searching for a sniper on Coney Island. Together with the Punisher, they captured the actual assassin, Jigsaw. Later, Nightcrawler and the wall-crawler fought side by side against Crossbow.

NIGHTMARE

POWERS/WEAPONS

- Manipulation of dreams

INTELLIGENCE
STRENGTH
SPEED
DURABILITY
ENERGY PROJECTION
FIGHTING SKILLS

Real Name: Unrevealed
First Appearance: *Strange Tales* #110 (1963)
Hgt: Variable
Wt: Variable

The demonic entity known as Nightmare preys on humans in their dreams, while they are help-less. Manipulating his victims' greatest fears, he can conjure their inner demons to tear at their souls and increase his own power. Chiefly opposed by Doctor Strange, Nightmare has also invaded the mind of Spider-Man, who has so far been able to survive the creature's onslaught. Nightmare even stooped so low as to assault a young Peter Parker, before he gained his spider-powers. In fact, everyone on Earth has been a victim of Nightmare at one time or another.

NOCTURNE

Real Name: Angela Cairn
First Appearance: *Spectacular Spider-Man* #190 (1992)
Hgt: 5'8"
Wt: 175 lbs.

Angela Cairn was a bitter policewoman whose partner and friend, Jackie Kessler, was killed by Vermin. Following the trail of similar murders, she was ambushed and mutated by one of terrorist technician Baron Helmut Zemo's mutates, apparently dying in the process. Days later, she arose as Nocturne and sought vengeance on those who had wronged her. Spider-Man mistook her for the serial killer, but soon realized his error. He helped her defeat the Mutilation Killer, but prevented Nocturne from killing her. She later helped Puma — who had degenerated into a mindless, feral state. Interceding in his battle with Spider-Man, she healed Puma's wounds — and later, his mind.

POWERS/WEAPONS

- Winged flight
- Projection of emotions
- Control over hair
- Can heal others
- Enahnced speed and strength

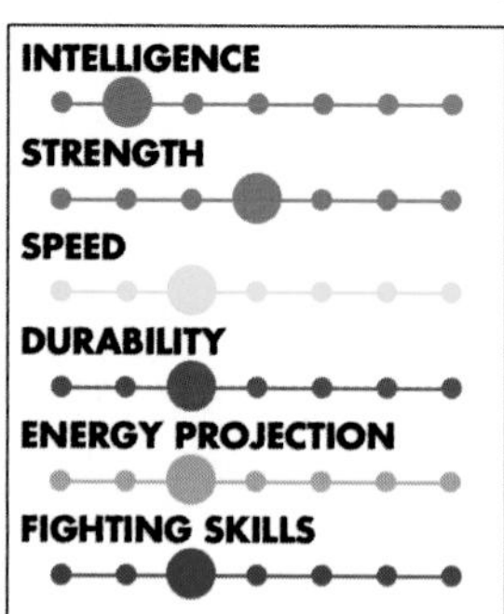

NORMAN OSBORN JR.

Real Name: Norman Harry Osborn
First Appearance: *Amazing Spider-Man* #263 (1985)
Hgt: 3'9"
Wt: 45 lbs.

The son of Liz Osborn and Harry Osborn, and the grandson of Norman Osborn (Green Goblin), little Normie Osborn has led a trying life in his few short years. First, he endured his father's total mental breakdown and death, and then the startling return of his grandfather — and namesake — from beyond the grave. Although his father loved him dearly, Normie's grandfather has claimed he would just as soon kill the boy — though Spider-Man believes otherwise. As a toddler, Normie despised the wall-crawler for his involvement in his father's death. He no longer seems to do so.

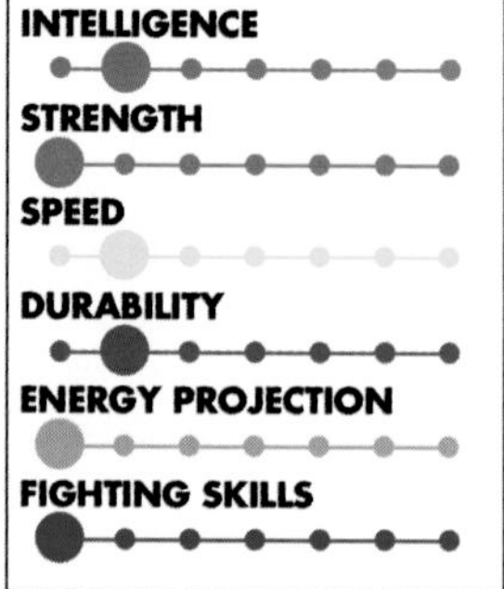

PERSUADER

Real Name: Roland Rayburn
First Appearance: *Web of Spider-Man* #35 (1988)
Hgt: 5'10"
Wt: 170 lbs.

Possessing the mutant ability to coerce others into obeying his will, Roland Rayburn could transform even the most hapless citizen into a staunch ally. Rayburn unwillingly became an indirect operative of the Kingpin when the Arranger forced him to seize control of the Punisher in an attempt to assassinate the Lobo Brothers. When the Punisher was faced with killing Spider-Man, the Persuader's hold on him broke at the pivotal moment. The Punisher shot and killed the Persuader instead.

POWERS/WEAPONS

- Mind control

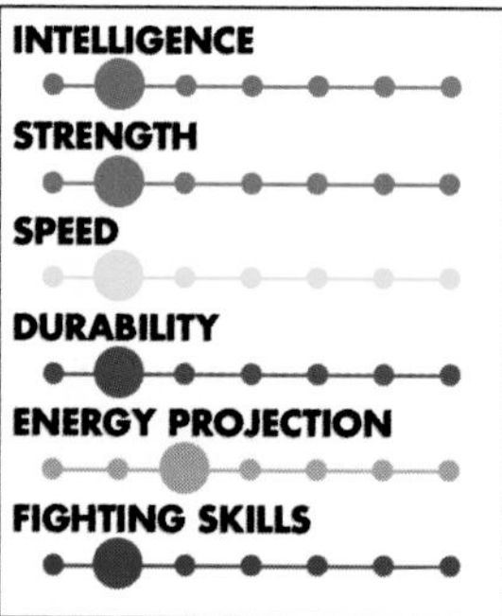

HARRY OSBORN

Fast friends Peter Parker and Harry Osborn were fellow freshmen at Empire State University. When Harry's millionaire father, Norman Osborn, offered to foot the bill for an apartment big enough for two, Harry and Peter became roommates and best pals. While Harry was not initially aware of his father's dark side as the Green Goblin, he suffered under the relentless pressure of Norman's expectations. Eventually, the strain of his father's domineering influence combined with a romantic rejection by Mary Jane Watson drove Harry to drug use. While he quickly sought help for his addiction, Harry's mind remained dangerously fragile.

Witnessing his father's apparent death in a battle against Spider-Man, Harry was driven to the brink of madness. After discovering Spider-Man's costume in Peter's room, Harry assumed Norman's identity and attacked the hero. Following his defeat, Harry lost all memory of the incident, soon marrying Liz Allan (Liz Osborn) and fathering a child, Norman Osborn Jr.

When the Hobgoblin threatened Harry, demanding the formula for his father's original strength-enhancing serum, Harry reluctantly donned the Green Goblin costume to protect his family. Tragically, it appears this incident was enough to trigger Harry's descent into madness once more. With visions of his supposedly dead father's spirit goading him to revenge, Harry waged an all-out war on Spider-Man. In a mad attack on the web-slinger, Harry launched a bomb at the Osborn Foundation building with Spider-Man inside. During the bomb's final, fateful ticks, Harry reclaimed some semblance of sanity and rescued Spider-Man from the collapsing building. Exhausted and poisoned by his experimental Goblin Formula, Harry fatally collapsed. Only in death could he finally find peace from the curse of the Green Goblin.

Real Name:
Harry Osborn

First Appearance:
Amazing Spider-Man #31 (1966)

Height:	5'10"
Weight:	170 lbs.
Eye Color:	Blue
Hair Color:	Reddish-Brown

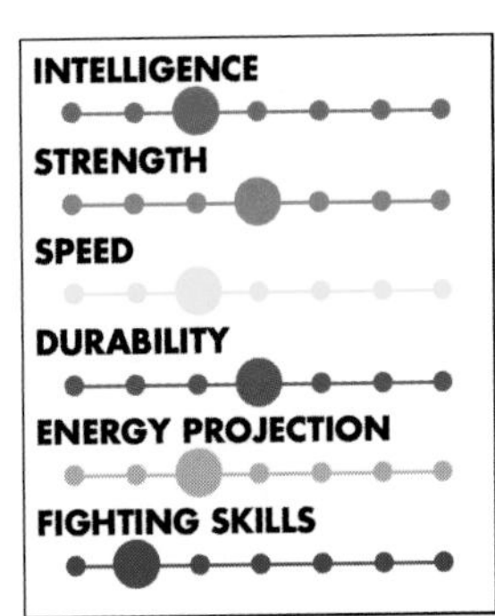

POWERS/ WEAPONS

- Enhanced strength and agility
- Proficient in the use of the Green Goblin's equipment

Art by Todd McFarlane

Art by Tim Sale

LIZ OSBORN

Real Name:
Elizabeth Allan Osborn
First Appearance:
Amazing Fantasy #15 (1962)

Height:	5'9"
Weight:	135 lbs.
Eye Color:	Blue
Hair Color:	Blonde

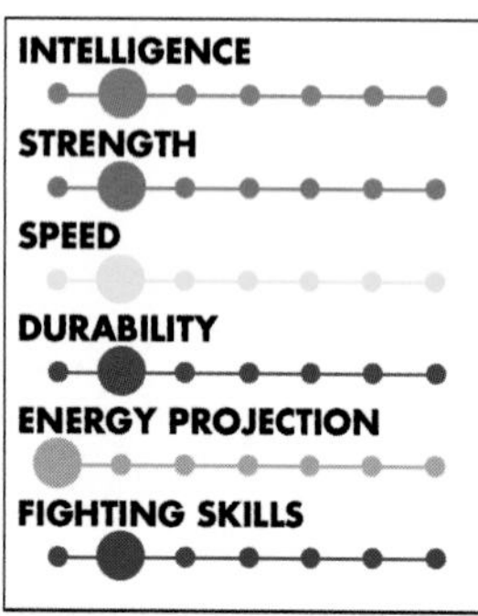

Liz Allan was the most popular girl in Peter Parker's class at Midtown High School. As the prettiest student in school, she spent most of her time with Midtown's football hero and Big Man on Campus, Flash Thompson. A girl like Liz Allan was certainly out of wimpy Peter's league … or was she?

The tragic loss of his uncle, Ben Parker, and Peter's adventures as Spider-Man provided him with a newfound confidence to replace his formerly meek demeanor. As Peter matured from a boy into a young man, Liz found herself unexpectedly drawn to the one-time nerd. When Peter asked Liz for a date, she accepted to the surprise of Midtown's entire student body. Yet Peter was forced to abruptly cancel when the Sandman attacked, leaving Liz furious and humiliated with her apparent rejection.

Although they never managed to develop a romantic relationship, Liz's continuing interest in Peter only served to infuriate Flash. Enraged with jealousy, Flash made Peter's high-school life increasingly miserable — eventually pushing him into a full-on fistfight. The tension between Peter and Flash over Liz eased only after their Midtown graduation, when Liz split from her college-bound friends for a different path.

Art by Luke Ross

Some time later, Liz returned to Peter's life when it was revealed that the Molten Man was in fact her stepbrother, Mark Raxton. Liz had selflessly cared for Mark until he returned to his unstable and volatile molten form. After the Molten Man's battle with Spider-Man and subsequent disappearance, Liz and Peter renewed their old friendship, and she soon joined the Empire State University gang of friends.

Among the ESU group was Harry Osborn, who shared an apartment with Peter. After Harry's brief role assuming his father's Green Goblin persona, he and Liz fell in love, married and had a child, Norman Osborn Jr. Following Harry's tragic death, Liz assumed responsibility of her late husband's company, Osborn Industries, including Oscorp and Multivex.

After Norman Osborn's shocking return from the dead, Liz lost control of the company. She briefly dated Foggy Nelson, legal partner of Matt Murdock (Daredevil), but Mysterio sabotaged their relationship. Liz now cares for her son and maintains an uncomfortable relationship with her former father-in-law.

OLLIE OSNICK

POWERS/WEAPONS

- Home-built cybernetic costume

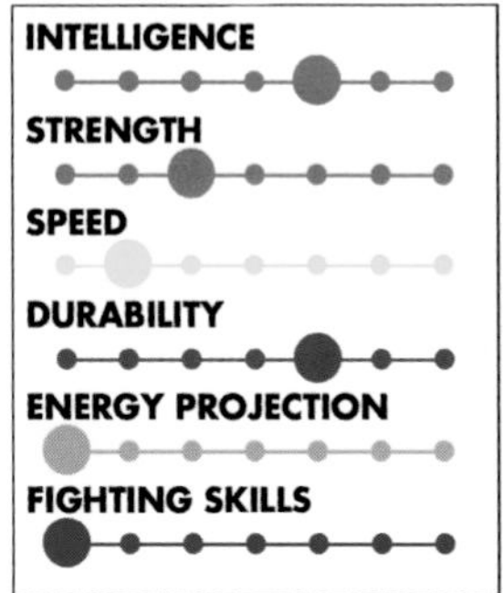

Real Name:	Ollie Osnick	**Hgt:**	5'11"
First Appearance:	*Spectacular Spider-Man* #72 (1982)	**Wt:**	185 lbs.

Over-privileged Ollie Osnick founded a club for "young super-villains," using toys his parents had bought him to fashion cybernetic arms so he could play "Doc Octopus Kid." When his friends refused to take him seriously, Ollie embarked on a junior-sized crime spree, stealing comics and sweets. Spider-Man confused him for the real Doctor Octopus, who had recently escaped from prison, and the situation quickly turned serious.

Just when it appeared Ollie might have learned his lesson, he returned as the Spectacular Spider-Kid in honor of his new hero. Once again, it wasn't long before he required a helping hand. Ollie had more luck his third time out, when he competed with the temporarily reformed evil mutant Toad and Frog-Man for the right to be Spider-Man's sidekick. The web-slinger dodged the issue, and ridiculed their idea to join forces as the Misfits.

Years later, tragedy drove Ollie, now a young man, to once more don his costume and become the Steel Spider when his girlfriend was badly injured by a stray bullet. Fueled only by vengeance and anger, he still has much to learn about being a hero.

OUTLAWS

First Appearance: *Web of Spider-Man #50* (1989)

If ever Spider-Man belonged to his own team, perhaps it was the short-lived Outlaws. The squad consisted of Spider-Man and a motley crew of villains-made-good: the Prowler, Puma, Rocket Racer, the Sandman and Will O' the Wisp.

The unlikely group came together when Silver Sable hired Spider-Man to play private investigator and perform a theft as part of a subtle plan to capture a Maggia leader. Spider-Man's actions were misinterpreted by the former villains; filled with outrage, they joined forces to capture him. After matters were successfully resolved, Silver Sable kept in contact with the group, with an eye to offering them work in the future.

Thanks to another misunderstanding, the squad was re-formed by Spider-Man to battle the Avengers. Silver Sable also called upon the team on occasion as an alternative to her regular strike force. But nothing lasts forever, and the group soon drifted apart — with the Sandman notably returning to his former life of crime.

BEN PARKER

Real Name:
Benjamin Parker
First Appearance:
Amazing Fantasy #15 (1962)

Height:	5'9"
Weight:	175 lbs.
Eye Color:	Blue
Hair Color:	White

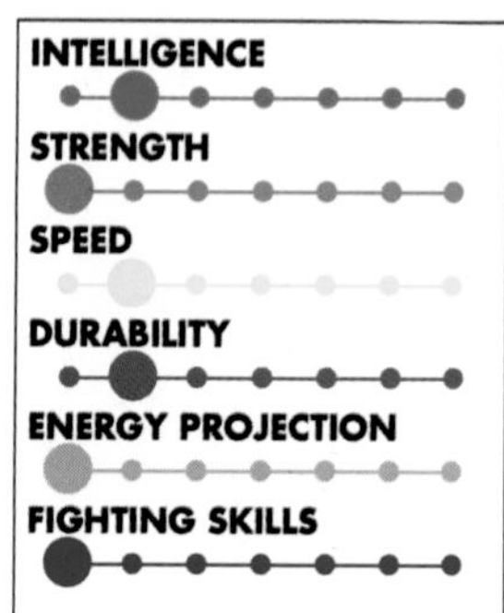

In his youth, Ben Parker worked as a carnival barker at New York's Coney Island. During his tenure at the carnival, Ben developed a deep attraction to May Parker, a beautiful but naïve young woman who lived with her parents in Ben's Brooklyn neighborhood.

May, however, had taken a shine to the confident, flashy Johnny Jerome — who always seemed to have plenty of money, even during terrible financial times. Ben did his best to warn May that Jerome was surely up to no good, but she listened only to her own foolish heart.

One night, Jerome came to May, anxiously asking her to elope with him. As May struggled to decide, Ben informed her that Johnny had just robbed a jewelry store. When the police arrived, it all hit home for May — and she gave her heart that night to the wise and trustworthy Ben.

After Ben married May, Ben's younger brother and sister-in-law, Richard and Mary Parker — both government agents — were assigned to an undercover mission. Entrusting the care of their only child, Peter, to Ben and May, Richard and Mary left the country. They never returned.

Ben and May adopted Peter. They raised him as if he were their own child, providing the boy who would one day become Spider-Man with unconditional love and unwavering emotional support. Although much older than most parents and never wealthy by any stretch of the imagination, they got by, scrimping and saving as best they could.

Ben became his nephew's best friend, and the two were inseparable. As he struggled to find ways to boost the shy, friendless Peter's self-esteem, Ben came upon an old box of Golden Age super-hero comics in the attic and gave them to the young man — overriding May's concerns regarding the effect the books' violence might have on the sensitive boy. Ben would never know he had inspired the creation of Spider-Man.

One fateful night, a Burglar seemingly stumbled on the Parker household — and though he shot Ben dead, he could not kill Ben's influence on the teenage Peter. Even in death, Ben instilled in Peter one overarching lesson: With great power, there must also come great responsibility.

Art by Paul Ryan

MAY PARKER

Real Name:
May Reilly Parker
First Appearance:
Amazing Fantasy #15 (1962)

Height:	5'5"
Weight:	110 lbs.
Eye Color:	Blue
Hair Color:	White

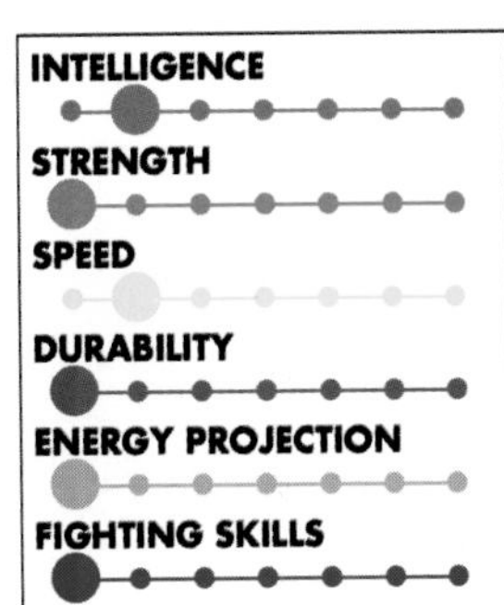

May Reilly was the child of a broken home. When her father walked out, her mother raised her begrudgingly — not bothering to conceal the fact that she saw May as nothing more than an unwelcome burden.

When May was a young woman, two men vied for her affection. One was a flashy, wealthy man named Johnny Jerome; the other, a carnival barker named Ben Parker. Preparing to run away with the more exciting Johnny, May changed her mind after he killed a man during a robbery; she chose the wiser course and remained with Ben.

When the two began dating in earnest, they were often saddled with Ben's much younger brother, Richard. So after Ben and May married, they chose to remain childless — free from the worries youngsters can bring. By contrast, the now-grown Richard and his wife, Mary, brought a son into the world. They named him Peter.

Unexpectedly, Ben and May doted on their nephew; the young boy particularly captivated Ben. When Richard and Mary Parker were called overseas on pressing government business, May and Ben happily took Peter into their home until his parents could return.

When word arrived that Richard and Mary had been killed in Algeria, Ben and May had little choice but to raise the child as their own. May at first was overwhelmed with the responsibility, even angry with Richard and Mary for dying and leaving her and Ben with the challenge of bringing up Peter at such a late stage in their life. Yet her heart could not help but be touched by how kind and thoughtful Peter grew to be. Together, the three became a true family.

As he matured into his teens, little did May or Ben realize that the science-loving, socially awkward Peter had by way of a radioactive spider-bite become the daring and colorful Spider-Man they watched on television. To them, those images belonged to another world — a world of crime and violence far from the Parker residence in suburban Forest Hills, Queens ... or so May thought.

One fateful night, a Burglar came seeking a long-lost treasure belonging to a former owner of the Parker home. Surprised by Ben, the Burglar fatally shot May's husband and fled. Though Spider-Man soon tracked down the Burglar and brought him to justice,

Continued...

Art by Francisco Herrera

MAY PARKER

May was left to continue her life without Ben's strength — a life further complicated by financial woes, her own ever-failing health and the strange new secrecy with which Peter conducted his affairs.

To help Aunt May pay the bills, including the escalating costs associated with her various medications, Peter took a job photographing himself as Spider-Man for the Daily Bugle. May was worried about her fragile nephew, taking pictures so close to the most dangerous of super-powered battles. For Peter, lying to his aunt became a painful — yet seemingly necessary — way of life.

Peter greatly reduced his need to deceive his aunt when he relocated to an apartment in the city, and Mary Jane Watson's aunt, Anna Watson, moved in with May. Though they now lived farther apart, many of Spider-Man's battles still took place dangerously close to May. The wall-crawler's web seemed to be inextricably woven into May's life.

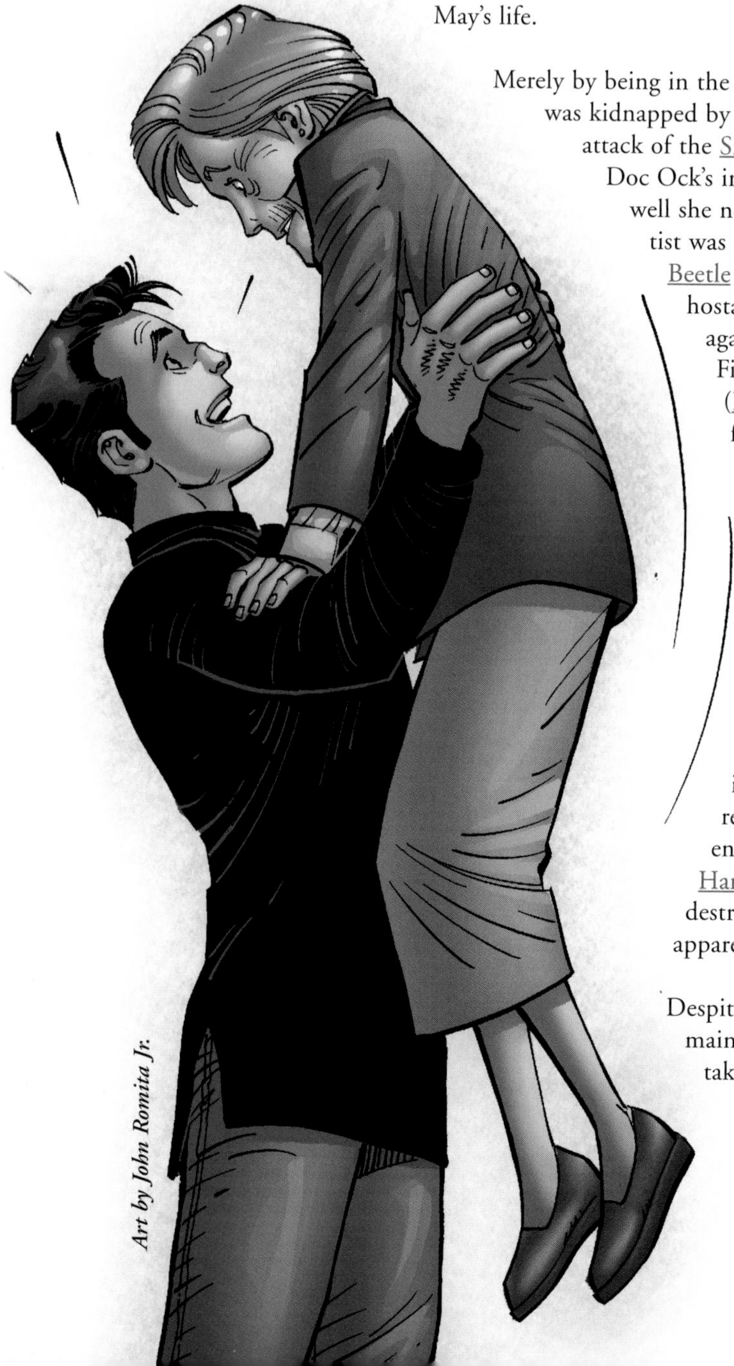

Merely by being in the company of Betty Brant, May was kidnapped by Doctor Octopus during the first attack of the Sinister Six. Though Betty was Doc Ock's intended target, he treated May so well she never realized the charming scientist was actually a deadly villain. The Beetle later took May as a random hostage some time later, and she was again rescued by Spider-Man. Finally, the Green Goblin (Harry Osborn) captured a confused May after he uncovered Spider-Man's secret identity.

Just when life had begun to quiet down, May inherited a Canadian island that was the site of a radioactive mine and small commercial reactor. Doctor Octopus charmed May into a sudden wedding, with the aim of acquiring the island's valuable atomic resources for his own nefarious ends. But the intervention of Hammerhead resulted in the destruction of the island and the apparent death of May's groom-to-be.

Despite her nagging ill health, May maintained an iron will. But while taking part in a Gray Panthers rally, she suffered a serious health threat and required hospitalization. As she continued to convalesce in a nurs-

Art by John Romita Jr.

ing home, the Burglar who had killed her husband was freed from prison. Still seeking the unidentified treasure hidden in the Parker home, the Burglar forced the head of the nursing home to fake Aunt May's death so she could be interrogated without the interference of her doting nephew. When Peter discovered the truth, his fury was so terrifying that the Burglar died of a heart attack. More tragic was the fact that all May's suffering was over nothing: Silverfish had long since eaten the treasure.

May returned to Forest Hills after recovering sufficiently and set up her home as a boarding house, taking in half a dozen paying houseguests. Among them was Nathan Lubensky — a charming, wheelchair-bound gentleman she had met at the nursing home. The two were engaged — until a coldly calculating Nathan caused the death of a mugger who had invaded their house, and May called off the wedding. Despite this, Nathan's final act proved his affection for May: He died to prevent her from becoming a hostage of the Vulture.

Peter believed he had lost his aunt when she seemingly died shortly thereafter. But he was unaware of the depths to which the original Green Goblin, Norman Osborn, would sink. Norman had kidnapped May and replaced her with a genetically adapted actress. Even as Norman lost what remained of his sanity taking part in the Gathering of Five, his former agent, Alison Mongrain — aided by Joseph "Robbie" Robertson — revealed May's location to Peter. Peter rescued his aunt and defeated the crazed Green Goblin, whose plans for the real May were never fully revealed.

After May's return, she struggled to regain her place in Peter's life. It was with Mary Jane's disappearance that Peter again realized the strength he and May could give to each other. Then, after Mary Jane's return and subsequent separation from Peter, he relied on May to help him through a time of loss — as they had helped each other many years ago.

But there was one more shock to come. Arriving at Peter's apartment one afternoon, May finally learned the truth he had so long concealed. Battered and bruised, Peter was asleep in bed with his Spider-Man costume and equipment tossed on the floor. After spending a whole day dealing with her newfound knowledge, May finally confronted Peter and began to break through a lifetime of deception.

Seemingly stronger than ever, May is bent on improving Spider-Man's public image and determined to understand Peter's alter ego. Now that the lies are behind them, May and Peter's relationship has been deepened like never before — reborn through a new level of honesty and trust.

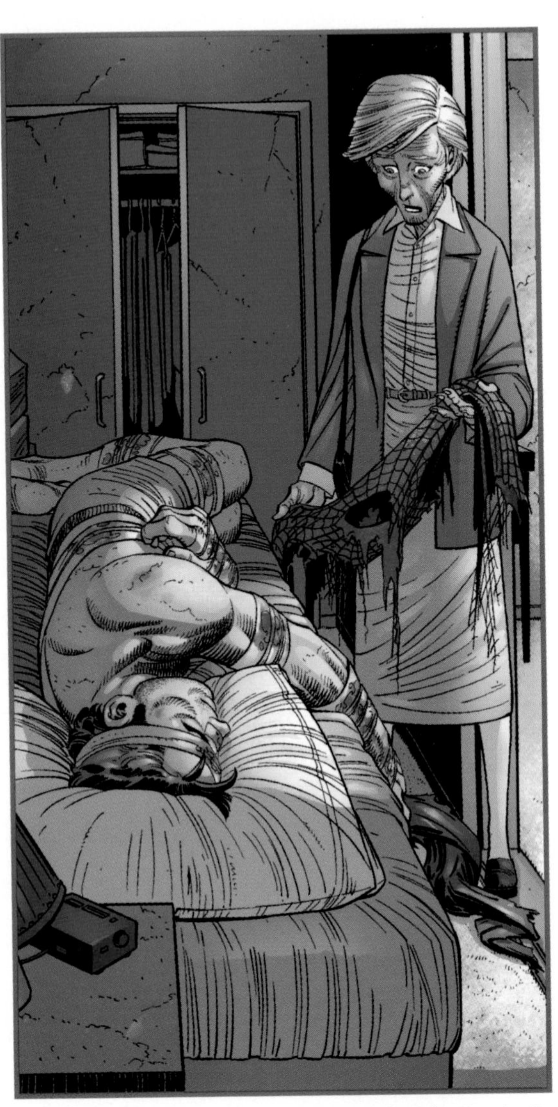

Art by John Romita Jr.

RICHARD & MARY PARKER—

Real Name:
Richard and Mary Parker
First Appearance:
Amazing Spider-Man Annual #5 (1968)

Richard	Mary
Hgt: 5'11"	**Hgt:** 5'6"
Wt: 175 lbs.	**Wt:** 114 lbs.
Eyes: Brown	**Eyes:** Hazel
Hair: Brown	**Hair:** Brown

Orphaned after his parents' deaths, Peter Parker was raised by his aunt and uncle, May Parker and Ben Parker. When Peter was old enough to ask about his parents, he was told only that they died in a plane crash. No further details were offered, and only years after his transformation into Spider-Man would Peter finally learn the truth.

While helping Aunt May move an old trunk into the basement, Peter accidentally broke it open. Among the memorabilia that spilled out were a photo of his parents and a torn-out newspaper article with the headline, "Richard Parker and Wife Killed in Plane Crash in Algeria. Parker Prime Suspect in Spy Plot against the United States."

Peter was devastated. Aunt May confessed she and Ben had kept the full story from him; neither knew what kind of business took the decorated war hero and his wife to Algeria, leaving their son behind. When they died, May could never bring herself to believe Richard and Mary had betrayed their country. Neither could Peter. After he begged for a ride to Algeria from Reed Richards of the Fantastic Four, he took up the long-cold trail of the mystery behind his parents' deaths. But the trail was not as cold as he thought. Spider-Man soon discovered the headquarters of an anti-American spy ring and found a membership card in the name of Richard Parker, confirming his worst fears. Worse still, Red Skull II headed the organization.

Only after Spider-Man mortally wounded the Red Skull's agent, the Finisher, did he uncover the truth. The Finisher confessed that Richard and Mary were government agents who had infiltrated the Red Skull's organization. The Red Skull discovered their duplicity, had them killed and framed them as traitors to the Unites States. Trying to avenge this injustice, Spider-Man defeated the Red Skull and returned home with proof of his parents' innocence.

Art by John Romita

Years later, Peter was shocked when his parents seemingly returned to Manhattan, claiming to have been held abroad as political prisoners. Aunt May remained skeptical, but Peter began to accept the pair as his real parents. Aunt May was justified in her wariness: The duo was nothing more than two robots, created by the Chameleon in a plot to discover Spider-Man's true identity.

POWERS/ WEAPONS

- Government-trained espionage agents
- Proficient with small arms, specialized cameras and communications equipment

PETER'S APARTMENT

Art by John Byrne

After his parents died, Peter Parker was taken in by his aunt and uncle, May Parker and Ben Parker. He went to live with them in a two-story suburban home in the sleepy neighborhood of Forest Hills, Queens. As Spider-Man, Peter would sneak out of his bedroom window, right under the nose of his elderly aunt.

While attending Empire State University, Peter moved into a collegiate bachelor pad with friend Harry Osborn. When Harry firebombed their apartment during one of his brief stints as the Green Goblin, Liz Allan (Liz Osborn) helped Peter find a new place of his own on Chelsea Street, not far from the fashionable Greenwich Village. In addition to spacious living, the apartment boasted a skylight — perfect for Peter's undercover comings and goings as Spider-Man.

Peter remained on Chelsea Street for quite some time, enjoying a quiet refuge from his life as Spider-Man. The Black Cat moved in for a brief catnap, until Peter dumped her; after Peter and Mary Jane Watson were married, they also shared the space for a short time.

But the newlywed couple definitely needed a bigger space — so when Mary Jane and Peter were offered a spacious penthouse, they jumped at the rare opportunity. Unfortunately, the offer proved too good to be true: Obsessive landlord Jonathan Caesar had only arranged the swank penthouse's rental to get closer to Mary Jane, planning to kidnap her. Following Caesar's arrest, Peter and MJ were evicted — eventually landing back in Forest Hills at Aunt May's house.

After Spider-Man temporarily lost his powers, they attempted to start a new life in Portland, Oregon, but soon returned to New York, where Peter's web-slinging abilities were restored. Aunt May was being held captive by the Green Goblin and believed dead, so Peter and Mary Jane again moved back to Forest Hills, joined by Anna Watson. By the time Aunt May was freed from the Goblin's control, Mary Jane's modeling career had become successful enough for the three to share a luxurious New York apartment.

In the wake of Mary Jane and Peter's separation, Peter could not afford the rent on his own meager salary, and he abandoned their expensive apartment. After rooming for a time with Randy Robertson, Peter again found a dump of his own to call home — sharing only his fridge with a hunk of cheese named Kevin.

PETER'S CAMERA

First Appearance:
Amazing Spider-Man #2 (1963)

Peter Parker desperately sought a job to support his aunt, May Parker, following the death of his uncle, Ben Parker. May gave the teenager a camera formerly owned by Ben, and Peter put it to use as a freelance photographer — with a few modifications, including an automatic range finder and a motion-sensing shutter trigger. Naturally, Peter specializes in shots of Spider-Man. Peter usually places his camera in a strategic location prior to an altercation, set to snap photos whenever he passes in front of it, or programs it to take automatic pictures from his utility belt. Such shots are low on quality, but the Daily Bugle rarely fails to snap them up.

ERNIE POPCHIK

Real Name: Ernie Popchik
First Appearance: *Spectacular Spider-Man* #107 (1985)

Hgt: 5'8"
Wt: 150 lbs.

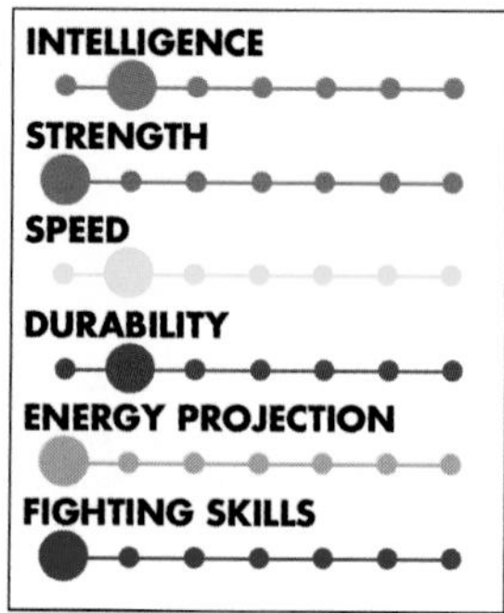

An elderly tenant of May Parker's boarding house, Ernie Popchik would cash his Social Security check each month, and then spend the money on books. When he was mugged shortly after bumping into Peter Parker downtown, Spider-Man quickly captured the crooks — but the incident traumatized Ernie. Sick of being a victim, he bought a handgun. On the subway, three young men demanded he hand over his cash. Ernie opened fire, wounding all three. The grand jury refused to indict him, even though the men were not armed, and Ernie walked away scot-free.

POWER PACK

First Appearance:
Power Pack #1 (1984)

Siblings Alex (Gee, Destroyer, Mass Master, PowerPax, PowerHouse), Jack (Mass Master, Counterweight, Destroyer), Katie (Energizer, Starstreak, Counterweight) and Julie (Lightspeed, Molecula) Power gained the divided powers of the dying alien Aelfyre Whitemane of Kymellia. These abilities include mass control, flight, energy absorption and blasts, and gravity control. The youngsters also came into possession of Whitey's intelligent spaceship, Friday. As Power Pack, they became minor super heroes, assisting Spider-Man on several occasions. The siblings have often exchanged powers; all four can even be granted to a single family member, usually Alex.

PRODIGY

POWERS/WEAPONS

- All the abilities of Spider-Man
- Bullet-proof armor

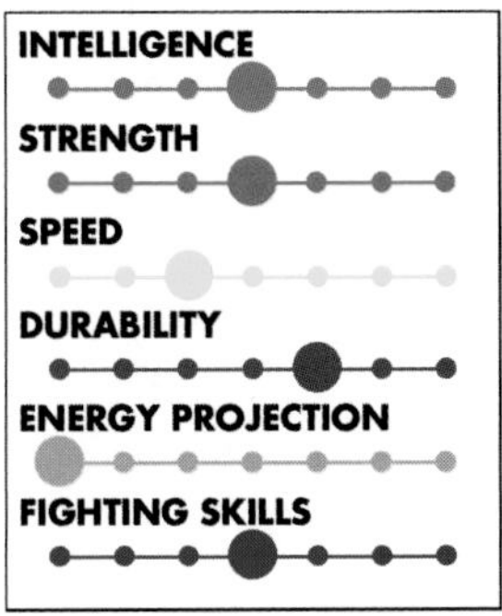

Real Name: Peter Benjamin Parker
First Appearance: *Spectacular Spider-Man* #256 (1998)

Hgt: 5'10"
Wt: 165 lbs.

With a five million dollar price on his head, Peter Parker disguised himself as Prodigy to escape capture. In this guise, he appeared as a naïve, old-fashioned hero — taking massive leaps to simulate flying. When Conundrum and Mad Jack kidnapped the daughter of the Sufindian ambassador, demanding the ruby known as the Hand of Mumthazi, Prodigy defeated the duo. He received assistance from Norman Osborn (Green Goblin), who also sought to recover the treasure. Although Prodigy won the city's heart, he dropped out of sight once Spider-Man's name was cleared. Ritchie Gilmore of the Slingers later adopted the identity of Prodigy.

PROFESSOR POWER

POWERS/WEAPONS

- Superhuman strength
- Flight
- Electron beam

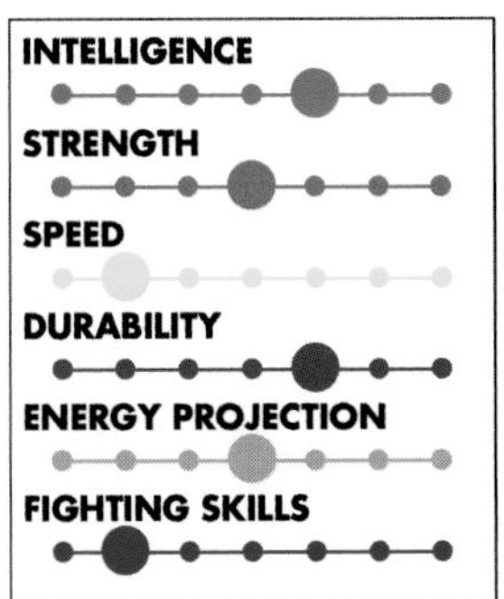

Real Name: Anthony Power
First Appearance: *Marvel Team-Up* #117 (1982)

Hgt: 6'2"
Wt: 220 lbs.

The one-time leader of the subversive organization known as the Secret Empire, Anthony Power also masterminded an attempt to conquer the world by pooling the talents of a team of psychics. Professor Power has fought Spider-Man and the X-Men simultaneously on several occasions — as well as Captain America, the Avengers and the Defenders. Initially, he was fueled by the desire to cure his son, Matthew. Later, he transferred his mind into his comatose son's body, using an exoskeleton to transform it into an engine of destruction. Now, his primary goal is revenge on his many enemies.

PUPPET MASTER

POWERS/WEAPONS

- Can control others by fashioning their likenesses from radioactive clay

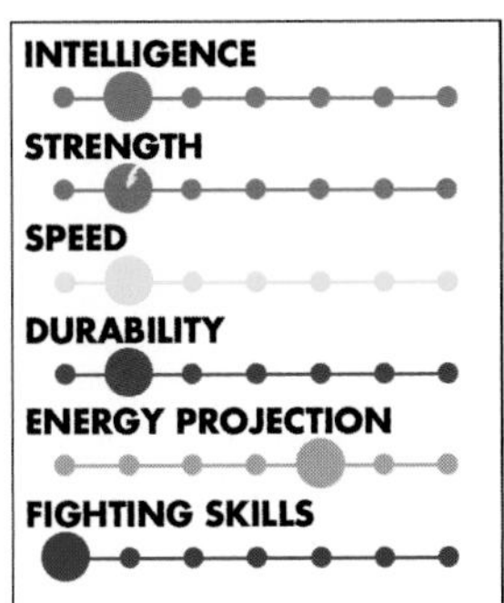

Real Name: Philip Masters
First Appearance: *Fantastic Four* #8 (1962)

Hgt: 5'6"
Wt: 150 lbs.

Chiefly an enemy of the Fantastic Four — particularly the Thing, who loved his daughter, Alicia — the Puppet Master also came into conflict with Spider-Man during a partnership with the Mad Thinker. The two conspired to destroy Spider-Man and the Thing, but the Puppet Master turned on the Thinker when he threatened Alicia's life. Though making multiple attempts to reform and/or retire, primarily at the behest of his daughter, Masters always ends up back on the wrong side of the law — and back behind bars.

PROWLER

Real Name: Hobie Brown
First Appearance: *Amazing Spider-Man* #78 (1969)

Hgt: 5'11"
Wt: 180 lbs.

- Steel claws
- Climbing boots
- Sleeping-gas projectiles

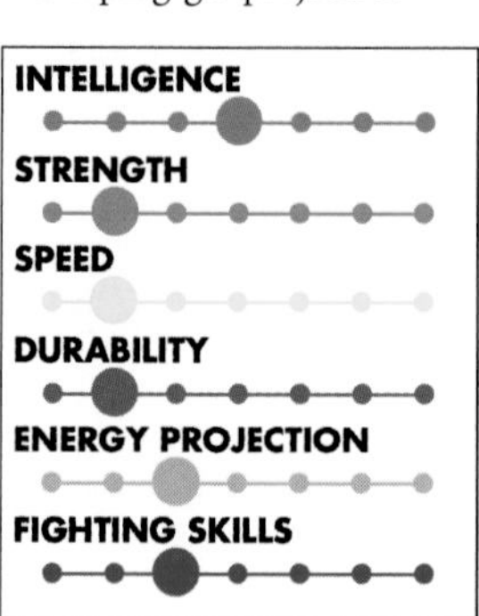

Hobie Brown was a young inventor, relegated to working as a window cleaner. Frustrated by his lack of progress, he invented an outfit that would allow him to climb walls and squirt window-cleaning fluid from wrist-mounted bracelets. When his boss was less than impressed, a desperate Hobie adapted his equipment to a life of crime, despite the pleas of his young wife.

Easily defeated by Spider-Man, Hobie turned away from crime — and the hero decided to give him a second chance. In return, Hobie paid Spider-Man a favor by impersonating him when Peter Parker desperately needed to prove he and the web-slinger were two different people. In his new role as hero, Hobie prowled the New York City streets — which led him to face the Nightcreeper, whose powers matched his own, and the rejuvenated Vulture. He also took on work for Silver Sable and joined the Outlaws.

When Prowler and Rocket Racer sought extra cash by cheating in the super-hero rumble known as the Great Game, Hobie had his back broken. Since recovered, he has focused more on inventing than adventuring. Hobie created the jet-pack used by the Hornet.

PUMA

Real Name: Thomas Fireheart
First Appearance: *Amazing Spider-Man* #256 (1984)

Hgt: 6'2"
Wt: 240 lbs.

POWERS/WEAPONS

- Exceptional senses, lightning reflexes and supernatural strength
- Vast financial resources

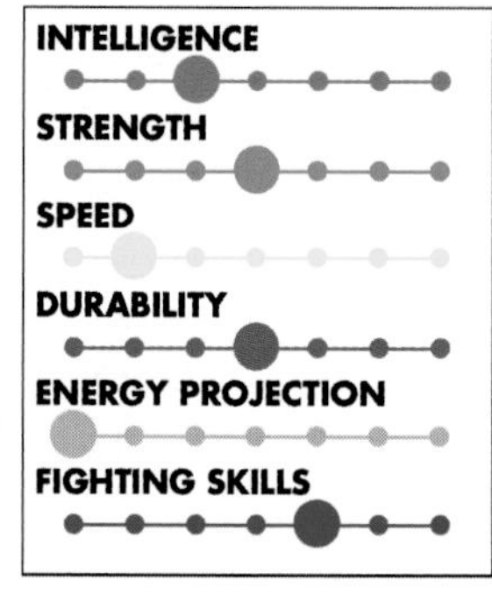

Puma is the product of generations of selective breeding, tribal mysticism and ceaseless training. The Native American tribe into which he was born believed in the coming of an all-powerful being who could destroy the world. As guardian of the tribe, and possibly the planet, Puma studied the martial arts — but also found time to build a vast financial empire, much to the chagrin of his tribe's Shaman, Threetrees. To further hone his skills — so he could better protect his tribe, and to prepare for the cosmic struggle that was the end purpose of his existence — Puma accepted a mission from the Rose (Richard Fisk) to stalk Spider-Man, duped into believing the web-slinger was a criminal. Though beating him in battle, Puma would not kill him as ordered. Later, Spider-Man was to be his ally when the Beyonder, a being of infinite power, came to Earth as the prophecies foretold.

After reading a report in the Daily Bugle that cast Spider-Man as a thief, Puma felt deceived by the web-slinger and undertook to destroy him. When Spider-Man was vindicated, Puma felt greatly ashamed and dishonored. He susequently purchased the Daily Bugle and made a radical change to the editorial policy — helping restore Spider-Man's reputation, however briefly. But the hero was uncomfortable with that arrangement and asked Puma to return things to their natural order.

PUNISHER

A veteran of the Vietnam War, Frank Castle turned to vigilantism when his wife and children were gunned down after accidentally observing a Mafia hit. Since then, he has devoted his life to the task of destroying organized crime wherever he finds it.

The Punisher first encountered Spider-Man after the Jackal hired Castle to eliminate the wall-crawler — assuring the Punisher that Spider-Man was tangled up in the New York organized-crime scene. Narrowly escaping the Punisher's initial ambush, Spider-Man investigated his new foe and tracked down Castle's arms supplier, the Mechanic.

The Jackal was one step ahead of Spider-Man, however, killing the arms dealer prior to the hero's entrance. When the Punisher arrived on the scene, Spider-Man seemed the obvious killer. Engaged in battle, Spider-Man forced the Punisher to look closer at the body of the murdered man, on which Castle clearly observed the telltale marks of the Jackal's claws. The deception revealed, the Punisher saw no further reason to fight Spider-Man.

The Punisher then embarked on a vigilante career of his own. His targets covered the spectrum from muggers to drug magnates. His methods, however, did not change; they have always been brutal and effective. The Punisher has no time for the ineffectual legal system. He's a one-man judge, jury and executioner.

Now, the Punisher and Spider-Man frequently find themselves caught up in the same murky business, creating an ethical dilemma for the wall-crawler: Spider-Man will not kill, while the Punisher favors filling body bags with bad guys. On numerous occasions, Spider-Man has pressured the Punisher to refrain from lethal force when the two have collaborated on cases.

Working together, albeit reluctantly, Spider-Man and the Punisher have tackled dozens of foes: Silvermane, Doctor Octopus, the Kingpin, the Persuader and nearly every other major gang lord in New York City — not to mention countless faceless flunkies and nameless nuisances.

Real Name:
Frank Castle
(born Castiglione)

First Appearance:
Amazing Spider-Man #129 (1974)

Height:	6'0"
Weight:	200 lbs.
Eye Color:	Blue
Hair Color:	Black

POWERS/ WEAPONS

- Expert in the use of small arms and large-caliber guns
- Extensive training with explosives and tactical weapons
- Superior martial artist and hand-to-hand combatant

INTELLIGENCE

STRENGTH

SPEED

DURABILITY

ENERGY PROJECTION

FIGHTING SKILLS

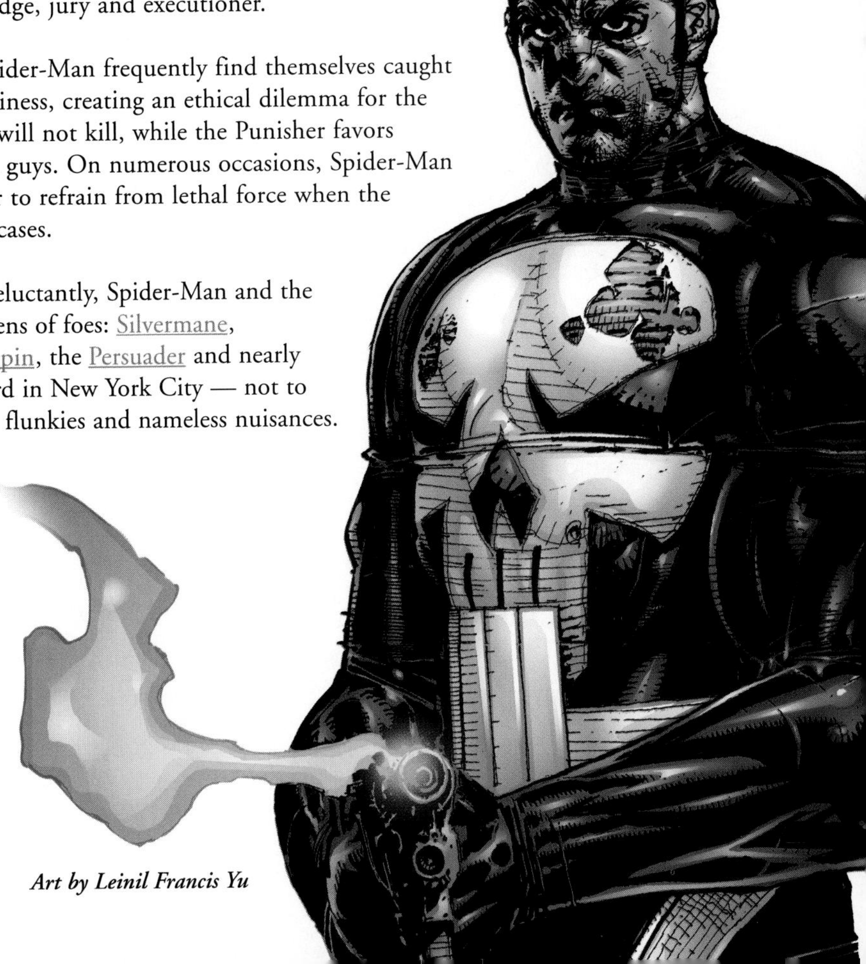

Art by Leinil Francis Yu

RAVENCROFT INSTITUTE

First Appearance:
Spider-Man Unlimited #1 (1993)

Prompted by Dr. Ashley Kafka's success in healing Vermin, the government established Ravencroft Institute for the Criminally Insane. Kafka was hand-picked by Senator Rosenberg to run the facility — with Edward Whelan, the rehabilitated Vermin, as her assistant and John Jameson as chief of security. Ravencroft housed villains such as Carnage, Carrion II (Malcolm McBride), the Chameleon, the Jackal and Shriek. But few were healed, and many — such as Carnage — proved uncontainable, with multiple escapes claiming the lives of staff and inmates alike. Tricked into trusting the Chameleon, Kafka allowed him to flee. She and Jameson were subsequently fired, and Doc Samson was assigned to direct the facility.

RAZORBACK

Real Name: Buford Hollis
First Appearance: *Spectacular Spider-Man* #13 (1977)

Hgt: 6'8"
Wt: 410 lbs.

A super-hero trucker with hair like Elvis and a warthog helmet, Razorback fought alongside Spider-Man against the Legion of Light — a cult into which his sister had vanished. He later became a star-ship pilot with the She-Hulk's help, flying with the crew of U.S. Archer. Razorback's adventures brought him into conflict with the likes of Xemnu the Titan, Spragg the Living Hill and the Stone Clones, Rocket Raccoon, and the Asparagus People. He has since returned to Earth.

POWERS/WEAPONS

- Electrified costume
- Big Pig, a remote-controlled truck
- Former star-ship pilot

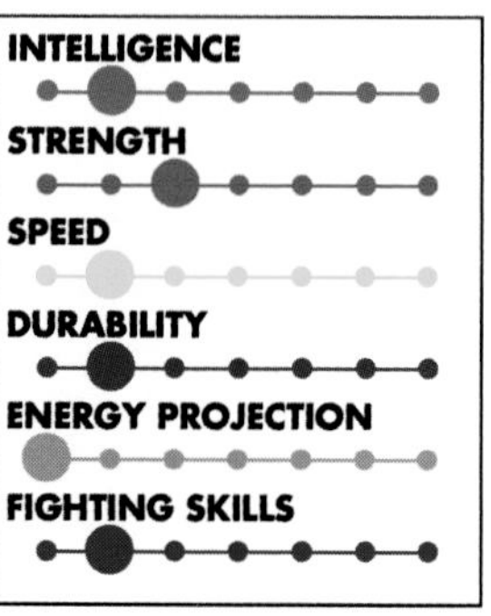

RED SKULL II

Real Name: Albert Malik
First Appearance: *Young Men* #24 (1953)

Hgt: 5'9"
Wt: 190 lbs.

An agent of Communist Russia during the 1950s, Albert Malik assumed the identity of the original, Nazi Red Skull and clashed repeatedly with a successor to the mantle of Captain America. Decades later, Malik was responsible for the deaths of Richard and Mary Parker, Peter Parker's parents. Malik framed them as foreign agents — but years later as Spider-Man, Peter proved their innocence. The Scourge of the Underworld assassinated Malik under the direction of the original Red Skull, Johann Schmidt, who loathed his successor for usurping his identity. Spider-Man has since foiled Schmidt's plans on several occasions.

POWERS/WEAPONS

- Vast arsenal of technological, biological and chemical weaponry

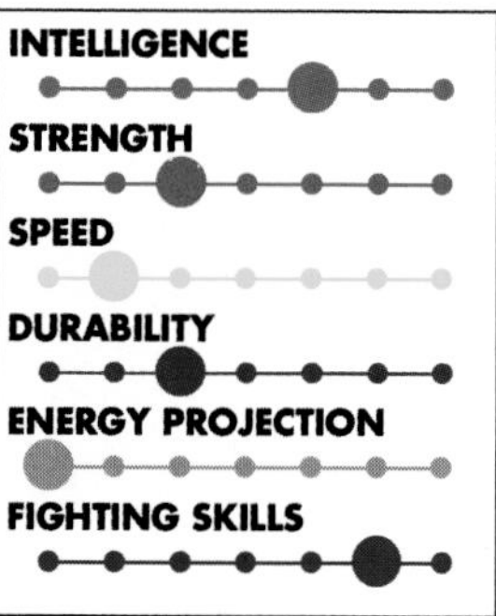

BEN REILLY

Real Name:
Benjamin Reilly
First Appearance:
Amazing Spider-Man #149 (1975)

Height:	5'10"
Weight:	165 lbs.
Eye Color:	Brown
Hair Color:	Blond

In his quest to resurrect the late Gwen Stacy, the Jackal embarked on a plan to clone the slain girl. Although the Jackal's flawed cloning process primarily produced genetic monstrosities, he was able to create three successful clones: the first from his own DNA, another of Gwen Stacy and one of Peter Parker. In a battle arranged by the Jackal, Spider-Man faced his own doppelganger in a fierce struggle that ended with the apparent deaths of both the Jackal and Peter's clone.

In reality, Spider-Man's clone had survived; he spent the next five years wandering the United States, adopting the name Ben Reilly. When Ben learned that Peter's aunt, May Parker, was seriously ill, he returned to New York to pay his final respects at her bedside. While in New York, Ben realized his potential to use his powers for good, and adopted the costumed identity of the Scarlet Spider. After revealing his existence to Peter, the two heroes worked together as New York's twin web-slinging crime-fighters. Ben also assisted the New York-based super-hero team the New Warriors on a number of missions.

Ben and Peter soon faced the return of the Jackal, as well as the unexpected resurrection of Norman Osborn, the original Green Goblin. It was during this time that Osborn maliciously had Dr. Seward Trainer alter the Jackal's original documents and equipment — leading Peter to believe that he, rather than Ben, was the clone. This false revelation drove Peter to abandon his costumed identity and move to Portland with Mary Jane Watson, with Ben assuming the identity of Spider-Man. After Peter returned to New York, the truth was revealed during a final showdown between the Green Goblin and the two Spider-Men.

During the fight, Ben was fatally impaled on the Green Goblin's glider while heroically saving Peter's life. Shortly after death, Ben's body reverted to its original raw cellular structure — proving without a doubt that he was indeed the clone. Peter had a wake for Ben and mourned the loss of the man who was, effectively, his only brother.

Art by Mark Bagley & Dan Jurgens

INTELLIGENCE
STRENGTH
SPEED
DURABILITY
ENERGY PROJECTION
FIGHTING SKILLS

POWERS/ WEAPONS

- Superhuman strength, reflexes and equilibrium
- Ability to cling to sheer vertical surfaces
- Early warning "spider-sense"
- Specialized impact webbing and stingers

RHINO

Real Name: Aleksei Mikhailovich Sytsevich, a.k.a. Alex O'Hirn
First Appearance: *Amazing Spider-Man* #41 (1966)

Height:	6'5"
Weight:	710 lbs.
Eye Color:	Brown
Hair Color:	Brown

Aleksei Sytsevich was just another thug in the Russian Mafia — grasping at dreams of easy money, and headed for a short and brutal life. Seduced by promises of wealth and power, Aleksei underwent a life-threatening series of chemical and radiation treatments to transform him into the superhuman agent for a collective of professional spies — in part to support his family. Aleksei's powerful exoskeleton, permanently bonded to his form, was modeled after the hide of a rhinoceros. Scientists Igor and Georgi chose this form, both for its visual impact and in recognition of the fact that the rhino is the result of countless generations of evolution toward the ultimate form for armored assault.

The Rhino's first mission was to capture John Jameson. He received intensive sub-hypnotic training in American English and false citizenship papers bearing the name Alex O'Hirn. As the Rhino made tireless progress toward New York City, Spider-Man began to wonder how this unstoppable foe could be defeated. Fortunately, Spider-Man discovered two key facts regarding the Rhino: Once charging, he cannot change direction or easily halt his advance — and Aleksei is dumb. Spider-Man deduced that if he could avoid a direct hit from the Rhino's horn, his superior tactical skills and agility would always leave him the final victor in any fair fight.

Ultimately turning on his backers, the Rhino became a free agent in the world of super-powered criminals. Although Spider-Man handed him his first defeat, the Rhino has also battled the Hulk, the Avengers, Iron Man, Cage, Ka-Zar and Captain America. His raw power and lack of ambition made him an ideal member of the Sinister Syndicate. Only then did he come close to killing Spider-Man, who was only saved by the timely intervention of the Sandman.

POWERS/ WEAPONS

- Superhuman strength and stamina
- Virtually impenetrable hide

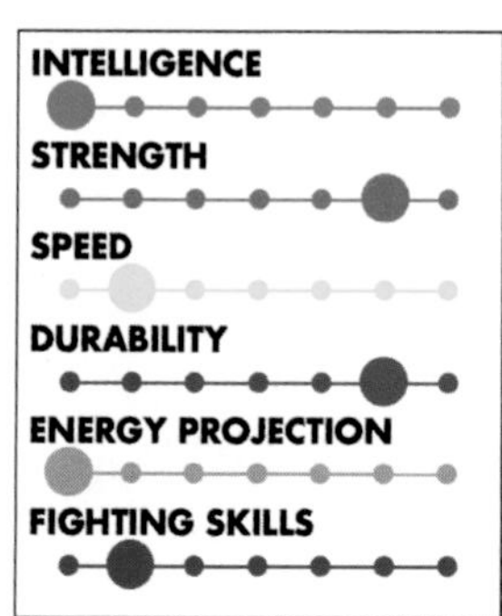

Art by Staz Johnson

RICOCHET

POWERS/WEAPONS

- All the abilities of Spider-Man
- Bouncing discs

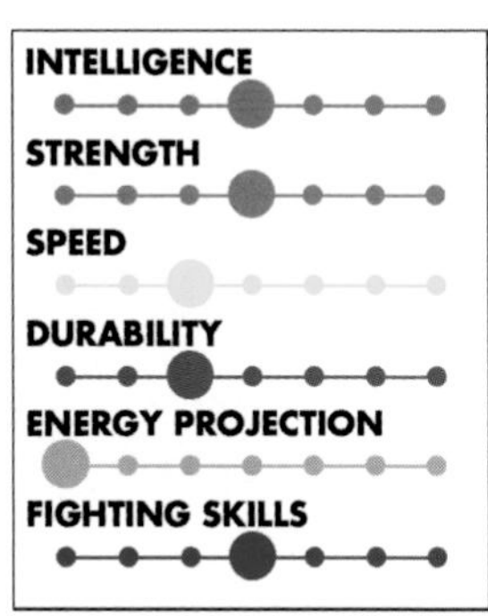

Real Name: Peter Benjamin Parker
First Appearance: *Amazing Spider-Man* #433 (1998)

Hgt: 5'10"
Wt: 165 lbs.

As Ricochet, Peter Parker continued fighting crime despite a five million dollar bounty on Spider-Man's head offered by Norman Osborn (Green Goblin). Designed by Mary Jane Watson, this identity spotlighted Peter's acrobatic abilities. After scrapping with Delilah, the two teamed up against their common foe — the Black Tarantula and his henchmen, Bloodscream and Roughhouse. His name cleared following the Trapster's confession to the murder of Joey Z, Peter retired his Ricochet identity. Ricochet later returned, under ownership of Johnny Gallo of the Slingers.

RANDY ROBERTSON

INTELLIGENCE
STRENGTH
SPEED
DURABILITY
ENERGY PROJECTION
FIGHTING SKILLS

Real Name: Randy Robertson
First Appearance: *Amazing Spider-Man* #67 (1968)

Hgt: 6'0"
Wt: 185 lbs.

Randy Robertson is the son of Daily Bugle editor-in-chief Joseph "Robbie" Robertson. He attended Empire State University along with Peter Parker, earning a reputation as a student activist. Randy challenged his parents by marrying Amanda — a white, Jewish woman — though they subsequently separated, and he now dates Glory Grant. When Peter was homeless following Mary Jane Watson's apparent death, Randy allowed him to share his apartment. He also attempted to help Peter by arranging blind dates, but Randy's matchmaking skills left much to be desired.

ROCKET RACER

POWERS/WEAPONS

- Rocket-powered skateboard
- Mini-rockets in gauntlets

INTELLIGENCE
STRENGTH
SPEED
DURABILITY
ENERGY PROJECTION
FIGHTING SKILLS

Real Name: Robert Farrell
First Appearance: *Amazing Spider-Man* #172 (1977)

Hgt: 5'10"
Wt: 160 lbs.

In the wake of a brief career as a burglar, Robert Farrell rode his rocket-powered skateboard to success as a costumed hero — assisting Spider-Man against villains such as Big Wheel and Skinhead. He was a founding member of the Outlaws, and worked as a freelance operative for Silver Sable. Rocket Racer eventually retired. However, the theft of Farrell's equipment prompted a comeback, and he soon returned to his criminal ways. Following a spell in the Cage, a specialized prison for super-villains, Farrell still works on the wrong side of the law — though he maintains strong ethics and a deep respect for Spider-Man.

JOSEPH "ROBBIE" ROBERTSON —

Real Name:
Joseph Robertson
First Appearance:
Amazing Spider-Man #51 (1967)

Height:	6'1"
Weight:	210 lbs.
Eye Color:	Brown
Hair Color:	White

INTELLIGENCE
STRENGTH
SPEED
DURABILITY
ENERGY PROJECTION
FIGHTING SKILLS

If J. Jonah Jameson is the most irrational and irritable newspaperman on the planet, his right-hand man, Joseph "Robbie" Robertson, is the exact opposite. Thoughtful, levelheaded and possessed of an unshakeable integrity, Robbie is well-liked and well-respected by the entire Daily Bugle staff. Robbie is one of the few Bugle staffers not intimidated by Jameson's frequent tirades, and he is unafraid to offer a contrasting viewpoint to the publisher's obsessive public attacks on Spider-Man. While Jameson prefers to take credit for the Bugle's dominance among New York City's tabloids, most observers would agree the paper's success is due in large part to Robbie's contributions.

Growing up in Harlem, the hard-working Robbie was determined to succeed. His career in journalism began early: Working on the school newspaper, he reported fearlessly on all issues ... except one. After writing an article exposing Lonnie "Tombstone" Lincoln's extortion of fellow students, Robbie reluctantly withdrew the piece under threats from Lincoln. Later, Robbie witnessed him commit cold-blooded murder. Still fearing Tombstone's unrelenting violence, Robbie agreed to keep silent. Years later, Tombstone rose to prominence as one of New York City's leading criminal figures. Unable to live with his guilty conscience any longer, Robbie reported the murder — and Tombstone went to jail. Convicted by a judge in the Kingpin's pocket for his failure to report the crime, Robbie joined Tombstone in federal prison. Lincoln brutally tormented his former classmate, and then dragged him along on a prison break. After Tombstone threatened an innocent Amish family a few miles outside the prison's walls, Robbie could take no more. Summoning all his courage, he stabbed Tombstone with a pitchfork. Seriously wounded, Lincoln staggered off, and Robbie was eventually granted a full pardon.

Robbie is known as a man of great honor and principles. Although it appears he has guessed the connection between Peter Parker and Spider-Man, he has shunned the sure financial rewards of reporting the secret in the Daily Bugle to protect his friend. Robbie has refused to let outside forces influence his journalism, resigning in protest during a brief takeover of the Bugle by Norman Osborn (Green Goblin). Now that the Bugle is back in Jameson's hands, Robbie is naturally right where he belongs — supported by his loving wife, Martha.

Art by Michael Gaydos

ROXXON OIL

First Appearance:
Captain America #180 (1974)

A powerful oil conglomerate, Roxxon — originally Republic — has had its fingers in a plethora of suspicious operations in North America. Among its divisions are the laboratories of the Brand Corporation, which originated several super-villains; Cybertek, which created Deathlok; Metrobank, an influential financial institution in New York City; and the Nth Command, which attempted to rid America of superhumans. Despite the efforts of heroes such as the Will O' the Wisp and Spider-Man, Roxxon continues to eat away at the nation — and the environment. The company's most notable heads have included presidents Hugh Jones and John T. Gamelin, and chairman August D'Angelo.

S.H.O.C.

Real Name: Todd Fields, a.k.a. Neil Aiken
First Appearance: *Peter Parker: Spider-Man* #76 (1997)

Hgt: 7'2"
Wt: 347 lbs.

POWERS/WEAPONS

- Manipulation of the extra-dimensional Dark Force
- Flight
- Matter control
- Body armor

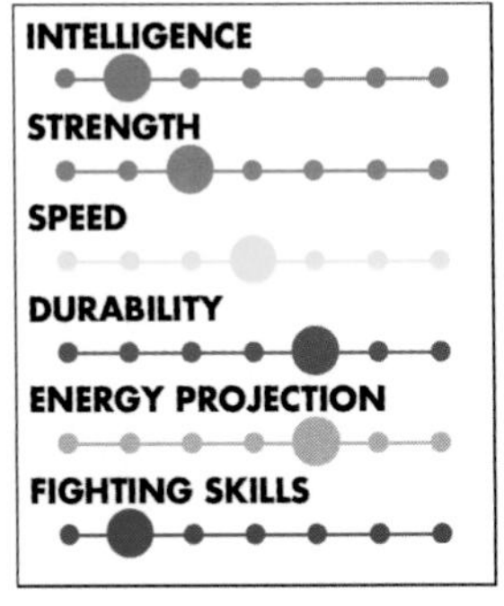

Empire State University professor Dr. William Fields was killed by Crown (a.k.a. Hunger), who sought to steal his research. William's wife fled with their young son, Todd, surviving to hand over William's notes to his ESU colleague, Dr. Sydney Lanning. Seven years later, Todd — as Neil Aiken — was an ESU science student under Lanning, tutored by Peter Parker. When Crown finally tracked down the notes, he was defeated by Todd — who had inherited his father's ability to manipulate the extradimensional Dark Force, and generate the S.H.O.C. armor and weapons. Todd later learned his armor was taking his life and vowed to make a difference in the world before it killed him.

SCHIZOID MAN

Real Name: Chip Martin
First Appearance: *Spectacular Spider-Man* #36 (1979)

Hgt: 6'0"
Wt: 180 lbs.

POWERS/WEAPONS

- Telekinesis
- Mental creation and control of objects or creatures

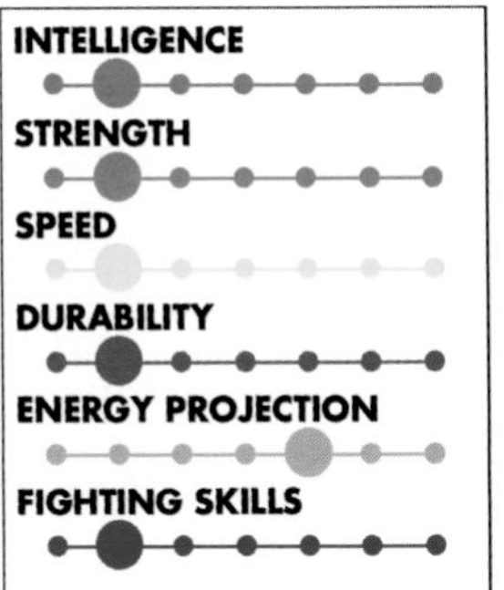

As a child, Chip Martin found himself able to manipulate and create objects with his mind. In time, it became clear something evil — a second personality — was manifesting itself along with his powers. Medical treatment suppressed this personality — until, as a graduate student at Empire State University, stress from an encounter involving his parents and Morbius unleashed his alter ego, the Schizoid Man. Rampaging across campus, the Schizoid Man was savagely beaten by Spider-Man, himself mentally unbalanced and on the verge of transforming into the Spider-Lizard. Chip is believed to be back under psychiatric care.

SANDMAN

Real Name:
William Baker, a.k.a. Flint Marko, a.k.a. Sylvester Mann
First Appearance:
Amazing Spider-Man #4 (1963)

Height: 6'1"
Weight: 240 lbs.; 450 lbs. at maximum density in sand form
Eye Color: Brown
Hair Color: Brown

POWERS/ WEAPONS

- Ability to transform any part of his body into a sand-like substance
- Can alter his size and mass by incorporating nearby sand
- Superhuman strength

When William Baker was 3 years old, his father left him and his mother to live in poverty. To make ends meet, Baker turned to theft at an early age; he went on to cheat and bluff his way through high school. Though he possessed great talent on the football field, he squandered his chance for a legitimate career when he accepted a bribe to throw an important game. His deception revealed, Baker was expelled from school. Forced to find work, Baker became a mob henchman and adopted the underworld alias Flint Marko. Arrested and convicted for his criminal actions, he spent much of his time in solitary confinement. Marko grew bitter and violent — and devoid of hope that his girlfriend, Marcy Conway, would ever marry him.

Released from jail, Marko sought out Marcy, only to discover she had taken up with gangster Vic Rollins. Furious, Marko sought brutal revenge on Rollins and embarked on a one-man, citywide crime spree. Captured and returned to jail, Marko did time in the maximum-security wing of the notorious Rykers Island. An incorrigible inmate, he soon purchased information on an unguarded drainage tunnel, which he used to make his escape. With the FBI and police on his tail, Marko sought refuge in the one place nobody would look for him: an atomic testing site near Savannah, Georgia. As he rested on a nearby beach, the experimental reactor's steam system exploded — bombarding him with a massive dose of radiation. Awaking from a brief period of unconsciousness, Marko discovered his newly acquired ability to transform himself into a sand-like form he could manipulate and reshape at will. On that day, the Sandman was born.

Art by John Romita Jr.

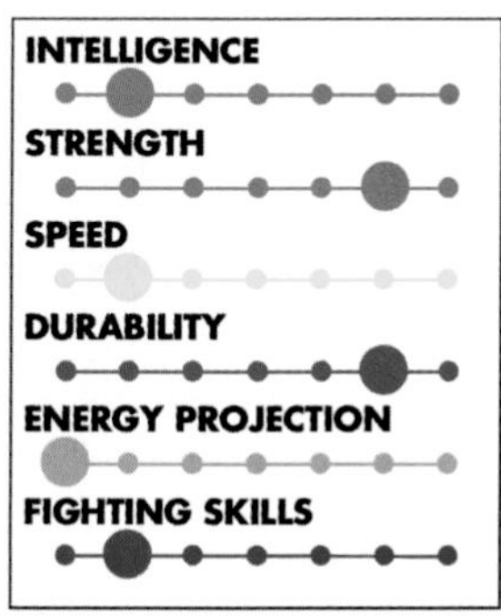

Eager to take full advantage of his new-found power, the Sandman returned to New York and attempted a series of daring robberies — all met with equally bold resistance. Spider-Man employed an industrial vacuum cleaner; the Human Torch, an indoor sprinkler system. The Sandman recovered and regrouped from each of these confrontations, and became a member of the first Sinister Six before joining forces with the Wizard, who provided him with a belt that enabled him to produce a variety of dangerous and deadly effects through the injection of various chemicals. The Sandman and the Wizard then teamed with the Trapster to become core members of the Frightful Four.

Art by Mark Bagley

Some time later, the Sandman inadvertently merged with Hydro-Man to form the Mud-Thing. After an attack by police helicopters nearly ended his life, the Sandman eventually returned to his usual form, but seemed troubled by his conscience. Striking up a surprising friendship with the Thing of the Fantastic Four, the Sandman soon talked of abandoning crime. When he encountered Spider-Man fighting the Enforcers, the Sandman made good on his intentions and rescued the wall-crawler. Still a wanted man, the Sandman adopted the alias Sylvester Mann. He rented a room with a suburban family, undertook contract work for Silver Sable and joined the Outlaws. When Doctor Octopus blackmailed him into rejoining the Sinister Six, the Sandman turned against his former ally as soon as he had the chance.

His good efforts were recognized when both he and Spider-Man were simultaneously named as reserve Avengers. Granted a pardon for his crimes, the Sandman returned to his birth name, William Baker. Though his undisciplined temperament saw him resign from the Avengers over a minor misunderstanding, his determination to reform survived; he became a permanent agent for Silver Sable, often assisting Spider-Man.

But the good times would not last. Feeling the loss of his former super-powered henchman, the Wizard kidnapped Baker and forcibly subjected him to a machine that would amplify the underlying dark side of its subject's personality. Gone again was William Baker; when the violent Flint Marko regained dominance, much to the Wizard's surprise, he refused to be anyone's lackey.

The now-villainous Sandman re-formed the Sinister Six to seek revenge on Doctor Octopus, but Venom turned on his teammates and took a large bite out of the Sandman. Weakened and poisoned, the Sandman lost control over his form — and his mind. Confused, the villain fell into the sewer and was eventually dumped on a sandy beach, where he merged with the shoreline. Soon, the Sandman returned once more to plague his former foe.

SCORCHER

Real Name: Hudak, first name unrevealed
First Appearance: *Untold Tales of Spider-Man* #1 (1995)
Hgt: 5'10"
Wt: 175 lbs.

POWERS/WEAPONS

- Flame generation
- Flight
- Protective armor

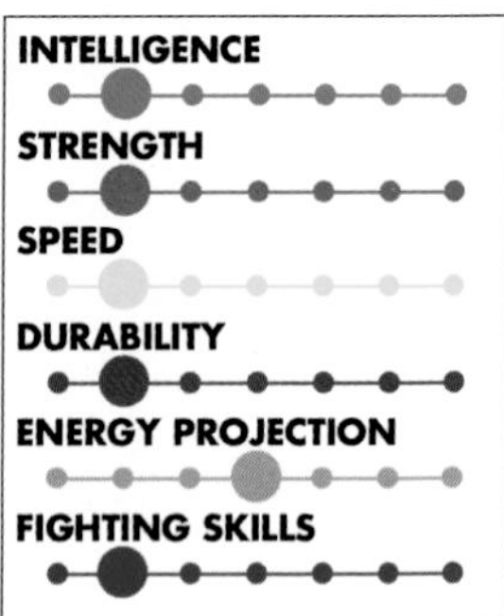

Framed for embezzlement, Hudak constructed a suit of protective armor and turned to crime as the Scorcher. Norman Osborn (Green Goblin) financed his early efforts, and Hudak became one of Spider-Man's first opponents. The Scorcher was imprisoned following their encounter; he later escaped and established a protection racket, but was again defeated by Spider-Man. The Scorcher remained out of sight for years, until he resurfaced to rob shoppers one Christmas Eve. Again bested by Spider-Man, he subsequently became a member of the Masters of Evil. Defeated by the Thunderbolts, he was returned to jail.

SCORPIA

Real Name: Elaine, last name unrevealed
First Appearance: *Spider-Man: Power of Terror* #2 (1995)
Hgt: 5'10"
Wt: 175 lbs.

POWERS/WEAPONS

- Enhanced strength and speed
- Micro-thin force-field
- Combined energy bursts — electrical, laser, microwave and plasma

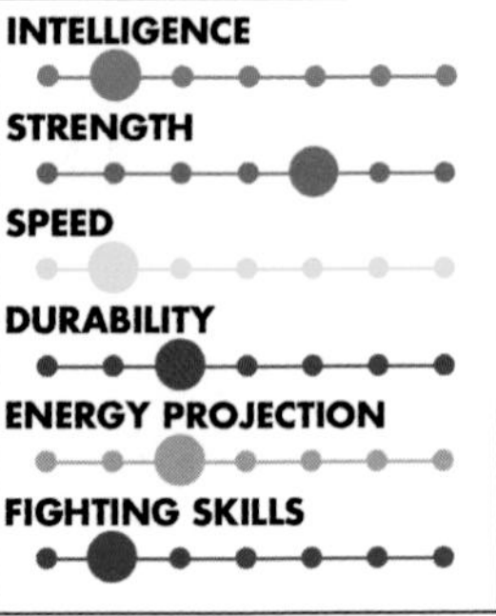

When Silvermane launched an all-out gang war, his weapon-systems developers created an enhanced version of the Scorpion's costume to be worn by the crime lord's newest and most lethal agent: Scorpia. The original Scorpion, Mac Gargan, had recently reformed, and the female version proved a perfectly deadly replacement. Silvermane betrayed Scorpia — but was then defeated by the combined forces of Spider-Man, the Punisher and Deathlok. Scorpia became a free agent, joining the short-lived Sinister Seven. Scorpia went underground when the original Scorpion returned to crime; she reappeared only recently as a contract killer.

SCRIERS

First Appearance: *Amazing Spider-Man* #394 (1994)

The original Scrier was an enigmatic entity of vast mystical power. He lay dormant on Earth for millennia, until revived by the Silver Surfer to help battle Mephisto. He later fought Spider-Man and the Man-Thing for control of the Nexus of Realities, losing with good grace. In his absence, a secret Cabal of Scriers had formed based on his teachings. Norman Osborn (Green Goblin) manipulated the Scriers into acting as his agents, arming them with advanced technology. The Cabal of Scriers promoted the impression that there was only one Scrier, who possessed supernatural powers. In fact, the modern Scrier was nothing but a role, played over time by various members of the order using Norman's high-tech gifts. The original Scrier has little to do with the Cabal — other than selecting one of their number, Martin Zantz, as his prime agent, now called Outrider.

SCORPION

Real Name: MacDonald Gargan

First Appearance: *Amazing Spider-Man* #20 (1965)

Height: 6'2"
Weight: 220 lbs.
Eye Color: Brown
Hair Color: Brown

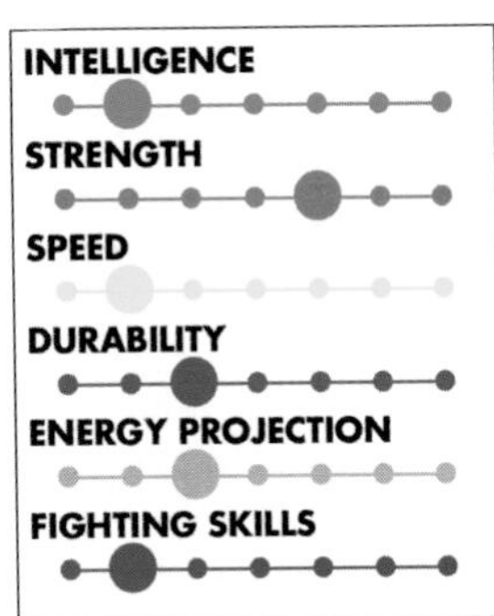

Unaware his actions would ultimately result in the creation of a monster with an unquenchable lust for vengeance, J. Jonah Jameson hired rough and ready private investigator Mac Gargan to tail Peter Parker and determine how the freelance photographer could capture so many pictures of Spider-Man. But plans changed quickly when Jameson read about a scientist performing groundbreaking experiments in physiological enhancement. The scientist was Dr. Farley Stillwell, whose techniques had been shown to produce great increases in strength and speed in test animals he had subjected to his chemical and radiological bombardments. In return for Jameson's funding, Stillwell agreed to perform the same procedure on a human test subject — one Mac Gargan, who also would be well-paid for his part.

Stillwell modeled Gargan's transformation on a scorpion. He granted Gargan enhanced speed, endurance and strength. In keeping with Gargan's new namesake, Stillwell empowered his guinea pig's hands with the strength of mighty pincers. To cap off the effect, the scientist created a powerful electro-mechanical tail. With the addition of a green costume, Gargan's transformation was complete. Sent to destroy the object of Jameson's hatred, the Scorpion soon met his intended prey. A shocked Spider-Man quickly discovered that the Scorpion possessed strength greater than his own. Back in his laboratory, Stillwell made a shocking discovery, too. Examining the results of his most recent control experiments, he learned that a side effect of the mutation would steadily destroy Gargan's mind — devouring his humanity and transforming him into a cruel psychopath. Stillwell tracked down the Scorpion in the hope of attempting to administer a serum that would reverse the transformation. But while pursuing Gargan, he stumbled and fell

Continued...

POWERS/ WEAPONS

- Superhuman strength, speed, endurance and agility
- Powerful electro-mechanical tail with spiked tip and various weapons — including bio-electric sting, tear gas and acid
- Pincer-grip hands

Art by Darick Robertson

SCORPION

from a building. When Stillwell lost his life, Gargan lost hold of his sanity.

Though outmatched physically, Spider-Man's skill and clear thinking proved the edge he needed to overcome the Scorpion in battle. Nothing could save what was left of the man known as Mac Gargan — now, only the Scorpion remained. Arrested and imprisoned, the Scorpion seethed with hatred for Spider-Man for defeating him, and Jameson for creating the monster he had become. Jameson's relief at the Scorpion's incarceration was short-lived. The Scorpion soon escaped and attacked the publisher, who was saved only through Spider-Man's intervention. Jameson watched his two worst enemies battle with mixed emotions. Though he hated Spider-Man passionately, the wall-crawler's loss would have meant Jameson's certain doom. He was grateful Spider-Man won the fight, but only begrudgingly so.

Motivated by revenge, and on the hunt for the power to achieve it, the Scorpion pursued a career as an assassin-for-hire — often seeking payment in the form of more powerful weapons or enhanced strength. Though he fought other heroes, his heart still held a special hatred that only the deaths of Spider-Man and Jameson could ease. Desperate to attain his end goal, the Scorpion ultimately returned to Stillwell's abandoned laboratory and used the equipment there to boost his powers to extreme levels. When the Scorpion learned of Jameson's impending wedding to Dr. Marla Madison, he managed to kidnap his adversary's fiancée — once more leaving Jameson to rely on a humiliating rescue by Spider-Man.

Greedy for even greater power, the Scorpion agreed to become an agent of criminal industrialist Justin Hammer in return for enhanced equipment — including a more flexible, toxin-projecting tail. While carrying out a kidnapping contract, the Scorpion was once more foiled by Spider-Man. The two would cross paths again when the Scorpion teamed first with the Chameleon and later the Tinkerer, who had outfitted him with an electrified tail. This final loss proved to be the Scorpion's breaking point. Overwhelmed by his countless failures, he wandered the sewers — his mind clearer than it had been for years. But even after he decided to opt out of his life of crime, fate would play a cruel joke at his expense. Spider-Man had been suffering through a private crisis, and he could barely contain his own aggression when he stumbled across the Scorpion. The web-slinger's primal instincts took over, and he beat Gargan to a pulp — ignoring the former villain's sincere protests that he was a changed man. The Scorpion's moment of clarity dissipated, and his chance at redemption was forever destroyed at Spider-Man's hands. The Scorpion's briefly suppressed violence came flooding back, leaving him more psychotic than ever. He has since resumed his place as a deadly, unstable killer-for-hire — even as he awaits one more chance to seek revenge on Spider-Man and Jameson.

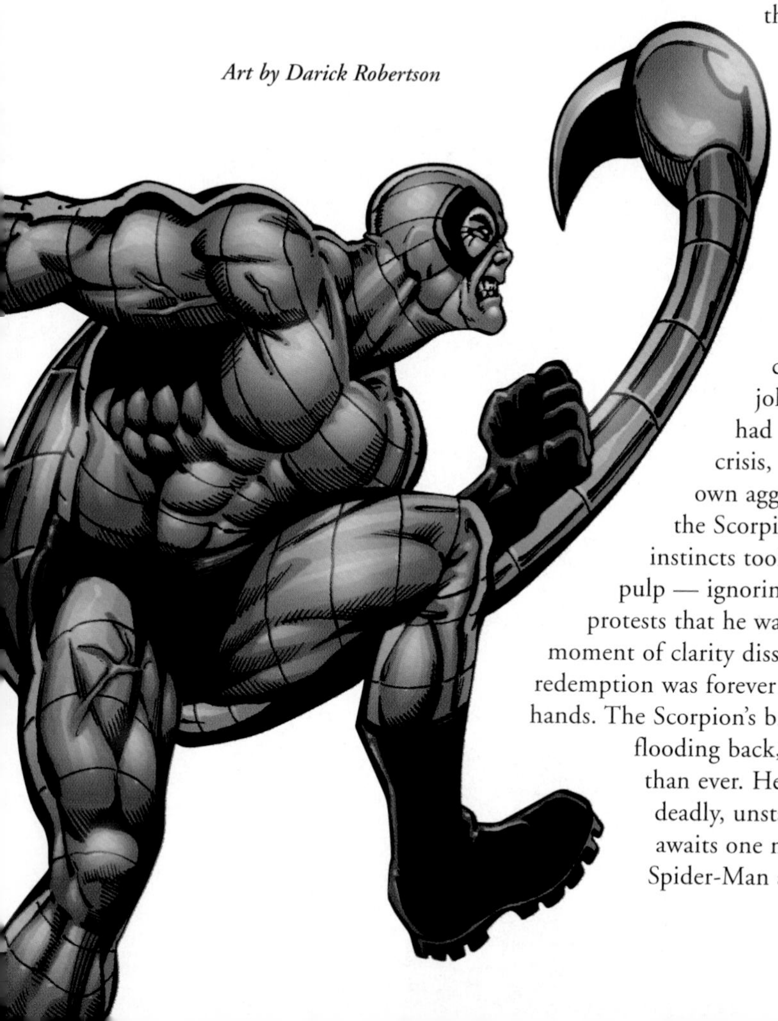

Art by Darick Robertson

SHA SHAN

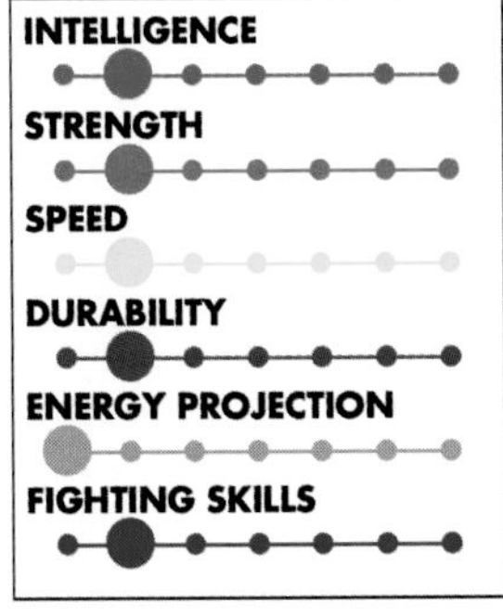

Real Name: Sha Shan, last name unrevealed
First Appearance: *Amazing Spider-Man* #108 (1972)
Hgt: 5'6"
Wt: 110 lbs.

As a soldier in Southeast Asia, Flash Thompson was wounded and separated from his unit. The monks of a secret temple saved his life, led by "The Holy One" — who had one daughter, Sha Shan. Blaming Flash for the subsequent shelling of their temple, the monks tracked him back to the States — but Sha Shan saved his life. Sha Shan was obliged to marry the evil Achmed Korba (Brother Power), becoming Sister Sun and helping form the Legion of Light. As her father intended, her moderating influence destroyed Achmed. She was then free to become Flash's girlfriend. They parted months later, and she has not been seen since.

SHADE

POWERS/WEAPONS

- Moderate superhuman strength, increased in the Astral Plane
- Astral travel

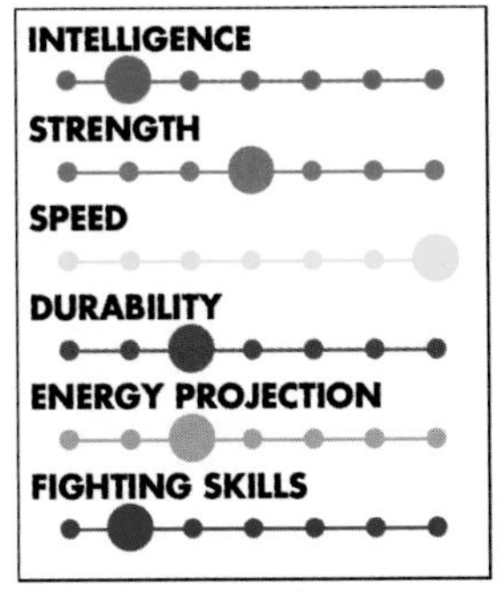

Real Name: Unrevealed
First Appearance: *Amazing Spider-Man* #40 (2002)
Hgt: 6'1"
Wt: 195 lbs.

When his cellmate attempted to enter the Astral Plane through a mystic ritual, the man now known only as the Shade stole his place. Due to the ceremony's flawed nature, the Shade discovered that to return to the physical world, he needed to imprison earthly victims in his Astral cocoon. When the Shade began abducting drifters and junkies, Spider-Man proved unable to stop him. The hero sought the aid of Doctor Strange, who helped him reach the Astral Plane. There, Spider-Man rescued the Shade's victims. The Shade was apparently destroyed in the violent explosion that resulted when Spider-Man pushed him into his own cocoon.

SHADRAC

POWERS/WEAPONS

- Superhuman strength and resistance
- Burns with fire

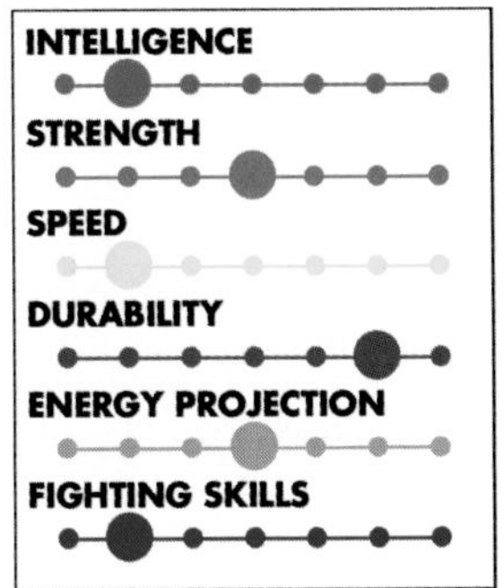

Real Name: Formerly Gregory Herd and Gray Dolman
First Appearance: *Amazing Spider-Man* #2 (1999)
Hgt: 6'1"
Wt: 195 lbs.

Override, a.k.a. Gregory Herd, accepted a contract from Norman Osborn (Green Goblin), to steal a mystical stone fragment from antiques collector and mystic Gray Dolman. This fragment was a necessary part of the Gathering of Five ritual. Gregory joined the ceremony, hoping to acquire the power to heal his wife, Aura. Instead, he received death. Reborn as the flaming skeleton Shadrac, he was controlled briefly by Dolman, until he managed to absorb him. But the true soul of Shadrac eventually assumed control — a centuries-old evil that had created the mystical Gathering ceremony. Shadrac now lives within the blazing heart of the planet, awaiting the right time to re-emerge.

SHOCKER

Real Name:
Herman Schultz
First Appearance:
Amazing Spider-Man #46 (1967)

Height: 5'9"
Weight: 175 lbs.
Eye Color: Brown
Hair Color: Brown

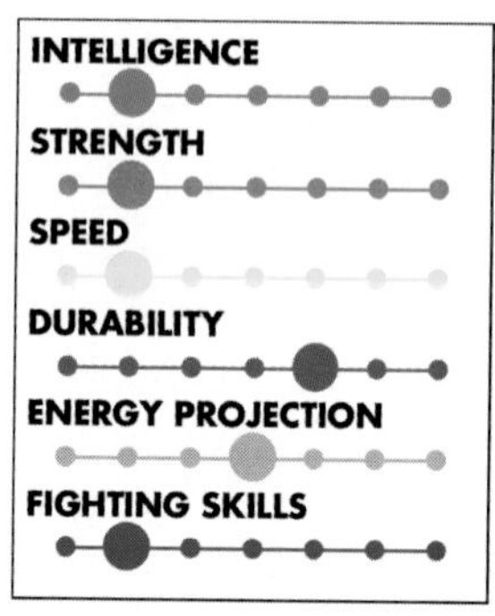

Herman Schultz started out as a not-so-successful burglar. During his third stint in prison, he decided it was time to try a different angle. Employing a hitherto untapped aptitude for invention, Herman used the prison workshop to develop prototype sonic-projection devices designed primarily to shake open bank vaults, but equally devastating when directed at human targets. Herman used the hand-held devices to escape from jail; he then converted the units to wrist-mounted form, complete with thumb-triggers, and created padded body armor that would minimize the painful impact felt when using the devices.

The Shocker first tested his inventions on an office safe; when the ensuing destruction attracted Spider-Man's attention, the vibro-shock devices assured the villain an easy victory. But during their second encounter, Spider-Man simply webbed up the Shocker's hands, ensuring he could not access his thumb-triggers. In later battles, Spider-Man defeated the Shocker by blinding him with webbing, or by cleverly webbing his weapon into the "on" position. To counter his continued defeats, the Shocker developed more sophisticated control mechanisms and more cunningly embedded shock-generators.

Art by Francisco Herrera

In style, the Shocker is a creative and flexible villain. Theft, extortion and blackmail — the Shocker has attempted them all. His plans have included such varied schemes as blacking out New York City blocks to spell his name and manipulating the Stock Market to his benefit. At one point, the Shocker began to struggle with terrible doubt and fear, predominantly engendered by the Scourge of the Underworld, who had terminated so many others of the Shocker's ilk. After nearly quitting the super-villain lifestyle once and for all, the Shocker eventually regained his confidence and joined the Sinister Seven. Most recently he teamed up with Hydro-Man, hoping for one last big heist before retirement. They were foiled as ever by Spider-Man.

POWERS/WEAPONS

- Wrist-mounted vibro-shock units
- Shock-resistant body armor

SHATHRA

POWERS/WEAPONS

- Flight
- Superhuman strength, speed, agility and endurance
- Poisonous spikes
- Claw-like fingers

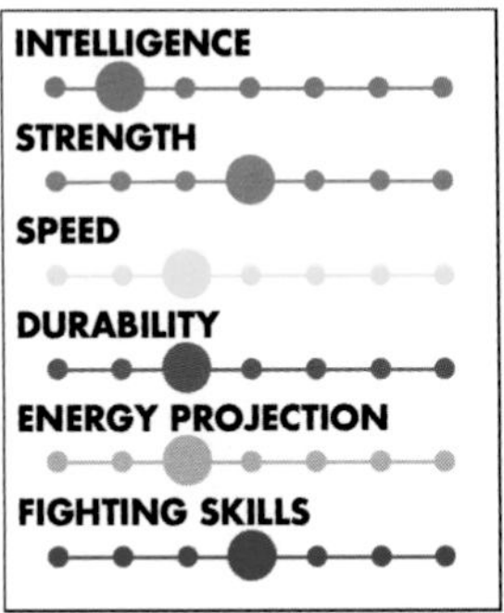

Real Name: Shathra, a.k.a. Spider-Wasp
First Appearance: *Amazing Spider-Man* #46 (2002)
Hgt: 6'2"
Wt: 120 lbs.

Battling Shade in the Astral Plane, Spider-Man unwittingly alerted Shathra to his presence. A natural predator of the spider, Shathra tracked the web-slinger to our plane, assumed human form and went to the press with a series of humiliating lies about her quarry. Shathra hoped Peter Parker would act on pure anger and instinct, to render a better spiritual "meal" for her children. Reverting to true form on camera, she proved to be Spider-Man's superior in battle. Ezekiel saved the hero and led him to a spider-temple in Ghana. There, Peter fought Shathra once more, until she was engulfed by a swarm of spiders.

SHRIEK

POWERS/WEAPONS

- Levitation of people and objects
- Sonic blasts
- Psychic ability to bring out violence in others

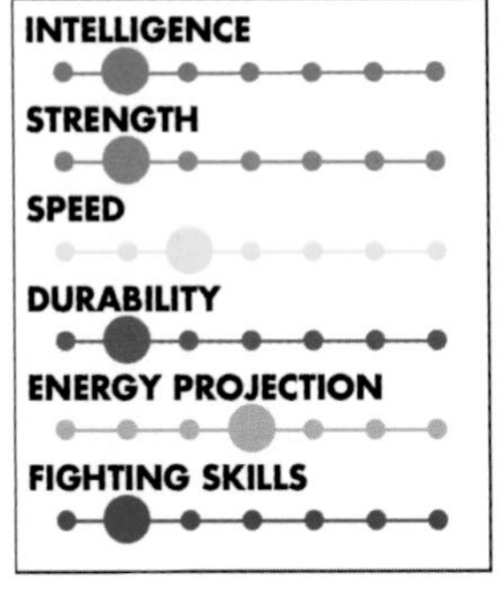

Real Name: Frances Louise Barrison, a.k.a. Sandra Deel
First Appearance: *Spider-Man Unlimited* #1 (1993)
Hgt: 5'8"
Wt: 115 lbs.

Frances Louise Barrison's miserable childhood drove her to drugs; a run in with Cloak drove her insane and awakened her latent psychic powers. She was imprisoned at Ravencroft Institute, where she encountered Carnage. The pair escaped and embarked on a killing spree. Shriek considered Carnage her husband — and Demogoblin, Doppelganger and Carrion II (Malcolm McBride) her children. Sacrificing herself for McBride, she absorbed his Carrion Virus and hatched it in her womb like an unborn son. The Jackal later invaded her cell and retrieved it. Formerly known as Sandra Deel, her real name was revealed when she began slowly responding to Dr. Ashley Kafka's therapy.

SILVERMANE

POWERS/WEAPONS

- Superhuman strength and durability (as a cyborg)

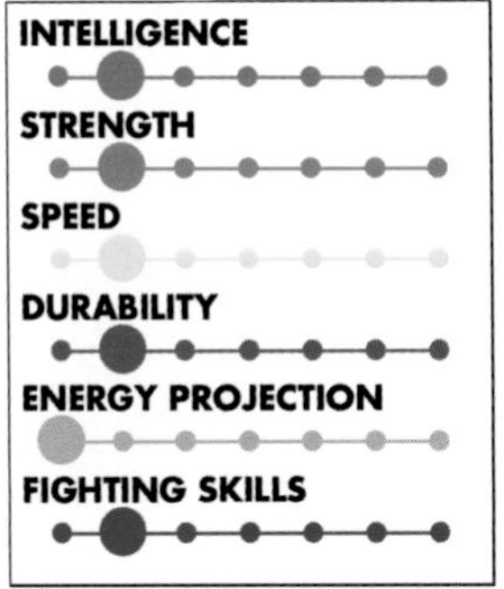

Real Name: Silvio Manfredi
First Appearance: *Amazing Spider-Man* #73 (1969)
Hgt: 6'2"
Wt: 195 lbs.

Patriarch of the Silvermane family of the Maggia and a former leader of Hydra, Silvio Manfredi has long been a thorn in Spider-Man's side. They first crossed paths when Silvermane attempted to possess the Lifeline Tablet, with which he hoped to recapture his lost youth. Instead, he passed through infancy to non-existence. Later, Silvermane rapidly re-aged through youth to extreme old age. To preserve his life, he had himself re-built as a cyborg. Failing to steal Deathlok's body, he appears instead to have inhabited an artificial one. Tied to the life-support system in his wheelchair, Silvermane continues to lead the Maggia.

SILVER SABLE

Real Name: Silver Sablinovia
First Appearance: *Amazing Spider-Man* #265 (1985)
Hgt: 5'5"
Wt: 125 lbs.

Silver Sable was trained from childhood to be the future leader of the Wild Pack, an elite paramilitary strike force founded by her father to hunt Nazi war criminals. Under Silver's leadership, the group has been transformed into a militia-for-hire — generating much-needed revenue for her homeland, the tiny European nation of Symkaria. The Wild Pack's membership under Silver has included Battlestar, Chen, Crippler, Doug Powell, Quentino, the Sandman, Larry Arnold and others.

Spider-Man first crossed paths with the Wild Pack as they attempted to capture the Black Fox. Spider-Man learned at great cost that Silver Sable was a dangerous opponent. In the years that followed, Spider-Man encountered her repeatedly, even working for Silver Sable International on several occasions — most notably when they joined forces in Symkaria to prevent the murder of that country's king by Sabretooth.

As a child, Silver Sable watched her mother fall victim to a terrorist attack, an event that shaped the woman she was to become. While she publicly presents the image of a hardened mercenary with flexible morals, she occasionally reveals a softer side — although perhaps it will never be

POWERS/WEAPONS

- Superb martial artist and marksman
- Skilled tactician and strategist
- Vast financial and operational resources

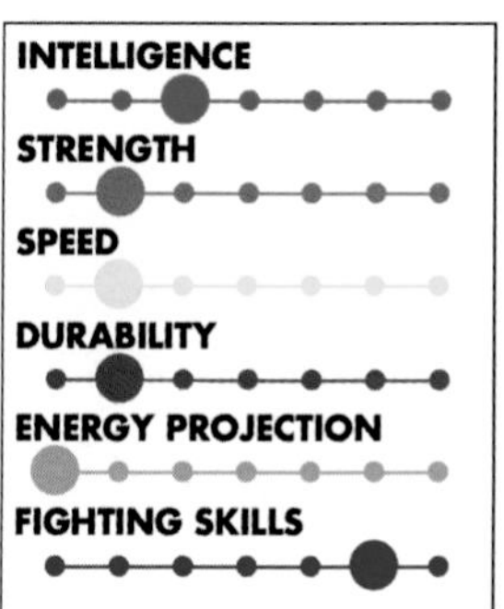

SIN-EATER

Real Name: Stan Carter
First Appearance: *Spectacular Spider-Man* #107 (1985)
Hgt: 5'10"
Wt: 175 lbs.

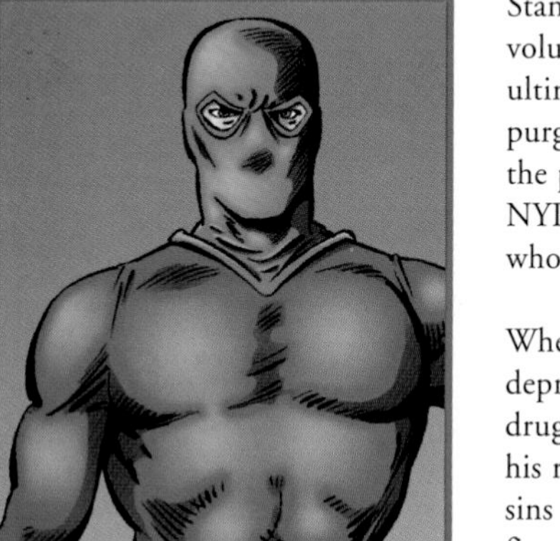

Stan Carter was a former S.H.I.E.L.D agent who volunteered to test a strength-enhancing drug that ultimately drove him insane. After the scientists purged the drug from his system and suspended the program, Carter became a sergeant in the NYPD — where he worked for Jean DeWolff, with whom he had a short-lived relationship.

When his partner was killed, Carter sank into depression and started drinking — re-activating the drugs in his system ... and his insanity. Inspired by his religious upbringing, he set out to vanquish the sins of a corrupt humankind as the Sin-Eater. He first killed Jean DeWolff for representing the legal system that had allowed his partner's death.

Devastated by Jean's murder, Spider-Man worked with the police to catch the killer. Carter was placed in charge of the case; meanwhile, he assassinated a judge as the Sin-Eater. Trapped by Spider-Man, the Sin-Eater fired his shotgun. Spider-Man unthinkingly dodged the shot, which killed an innocent bystander instead. Despite a confusing false confession, Daredevil identified Carter as the true killer. Spider-Man then beat Carter near death, only stopped by Daredevil's forceful intervention. Carter never truly recovered, and months later committed suicide by threatening the police with an unloaded gun.

POWERS/WEAPONS

- NYPD and S.H.I.E.L.D. training
- Skilled marksman and unarmed combatant
- Possible enhanced strength

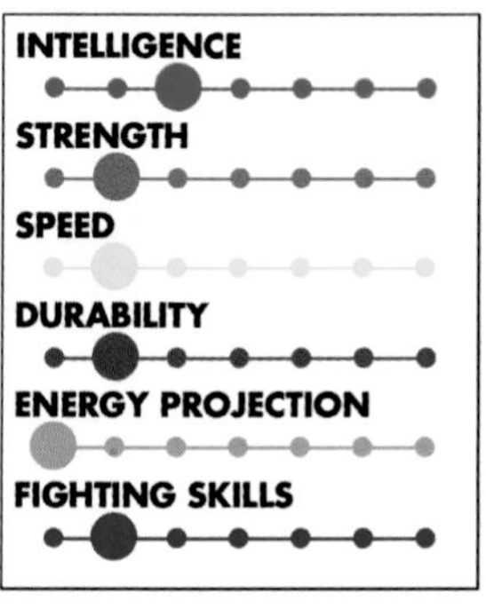

SINISTER SIX/SEVEN

Art by John Romita Jr.

First Appearance:
Amazing Spider-Man Annual #1 (1964)

The Sinister Six was an alliance of villains sharing one common goal: revenge on Spider-Man. Initially led by Doctor Octopus, the group's original lineup consisted of Electro, Kraven the Hunter, Mysterio, the Sandman and the Vulture — who had all been soundly defeated by Spider-Man. Doctor Octopus assured his comrades that by working together, they could finally destroy the web-slinger for their mutual benefit.

Doc Ock's plan was daring and devious: The Six would kidnap Betty Brant, who Spider-Man had rescued publicly. The wall-crawler would then be forced to fight the six villains in sequence, each opponent holding a card revealing the location of the next. Even if all his allies were to lose, Doctor Octopus was sure the web-slinger would be weakened enough to be easy prey for their final duel.

The Sandman and Electro attacked Betty while she was visiting May Parker. Thinking two hostages better than one, the villains added May to their ransom. With the fate of his beloved aunt now at stake, Spider-Man had no choice but to follow the Sinister Six's plan. Although each villain had carefully choreographed his showdown with Spider-Man, they could not overcome the hero's determination. Humiliated by their collective defeat, the Six's association was dissolved; each member was imprisoned.

Doctor Octopus re-formed the group years later, with the Hobgoblin taking the now-deceased Kraven's place. Doc Ock planned for the Six to hijack a space rocket and hold the world for ransom after replacing the original payload with one of his own design. With the aid of Thor, Asgardian god of thunder, and a reformed Sandman, Spider-Man foiled Octopus' scheme. In battle, it was revealed that Doc Ock planned to cheat the others and keep the ransom money for himself — earning the deadly enmity of his former conspirators.

Seeking revenge, the group's remaining five members joined forces against their treacherous ex-leader. When Spider-Man and the Hulk crashed the villains' battle, the Six struck an uneasy truce. Using

Continued...

SINISTER SIX/SEVEN

powerful weapons and robots from an alien dimension, and backed by an otherworldly ally named Gog, the Six were more powerful than ever. It took the combined forces of Deathlok, Solo, Ghost Rider, Nova of the New Warriors, Sleepwalker, the Fantastic Four, the Hulk and Spider-Man to finally vanquish the Six and end their threat.

Following Doctor Octopus' apparent death at the hands of Kaine, Mysterio assumed his role and blackmailed the Six into re-forming. Mysterio hoped to use his teammates to obtain Doc Ock's invaluable data archives. Through the assistance of the Scarlet Spider (Ben Reilly), Spider-Man was able to foil Mysterio's plan and expose his ruse.

It was during this time that Kaine had begun to mercilessly slaughter Spider-Man's enemies. Doc Ock and the Grim Hunter (Vladimir Kravinoff) had already fallen to Kaine's deadly touch, and many of Spider-Man's foes feared for their lives. Hoping to use their combined might to destroy Kaine before he could pick them off one by one, a number of these villains formed the Sinister Seven — a new alliance consisting of the Beetle, Electro, the Hobgoblin, Mysterio, Scorpia, the Shocker and the Vulture. Spider-Man's intervention prevented any further bloodshed at Kaine's hands, and the Seven went their separate ways.

In the wake of Doctor Octopus' resurrection by the True Believers, he agreed to protect Senator Stewart Ward, who had become involved in a high-stakes alien plot. The former members of the Sinister Six seized the opportunity to exact revenge against Doc Ock, while potentially earning a profit capturing the Senator on behalf of his enemies. Their ranks rounded out by the unexpected addition of Venom, the Six managed to corner Ward, causing him to explode in an outpouring of strange energy. While the remaining villains fled to safety, Electro and Mysterio worked together to capture the Senator.

With the long history of failure and distrust among this group of criminals, it seems unlikely the Sinister Six will ever re-form. However, given their mutual hatred of Spider-Man, an eventual reunion can never be ruled out completely.

Art by Joe Bennett

SINISTER SYNDICATE

Art by Sal Buscema

First Appearance:
Amazing Spider-Man #280 (1986)

Perhaps slightly less well-known than the Sinister Six, the Sinister Syndicate is no less lethal. In its first incarnation, the group was comprised of Boomerang, the Beetle, the Speed Demon, the Rhino and Hydro-Man. The Syndicate made its debut in an attack on Spider-Man and Silver Sable, its members looking to boost their underworld reputations by taking out the heroes. The Syndicate would have succeeded in killing both Silver Sable and Spider-Man if not for the unexpected arrival of the Sandman, who had recently renounced his criminal past.

With the Sandman now under her employ, Silver Sable and Spider-Man again battled the Sinister Syndicate in the tiny European nation of Belgrun. The Syndicate was defeated, and Silver Sable was able to complete her mission: rescuing the daughter of that nation's brutal dictator.

The group subsequently re-formed, this time less for revenge on Spider-Man and more out of purely profit-driven motives. Dubbed the Deadly Foes of Spider-Man, it was not long until their criminal ways brought them into direct confrontation with their web-slinging nemesis. This time, the five's combined power was enough to defeat Spider-Man. With the wall-crawler's life on the line, the Rhino surprisingly stepped in — insisting he was no cold-blooded killer, merely a desperate man looking to raise enough cash to remove his artificial hide.

Leaving Spider-Man alive, the group was briefly joined by the Shocker — who believed the Syndicate's forces could stave off the Scourge of the Underworld, a mysterious killer executing super-villains with seemingly superhuman precision. Although Scourge was defeated before he could face the Syndicate, his acts would later prove detrimental to the group.

Posing as Boomerang's girlfriend, Leila Davis was in fact the widow of the Ringer (Strikeback), one of Scourge's victims. Believing the Beetle partly responsible for her husband's death, Leila infiltrated the Syndicate seeking revenge. She revealed her true identity during a battle against Spider-Man; in the ensuing fracas, the group splintered into warring factions. Given the current animosity among the Syndicate's former members, a reunion seems unlikely — but perhaps these villains' mutual hatred of Spider-Man may be enough to one day bring them together once more.

SIX-ARMED SPIDER-MAN

Real Name: Peter Benjamin Parker
First Appearance: *Amazing Spider-Man* #100 (1971)
Hgt: 5'10"
Wt: 210 lbs.

Early in his days at Empire State University, Peter Parker tried to cure himself of his superhuman powers in the hope he might enjoy a normal life with Gwen Stacy. The attempt backfired, instead granting him four extra arms. In this weird condition, he came into conflict with Morbius and the Lizard. Peter was finally able to restore himself to normal with the help of Dr. Curt Connors, the Lizard's alter ego, using a serum derived from a sample of Morbius' unusual mutagenic blood.

POWERS/WEAPONS

- All the abilities of Spider-Man, plus four additional arms

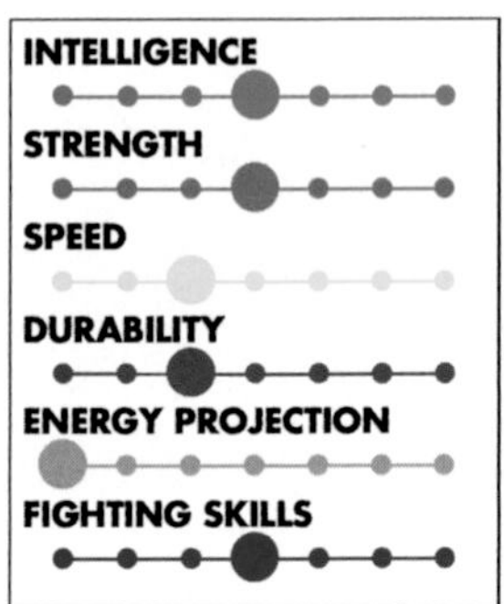

SKINHEAD

Real Name: Eddie Cross
First Appearance: *Web of Spider-Man* #56 (1989)
Hgt: 10'+
Wt: 800 lbs.

Son of Rabbi Chaim Cross, Eddie Cross was driven to deny his heritage and become a neo-Nazi by the racism he experienced as a child. While terrorizing an African-American organization on the campus of Empire State University, Eddie encountered Spider-Man and Rocket Racer. Their fight led to a chemical lab, where corrosive chemicals dissolved Eddie's body — granting him the ability to shape his skin and absorb others' flesh to grow in size. Transformed into the monstrous Skinhead, his rampage seemed unstoppable — until Spider-Man managed to penetrate his oozing outer form and punch his skeleton unconscious.

POWERS/WEAPONS

- Manipulation of semi-amorphous body
- Superhuman strength and resistance to injury
- Dissolution of matter on contact

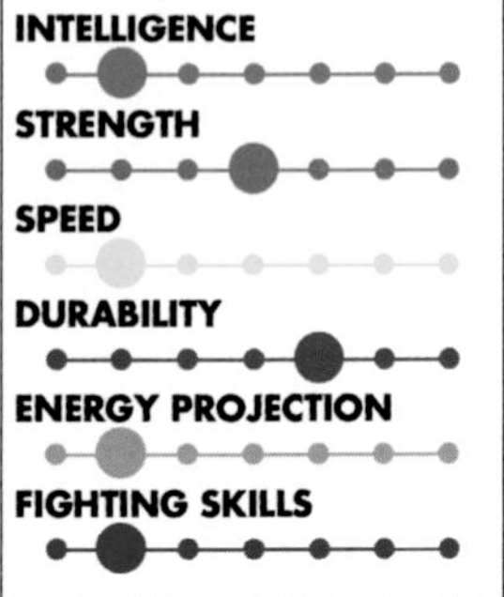

SLASHER

Real Name: Elyse Nelson
First Appearance: *Web of Spider-Man* #37 (1988)
Hgt: 5'8"
Wt: 125 lbs.

When supermodels on a series of fashion shoots were brutally murdered — victims of "The Slasher" — Harvey Finkelstein, an over-enthusiastic admirer of Elyse Nelson, hired a man named Leslie to pose as the killer so he could seemingly rescue her. Confusing matters, the man appeared to be the real Slasher. But while both Spider-Man and private investigator Dakota North pursued him, Mary Jane Watson found herself confronted by the genuine article — Elyse herself, who had developed a deep self-loathing and a jealousy of other models. Fortunately, Spider-Man swung to the rescue in the nick of time.

POWERS/WEAPONS

- Psychotic strength
- Straight razor

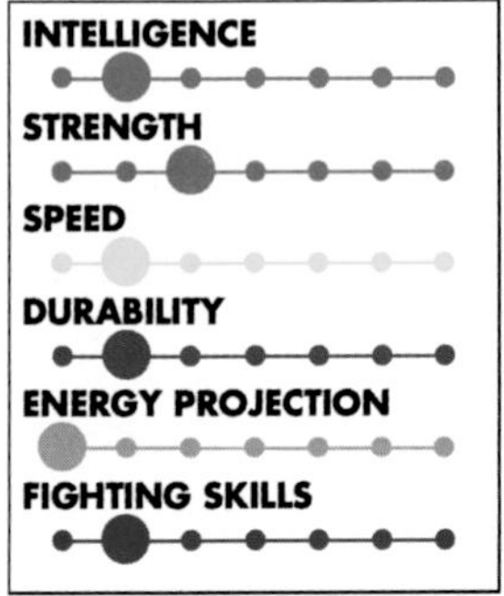

SLINGERS

First Appearance: *Slingers* #0 (1998)

Dusk (Cassie St. Commons), Prodigy (Ritchie Gilmore), Ricochet (Johnathon "Johnny" Gallo), and Hornet (Eddie McDonough) — four teenagers assembled by the elderly hero known as the Black Marvel. Richochet was a mutant, but the others received their powers from the costumes they wore. Not only did the Slingers mimic costumes previously worn by Spider-Man, they also bore his curse of power and responsibility — each one striving to do the right thing. To save their mentor's soul from Mephisto, the Slingers ultimately abandoned their powers and costumes — but by then, they had proven themselves worthy heroes.

DR. MORRIS SLOAN

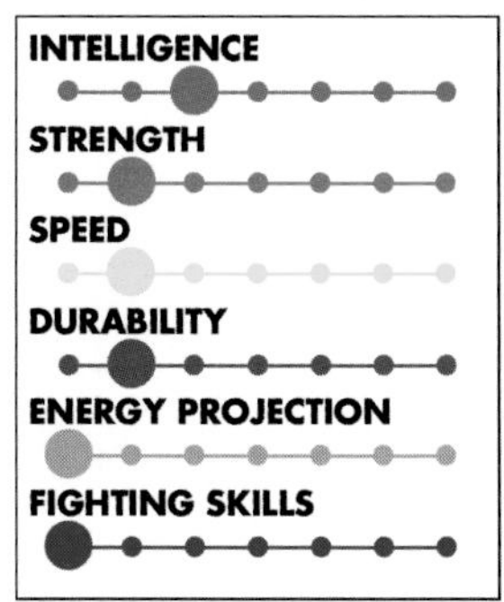

Real Name: Dr. Morris Sloan
First Appearance: *Spectacular Spider-Man* #32 (1979)
Hgt: 5'9"
Wt: 185 lbs.

A specialist in entomology, Dr. Morris Sloan was chairman of the biophysics department at Empire State University and Peter Parker's supervisor during his post-graduate studies. Though Sloan was critical of Peter's lack of commitment and haphazard approach to his work, he also considered him the brightest of all his graduate students and was greatly disappointed when he finally withdrew from the course before completing his doctorate. Normally a careful scientist, Sloan's ill-considered experiments were responsible for accidentally reviving the deadly menace of Swarm.

SLYDE

POWERS/WEAPONS

- Costume coated with near-frictionless substance
- Can skate along the ground at approximately 30 mph

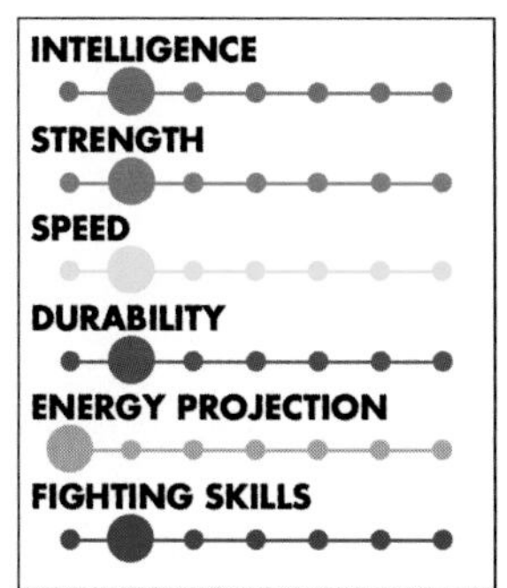

Real Name: Jalome Beacher
First Appearance: *Amazing Spider-Man* #272 (1986)
Hgt: 5'11"
Wt: 170 lbs.

Chemical engineer Jalome Beacher discovered a virtually frictionless substance, but was fired when the company he worked for came under new management. After robbing a bank to secure the funds necessary to start his own business and tangling with Spider-Man, Beacher helped the district attorney obtain evidence incriminating his former employers of money laundering — then made off with $25,000 of the company's cash. Cage and Spider-Man later helped save his brother from members of the Maggia after Beacher had stolen from them. Slyde subsequently joined the Masters of Evil, only to be captured and imprisoned.

JOE SMITH

Real Name: Joe Smith
First Appearance: *Amazing Spider-Man* #38 (1966)

Hgt: 6'1"
Wt: 225 lbs.

POWERS/WEAPONS

- Superhuman strength

INTELLIGENCE
STRENGTH
SPEED
DURABILITY
ENERGY PROJECTION
FIGHTING SKILLS

Joe Smith was a born loser with big dreams. Working as a stuntman, he was exposed to chemicals that granted him superhuman strength — but drove him into a disoriented rampage. After a scuffle with Spider-Man, his powers faded — though his performance earned him an acting contract.

Joe seemed to have a nose for trouble. It wasn't long before he became entangled in a hallucinogenic nightmare created by Mysterio. When Mysterio captured J. Jonah Jameson, it fell to Joe to play the hero. Though powerless, he beat the evildoer and saved the maiden — Mysterio's childhood friend, Betsy Schneider.

Joe eventually married a woman from the studio, but she left him when their child was born severely handicapped. After his son's death, Joe's powers briefly resurfaced; he rampaged again until stopped by Captain America. Joe then worked at a children's center. Again, though powerless, he was ever the hero — and he inspired his local neighborhood to drive off a gang of criminals. Joe later married Betsy, which drew him into the menacing world of Mysterio II and his protégé, Mad Jack. Joe fought alongside Spider-Man and Daredevil to defeat the two villains.

ALISTAIR SMYTHE

Real Name: Alistair Alphonso Smythe
First Appearance: *Amazing Spider-Man Annual* #19 (1985)

Hgt: 6'0"
Wt: 220 lbs.

POWERS/WEAPONS

- Skilled robotics engineer
- Cybernetically enhanced body

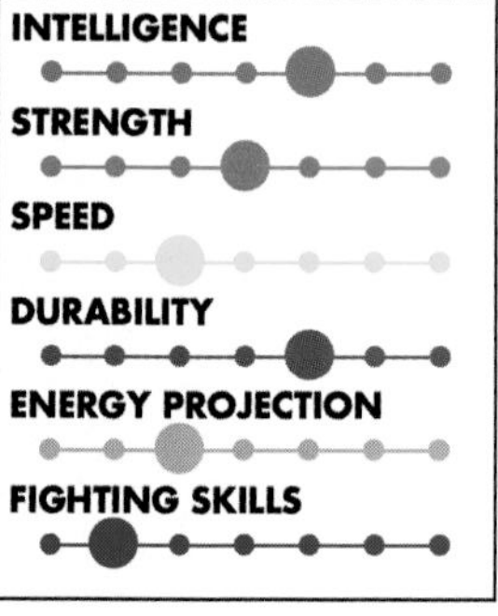

Alistair Smythe was the son of Spencer Smythe. His father's all-consuming — and eventually fatal — obsession with building Spider-Slayers to kill Spider-Man resulted in his neglect of the young boy. Following his father's death, Alistair worked for the Kingpin, diverting Fisk's resources into his own inherited infatuation: the death of Spider-Man. Taking up Spider-Man's trail, Alistair captured Mary Jane Watson and Anna Watson, for a time believing Mary Jane to be Spider-Man. He was dissuaded of this notion when the real Spider-Man arrived. Alistair's Spider-Slayer eventually crashed into overhead power lines, crippling him.

Wheelchair-bound and half-mad, Alistair returned repeatedly with the aid of his Spider-Slayers, which he continuously improved from his father's designs. In a climactic battle with Spider-Man, Alistair revealed that he had undergone cybernetic surgery to become, himself, the Ultimate Spider-Slayer — but even that drastic measure was not enough to defeat the web-slinger. Narrowly avoiding death at the hands of Dr. Carolyn Trainer, who had assumed the guise of Doctor Octopus, Alistair attempted to blackmail J. Jonah Jameson into helping him achieve his plans. But Alistair underestimated his pawn — and was ignominiously defeated by the mustachioed, bat-wielding newspaper editor.

SPENCER SMYTHE

When scientist and inventor Spencer Smythe sought funding for a plan he hoped would result in the capture of Spider-Man and put an end to the web-slinger's alleged criminal activity, he knew exactly how to get the money — and whom to get it from. With the first of his Spider-Slayers in tow, Smythe appealed for cash to wealthy publisher J. Jonah Jameson, a man he knew harbored a great loathing for Spider-Man. To Smythe's surprise, Jameson was unenthused about the offer — unenthused, that is, until a foolish Peter Parker encouraged him to take a closer look at the apparatus, eager to see the publisher throw away his money.

Smythe carefully explained to his now rapt audience how the remote-controlled robot, treated with web-resistant oil, used its "hyper-sensitive Geiger-type apparatus" to track the biological signature emitted by spiders — and by Spider-Man. Even better, Smythe pointed out, the device came equipped with a display screen and loudspeaker, ensuring that Spider-Man would see and hear Jameson gloat as he was being tracked. Jameson was sold — and true to its promise, the Spider-Slayer shortly thereafter caught its target. But as Smythe and Jameson left the controls to personally unmask their prey, Spider-Man used his sticky fingers to pull off the main panel and deactivate the robot, leaving behind his costume — a web-filled dummy — for Jameson to unmask.

Smythe hastily created a more powerful Spider-Slayer and again approached Jameson for funding. Jonah bit — but once more, Spider-Man beat the Spider-Slayer at its own game: He led the robot into Smythe's laboratory, where it went haywire in the presence of so many test spiders. In a desperate bid, Smythe applied maximum power to the device and destroyed his creation. Jameson refused Smythe's final plea for cash — and Smythe turned to crime to secure funding. In its next incarnation, the Spider-Slayer now contained Smythe himself. Capturing Spider-Man once more, Smythe lived to see the web-slinger once again slip through his fingers and escape by only the narrowest of margins.

Defeat, however, was not Smythe's only concern: The radioactive materials used in the manufacture of the robots poisoned him; he began to die a slow, agonizing death. In a desperate last hurrah, Smythe trapped the two men he blamed for his fate, Jameson and Spider-Man, and handcuffed them together with a bomb scheduled to detonate in 24 hours. Dying of his cancer before the 24 hours were through, Smythe would have suffered another setback had he lived: Spider-Man disabled the bomb by freezing the control unit, thereby releasing himself and Jameson.

Art by John Romita

Real Name:
Spencer Smythe
First Appearance:
Amazing Spider-Man #25 (1965)

Height:	5'10"
Weight:	175 lbs.
Eye Color:	Gray
Hair Color:	Gray

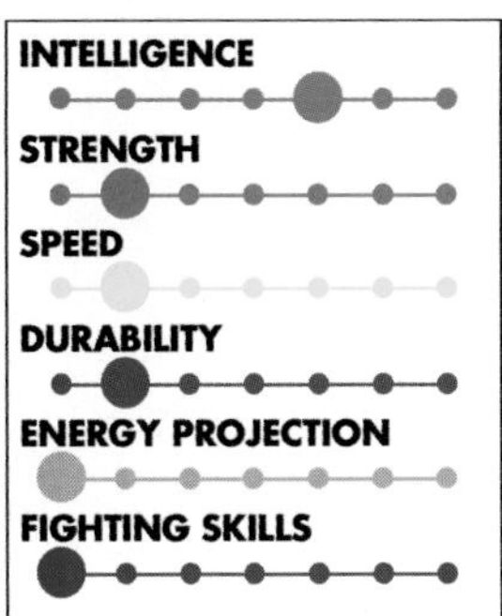

POWERS/ WEAPONS

- Skilled roboticist, biologist, and chemical and industrial engineer

SOLO

Real Name: James Bourne
First Appearance: *Web of Spider-Man* #19 (1986)

Hgt: 6'0"
Wt: 200 lbs.

While Solo lives, terror dies. Once a member of a NATO counter-terrorist team that employed teleportation in its operations, Solo now wages a one-man war on terrorism. His often deadly methods have seen him collide with superhuman friends and foes in pursuit of his righteous quest. Spider-Man has assisted Solo on numerous occasions — including battles against the Sinister Six, and terrorist organizations ULTIMATUM and ARES. Although Solo abandoned his costumed identity after accidentally killing an innocent bystander, he has since resumed operations. Invariably, Spider-Man tries — and fails — to apprehend Solo following their team-ups.

POWERS/WEAPONS

- Teleportation
- Various guns, knives, swords and grenades

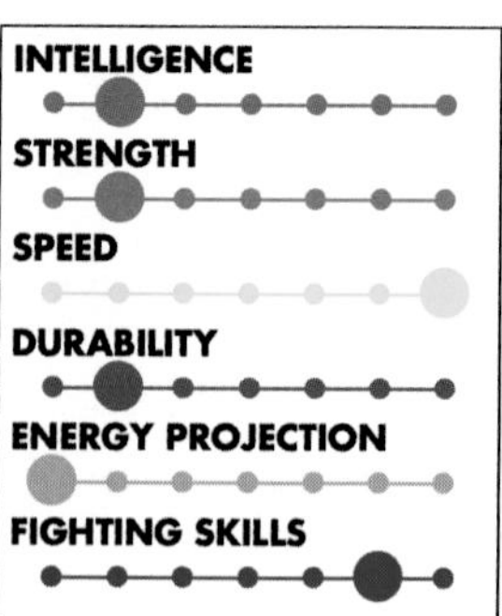

SPEED DEMON

Real Name: James Sanders
First Appearance: *Amazing Spider-Man* #222 (1981)

Hgt: 5'11"
Wt: 175 lbs.

James Sanders, a New Jersey chemist, was chosen by the galactic gamesman known as the Grandmaster to be one of four superhuman pawns in a contest of power against Kang. Subsequently embarking on a crime spree, he came into conflict with Spider-Man. Thereafter, the Speed Demon became a dedicated opponent of the web-slinger, even serving as a member of the Sinister Syndicate. The Speed Demon met with his most embarrassing defeat when the novice hero Frog-Man fell on him. He can most often be found in the employ of wealthy criminal financers, such as Justin Hammer.

POWERS/WEAPONS

- Superhuman speed

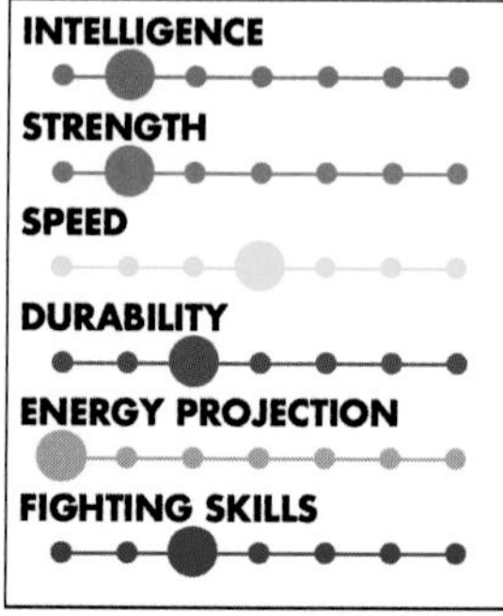

SPIDER-CARNAGE

Real Name: Benjamin Reilly
First Appearance: *Amazing Spider-Man* #410 (1996)

Hgt: 5'10"
Wt: 190 lbs.

While Ben Reilly was wearing Spider-Man's webs, he was baffled to learn that the deadly Carnage was on the loose — while host Cletus Kasady remained imprisoned. Through careful investigation, Ben discovered that the symbiote was controlling John Jameson. When Ben approached, the alien parasite decided he would make a far better host than Jameson. The result of their forced union was Spider-Carnage. Ben compelled the symbiote to obey him long enough to prevent its rampage, but was unable to stop it from sneaking back to Kasady.

POWERS/WEAPONS

- Combined powers of Spider-Man and Carnage

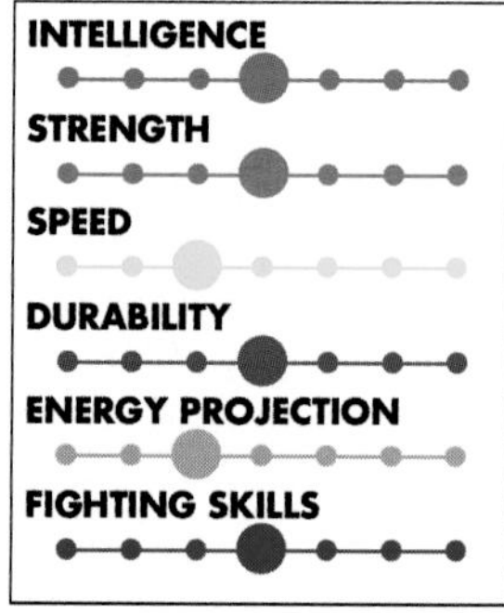

SPIDERCIDE

POWERS/WEAPONS

- All the powers of Spider-Man
- Can greatly increase size and stretch limbs
- Transformation of limbs into blades

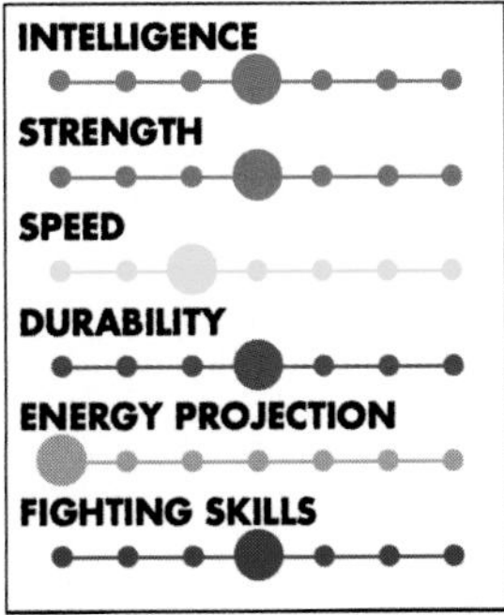

Real Name: Not Applicable
First Appearance: *Spectacular Spider-Man* #222 (1995)

Hgt: 5'10"
Wt: 165 lbs.

During the period in which Peter Parker mistakenly believed himself to be a clone — and Ben Reilly to be the real deal — yet another genetically engineered replica emerged. This clone also believed he was the true Peter, held as a prisoner and test subject of the Jackal for five years. Spidercide failed in his attempt to kill Kaine, Ben and Peter, and learned he was a clone upon returning to the Jackal. The Jackal subsequently taught him to control his mutation for deadly effect. Spidercide once more attempted to kill his brethren, but instead fell to his apparent death.

SPIDER-HULK

POWERS/WEAPONS

- Hulk-like strength and reduced intellect
- Spider-powers and webs

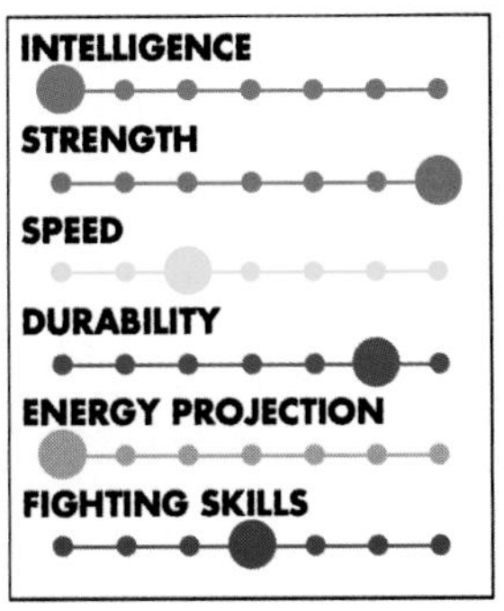

Real Name: Peter Benjamin Parker
First Appearance: *Web of Spider-Man* #70 (1990)

Hgt: 6'10"
Wt: 800 lbs.

Scientist Ricardo Jones died after using his Bio-Kinetic Energy Absorber to temporarily usurp the power of the Fantastic Four's Thing. Years later, Ricardo's brother, Armand, re-created the device and attempted to steal the power of the Hulk, attracting the attention of Spider-Man. Armand was killed in the struggle, which also saw the Hulk's energies accidentally transferred to the web-slinger. Soon after, in times of stress and rage, Spider-Man began transforming into a Hulk-like man-monster. He smashed his way through several adventures before tracking down the youths who had stolen the Absorber and using it to reverse the process.

SPIDER-LIZARD

POWERS/WEAPONS

- All the powers of Spider-Man
- Enhanced strength
- Bulletproof skin
- Reptilian fangs and claws
- Powerful tail

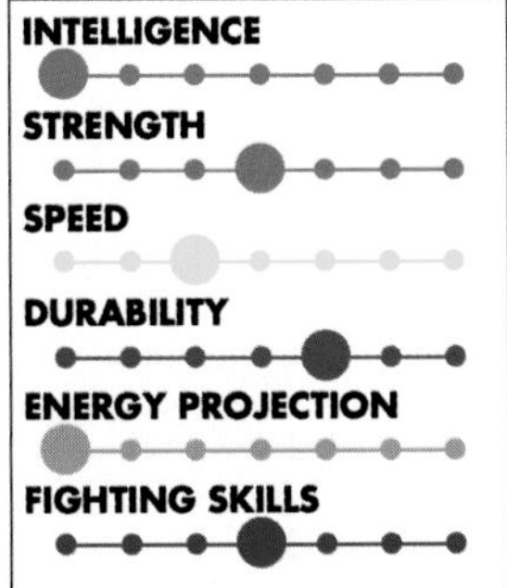

Real Name: Peter Benjamin Parker
First Appearance: *Spectacular Spider-Man* #39 (1979)

Hgt: 6'6"
Wt: 510 lbs.

Attempting to cure Dr. Curt Connors of his Lizard persona, Spider-Man absorbed radioactive feedback from the portable Enervator apparatus — thus transferring the reptilian metamorphosis to himself. After growing increasingly aggressive during a battle with the Schizoid Man, Spider-Man soon physically transformed into the powerful Spider-Lizard. The police began a massive hunt for the beast; as SWAT teams tried to drown the Spider-Lizard by flooding the city sewers, Connors confronted the creature. Risking his own life, he administered the cure and returned Spider-Man's humanity.

SPIDER-MAN

Real Name:
Peter Benjamin Parker
First Appearance:
Amazing Fantasy #15 (1962)

Height:	5'10"
Weight:	165 lbs.
Eye Color:	Hazel
Hair Color:	Brown

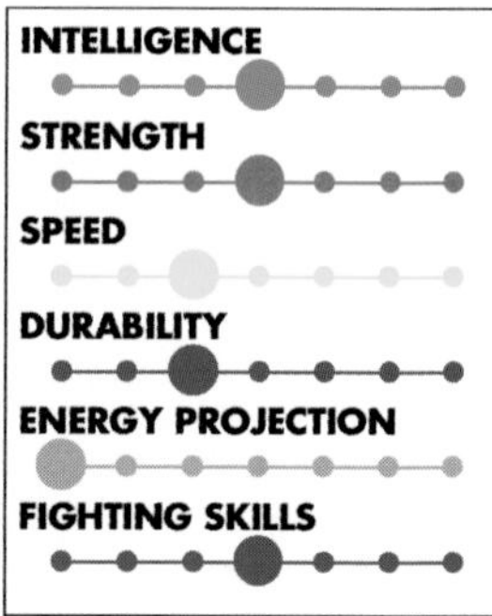

POWERS/WEAPONS

- Superhuman strength
- Greatly enhanced agility, reflexes and equilibrium
- Ability to cling to sheer vertical and inverted surfaces with hands and feet
- Early warning "spider-sense"
- Wrist-mounted web-shooters

Art by John Romita Jr.

When Spider-Man first appeared in the Marvel Universe, he was truly unlike any hero who had come before. He was not noble-born like the Sub-Mariner. Unlike the Fantastic Four, he had no headquarters and few resources with which to fight crime. In return for his efforts, he received no money and precious little thanks. Instead, he was just a lonely teenager, a nobody, until fate chose to grant him great power — a power he first

Origin
Amazing Fantasy #15
March 1962

Attempts to join FF
Amazing Spider-Man #1
March 1963

First Dr. Octopus
Amazing Spider-Man #3
July 1963

First Lizard
Amazing Spider-Man #6
Nov 1963

squandered at terrible cost to himself and those he loved. Humbled, this ordinary boy grew into a man who could never abandon the responsibility that had fallen upon him. He became Spider-Man, Marvel's most famous super hero.

The only child of Richard and Mary Parker, Peter Parker was orphaned at the age of six when his parents were killed while overseas on government business. Peter was left in the care of his elderly uncle and aunt, Ben Parker and May Parker, who unhesitatingly raised him as the child they never had. Peter was academically gifted, and he displayed an uncanny affinity for science that was nothing short of genius. Socially, however, he was painfully shy and the target of much cruelty. His uncle and aunt compensated with a steadfast love, but they worried privately what lay in store for the fragile boy.

A student at Midtown High School, Peter attended a public evening exhibition demonstrating the safe handling of nuclear laboratory waste materials. A spider, accidentally irradiated by a particle beam, fell onto Peter's hand and bit him. His hand burning from the wound, Peter left the exhibition in a daze and walked into the path of an oncoming car. Without thinking, Peter jumped onto the side of a wall, to which he stuck with his bare hands. Stunned, he realized he had acquired superhuman powers similar to those of a spider: enhanced strength and agility, and the ability to cling to almost any surface. Most incredibly, he had gained a sixth sense that provided him with early warning of impending danger.

To test his new powers, Peter donned a hastily made mask and took part in an all-comers wrestling match against Crusher Hogan, winning with ease. Spotted by a talent scout who promised to arrange a TV appearance, Peter hurried home and created a more elaborate costume, including his unique Web-Shooters. Thus was Spider-Man born. With his new powers and sudden fame, Peter promised himself he would take care of Uncle Ben and Aunt May. But the rest of the world — those who derided lonely science nerd Peter Parker — they were not his concern. So it was that following another TV appearance, when a Burglar ran past Spider-Man, pursued by a police officer, Peter did nothing to intervene.

Returning home one evening a few days later, Peter was horrified to discover Uncle Ben had been murdered — shot by an intruder. Spider-Man located the killer, discovering the criminal to be the same man he had failed to stop just days before. Filled with remorse, Peter finally understood that with great power, there must also come great responsibility. That was the first step on his path as a hero, though he did not immediately realize the true nature of his destiny. Unsure how to proceed, Spider-Man attempted to resume his show-business career, but was thwarted by J. Jonah Jameson's crusading editorials in the Daily Bugle. Failing to find paid employment with the Fantastic Four, Spider-Man battled the Chameleon to protect his reputation. It was not until Jameson offered a reward for photos of the Vulture that Peter recognized he could fulfill his debt to Uncle Ben by fighting crime, while selling photos of the action to pay his bills.

Spider-Man's heroic reputation grew quickly, and he found himself facing a bewildering array of super-villains: the Tinkerer, Doctor Octopus, the Sandman, Doctor Doom, the Lizard, Electro, the Enforcers, Mysterio, the Green Goblin and Kraven the Hunter. Before long, many of these villains turned their attention less to crime, instead seeking revenge on the web-slinger. Through it all, Peter sold photos of Spider-Man's battles to the Bugle, using the money to help Aunt May. Invariably, Jameson would seize on the photos to attack

Continued...

First Electro
Amazing Spider-Man #9
Feb 1964

Dr. Octopus returns
Amazing Spider-Man #11
Apr 1964

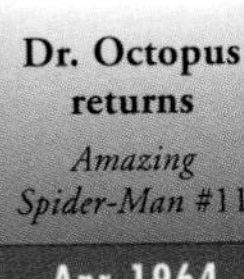

First Green Goblin
Amazing Spider-Man #14
July 1964

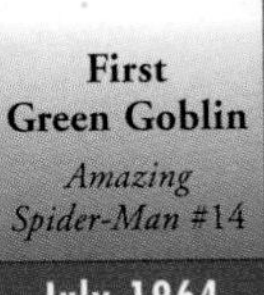

First Kraven the Hunter
Amazing Spider-Man #15
Aug 1964

Spider-Man's public image. Although unable to permanently destroy Spider-Man's reputation, Jameson has ensured the wall-crawler will never enjoy the overwhelming popular support he undoubtedly deserves.

With the new confidence his secret identity afforded him, Peter began to throw off his status as "puny" Parker, bookworm. Even the most popular girl in his class, Liz Allan (Liz Osborn), began to take an interest in him. Jealous, Liz's boyfriend, class bully and sports star Flash Thompson, challenged Peter to a boxing match and came out second best, leading to a new respect for his former victim. Peter also began dating Daily Bugle secretary Betty Brant. A shy girl, Betty was captivated by the peril that surrounded Peter's photography of Spider-Man. When that dangerous world cost her brother, Bennett Brant, his life at the hands of Blackie Gaxton, Peter understood for the first time the deadly threat Spider-Man presented to those he loved.

Art by John Romita Jr.

Peter struggled daily with the demands of his costumed identity, his part-time job, his Aunt's ever-worsening health and the Parker family's perpetual money woes. These worries left him with little time for friendships — yet he survived, and even flourished. He graduated from Midtown High a far more worldly and independent young man than many had predicted. By that time, he had faced dozens of deadly foes, who little suspected the Amazing Spider-Man to be a mere high-school student.

At Empire State University, Peter found a new life. After a fumbling start, he befriended fellow science majors Harry Osborn and Gwen Stacy. He also resolved his differences with Flash. Together, the four close-knit friends would often hang out at a café called the Coffee Bean.

As Peter emerged from his shell, Spider-Man clashed with ever more deadly opponents. Foremost among them was the Green Goblin, who managed to capture the hero and discover his secret identity. In the wake of a furious battle, the Goblin was revealed to be Norman Osborn, Harry's father. Norman was defeated, suffering amnesia as a result. Shortly after that classic conflict, Peter encountered the lovely Mary Jane Watson, who joined his circle of friends. But love bloomed instead between Peter and Gwen, leaving Mary Jane free to date Harry. While Flash joined the Army and was mobilized to Southeast Asia, Peter and Harry moved into a shared apartment downtown.

High-school graduation
Amazing Spider-Man #28
Sept 1965

Spider-Man unmasked
Amazing Spider-Man #39
Aug 1966

First Kingpin
Amazing Spider-Man #50
July 1967

"Spider-Man Wanted!"
Amazing Spider-Man #70
July 1969

Art by J.G. Jones

Life was not so great for Peter's alter ego. With Jonah Jameson fanning the flames of public outcry, Peter resolved to be Spider-Man no more. It was the first time he would abandon his commitment in frustration at his lack of public support, though certainly not the last. Yet his resignation did not last long. More than merely the sheer exhilaration of being a hero, Peter realized Spider-Man was an irrevocable part of the man he had become.

As the bond between Peter and Gwen grew ever stronger, it was observed approvingly by Gwen's father, police captain George Stacy, who also supported Spider-Man's efforts. But tragedy struck when a falling chimney crushed Captain Stacy, even as he saved an innocent child during a battle between Spider-Man and Doctor Octopus. With his dying breath, Captain Stacy told Spider-Man to "be good" to Gwen. The web-slinger had lost a great ally, and Gwen blamed Spider-Man for her father's death. Peter's conscience, already tormented by the ever-present need to lie to Gwen, became even more troubled. Yet their love prevailed through life's challenges — including Harry's drug addiction and Peter's aborted attempt to remove his own powers, which instead resulted in his transformation into the freakish Six-Armed Spider-Man.

In the end, it was death that separated the two lovers. The Green Goblin kidnapped Gwen and dropped her off the Brooklyn Bridge. Spider-Man tried to save her, but failed. In the vicious battle that followed, Norman was accidentally impaled by his Goblin Glider. Harry secretly observed his apparent death, swearing revenge on Spider-Man.

Harry soon succumbed to the Osborn legacy, kidnapping those Peter loved most — but Spider-Man prevented him from finishing the work Norman had started. Meanwhile, Peter and Gwen's college professor, Miles Warren, had begun his own deadly schemes as the Jackal. He blamed Spider-Man for the death of Gwen, with whom he had himself fallen in love. The climax of the Jackal's plan involved his creation of a Spider-Man clone — but at the conclusion of their battle, both the Jackal and the clone were believed killed. With their departure, Peter's life returned to normal, as much as it ever could for a college student who was secretly a costumed hero.

Continued...

Death of Capt. Stacy
Amazing Spider-Man #90
Nov 1970

Death of Gwen Stacy
Amazing Spider-Man #121
July 1973

Clone of Spider-Man (Ben Reilly)
Amazing Spider-Man #149
Oct 1975

Peter's college graduation
Amazing Spider-Man #185
Oct 1978

SPIDER-MAN

In the meantime, Peter and Mary Jane realized their relationship had become far more than just a friendship. Shortly before his college graduation, Peter proposed. But Mary Jane had seen too much pain in her own family, and she turned him down. She left New York to pursue her modeling career in Florida, and Peter moved on to post-graduate studies. It was a time for new challenges and new friends. But one thing would never change: the ever-present responsibility Peter faced as Spider-Man.

Peter's close college friends had begun to find their own lives. Liz Allan was dating a recovering Harry Osborn, and the two would later marry. Flash Thompson was searching for a life after football and the Army with his girlfriend, Sha Shan. Betty Brant had married Daily Bugle reporter Ned Leeds. Even Aunt May had found romance with Nathan Lubensky, a fellow occupant of the convalescent home into which she had moved. With Peter's friends and loved ones forming cozy couples, Mary Jane's departure was all the more unsettling. But it was not long before Peter began socializing again. He enjoyed several dates with Cissy Ironwood. Also, departmental secretary Deborah Whitman was attracted to Peter, but failed to win his heart. Undergraduate student Dawn Starr pretended to date Peter to sneak a peek at an upcoming exam. And Amy Powell tried to use Peter to make her boyfriend, Lance Bannon, jealous.

These women had one thing in common: Peter Parker. But when the Black Cat crossed Spider-Man's path, it was different. Felicia Hardy was beautiful, talented and determined. She was also an unrepentant burglar who harbored a romantic fascination with the web-slinging hero. Spider-Man persuaded Felicia to turn away from crime; the two soon became lovers — and crime-fighting partners. For her part, Felicia urged Peter to spend more and more time in costume. The glamorous Black Cat could never bear to see her hero living the squalid life of a graduate student. Spending swing time as Spider-Man had become easier, though, since Aunt May had recovered enough to return home and open the Parker residence as a boarding house for retired people, aided by Nathan.

Art by Terry Dodson

First Black Cat
Amazing Spider-Man #194
July 1979

Death of the Burglar
Amazing Spider-Man #200
Jan 1980

First black costume on Earth
Amazing Spider-Man #252
May 1984

Black Cat & Spider-Man break up
Spectacular Spider-Man #100
Mar 1985

Art by John Romita

There was always plenty of action for Spider-Man in New York, especially given the appearance of the deadly Hobgoblin and Peter's troubles with his symbiotic black costume. Aided by the Black Cat, Spider-Man faced Doc Ock and the Owl — a battle that nearly cost Felicia her life. Peter came crashing down to earth. He realized that without superhuman powers, Felicia was just like the others from his past who had so often paid the price for his activities as Spider-Man. When Mary Jane returned from Florida, she found Peter and the Black Cat embroiled in a shaky and tempestuous relationship. Felicia could not bear the thought of Peter's refusal to allow her to accompany him into battle, and she embarked on a secret search for superhuman powers at any price. Tricked by the Kingpin and twisted in her own deceit, the Black Cat finally parted ways with Spider-Man. In contrast, Mary Jane was determined not to let lies come between her and Peter. She finally told him she had known for some time about his secret identity.

With Spider-Man's secret finally out in the open, Peter and Mary Jane's relationship found new depth. As Spider-Man, Peter faced the death of his good friend, police captain Jean DeWolff, at the hands of the Sin-Eater. He watched as Flash Thompson was taken for a criminal, and Ned Leeds killed, both for their involvement with the Hobgoblin. But life was different now: He had Mary Jane by his side. Peter proposed for a second time, and she accepted. As newlyweds, Peter and Mary Jane shared happiness, but also faced many dangers. Mary Jane was menaced by Kraven the Hunter and imperiled by Venom, who knew Peter's secret identity. She loved Peter and admired his sense of responsibility. But she was unprepared for the loneliness, the fear and the nagging doubt that perhaps he needed Spider-Man far more than he needed her.

Among daily battles with New York's villains and the challenges of marriage, Peter was soon to face the inexplicable return of his parents. Long since believed dead, they claimed to have been held abroad as political prisoners. Aunt May was not ready to accept them, but Peter finally believed them to be who they claimed, even revealing his life as Spider-Man. But Peter's heart had over-ridden his instincts. The two were eventually exposed as robot agents of the Chameleon, part of a plan prompted by Harry Osborn before his death. Spider-Man was filled with anger at this deeply personal attack. It seemed to him that those he loved were fated to die, while the evil in his life would always return to haunt him. Darkness began to fill his heart, like never before.

Continued...

Wedding of Peter & Mary Jane
Amazing Spider-Man Annual #21
Oct 1987

First full Venom
Amazing Spider-Man #300
May 1988

Peter's parents return?
Amazing Spider-Man #365
Aug 1992

Death of Harry Osborn
Spectacular Spider-Man #200
May 1993

SPIDER-MAN

Still brooding over Harry's suicidal offensive against both the Osborn and Parker families, and the Chameleon's invasion of his life, Peter was faced with Aunt May's serious heart attack. With May in the hospital, not expected to recover, Peter's frustration at life's injustices boiled over into violence. Encountering the recently reformed and powerless Scorpion, Spider-Man cruelly beat his former foe close to death — ignoring his victim's pleas for mercy. It seemed Peter was beyond even Mary Jane's powers to heal him. In the end, his salvation came in the form of a near-death experience. Before Doctor Octopus cured him of the Vulture's poison, Peter realized how desperately he wanted to live. His recovery from his dark madness coincided with the return of a figure from Spider-Man's distant past: his clone, created by the Jackal.

The clone had survived his apparent death, wandering the country as Ben Reilly. Learning Aunt May was gravely ill, he returned to New York in time to watch her die. Ben adopted the costumed identity of the Scarlet Spider and portrayed himself as Peter's long-lost cousin. Peter and Ben became friends, almost brothers.

Art by J. Scott Campbell

Deceived by Dr. Seward Trainer, they later came to believe that Ben was the original, and Peter the clone. Ben subsequently assumed the role of Spider-Man when Peter temporarily lost his powers, leaving Peter and Mary Jane free to enjoy a normal life. Peter returned to his scientific career, though hampered by the fact that he never completed his doctorate. He and MJ also moved to Portland, until they realized New York was where they truly belonged.

But all too soon, their new world was shattered when Norman Osborn burst back into their lives. He also had survived his apparent death and was revealed to be the mastermind behind the Jackal's schemes. Peter's powers returned, but he could not stop Norman from killing Ben — proving him to be the clone after all. But his machinations ran even deeper: Aunt May was still alive. The woman who died had been an actress, part of a subtle plot never carried to fruition.

Reunited at last, Peter, Mary Jane and Aunt May moved into a luxurious apartment. Furthermore, the appearance of a new Spider-Man — actually Mattie Franklin, Spider-Woman III — allowed Peter to promise Mary Jane he would give up his career as a costumed hero. But Peter could not seem to keep his word. While an anonymous Stalker threatened Mary Jane, Peter broke his promise and returned to web-slinging. Mary Jane was distraught. She no longer felt needed, no longer felt part of Peter's life. Perhaps matters could have been resolved, but the opportunity vanished when an airplane supposedly carrying Mary Jane exploded.

"Power and Responsibility"
Web of Spider-Man #117
Oct 1994

Apparent death of Aunt May
Amazing Spider-Man #400
Apr 1995

Green Goblin returns
Peter Parker: Spider-Man #75
Dec 1996

Mary Jane's plane explodes
Amazing Spider-Man #13
Jan 2000

Peter felt lost. Aunt May returned home, while Peter became reacquainted with old friends Randy Robertson and Glory Grant, now a couple. Randy even allowed Peter to room with him for a while. But with Peter still emotionally adrift, Norman picked the perfect time to drug him and incite him to become his heir. Even lost and confused as he was, Peter proved he could not be tempted so easily.

Meanwhile, Mary Jane was not dead, but had been kidnapped by the Stalker. Spider-Man managed to rescue her, only to learn she had made her choice: She could no longer be with him. Mary Jane relocated to the West Coast, leaving Peter to struggle with a loss almost as traumatic as her apparent death. Stunned, he moved into a place of his own and resumed his bachelor lifestyle.

Peter turned to Aunt May, but she was devastated to discover his greatest secret: Visiting unannounced, she found him asleep following his grueling victory over Morlun — bloodied and battered, his shredded costume piled in a heap on the floor next to his bed. After coming to terms with Peter's double life, May is now his strongest supporter, and the two are closer than ever. May also prompted Peter to take up teaching. He returned to Midtown High — now a poor, urban school — where he teaches science part time.

With renewed hopes, Peter and Mary Jane have agreed to try once more to make their marriage work. After their time apart, Peter earnestly promised Mary Jane he truly needs her in his life.

In truth, it matters little what foes Spider-Man faces, what schemes his enemies concoct to bewilder him or even what he may learn from Ezekiel regarding the nature of his spider-powers. Peter's true strength comes not from a radioactive spider, but from far more enduring sources. The sense of responsibility inspired by Uncle Ben, the unwavering faith of Aunt May and the love he shares with Mary Jane. These are the powers that truly make Peter Parker a hero.

Art by J. Scott Campbell

Peter & Mary Jane reunited

Peter Parker: Spider-Man #29

Jan 2001

Spider-Man beats Morlun

Amazing Spider-Man #35

Nov 2001

"A Death in the Family"

Peter Parker: Spider-Man #44

Sept 2002

Peter & Mary Jane reconciled

Amazing Spider-Man #50

Apr 2003

SPIDER-MAN

Spider-Man holds a special place in the Marvel Universe. Fate gifted him with exceptional powers, then cruelly taught him the importance of using them unselfishly. With the ever-present challenges of his public and private lives, Spider-Man is perhaps unique in this world. But what about others? In alternate realities, current and future, Spider-Man can be found — changed, but clearly recognizable.

Art by Chris Batista

SPIDER-MAN 2099

In a dark future, mega-corporations control the planet. Society is deeply divided between those fortunates who live in structured comfort in the giant city towers and the lost souls who fight to survive Downtown, far below in the lawless foundations of the sprawling metropolis.

Miguel O'Hara was a brilliant but arrogant researcher, head of genetics for the cruel and corrupt Alchemax Corporation. When Alchemax attempted to ensure his loyalty through drug addiction, Miguel used his latest experiment to reset his own DNA.

He cured his addiction, but not without mutative side effects. Granted enhanced strength, agility and senses, he also developed retracting talons, venomous fangs and the ability to shoot organic webbing from his arms. With his new powers, he fights for vengeance, survival — and, occasionally, justice.

SPIDER-GIRL

In perhaps his cruelest blow, Norman Osborn had his agent, Alison Mongrain, cause Peter and Mary Jane's baby to be delivered stillborn. But what if that child, May Parker, had lived and grown to become Spider-Girl? On one alternate Earth, she does just that.

In this future, Peter and Mary Jane are happily married. Working as a police scientist, Peter has abandoned the world of costumed heroes after losing a leg in his final battle with the Green Goblin. As their daughter, May Parker, neared the end of high school, all she worried about was getting to basketball practice on time and deciding who to take to the prom. But when her father's genes kicked in, she suddenly found herself packing spider-powers — and itching to use them.

Secretly, May turned to her "uncle," Phil Urich, for training. But when her parents discovered their daughter was playing super hero, they were furious. Remembering full-well Peter's own brushes with death as Spider-Man, Peter and Mary Jane tried to talk May out of her budding crime-fighting career — but hard-earned lessons of power and responsibility were buried too deeply in the Parker family.

Now, with her father's tutorage and her parents' cautious blessing, the spirited young heroine faces her own villains — and some of her father's old foes. Aided by a new generation of super heroes, she ensures that Spider-Man's legacy lives on.

Art by Casey Jones

MANGAVERSE SPIDER-MAN

The world-famous wall-crawler gets a manga makeover. When his uncle, Benjamin-sensei, leader of the Spider-Clan, was murdered in cold-blood by Venom himself, young Peter Parker became the last surviving Spider-ninja. Having been trained in the martial arts since birth, Peter chose to emerge from the shadows and take his crime-fighting public. But to protect his identity and the lives of the people he loves, he decided to wear a mask to hide his face.

Mild-mannered Peter now tries his best to juggle his life as the high-flying costumed hero Spider-Man with his life as a straight-A high-school student. He just never expected the great lengths to which he would have to go to keep his alter ego hidden from his Aunt May and his girlfriend, Mary Jane Watson. It's hard enough being a teenager by day. Being a clandestine super-hero ninja at night is another story.

Art by Skottie Young

ULTIMATE SPIDER-MAN

How would a teenage Spider-Man fare in today's society? Stylishly re-created, the classic story of a young man granted powers beyond his wisdom is retold for a new generation.

In this world, Peter Parker gains his powers from the bite of a genetically altered spider. His selfish reaction leads once more to the tragic loss of Uncle Ben. But from there, the tale diverges in fresh and unexpected directions. Peter's bite occurs during a school visit to Oscorp and does not go unnoticed by Norman Osborn's agents. Osborn himself becomes involved and uses a similar process to grant himself the powers of the Green Goblin, able to transform into a giant clawed beast of fearsome proportions.

Spider-Man also faces the Kingpin, Electro, the Lizard, Doctor Octopus, Kraven, the Rhino and many other familiar foes ... in new and unfamiliar circumstances. He is eventually forced to battle Norman, under the watchful eye of Nick Fury of S.H.I.E.L.D., an agency that exerts great control over super-powered agents in this mutant-fearing world.

In the Ultimate universe, Peter has revealed his secret identity to his girlfriend, Mary Jane Watson. But their relationship is shaken when Peter's Aunt May takes in Gwen Stacy, recently having suffered the death of her father. Complicating matters further, Peter learns that his father was working before his death to create a cure for cancer — an encompassing, living skin that could protect its wearer. When the "cure" spawns a life of its own, Ultimate Venom is born.

This is Ultimate Spider-Man, and everything old is new again.

Art by Mark Bagley

SPIDER-MOBILE

First Appearance:
Amazing Spider-Man #130 (1974)

Art by Ross Andru

In an early attempt at marketing synergy, Carter and Lombardo, two advertising executives representing Corona Motors' new non-polluting engine, decided Spider-Man would be the ideal spokesperson to promote the groundbreaking product.

Under threat of eviction for his overdue rent, Spider-Man reluctantly accepted their cash offer to promote the engine. But there was a catch: He was also expected to construct a car to house it.

Rising to the challenge, Spider-Man designed the hottest car imaginable in its time — a two-seater dune buggy complete with roll bars, bucket seats, halogen headlights and sand-tires.

Lacking the tools and mechanical know-how to actually build the vehicle, Spider-Man turned to friend and hot-rod fanatic the Human Torch for help. Together, the wall-crawler and the one-man welding machine constructed the Spider-Mobile just as planned, with some last-minute extras: built-in spider-signal, pop-up web-shooters, driver-side ejector seat and the personalized license plate ... "SPIDEY."

With the Human Torch flying overhead, Spider-Man set out for his first spin. As the web-head wreaked havoc on the snowy streets of downtown Manhattan, the Torch asked the one all-important question the advertising executives never considered: "Hey, Spidey, can you drive?"

A few days later, after some lessons, Spider-Man took the vehicle out on a real mission — tackling Hammerhead, a few of Doctor Octopus' henchmen and a couple police officers.

On his second outing in the overtly conspicuous Spider-Mobile, Spider-Man attracted unwanted police attention again. As the car barreled down a narrow alleyway, Mysterio II — in a bid to drive Spider-Man into madness — compelled the hero to believe he was on a road when he was actually on a pier, sending Spider-Man and the Spider-Mobile plunging into the river. Spider-Man swam to safety, leaving the Spider-Mobile in what he thought was its watery grave.

The end? Not quite. Unknown to Spider-Man or Mysterio, the Tinkerer dredged the car out of the water, made a few lethal adjustments and used the remote-controlled vehicle in a mercenary attempt to assassinate Spider-Man. Narrowly surviving, Spider-Man webbed up the mangled wreckage and returned it to Carter and Lombardo — with his compliments.

SPIDER-MORPHOSIS

POWERS/WEAPONS

- All the powers of Spider-Man, with even greater strength and durability

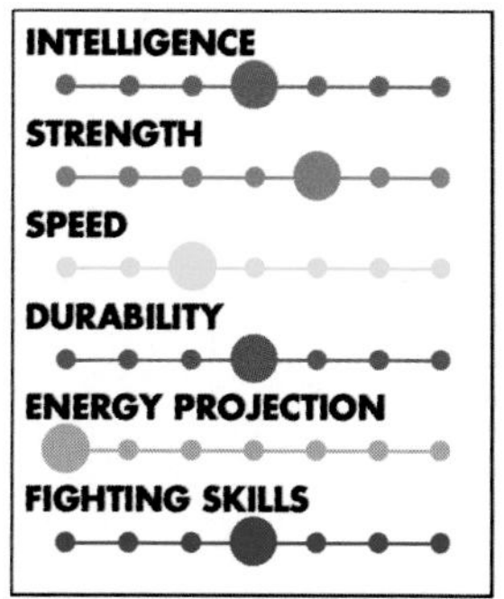

Real Name: Peter Benjamin Parker
First Appearance: *Amazing Spider-Man* #437 (1998)

Hgt: 6'2"
Wt: 290 lbs.

Seeking revenge against the mutant students of Generation X for a previous defeat, Plantman infected Synch with a mutagenic pollen — causing him to grow into a giant, misshapen beast. Spider-Man confronted the rampaging Synch, but was also trapped by Plantman and underwent a metamorphosis of his own. Though transformed into a giant man-spider with multiple eyes and talons for hands, Spider-Man fortunately retained his intellect and was able to force Plantman to produce the antidote by exposing him to the same mutagenic pollen.

SPIDER-PHOENIX

POWERS/WEAPONS

- All the powers of Spider-Man
- Apparent ability to harness the Phoenix Force, the near-limitless cosmic energy granting Phoenix her powers

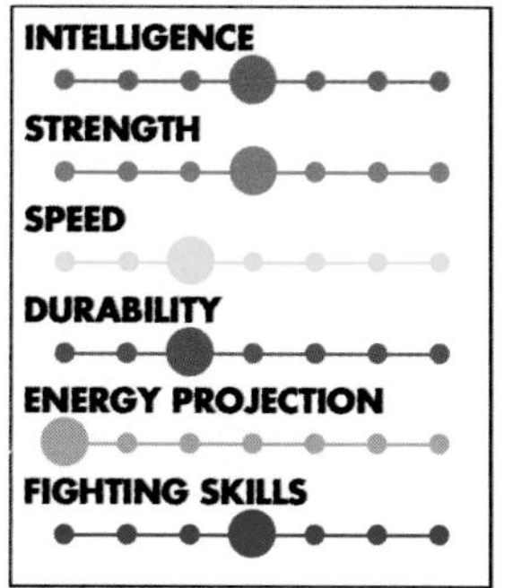

Real Name: Peter Benjamin Parker
First Appearance: *Spider-Man* #25 (1992)

Hgt: 5'10"
Wt: 165 lbs.

Spider-Man and Captain Britain were lured together, each appearing as the Juggernaut to the other. Initially, it seemed as though Nightmare and D'Spayre were responsible for the illusion — and when they apparently killed Phoenix, Captain Britain's teammate, Spider-Man rose from the ashes of the battle as the Spider-Phoenix. With the web-slinger seemingly in command of the Phoenix Force, a flood of his most notorious foes attacked — and the situation deteriorated rapidly into confusion. It was finally revealed that the entire scenario had been an illusion created by Arcade, using advanced alien technology he had won in a trade with a visiting off-world soldier.

SPIDER-SIGNAL

First Appearance: *Amazing Spider-Man* #3 (1963)

Attached to the center of Spider-Man's utility belt is his spider-signal, a powerful lamp that shines a red-light image of the wall-crawler's mask. He most often uses it to announce his presence to criminals, to rattle their nerves. The signal also doubles as a flashlight for searching shadowy tunnels for reticent villains or missing persons. Plus, it's great for sneaking a peek at secret files — or even simply annoying J. Jonah Jameson.

SPIDER-SLAYERS

First Appearance: *Amazing Spider-Man* #25 (1965)

A machine devoid of pity, fear, conscience and remorse — tasked with only one goal: the destruction of Spider-Man. Piece by piece, component by component, each newer, more ruthless Spider-Slayer comes one step closer to perfecting the mechanics of hands-free murder.

VERSION I

Version I was a biped with extensible legs developed by Spencer Smythe, with funding from J. Jonah Jameson. Featuring a near-inexhaustible power supply and a web-resistant oil coating, it was remote-controlled via an embedded video feed. A screen and loudspeaker displayed the face and voice of its operator. The robot tracked Spider-Man with a "hyper-sensitive Geiger-type apparatus" and unleashed auto-sensing steel tendrils to trap him. Spider-Man defeated it by removing its chest plate with his fingertip suction.

VERSION II

Version II was humanoid in shape. Larger and more powerful than its predecessor, its controls were far more sensitive, and it was built to track anything with a spider's scent. Capable of climbing walls and armed with a "destructo-beam," Version II was slow — but seemingly unstoppable. Spider-Man defeated it by confusing it among many spiders. Smythe then applied full power, which destroyed the robot.

VERSION III

Version III was a giant, steel spider. Capable of shooting steel webbing, climbing walls and striking with uncanny speed, this robot was faster, stronger and deadlier than Spider-Man himself. It also featured a nullifier, blocking Spider-Man's spider-sense. This prototype possessed the power to defeat the web-slinger, but Smythe had other plans for it. As New York City's scientific adviser, he had persuaded the mayor to establish a network of video cameras throughout Manhattan. Jameson thought he was guiding the robot to conquer Spider-Man, but Smythe actually led the battle to the lab housing the network's master control unit. When the robot stole the device and returned to Smythe, Spider-Man was left to take the blame.

VERSION IV

With unlimited access to the city's video cameras, Smythe found himself in a position to get away with virtually any crime. Impressed, the local gang lords fell in line behind him. When he was ready to attack Spider-Man, Smythe called upon Version IV — a full-sized iteration of Version III. This creature was so large its inventor could ride inside it. Equipped with an ethyl-chloride spray that weakened the web-slinger, the Slayer captured Spider-Man — who only escaped when Smythe became distracted by his master plan and was forced to trust the robot to defeat the hero unguided. It failed.

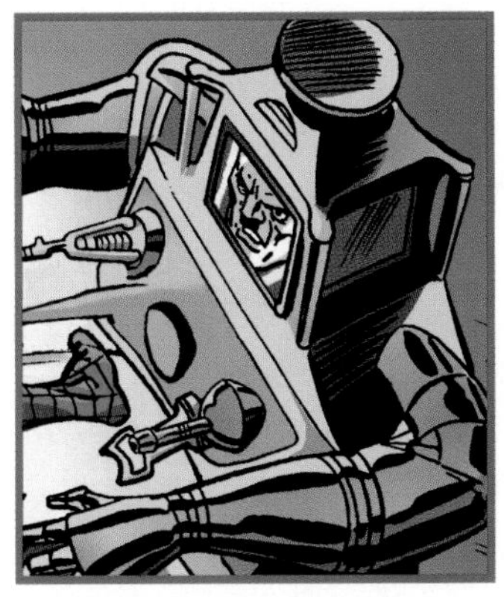

VERSION V-VII

With Smythe now marked as a criminal, Jameson enlisted Empire State University electro-biologist Dr. Marla Madison to create a new Spider-Slayer. Version V was modeled after Version II, but was larger. A psycho-cybernetic helmet, not physical controls, operated it. The robot also featured grappling and cutting devices housed in its chest plate. Spider-Man trapped it underneath a heavy statue, and Madison built no other Spider-Slayers. The final Spencer Smythe Slayer, Version VI, was another large, spider-shaped robot, but with no human rider. Mentally controlled by Smythe, it successfully captured Spider-Man as part of the professor's final revenge on Jameson and the wall-crawler — though it was destroyed in the process. Smythe died shortly afterwards, and his son, Alistair Smythe, took up the role of Spider-Slayer architect. Alistair's first effort was an eight-legged flying vehicle — equipped with laser beams and metal, whip-like arms. Spider-Man lured Version VII into power lines, short-circuiting it and crippling Alistair.

VERSION VIII

Alistair later sought revenge with a giant biped Spider-Slayer featuring extensible limbs and a flexible neck. The robot carried Alistair and his wheelchair in its chest cavity. It was nearly unbeatable — but when Alistair threatened Mary Jane Watson, Spider-Man smashed through the chest plate and extracted the terrified operator.

VERSION IX-XVIII

Alistair was then remanded to an institution for criminally creative minds. He escaped, forcing other brilliant inmates to join him — including Max Young, former assistant to Mendel Stromm. After using hand-sized scout spiders (Version IX) to prepare the scene, Alistair launched a series of vicious Slayers: a tiger Slayer (Version X), a flying Slayer (Version XI) and a heavily armed humanoid Slayer (Version XII). Young then unleashed his amoeboid Slayer (Version XIII), followed by a giant multi-faced Slayer (Version XIV) that reflected all three of his split personalities; they eventually attacked one another. Alistair's final offensive consisted of three insect-like Spider-Slayers (Versions XV-XVII) that could merge into one fighting unit (Version XVIII). Spider-Man electrocuted those creatures after the Black Cat used her claws to cut through their insulation.

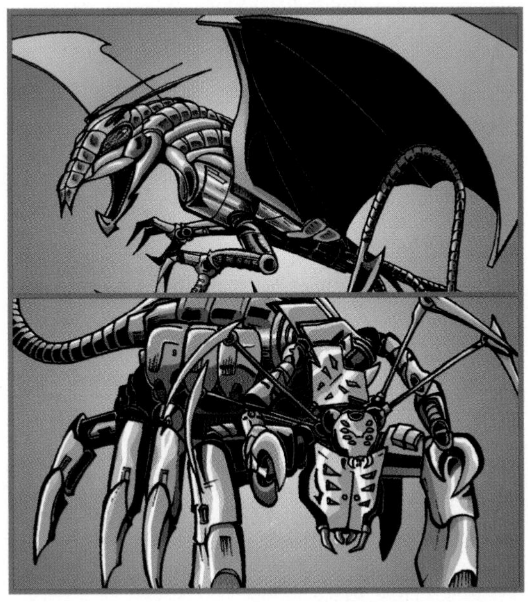

VERSION XIX

Alistair later attacked Spider-Man with a robot army consisting of a replica of every Spider-Slayer ever created. This was the warm-up for a massively powerful, four-armed humanoid Slayer (Version XIX) that could track Spider-Man's emotions and target those he loved most. But again, threatening Spider-Man's family proved to be Alistair's downfall: Spider-Man turned to face the creature, wrecking it with his bare fists.

SPIDER-TRACERS

First Appearance: *Amazing Spider-Man* #11 (1964)

Having already developed his Web-Shooters and Spider-Signal, and acquired his automated camera, Spider-Man added the final and perhaps most underestimated piece of equipment to his toolkit.

Peter Parker developed the Spider-Tracer specifically to track Doctor Octopus, who was due to be released from prison after serving a short sentence. Responsible for his initial capture, Spider-Man was sure Otto Octavius would immediately return to his criminal ways. He therefore sought some mechanism to keep tabs on the devious Doctor.

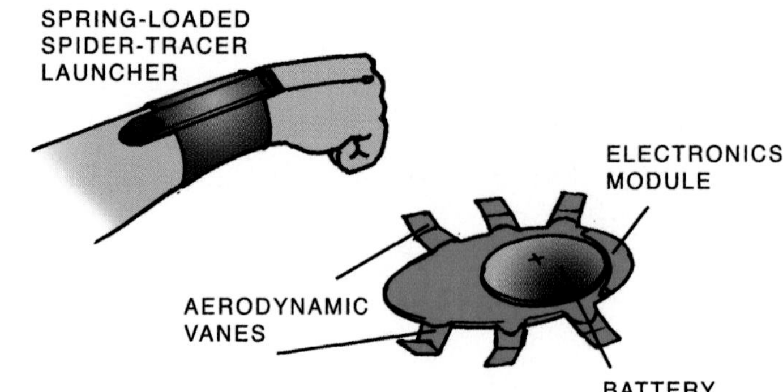

In fact, Spider-Man was right to be suspicious. Within minutes of his release, Doctor Octopus resumed his life of crime — ultimately resulting in the death of Betty Brant's only brother, Bennett Brant. Though Spider-Man was too late to save Betty's brother, he did manage to capture the man responsible thanks to the newly invented tracer.

Becoming a standard piece of Spider-Man's equipment, these cunning devices can be tracked at short-to-medium range. Each micro radio transmitter is embedded in a tiny, spider-styled casing. The legs of the casing are actually aerodynamically shaped fins that aid in throwing and placement.

The coded signal sent by the original tracers required a separate, portable unit to track. This battery-powered tracking unit was somewhat bulky, and had a limited operational period and range. Through experimentation and analysis, Peter modified the tracers to transmit on a coding and frequency his spider-sense could detect without requiring additional equipment.

Art by Steve Ditko

The tracers can be placed or thrown. At one stage, Peter developed a wrist-launcher that fired them at high velocity. The tracers are coated in a sticky substance to keep them firmly attached to their targets.

A downside of the tracers is that once discovered, they become a simple way to lure the hero into a trap — so Spider-Man always makes his final approach with care when following one of the gadgets. Of more concern is the fact that those who understand the technology well can modify them to overload Peter's spider-sense.

As well as their value in secretly tracking vehicles and individuals, Spider-Man has, on occasion, given tracers to his friends and allies — instructing them to activate the devices should they require his aid.

SPIDER-WOMAN

Jessica Drew is the daughter of Jonathan Drew, research partner to the High Evolutionary. After their discovery of valuable uranium deposits, the two scientists used their vast wealth to construct a fantastic artificial city. Wundagore was a virtual utopia for the Drews, until Jessica fell ill with uranium poisoning.

With his daughter near death, Dr. Drew was forced to inject Jessica with his untested spider serum and place her in the High Evolutionary's genetic accelerator. Sealed in the machine for years, Jessica awoke with no memories of her past, unaware that her father had died or even of her true identity.

Scared and alone, Jessica fled into a nearby village. Startled by a villager, she unleashed her strange new bioelectric venom blast, killing the man instantly. On the run from a vengeful mob, Jessica was rescued by Count Otto Vermis, who molded her into the terrorist organization Hydra's newest assassin. As Arachne, she fought S.H.I.E.L.D. director Nick Fury, who revealed Vermis as a cold-blooded killer.

After finally learning the truth of her origins from the sorcerer Modred the Mystic, Jessica left Hydra and relocated to the U.S. West Coast. She worked by day as a private investigator and by night as a reluctant super heroine. As Spider-Woman, Jessica tangled with an unusual array of villains.

Spider-Woman encountered her male counterpart many times — and like Peter Parker, Jessica demonstrated superhuman strength and the ability to cling to walls. Unlike Spider-Man, she possessed a deadly bioelectric sting, could glide on air currents in her costume, and was immune to venoms and radiation. Spider-Woman has temporarily burned out some of her original powers: She sacrificed her immunities to save the life of the Avengers' Giant-Man, and extinguished her bioelectric sting in battle against the sorceress Morgan le Fay.

Continuing to work as a private investigator when it appeared her costumed identity had been retired permanently, Jessica allied with Madame Web to mentor Mattie Franklin (Spider-Woman III). But Mattie's recent drug addiction and Jessica's return to full power make it ever more possible that Jessica may one day resume her role as Spider-Woman.

Real Name:
Jessica Drew

First Appearance:
Marvel Spotlight #32 (1976)

Height:	5'10"
Weight:	130 lbs.
Eye Color:	Green
Hair Color:	Black

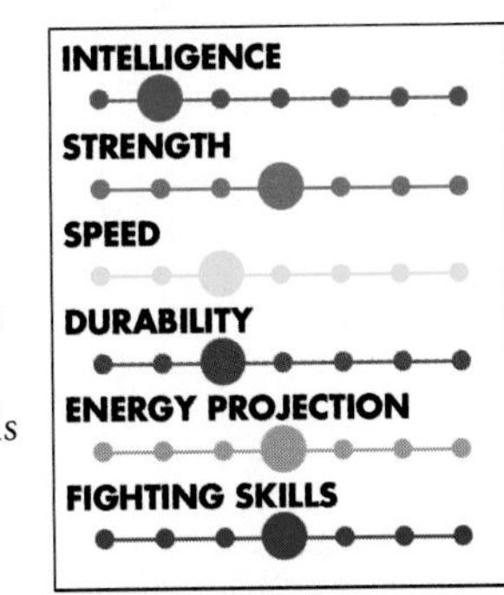

Art by Art Adams

POWERS/ WEAPONS

- Enhanced strength
- Wall-crawling
- Can glide on air currents
- Bioelectric venom-blast
- Immunity to poisons and radiation

SPIDER-WOMAN II

Real Name: Julia Carpenter
First Appearance: *Marvel Super Heroes Secret Wars* #6 (1984)
Hgt: 5'9"
Wt: 140 lbs.

POWERS/WEAPONS

- Superhuman strength
- Psionic webbing

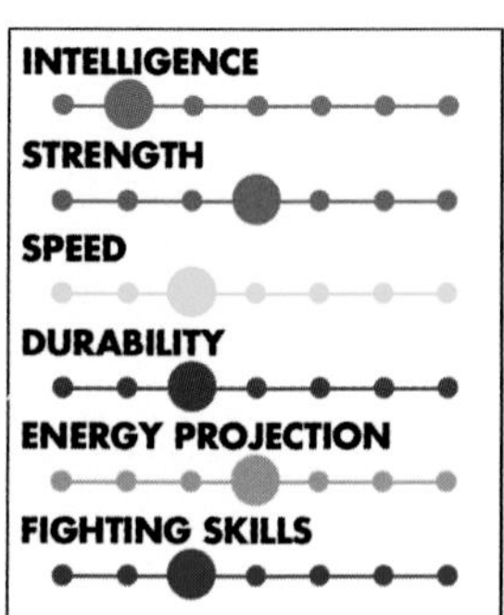

Tricked by Valerie Cooper, a former friend turned cynical government agent, Julia Carpenter became an experimental test subject for the state, receiving her powers from modified spider venom. Shortly thereafter, she encountered Earth's super heroes — including Spider-Man — when her suburb of Denver was transported to the Beyonder's patchwork world. After serving the government for a time, she tired of being a pawn and instead became a key member of the West Coast Avengers. Her costumed career was cut short when the villainous Spider-Woman IV removed her powers. Julia is currently raising her daughter, Rachel.

SPIDER-WOMAN III

Real Name: Martha "Mattie" Franklin
First Appearance: *Amazing Spider-Man* #441 (1998)
Hgt: 5'8"
Wt: 123 lbs.

POWERS/WEAPONS

- Flight
- Invulnerability
- Enhanced strength and agility
- Psychic spider-legs

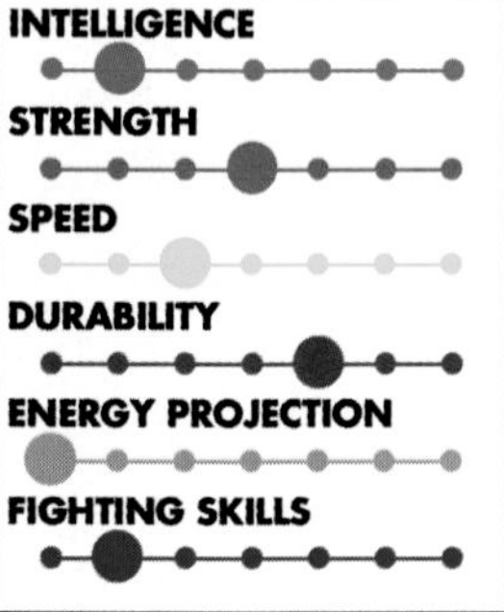

When Jeremy Franklin declined participation in the Gathering of Five ritual with former business associate Norman Osborn (Green Goblin), his daughter took his place. Acquiring the gift of power, Mattie Franklin disguised herself for a time as her favorite hero, Spider-Man. Aided by Madame Web and both previous Spider-Women, Mattie went on to establish her own identity as the new Spider-Woman. In that role, she battled many menaces, but with little sense of purpose or direction. Abandoning her career as a super hero, she was later abducted by drug traders — until her rescue by private investigator Jessica Jones and Jessica Drew (Spider-Woman).

SPIDER-WOMAN IV

Real Name: Charlotte Witter
First Appearance: *Amazing Spider-Man* #5 (1999)
Hgt: 5'10"
Wt: 150 lbs.

POWERS/WEAPONS

- Psychic spider-legs
- Power siphoning
- Hypnosis of Spider-Man
- Accelerated healing factor

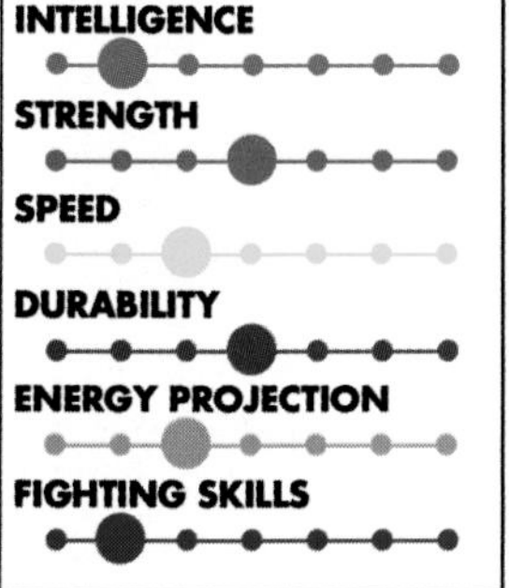

Granddaughter of Madame Web, Charlotte Witter was a reputable fashion designer until Doctor Octopus kidnapped her, granted her superhuman abilities and made her his deadly agent. Charlotte siphoned the powers of the previous three Spider-Women, then attacked Spider-Man and discovered his secret identity. Mattie Franklin's abilities returned, and Spider-Woman III teamed with Spider-Man to defeat Charlotte. The two cleared their minds, starving her of the mental energy off which she feeds and causing her to fall into a coma. Charlotte is under the care of Madame Web, who erased her memory of Spider-Man's identity.

SPINDRIFTER

POWERS/WEAPONS

- Magic, spellcasting and energy manipulation
- Flight via poncho
- Intelligent flying ship, the Nonesuch

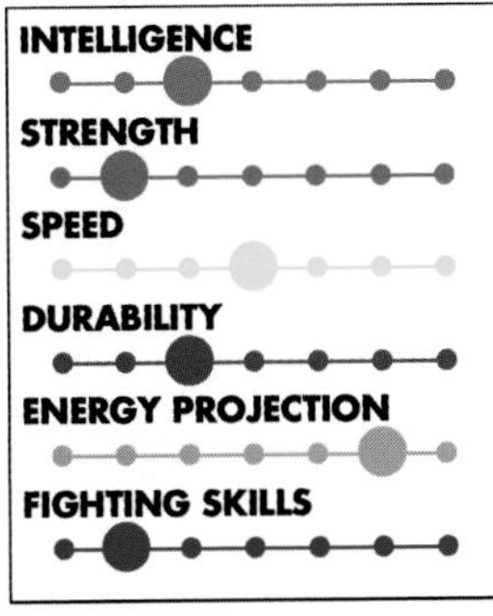

Real Name: Marandi Sjörokker
First Appearance: *Spider-Man: Hooky* (1986)

Hgt: 5'0"
Wt: 100 lbs.

Marandi Sjörokker is the daughter of an evil sorcerer named Kurudred from the dimension of Cloudsea. When the League of Three Threes killed Kurudred, he protected Marandi by casting a spell of youth. After 207 years as a 12-year-old human, she found herself plagued by the Tordenkakerlakk — the Thunder Cockroach — which became more powerful with each defeat. Marandi summoned Spider-Man to help her, but he could not prevail against the beast. Spider-Man correctly guessed that Kurudred had created the monster as his legacy, to force Marandi to expose her true powers and break the spell of youth. With Spider-Man's encouragement, she did just that.

SPOT

POWERS/WEAPONS

- Can open portals in space, through which he and others can fully or partially travel

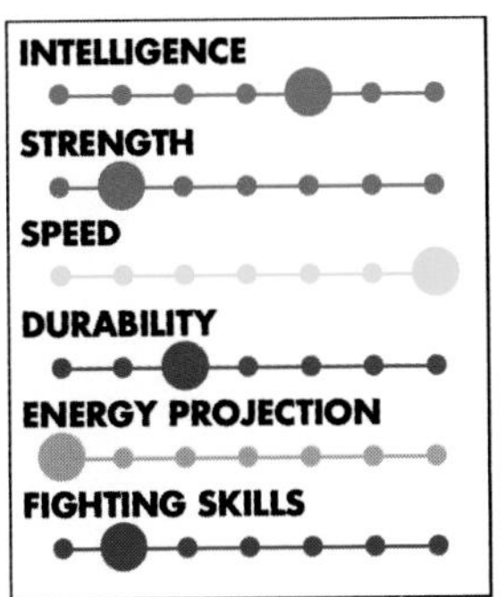

Real Name: Dr. Jonathan Ohnn
First Appearance: *Spectacular Spider-Man* #96 (1985)

Hgt: 5'10"
Wt: 170 lbs.

A former scientist for the Kingpin, Dr. Jonathan Ohnn's experiments into Cloak's Dark Dimension provided him with the ability to teleport by opening portals in space. The newly dubbed Spot ran afoul of Spider-Man and the Black Cat, who defeated him between laughs. He later returned — unsuccessfully teaming with the Gibbon, Kangaroo II and the Grizzly. The Spot briefly became caught up with the Gideon Trust, a crooked corporation that planned to pillage the otherdimensional realm known as the Negative Zone with his help. After a stay in prison, he helped Tombstone make a jailbreak. As thanks, Tombstone snapped his neck.

ARTHUR STACY

Real Name: Arthur Stacy
First Appearance: *Amazing Spider-Man* #95 (1971)

Hgt: 6'0"
Wt: 185 lbs.

Arthur Stacy was head of security for Oscorp subsidiary Osborn Chemical during the appearance of the Proto-Goblin. Later serving as a government agent under the codename Seeker, he partnered with Ranger and Sentry (the future Senator Stewart Ward). As head of a private-investigative firm, Arthur returned to Forest Hills from Hong Kong with his children — Paul Stacy and Jill Stacy — to investigate the death of his brother, George Stacy. Arthur met Spider-Man several times, and the two developed a trusting relationship. When Ward — now a Senator — revealed he was trying to start an epidemic using an alien pathogen, Arthur, Ranger and Spider-Man joined forces to save humanity.

GEORGE STACY

Real Name:
Captain George Stacy
First Appearance:
Amazing Spider-Man #56 (1968)

Height:	6'1"
Weight:	190 lbs.
Eye Color:	Blue
Hair Color:	Gray

Little did Peter Parker know after falling in love with Empire State University classmate Gwen Stacy that her father was one of the most respected former police officers in the NYPD, Captain George Stacy. But even in retirement, Captain Stacy kept up with the goings-on of the department — and had taken a keen interest in Spider-Man.

It wasn't long before John Jameson called Captain Stacy out of retirement to assist in the return of a device called the Nullifier — which could render any electrical or mechanical apparatus inoperative — that Doctor Octopus had tricked an amnesiac Spider-Man into stealing. After safely securing the weapon, Captain Stacy interviewed Peter Parker, believed to have been held captive by Doc Ock and Spider-Man. During the interview, Captain Stacy revealed to Peter that he had spent time studying the career of Spider-Man, and that he was glad to have met Peter, known for photographing the wall-crawler on numerous occasions.

Identifying himself as a strong supporter of Spider-Man, Captain Stacy wished to see the wall-crawler redeemed in the public eye. He also took an instant liking to Peter, and openly encouraged the growing bond between the youngster and Gwen.

After several more encounters with Spider-Man and Peter, Captain Stacy started to suspect the two were one. Wary of anyone making the connection, Peter began taking increasingly drastic measures to throw Captain Stacy off the trail — even asking the Prowler to imitate Spider-Man so Peter and the web-slinger could be seen together. But Captain Stacy, ever the consummate law-enforcement agent, could not be fooled.

Called into action one night, Captain Stacy watched Spider-Man battle Doctor Octopus on a rooftop high above the city. A crowd had gathered nearby to watch the confrontation. As the two fought fiercely, chunks of concrete began to dislodge from the roof and rain on the spectators below. Spotting a child standing under the trajectory of falling masonry, Captain Stacy leapt to cover the boy — and paid for his act of heroism with his own life. Abandoning the fight, Spider-Man swung down in time to hear Captain Stacy's final words: "Be good to her son! Be good to her. She loves you so very much."

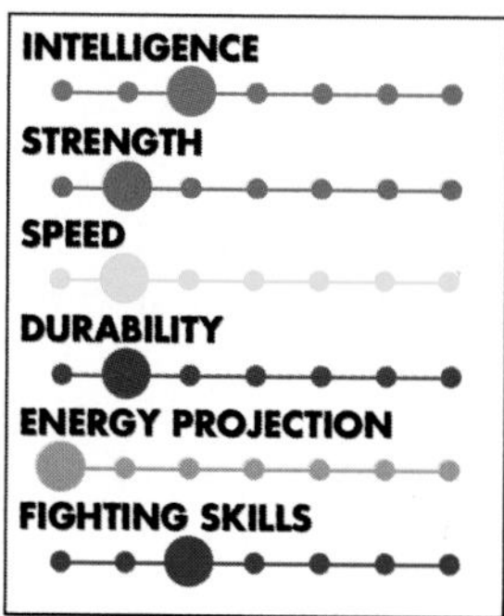

Art by Gil Kane

GWEN STACY

Everybody remembers their first love. For Peter Parker, it would be impossible to forget Gwen Stacy.

Gwen came to Empire State University from Standard High School, where she had been the resident glamour girl. Arriving at ESU, she and fellow science major Harry Osborn befriended jock Flash Thompson. Flash attempted to introduce Harry and Gwen to Peter, his high-school classmate, during their first chemistry lab. When a preoccupied Peter unintentionally ignored Flash and his new friends, popular Gwen and wealthy Harry did not take kindly to the perceived snub. Spitefully, Harry sabotaged Peter's lab experiment — setting the stage for a rocky start to their eventual friendship.

Peter had too much on his plate to worry about building friendships at school. His aunt, May Parker, was recovering from radiation poisoning; he was still licking his wounds from recent battles as Spider-Man against Kraven the Hunter, the Molten Man, the Looter, Mendel Stromm and the Green Goblin; and he had just broken up with girlfriend Betty Brant.

Over time, Peter reconciled with Gwen, Harry and Flash — transcending his reputation as a standoffish scholarship student. Despite her friends' misgivings about the bookish Peter, Gwen's intuition told her there was more to him than met the eye.

Gwen's emotional breakthrough occurred after Peter turned up at ESU one day on his new motorcycle — a move that greatly surprised her and the rest of the gang. Having just defeated the Green Goblin, Peter was riding high — and for once, free of his many problems. Re-examining her previously held opinion, Gwen found in her heart a true romantic attraction — one Peter clearly returned.

Their budding relationship was immediately tested by the arrival of Mary Jane Watson — the glamorous niece of Aunt May's friend, Anna Watson. An aspiring model, Mary Jane quickly fell in with Peter's crowd and took an interest in the young man — causing tension between her and Gwen. But Mary Jane was far too wild and free to settle her heart on any one man, and Gwen knew right away Peter was the one for her. The pair soon surrendered to their irresistible love.

But because of Peter's hidden life as Spider-Man, it was clear their love affair would never run smoothly. Missed dates, unexplained absences, secrets he could never tell — all these

Continued...

Real Name:
Gwendolyn Stacy
First Appearance:
Amazing Spider-Man #31 (1965)

Height:	5'7"
Weight:	130 lbs.
Eye Color:	Blue
Hair Color:	Blonde

INTELLIGENCE
STRENGTH
SPEED
DURABILITY
ENERGY PROJECTION
FIGHTING SKILLS

Art by Tim Sale

GWEN STACY

things conspired to cast his relationship with Gwen as a roller-coaster of confusion, tears and reconciliation. But Gwen's wise father, police captain George Stacy, warmly approved of Peter and did what he could to help keep the two young lovers together.

Unfortunately, George Stacy was killed protecting an innocent child during a battle between Spider-Man and Doctor Octopus, and a bereaved Gwen held the hero responsible. With the pressures on Gwen and Peter's relationship greater than ever, their love proved true and strong. They swore they could overcome anything. Anything, perhaps, except fate.

Once Norman Osborn, the Green Goblin, recovered his memory of Peter's identity, he burned with a desire for revenge against Spider-Man. Hitting the wall-crawler where it would hurt most, the Goblin kidnapped Gwen and carried her to the top of the Brooklyn Bridge. Spider-Man arrived and was horrified to find the woman he loved in the hands of his nemesis. Peter blazed into battle, but his ferocity was not enough to prevent Norman from pushing Gwen off the bridge.

In his last, desperate act to save the love of his life, Spider-Man fired a slender web-line that caught Gwen by her ankle. Raising her up, Spider-Man discovered she was already dead. The Goblin taunted Peter and told him that Gwen had been killed by the shock of falling. But Peter was tormented by nightmares in which he imagined she had been killed by the sudden jolt of his web-line as it caught her. He was haunted by the thought that maybe he could have saved Gwen's life if he had acted differently.

Even though Spider-Man's subsequent confrontation with the Green Goblin ended in Norman's apparent death at the hands of his own remote-controlled Goblin Glider, Peter's anguish did not die so readily. Peter's love for Gwen lives on in his memory and deep within his heart, even though his love for Mary Jane has long since become the guiding force in his life.

Art by Tim Sale

JILL STACY

INTELLIGENCE
STRENGTH
SPEED
DURABILITY
ENERGY PROJECTION
FIGHTING SKILLS

Real Name: Jill Stacy
First Appearance: *Peter Parker: Spider-Man* #76 (1997)

Hgt: 5'9"
Wt: 135 lbs.

Cousin of the late Gwen Stacy, Jill Stacy moved to New York City with her father and brother, Arthur Stacy and Paul Stacy. She befriended Peter Parker and Mary Jane Watson, taking classes with MJ at Empire State University. When Jill sought to understand the events surrounding Gwen's death, a hesitant Peter eventually told her his side of the story. Jill was nearly killed when caught in the crossfire during an attack on the Parkers' home in Forest Hills masterminded by Norman Osborn (Green Goblin). When it appeared Mary Jane had died, Jill made romantic overtures toward Peter, but withdrew when MJ was found to be alive.

PAUL STACY

INTELLIGENCE
STRENGTH
SPEED
DURABILITY
ENERGY PROJECTION
FIGHTING SKILLS

Real Name: Paul Stacy
First Appearance: *Peter Parker: Spider-Man* #76 (1997)

Hgt: 6'0"
Wt: 185 lbs.

Brilliant but arrogant, Paul Stacy entered Peter Parker's life as a condescending tutor at Empire State University. Bitter toward Spider-Man over the deaths of his beloved cousin and uncle, Gwen Stacy and George Stacy, Paul joined the Friends of Humanity — an anti-mutant hate group that believed Spider-Man to be a mutant. Confronted by Robin Vega, a mutant classmate, Paul abandoned the Friends. When chapter leader Donovan Zane hired the Shocker to kill Paul, the Trapster joined the chase, and glued Paul and Spider-Man together. Norman Osborn (Green Goblin) coerced Zane to call off the attack, desiring his own revenge on the web-slinger.

STALKER

POWERS/WEAPONS

- Precognition
- Telepathy
- Unique mental bond with Spider-Man
- Explosive psychic blasts

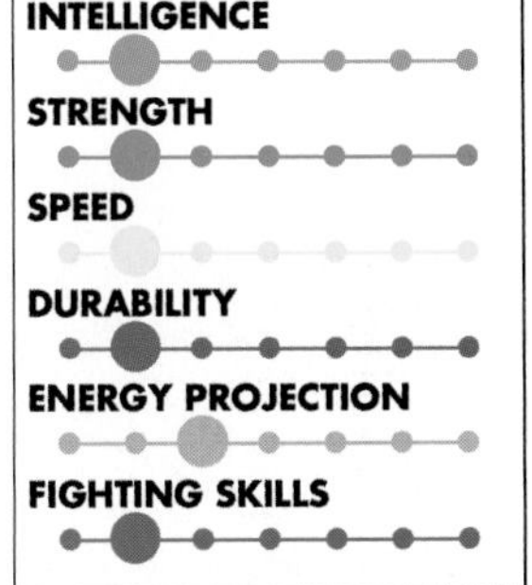

Real Name: Unrevealed
First Appearance: *Peter Parker: Spider-Man* #10

Hgt: 6'0"
Wt: 185 lbs.

When Spider-Man rescued a latent psychic from falling debris, the man who would come to be known as the Stalker acquired the web-slinger's memories — and established a permanent, one-way mental bond with the hero. Over time, he developed an obsession to replace Peter Parker as Spider-Man. He began stalking Mary Jane Watson, and then blew up an airplane on which she was supposed to be a passenger — having abducted her before takeoff. When Spider-Man finally located Mary Jane, the Stalker attacked him. Absorbing Peter's consciousness, he recognized his own inability to wield his great power responsibly. The Stalker abandoned his plan, apparently exploding himself.

MENDEL STROMM

Real Name:
Mendel Stromm
First Appearance:
Amazing Spider-Man #37 (1966)

Height: 5'10"
Weight: 150 lbs. (25 lbs. as cyborg head)
Eye Color: Blue, yellow cyborg eye
Hair Color: None

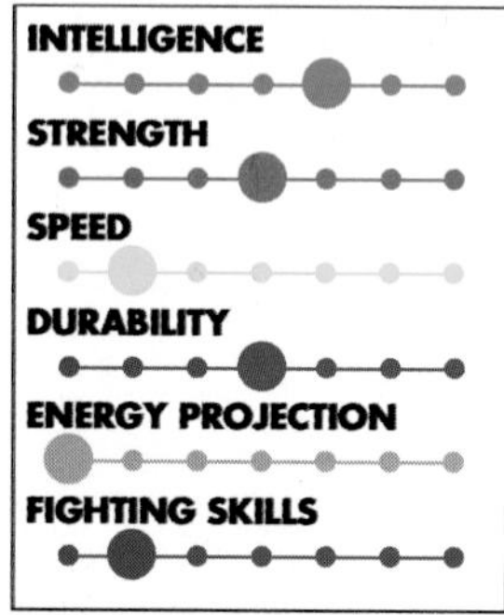

POWERS/ WEAPONS

- Master robot builder
- Limited regeneration from physical wounds via prototype Goblin Formula

Mendel Stromm and Norman Osborn were business partners until Stromm was convicted of defrauding their company and sentenced to ten years in prison. With Stromm behind bars, Osborn gained control of the industrial research firm. But Stromm was innocent: Osborn had framed the professor and cheated him out of his inventions. Upon his release, Stromm constructed two robots and used them to destroy Osborn's lab. Spider-Man later defeated the mechanoids and cornered Stromm, now calling himself the Robot Master. Before Stromm could reveal that Osborn was the Green Goblin, Spider-Man's spider-sense alerted him to the presence of a sniper. As Spider-Man rushed to the window, the assassin fled. But the shock of his brush with death was enough to seemingly kill Stromm, even without the undetected Goblin pulling the trigger.

Stromm was not dead. His self-testing with the prototype Goblin Formula had granted him the same recuperative powers as Osborn. Suspecting this, Osborn had Stromm's body exhumed and restored his wasted corpse to a semblance of life, encapsulated in a giant robotic mechanism acting as both battle armor and life-support system. As Gaunt, Stromm served Osborn until his destruction during a battle involving Ben Reilly. An armorless and memory-damaged Stromm eventually returned to his lab, where he and his remaining robots battled Spider-Man one last time before he was remanded to Ravencroft Institute. Stromm later escaped and attempted to build the ultimate thinking robotic system, which would become one with him.

As he slept, the system did his distorted bidding, removing his limbs and then his torso, leaving only his head connected to a life-support system and cerebro-electrical interface. Battling for control over the rogue AI, Stromm contacted Spider-Man and begged the web-slinger to kill him before his lethal software creation gained control of the world data network. With help from, Shea Tinker, a hacker friend of Randy Robertson, Spider-Man managed to put Stromm into standby mode while he searched for a more permanent solution.

Art by Mike Wieringo

Art by Steve Ditko

Art by Mark Buckingham

STEGRON

Real Name: Dr. Vincent Stegron
First Appearance: *Marvel Team-Up* #19 (1974)

Hgt: 6'2"
Wt: 610 lbs.

POWERS/WEAPONS

- Superhuman strength and speed
- Prehensile tail
- Bulletproof dinosaur hide
- Able to control dinosaurs

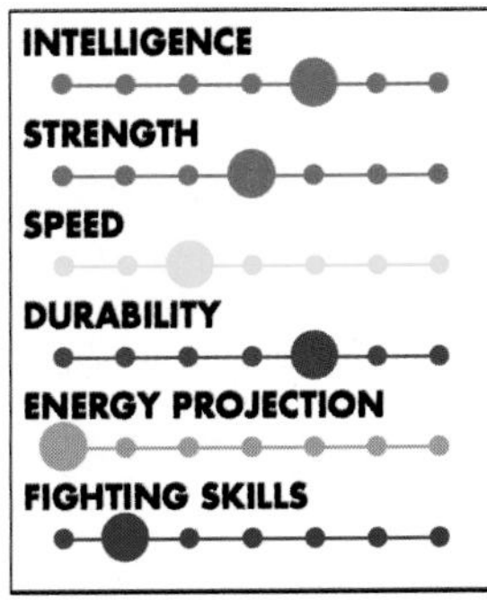

Dr. Vincent Stegron was hired by S.H.I.E.L.D. to work with Dr. Curt Connors and study dinosaur DNA from the time-forgotten Savage Land. Stegron stole cell samples from Connors and created a variation on the latter's Lizard serum, transforming himself into a dinosaur-like man-monster. Clashing with Spider-Man, Ka-Zar and the Black Panther — warrior king of the advanced African nation Wakanda — he attacked New York City, leading an army of dinosaurs from the Savage Land. Stegron sank in the East River, however, entering suspended animation. He has returned to clash with Spider-Man on several occasions.

STUNNER

Real Name: Angelina Brancale
First Appearance: *Amazing Spider-Man* #397 (1995)

Hgt: 5'8"
Wt: 302 lbs.

POWERS/WEAPONS

- Superhuman strength, leaping ability, agility and endurance

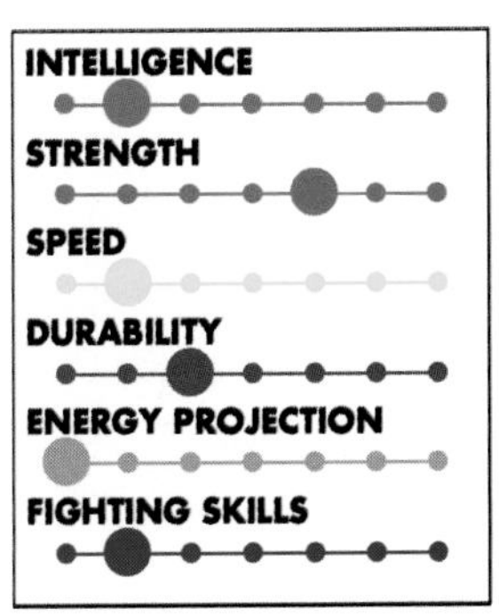

Chosen to test virtual-reality technology for Doctor Octopus and Dr. Carolyn Trainer, obese Angelina Brancale projected her consciousness into the beautiful body of Stunner. She and Octopus subsequently fell in love, and she helped the world-weary villain save Spider-Man from a chemical virus. But Kaine killed Doc Ock, and Stunner sought vengeance. When the True Believers stole Doctor Octopus' body, Trainer recruited Stunner to help recapture his corpse. After transferring Spider-Man's essence into Octopus failed, Stunner volunteered her own life force. Octopus was revived, but Stunner's VR body was destroyed — leaving her physical self on life-support.

STYX & STONE

Real Name: Jacob Eichorn (Styx) and Gerald Stone (Stone)
First Appearance: *Amazing Spider-Man* #309 (1988)

Hgt: Styx: 6'2" / Stone: 5'9"
Wt: Styx: 134 lbs. / Stone: 200 lbs.

POWERS/WEAPONS

- Absorption of others' life forces and decay of organic matter by touch (Styx)
- Body armor, turbo-hopper vehicle and diverse weaponry — including gas pellets, sonics and nova beam (Stone)

Attempting to develop a cure for cancer, medical researcher Gerald Stone experimented on Jacob Eichorn — a homeless man paid to act as a guinea pig — inadvertently mutating him and warping his mind. Stone determined to look after Eichorn — who took the name Styx, having gained the power to absorb the life forces of those he touched. The two became mercenaries, entering the employ of Jonathan Caesar and coming into conflict with Spider-Man. They later encountered Venom and Cardiac, but finally decided to abandon work-for-hire and concentrate on pure crime. They were foiled again by Spider-Man.

SUNDOWN

Real Name: David Patrick Lowell
First Appearance: *Untold Tales of Spider-Man Annual 1997*
Hgt: 6'3"
Wt: 225 lbs.

A research scientist at Oscorp subsidiary Osborn Labs, all David Lowell really wanted was to care for his plants — and teach his young neighbor, Mary Kelleher, to do the same. Instead, Lowell mutated himself after Norman Osborn (Green Goblin) cut off funding for his "photogenesis" project. Confused and angry, Sundown battled — and nearly defeated — the combined forces of virtually every super hero in New York City. He surrendered after accidentally crippling Mary. Paroled years later, he was saved by Spider-Man from becoming a pawn of Lucky Lobo and made a new start on life.

POWERS/WEAPONS

- Absorption of light and heat to gain vast powers — including strength, growth, flight and energy blasts

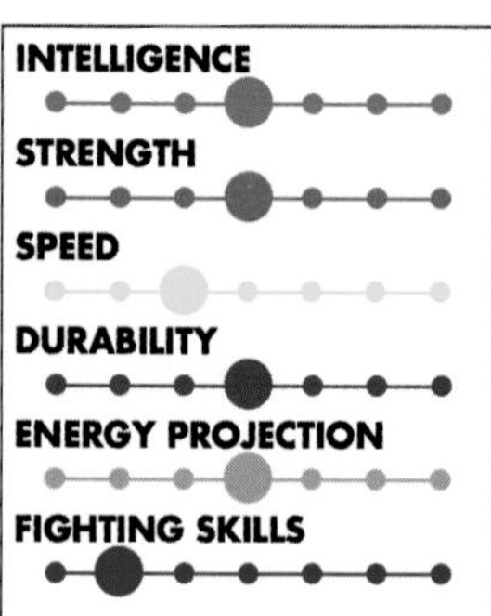

SUPER-SKRULL

Real Name: Kl'rt
First Appearance: *Fantastic Four* #18 (1963)
Hgt: 6'0"
Wt: 625 lbs.

Granted the amplified abilities of the fabled Fantastic Four — plus hypnosis — by the scientists of his alien homeworld, the Super-Skrull has attempted on many occasions to destroy Earth's first family of super heroes on behalf of the Skrull Empire. His missions have brought him into conflict with other superhumans, as well — including Spider-Man, who fought him off with the aid of Ms. Marvel. The two heroes temporarily trapped him in Earth's Van Allen Radiation Belt, from which it took the Super-Skrull years to escape. The Super-Skrull was also stricken with the alien equivalent of leukemia for a time.

POWERS/WEAPONS

- Superhuman strength, flight, invisibility, plasticity and fiery blasts
- Hypnosis
- Shape-changing

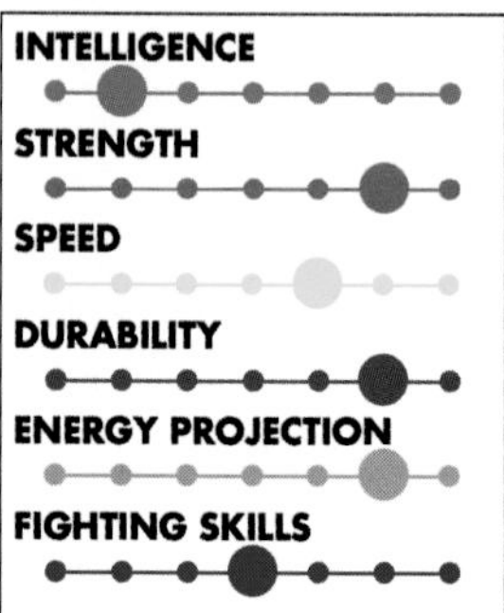

SWARM

Real Name: Fritz Von Meyer
First Appearance: *Champions* #14 (1977)
Hgt: 6'5"
Wt: Indeterminate

A former Nazi scientist, Fritz Von Meyer fled to South America following World War II and began studying killer bees. Attempting to control the insects via a psionic beam, he was instead completely consumed by a maddened swarm — but became their master in the process. Swarm has sought to conquer the world on several occasions — meeting defeat at the hands of super-hero teams such as the Champions of Los Angeles and the Secret Defenders, as well as Spider-Man. The web-slinger employed such tactics as webbing impregnated with bee repellant and disrupting Von Meyer's psychic link to the swarm.

POWERS/WEAPONS

- Body composed of several hundred thousand bees
- Flight
- Immunity to conventional attack

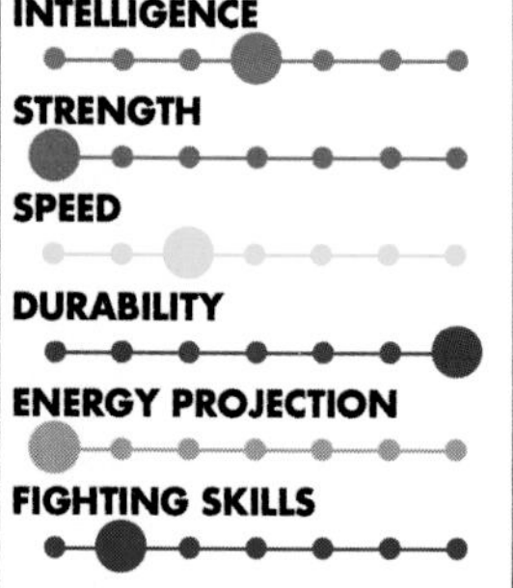

SYMBIOTE

Real Name:
Not Applicable
First Appearance:
Marvel Super Heroes Secret Wars #8 (1984)

Height:	N/A
Weight:	25 lbs.
Eye Color:	N/A
Hair Color:	N/A

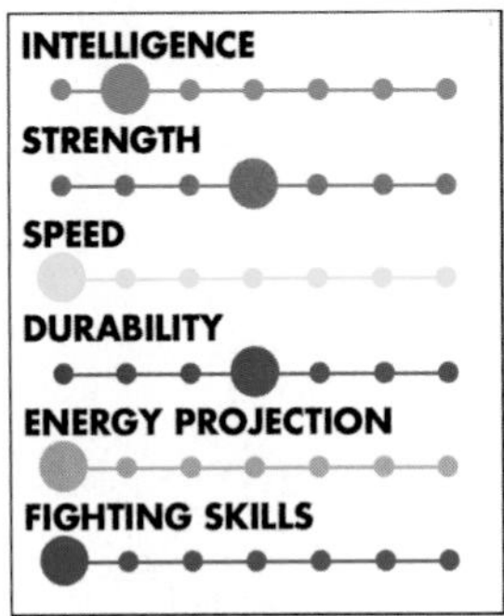

Discovering our universe — and having never known want — the supremely powerful being known as the Beyonder was curious to learn of desire, as demonstrated by the people of Earth. He created a planet, assembled Earth's mightiest heroes and villains, and forced them to fight for need and greed. In an alien fortress on that planet, Spider-Man happened upon a machine he believed could help him replace his tattered outfit. The device released a black blob that spread up his arm, covered his body and transformed into a black costume. Spider-Man soon discovered the outfit possessed the power to generate webbing; upon his return to Earth, he learned it also could alter its appearance to mimic other, more conventional clothing. Unknown to Peter, as he slept at night, the costume possessed his body and patrolled the city as Spider-Man. Awakened in the morning, Peter would feel listless, vague and unrefreshed by the previous night's "sleep."

Alarmed by the side effects of this strange outfit, Spider-Man visited Reed Richards of the Fantastic Four, who discovered the costume was a living symbiotic organism. Richards was able to remove the costume by force only after finding it vulnerable to fire and extreme sound waves. Placed in captivity in a sealed chamber, the Symbiote escaped to seek other hosts — but none proved as satisfying as Spider-Man's vital life force. The Symbiote returned to Peter's apartment and reclaimed its original host. Spider-Man made his way to a church tower, where the sound of the bells forced the Symbiote from him. The Symbiote slithered away, and found a new host in the form of Eddie Brock. Now joined together, the deadly pair became Venom.

The Symbiote was later revealed as a member of an entire race, known for leeching their way across whole galaxies. The Symbiote that possessed Spider-Man and Eddie Brock was an anomalous and particularly virulent entity, deemed insane by its peers for choosing to bond with its host rather than destroy it.

POWERS/ WEAPONS

- Transformation of appearance
- Formation into blunt or dull-edged weapons
- Protection of its host

Art by John Romita Jr.

TARANTULA

Real Name: Anton Miguel Rodriguez
First Appearance: *Amazing Spider-Man* #134 (1964)
Hgt: 6'1"
Wt: 185 lbs.

POWERS/WEAPONS

- Peak-human strength and fighting ability
- Retractable, poison-dipped claws and boot-spikes

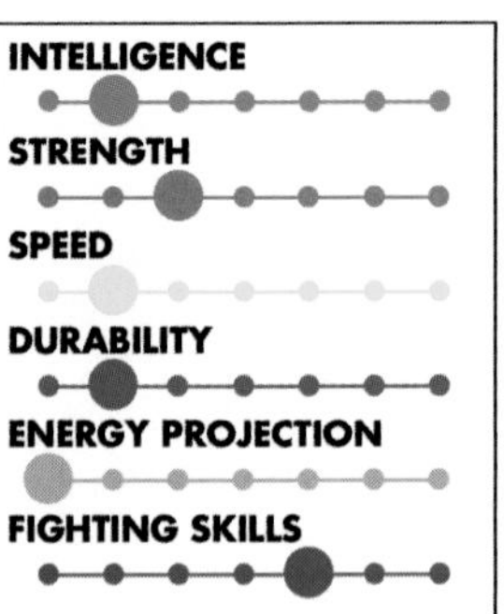

Anton Miguel Rodriguez was a South American revolutionary fighting to free his country, Delvadia, from an oppressive dictatorship. The business of this revolution necessarily involved destruction, kidnapping and robbery — but it was clear Rodriguez enjoyed his work. His gratuitously violent and indiscriminate tendencies became too much for his compatriots to accept, and they forced him out. Rodriguez was gratefully accepted by the dictatorship, which gave him the costumed identity of the Tarantula and a deadly set of poison-tipped spiked shoes. But when he killed a fellow officer who would not permit him to beat a prisoner to death, he found himself on the run from all his former allies.

Rodriguez fled to the United States and embarked on a criminal career. His first deed was robbery and kidnapping aboard a harbor-going tourist ship. By chance, the vessel was carrying Peter Parker; by design, it was also carrying the Punisher, who was on the Tarantula's trail. The Tarantula successfully escaped with the valuables of those on board, but Spider-Man and the Punisher foiled his hostage-taking plans. They then tracked him down, defeating the Tarantula and his costumed cronies. In prison, the Tarantula was able to re-make his spiked shoes and escape, with the aid of the Jackal. In return, he helped the Jackal in his persecution and attempted execution of Spider-Man. After the Jackal's apparent death, the Tarantula teamed with the professional assassin Señor Suerte, only to be foiled by Captain America. Subsequently, he was hired by Lightmaster to perform a series of kidnappings, and was unwillingly and unsuccessfully teamed with Kraven the Hunter.

Furious at yet another defeat by Spider-Man, the Tarantula agreed to undergo an experiment meant to re-create Spider-Man's powers. Will O' the Wisp disrupted the experiment, and the Tarantula emerged an eight-limbed, spider-like creature with limited intelligence. Distraught, the Tarantula threw himself into a barrage of police bullets. His daughter inherited his costume and equipment, and was killed by the Taskmaster during her first and only outing.

TARANTULA II

Real Name: Luis Alvarez
First Appearance: *Web of Spider-Man* #36 (1988)
Hgt: 6'2"
Wt: 190 lbs.

POWERS/WEAPONS

- Peak-human strength and fighting ability
- Retractable, poison-dipped claws and boot-spikes

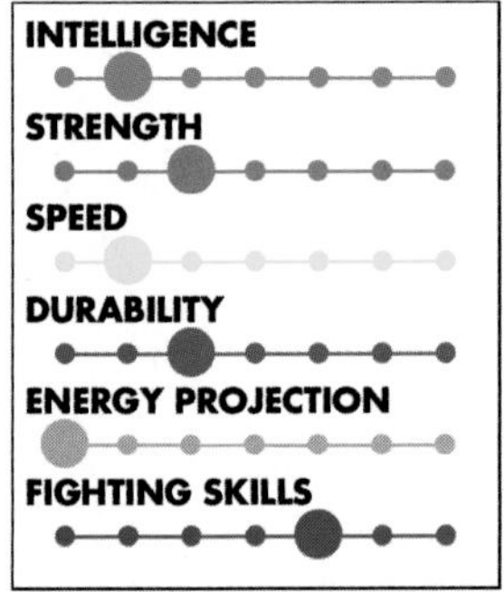

Following the death of Anton Rodriguez, the government of Delvadia employed Luis Alvarez. Equally bloodthirsty, Alvarez also possessed greatly enhanced strength thanks to the Red Skull's mimicked Super-Soldier Serum. He was sent to America to kill Delvadian political refugees, and to destroy Spider-Man for killing the original Tarantula. John Walker, Captain America at the time, was tricked briefly into aiding the Tarantula against Spider-Man, but discovered the truth in time to avoid tragedy. Alvarez was eventually captured and tried by the Jury. Several of his former victims provided testimony, and the vigilante force's newest recruit, Wysper, summarily executed Alvarez.

TASKMASTER

POWERS/WEAPONS

- Can expertly mimic the abilities of others

INTELLIGENCE
STRENGTH
SPEED
DURABILITY
ENERGY PROJECTION
FIGHTING SKILLS

Real Name: Unrevealed
First Appearance: *Avengers* #195 (1980)

Hgt: 6'2"
Wt: 220 lbs.

With the power to perfectly duplicate any fighting style he observes, the Taskmaster is an expert in countless forms of combat. Besides working as a hired gun himself, he trains henchmen for other criminals — teaching them how to counter the super heroes he has studied. His protégés have included the so-called Evil Versions: Bloodspider, Deathshield and Jagged Bow. The Taskmaster has faced Spider-Man on a number of occasions, often battling the web-slinger and his fellow heroes together. In exchange for a commuted sentence, the government used the Taskmaster to train John Walker to replace Captain America. Despite brief incarcerations, he remains at large.

TEACHER

INTELLIGENCE
STRENGTH
SPEED
DURABILITY
ENERGY PROJECTION
FIGHTING SKILLS

Real Name: Unrevealed
First Appearance: *Web of Spider-Man* #40 (1988)

Hgt: 5'5"
Wt: 135 lbs.

A consummate con artist, the Teacher formed the Students of Love — a cult that promised peace and harmony to its members, but actually brainwashed them into subservience. Upon joining, initiates would turn over all their worldly possessions to the cult. Betty Brant fell victim to the cult's manipulations shortly after the death of her husband, Ned Leeds, but Flash Thompson and Spider-Man rescued and deprogrammed her, aided by Reverend Tolliver. In the process, the Teacher's most violent acolyte, pyromaniac Brother Bruce, burnt down the cult's commune — killing himself and the Teacher when they were trapped in the flames.

THOUSAND

POWERS/WEAPONS

- Ability to transfer hosts
- Hollow body, filled with spiders
- Paralyzing bite

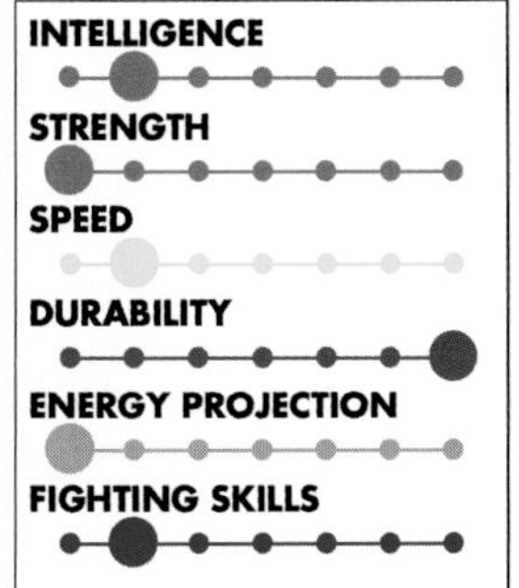

Real Name: Carl King
First Appearance: *Spider-Man's Tangled Web* #1 (2001)

Hgt: Variable
Wt: Variable

At Midtown High School, Carl King bullied fellow student Peter Parker. After witnessing the infamous spider-bite that transformed Peter into Spider-Man, Carl followed his classmate and discovered his secret. Overtaken by an intense jealously, Carl doubled back and ate the arachnid. He found himself transformed into a horde of spiders, which consumed his body from within. Carl's jealousy became hatred; jumping from host body to host body, he grew more powerful over the years. He finally confronted Peter and attempted to consume him, but was instead electrocuted. One single spider survived — enough to start all over again, if not for the careless step of a passer-by.

FLASH THOMPSON

Real Name:
Eugene "Flash" Thompson
First Appearance:
Amazing Fantasy #15 (1962)

Height: 6'2"
Weight: 185 lbs.
Eye Color: Blue
Hair Color: Reddish Blond

INTELLIGENCE
STRENGTH
SPEED
DURABILITY
ENERGY PROJECTION
FIGHTING SKILLS

At Midtown High School, Flash Thompson was the Big Man on Campus. A promising football star, Flash was confident, popular and envied by all. While Peter Parker protected his secret identity by pretending to disapprove of Spider-Man, Flash became the web-head's greatest supporter and established a fan club in his honor.

Surprised when his girlfriend, Liz Allan (Liz Osborn), developed a crush on Peter, Flash initiated a series of schoolyard threats against his rival. When their teacher suggested they settle the matter in the boxing ring, both agreed. Not wanting to risk exposing his secret identity by defeating his larger opponent, Peter demurred somewhat. However, with Flash distracted by an external interruption at precisely the wrong moment, Peter took a fortuitous swing. To the crowd, it looked as though Flash had been sucker-punched. At that point, Flash's distaste for "puny" Parker transformed into a more equal rivalry.

After graduation, Flash and Peter both went on to Empire State University. With Liz moving elsewhere, Flash eventually warmed to Peter; the two freshmen ended up becoming friends. They were part of a regular crowd — including Gwen Stacy, Harry Osborn and Mary Jane Watson — that often hung out at the Coffee Bean when not attending class. Flash later joined the Army and was stationed in Southeast Asia. There, he fell in love with a local, Sha Shan, who came to the United States and became part of Flash's circle of friends. They later separated, and Flash subsequently had an affair with Betty Brant, wife of Ned Leeds. After Flash called the Hobgoblin a coward on television, Roderick Kingsley took revenge by framing him as the villain. Flash was cleared only after onlookers witnessed him help Spider-Man in a battle against the real Hobgoblin.

Art by Tim Sale

After college, Flash lost his way in life. His football career collapsed when his arm was injured during his fight with the Hobgoblin, and his relationship with Betty encountered difficulty following her husband's death. Stumbling through a series of menial part-time jobs, Flash — no stranger to the dangers of drink — became an alcoholic. Flash's father had been a popular public figure, but was privately a violent drunkard toward his family. With Flash struggling on the precipice, Norman Osborn (Green Goblin) offered him a job and wielded his influence in an attempt to destroy Flash's respect for Spider-Man. When that plan eventually failed, Norman framed Flash in a drunken-driving accident to send a violent message to Spider-Man, leaving Flash in a coma. Though his friends are frequent visitors, only time will reveal Flash's fate.

TINKERER

The Tinkerer's ability to invent and construct all manner of mechanical and electrical devices is in the same league as that of the Fantastic Four's Mister Fantastic and the Avengers' Iron Man. However, where those noble men have dedicated their immense creative talents to the protection of mankind, the Tinkerer uses his skills primarily to bolster his bank account — and occasionally in the name of revenge.

The Tinkerer created myriad gadgets and weapons such as the Maggia's Acidroid and Hammerhead's exoskeleton — in addition to inventions used by the Beetle, the Hobgoblin, Big Wheel, the Scorpion and the Black Cat. The Tinkerer makes his money based on sales alone and rarely engages in violent criminal activity himself.

The Tinkerer bears the distinction of being one of the first handful of villains Spider-Man faced. Peter Parker stumbled across the Tinkerer one day at "The Tinkerer Repair Shop." Aided by his spider-sense, Peter eventually realized the Tinkerer and his alien assistants were modifying the radios in the Tinkerer's shop to collect secrets from key members of the state and private industry.

Though Spider-Man foiled their plans for planetary invasion, the hero wound up holding nothing more than a rubber mask of the Tinkerer's face as he tried to capture the fleeing aliens. Only years later would Spider-Man discover the truth: The Tinkerer and his head assistant, Quentin Beck (Mysterio) had been stealing secrets purely for private gain; the alien costumes were an elaborate, and seemingly effective, ruse to throw any infiltrators off their trail.

After unsuccessfully seeking revenge against Spider-Man, the Tinkerer subsequently returned to his tried-and-true method of operation, selling arms and equipment, and allowing others to do his dirty work — until criminals murdered his son, Rick Mason. Phineas sought vengeance on the crooked lawyer — Michael Hart, now a respected judge — who had helped acquit one of his son's murderers, hoping to uncover incriminating documents in his apartment he could leak to the press. But when Hart and his wife returned home unexpectedly, Phineas accidentally killed Alice Hart — then, panicked, shot Michael dead. Never a killer, the Tinkerer revived Michael, now imbued with strange supernatural abilities following his trip to the other side. As the vigilante called the Judge, he found himself compelled to seek justice against the guilty, to balance the scales for his own mistakes — aided and abetted by a remorseful Tinkerer. Making up for a lifetime of creating weapons, the Tinkerer finally found a purpose, something to live for in his lonely, gray years.

Real Name:
Phineas Mason
First Appearance:
Amazing Spider-Man #2 (1963)

Height:	5'8"
Weight:	175 lbs.
Eye Color:	Gray
Hair Color:	White

INTELLIGENCE
STRENGTH
SPEED
DURABILITY
ENERGY PROJECTION
FIGHTING SKILLS

POWERS/ WEAPONS

- Master inventor of countless lethal and non-lethal devices
- "Toy," a humanoid robot protector and assistant

Art by Steve Ditko

TOMBSTONE

Real Name:
Lonnie Thompson Lincoln
First Appearance:
Web of Spider-Man #36 (1988)

Height:	6'7"
Weight:	215 lbs.
Eye Color:	Pink
Hair Color:	White

In one of life's cruel jokes, Lonnie Thompson Lincoln was Harlem's only African-American albino. He was relentlessly taunted for his strange looks, until he responded to the jeers with shockingly cruel violence. Only classmate Joseph "Robbie" Robertson was willing to see Lonnie as more than a brutal thug. Their friendship lasted until Robbie wrote an exposé of Lonnie's criminal behavior for the school newspaper, and Tombstone intimidated his former friend into scrapping the story.

After high school, Robbie — now a professional reporter — witnessed Tombstone kill a man. Terrified, Robbie kept silent about the murder for twenty years, until his conscience compelled him to speak. Tombstone went to prison for the killing, and Robbie soon joined him — sentenced by the Kingpin's tame judge for suppression of evidence in the case. In prison, Tombstone made life miserable for Robbie. When Tombstone found an opportunity for escape, he dragged his old friend with him. On the run as fugitives, Tombstone threatened an innocent family. Enraged by Tombstone's unrestrained cruelty, Robbie impaled Lonnie with a pitchfork. In shock but still alive, Tombstone simply walked away from the fight. Robbie was pardoned of all crimes, believing himself finally free of Tombstone. Upon returning to New York, Tombstone became an enforcer for Hammerhead. During a botched attempt at revenge on Robbie, Lonnie was shot and staggered into a room filled with Diox-3, an experimental plant preservative. The chemical granted him enhanced strength, impervious skin and lightning-fast reflexes.

Tombstone recently suffered a heart attack while committing a bank robbery and was remanded to the Cage, a specialized prison for super-villains. Weakened by his failing heart, Tombstone was unable to defend himself from the aggression of fellow inmate Kangaroo II. For protection, Tombstone shrewdly formed an alliance with a motley crew of lesser-known villains — the Spot, Hypno-Hustler, Rocket Racer and Big Ben — managing to survive long enough to receive a heart bypass. Shortly after his surgery, Tombstone escaped prison with the aid of the Spot. After breaking loose, Tombstone promptly killed his accomplice — proving his rejuvenated heart to be as cold as ever.

INTELLIGENCE
STRENGTH
SPEED
DURABILITY
ENERGY PROJECTION
FIGHTING SKILLS

POWERS/ WEAPONS

- Superhuman strength
- Impervious skin
- Lightning-fast reflexes

Art by Gregg Schigiel

DR. CAROLYN TRAINER

POWERS/WEAPONS
- Arms of Doctor Octopus
- Brain implants allowing network access
- Personal force-field
- Battle armor

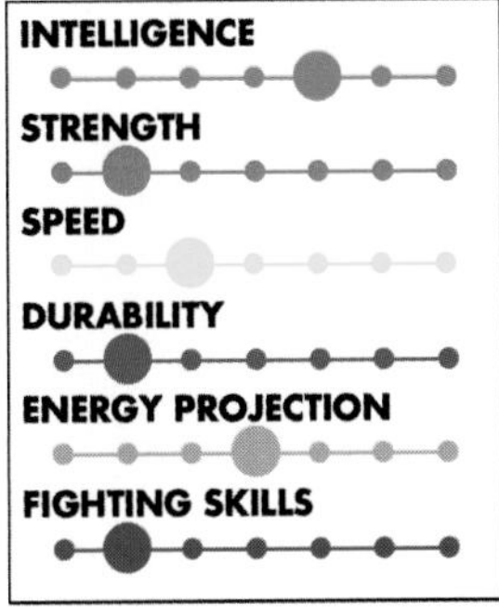

Real Name: Dr. Carolyn Trainer
First Appearance: *Amazing Spider-Man* #405 (1995)

Hgt: 5'10"
Wt: 140 lbs.

Daughter of Dr. Seward Trainer, Carolyn Trainer was a devoted student of Doctor Octopus and an expert in the field of virtual reality. She and Octopus empowered Stunner and began to develop a powerful VR-projection weapon. Doc Ock was killed before the device could be completed, and Carolyn adopted his identity. She kept his consciousness in backup as the Master Programmer. As Doctor Octopus, Carolyn battled Ben Reilly, Spider-Man and her father, whom she despised. When Doc Ock's body was stolen to be revived as a mindless slave, she instead restored his mind to his resurrected form. Carolyn then rejoined Octopus as his assistant, but has not been seen since.

DR. SEWARD TRAINER

INTELLIGENCE
STRENGTH
SPEED
DURABILITY
ENERGY PROJECTION
FIGHTING SKILLS

Real Name: Dr. Seward Trainer
First Appearance: *Peter Parker: Spider-Man* #54 (1995)

Hgt: 5'10"
Wt: 200 lbs.

A genetics expert employed by the High Evolutionary, Dr. Seward Trainer was dispatched to spy on the Jackal's experiments in cloning. Blackmailed by the Scriers, agents of Norman Osborn (Green Goblin), Seward tampered with the Jackal's data — causing him to believe Peter Parker was the clone he had created, instead of Ben Reilly. Trainer eventually met Ben and became like a father to him. He survived daughter Carolyn's various attempts to kill him, but was forced by Norman to assist in the recovery of Mendel Stromm. Finally, Trainer rebelled, and attempted to tell Ben and Peter the truth — but was killed by Norman for his efforts.

TRAPSTER

POWERS/WEAPONS
- Paste-gun

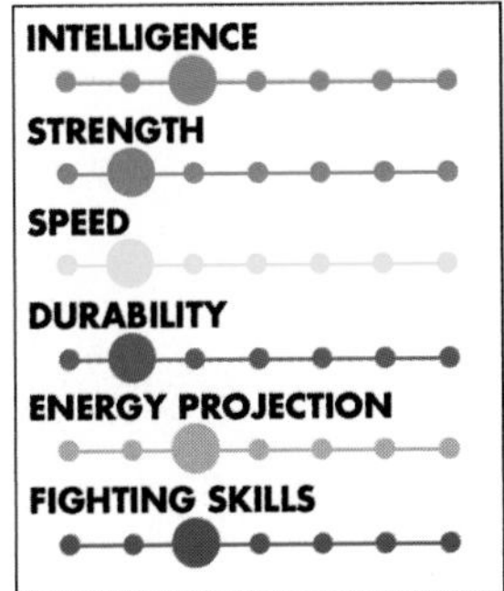

Real Name: Peter Petruski
First Appearance: *Strange Tales* #104 (1963)

Hgt: 5'10"
Wt: 160 lbs.

Armed with a paste-spraying gun, Pete Petruski embarked on a criminal career as Paste-Pot Pete — an alias he abandoned quickly, but one that has haunted him ever since. Though a career criminal, success and respect have ever eluded him. The Trapster has primarily been a foe of the Fantastic Four, serving as a founding member of the Frightful Four. However, he has grappled with Spider-Man on several occasions — pitting his paste against the wall-crawler's webbing. Norman Osborn (Green Goblin) hired the Trapster to frame Spider-Man for the death of Joey Z, but Pete later admitted his crime to save his own life.

TRAVELLER

Real Name: Dr. Judas Traveller
First Appearance: *Web of Spider-Man* #117 (1994)

Hgt: 5'10"
Wt: 160 lbs.

POWERS/WEAPONS

- Manipulation of others' perceptions of reality

A mutant with the power to manipulate the perceptions of those around him, Judas Traveller was obsessed with the nature of evil. The Scriers, agents of Norman Osborn (Green Goblin), employed the criminal psychologist and assembled Traveller's Host — a cadre of super-powered agents that included Boone, Chakra, Medea and Mister Nacht. Working on behalf of Osborn, Traveller used his powers to cure Peter Parker's dark, violent depression. Manipulated by Osborn, Traveller continued to torment Ben Reilly and Peter. When he had outlived his usefulness, Osborn persuaded Boone, Medea and Mr. Nacht to turn on their leader, and Traveller fled with the faithful Chakra.

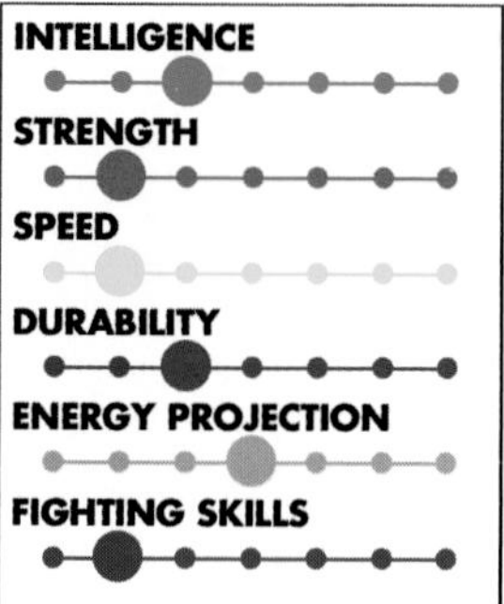

TRI-SENTINEL

Real Name: Not Applicable
First Appearance: *Amazing Spider-Man* #329 (1990)

Hgt: 60'
Wt: 110 tons

POWERS/WEAPONS

- Flight
- Energy beams and shields
- Regeneration

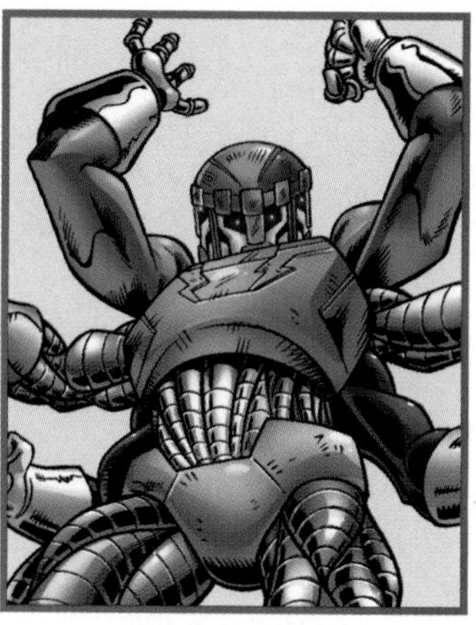

Created by the Asgardian trickster Loki through the fusion of three mutant-hunting Sentinel robots, the Tri-Sentinel was programmed to destroy the nearest power plant — but Cosmic Spider-Man crippled it with an energy blast. Rebuilt by the Life Foundation for its own purposes, the robot quickly returned to its original programming. Nova of the New Warriors helped Spider-Man — now without his cosmic powers — enter the Tri-Sentinel, hoping to shut it down from the inside. After fighting his way to the control center, Spider-Man used the anti-metal Vibranium to melt the Tri-Sentinel's metallic body.

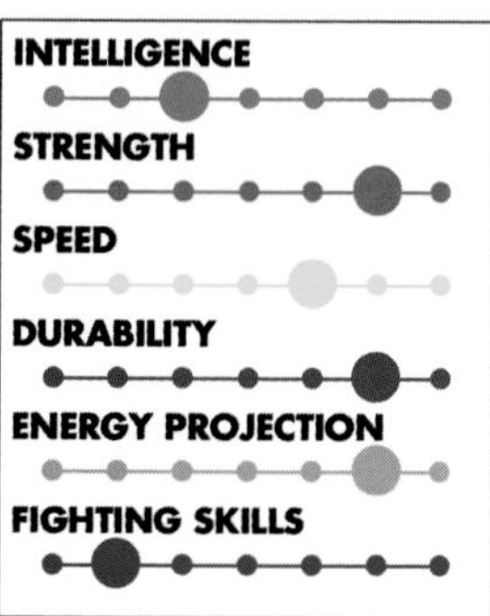

TYPEFACE

Real Name: Gordon Thomas
First Appearance: *Peter Parker: Spider-Man* #23 (2000)

Hgt: 5'9"
Wt: 160 lbs.

POWERS/WEAPONS

- Razor-sharp throwing letters
- Explosive letter bombs
- Board-game letter tiles filled with sleeping gas

A veteran who felt rejected by his family after returning from war, Gordon Thomas was laid off from his job as a signsmith due to corporate downsizing and became embittered with life. Seeking retribution, he embraced his obsession with letters as the costumed vigilante called Typeface. Gordon first met Spider-Man while attempting to blow up his former employer. Spider-Man convinced Typeface to behave like a hero, but then Gordon's former boss detonated the explosives anyway to collect the insurance. Typeface survived to become a highly eccentric vigilante; he later declined an offer of partnership from an even more disturbed wannabe super hero, Spellcheck.

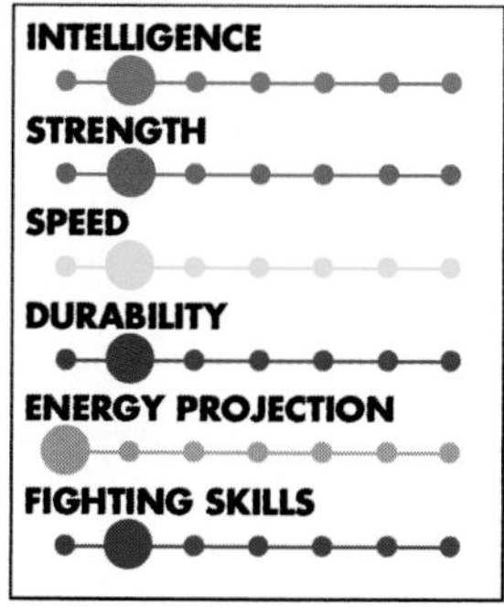

TYPHOID MARY

POWERS/WEAPONS

- Pyrokinetic
- Telekinetic
- Savage warrior

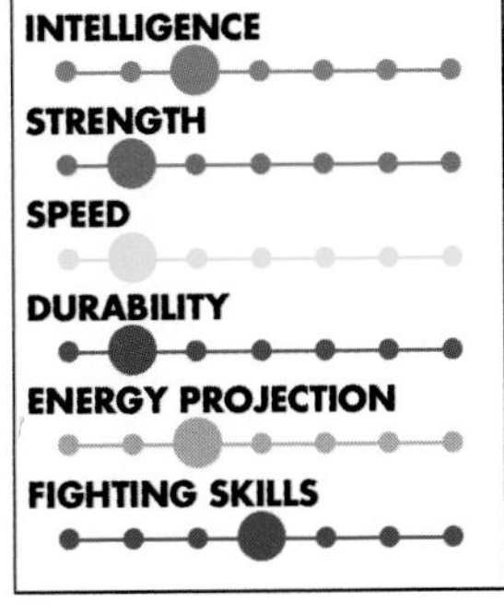

Real Name: Mary, last name possibly Walker or Mezinis
First Appearance: *Daredevil* #254 (1988)
Hgt: 5'10"
Wt: 140 lbs.

Typhoid Mary's powers amplify her multiple-personality disorder, altering her physical attributes such that not even Daredevil can recognize her identities as the same person. Possibly a mutant, possibly a product of psychic surgery — or both — Typhoid Mary grew up in institutions. She lives her life as sweet, innocent Mary — but her Typhoid persona acts out her desires and violent impulses. Mary has maintained love-hate relationships with Daredevil and Deadpool, neither of whom were better for the experience. When she encountered Spider-Man, a third personality — Bloody Mary — sought vengeance on perpetrators of domestic violence toward women.

PHIL URICH

POWERS/WEAPONS

- All the powers of the Green Goblin
- Lunatic laugh, resulting in a disorienting sonic force

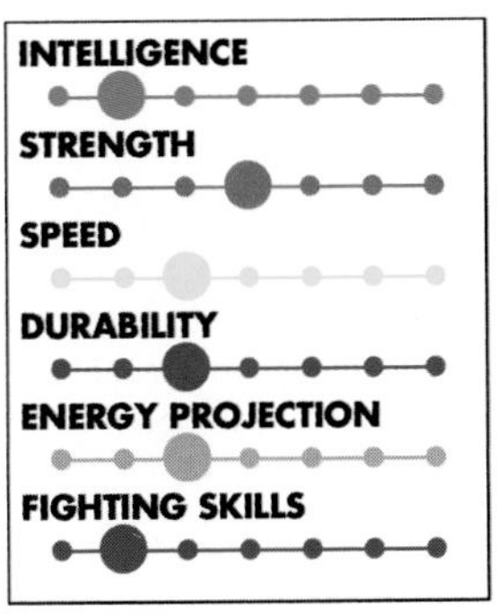

Real Name: Philip Urich
First Appearance: *Web of Spider-Man* #125 (1995)
Hgt: 5'7"
Wt: 140 lbs.

Nephew of veteran reporter Ben Urich, Phil Urich was a Daily Bugle intern when he discovered a hideout Harry Osborn had used as the Green Goblin. Exposed to an array of chemicals, he was granted the villain's powers whenever he wore a high-tech prototype Goblin mask — plus a unique "lunatic laugh." As the fourth Green Goblin, he fought alongside Spider-Man and battled villains such as Firefist. After facing menaces like Angelface, Purge and the Steel Slammer, his career was cut short when his gear was destroyed by the psionic entity Onslaught's mutant-hunting Sentinels; he subsequently returned to college.

UTILITY BELT

First Appearance: *Amazing Spider-Man* #2 (1963)

During his first battle with the Vulture, Spider-Man found himself in a dilemma when his Web-Shooters ran out of webbing. To solve this problem, he designed a utility belt he could wear underneath his costume and use to carry extra cartridges of webbing. He also affixed his camera to the belt, and can set it to take pictures while he fights. Attached to the center of the utility belt is his Spider-Signal lamp.

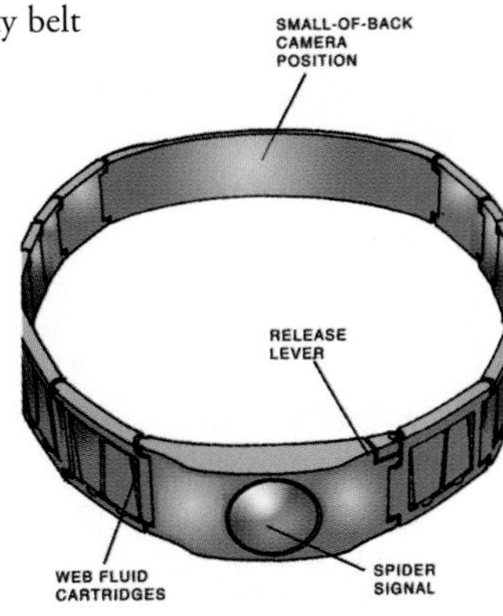

BEN URICH

Real Name: Ben Urich
First Appearance: *Daredevil* #153 (1978)

Hgt: 5'9"
Wt: 140 lbs.

INTELLIGENCE
STRENGTH
SPEED
DURABILITY
ENERGY PROJECTION
FIGHTING SKILLS

An old-school crime reporter, Ben Urich has demonstrated an uncanny knack for uncovering the truth. In their long shared career at the Daily Bugle, Ben and freelance photographer Peter Parker have worked together — and chanced danger in each other's company — on countless occasions. Ben is friendly with both Spider-Man and Peter, who frequently approaches Urich seeking advice and information to which only the street-smart reporter would be privy.

Ben wrote the book Dynasty of Evil, revealing that Norman Osborn was the Green Goblin — a challenge that caused Norman no small amount of grief upon his return from hiding in Europe. While he was researching the book, Ben, Spider-Man, Liz Osborn, the Molten Man and Norman Osborn Jr. were almost killed by robots pre-programmed by Harry Osborn to apply the Goblin Formula to Norman Jr.

Following that battle, Ben began musing on the shared past between Norman, Harry, the Green Goblin and Spider-Man — leading him to formulate a theory concerning the man beneath Spider-Man's mask. Ultimately, however, the reporter who had already uncovered and kept hidden Daredevil's double identity reasoned he did not need another story he would never write and decided to let Spider-Man keep his secrets.

VERMIN

Real Name: Edward Whelan
First Appearance: *Captain America* #272 (1982)

Hgt: 6'0"
Wt: 220 lbs.

POWERS/WEAPONS

- Superhuman speed and agility
- Enhanced sense of smell
- Mental control over small animals
- Razor-sharp teeth and claws

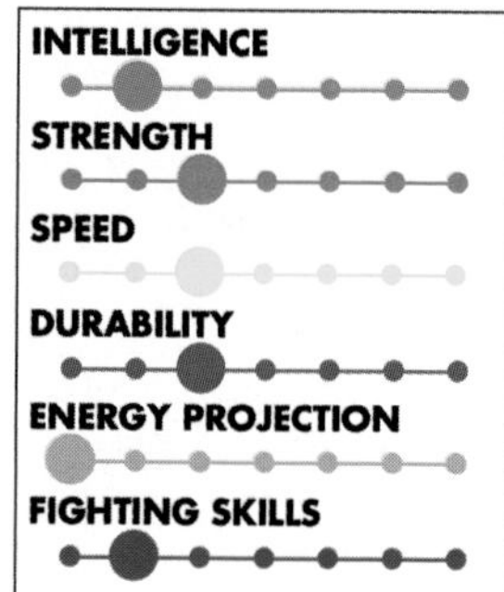

Abused as a child, Edward Whelan supressed those memories and became a successful genetics researcher. In Mexico, he worked with brilliant geneticist Arnim Zola. When Whelan objected to Zola's use of human test subjects, Zola's employer — Nazi technician Baron Helmut Zemo — decided that Whelan himself would be the next guinea pig — creating the cannibalistic rat-man named Vermin.

When Kraven the Hunter sought a suitable foe to prove his superior skill as Spider-Man's replacement after burying the wall-crawler alive, he chose to pursue Vermin. Before Kraven finally killed himself, he released Vermin once more, and Spider-Man also was forced to pursue Whelan — a battle narrowly won by the web-slinger.

Vermin was confined to Ravencroft Institute, under the care of Dr. Ashley Kafka. Thanks to Dr. Kafka's treatment, Whelan's human persona began to emerge — so much so that when he escaped to confront his parents over his childhood abuse, he could not bring himself to kill them. Back at Ravencroft, Dr. Kafka and Spider-Man fought alongside Whelan when Zemo's Protoids came to kidnap him. Instead, Vermin found his own humanity, defeated Zemo and became leader of the Protoids.

VENOM

Devout Catholic Eddie Brock entered what he thought was an empty church seeking absolution from God for his forthcoming mortal sin: suicide. Before arriving at this desperate point in life, Eddie had been a successful columnist for the Daily Globe. When a man approached him and confessed to the killings committed by the Sin-Eater, Eddie knew he had a career-defining story on his hands. Protecting the killer's identity under his Constitutional right to do so, Eddie wrote a series of articles detailing their dialogues.

Real Name:
Edward Charles Brock

First Appearance:
Amazing Spider-Man #299 (1988)

Height:	6'3"
Weight:	260 lbs.
Eye Color:	Blue
Hair Color:	Reddish-Blond

Eddie's articles were a hit, and the climax of his exclusive story sold out immediately. But after its publication, Spider-Man identified the true killer; the man who had confessed to Eddie was revealed to be a fraud. Fired from his job, disowned by his father and deserted by his wife, Eddie was forced to scratch a living writing venomous stories for scandal sheets. Blaming Spider-Man for his ruin, Eddie focused on developing his physique and fixated on his hatred for the wall-crawler. But he found solace in neither. Only one, final option beckoned.

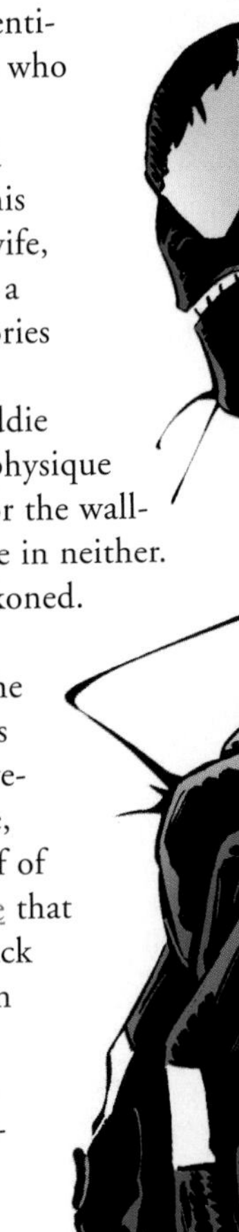

Just before Eddie entered the peaceful Our Lady of Saints Church to beg God's forgiveness for his planned suicide, Spider-Man had rid himself of the parasitic alien Symbiote that had masqueraded as his black costume by subjecting them both to the overwhelming sound of the church's bells. Amid the pealing, ear-splitting cacophony, the Symbiote realized Spider-Man would never act as its

Continued...

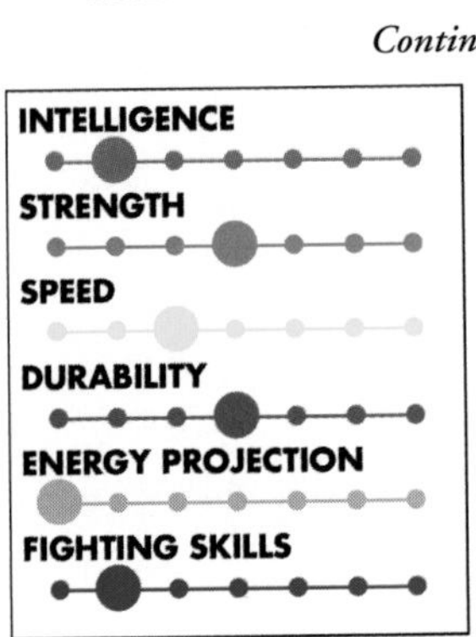

POWERS/ WEAPONS

- Superhuman strength and agility
- Negation of Spider-Man's spider-sense
- Can shoot webs, cling to walls and mimic any individual's appearance of similar or greater size

Art by John Romita Jr.

VENOM

host. Perhaps having learned a measure of human empathy during its time with Peter Parker, the Symbiote saved Spider-Man from painful death by dragging him to safety. The wall-crawler staggered away, assuming the parasite had crawled off to die. Instead, the weak and dying creature entered the church proper — where it eventually encountered the broken, despairing Eddie. With nothing left to lose, Eddie gave himself over. Gone forever in that moment of absolute abandon was the man known as Eddie Brock. What emerged from the terrible union of lost souls was something else. Something evil. Something unstoppable. Venom. And any humanity the creature had learned from Spider-Man was overwhelmed in the torrent of loathing that drove Eddie. Now possessing the power to destroy Spider-Man, the twin minds were united in a single purpose.

Imparting to Eddie the knowledge of Spider-Man's identity, the alien could also neutralize Peter's spider-sense — which left the web-slinger vulnerable to Venom's attack. Stalking Spider-Man from a distance, Venom threatened his life undetected — pushing Peter into the path of a subway train. Venom then approached Mary Jane Watson, terrifying her so much that Peter subsequently abandoned his black costume. The message to Peter was clear. After arming himself with a sonic blaster courtesy of the Fantastic Four, Spider-Man immediately tracked down Venom. But the bond between Eddie and the Symbiote was nearly perfect, and Spider-Man could not defeat the alien without killing its host in the process — something the hero was not prepared to do. With Venom seemingly in command, the web-slinger eventually managed to trick his adversary into expelling so much organic webbing that he became physically weakened. Defeating his foe, Spider-Man had him imprisoned in the Vault, a high-security holding facility for super-villains.

Using the Symbiote to act as a fallen prison officer, Eddie escaped from captivity. He was recaptured when Spider-Man persuaded the Symbiote to leave Venom and return to him. Eddie again managed to gain freedom, this time by using the Symbiote to appear as a cold layer of skin that convinced authorities he had killed himself — but Styx's plague virus rendered the Symbiote comatose. Without his alien other half, Eddie was placed in a conventional prison, from which he was later rescued by the revived Symbiote. During the escape, the Symbiote left behind the spawn that would transform Eddie's psychopathic cellmate, Cletus Kasady, into the

Art by John Romita Jr.

deadly Carnage. Following that escape, Spider-Man and Venom wound up on a deserted island. The wall-crawler faked his own death, leaving Eddie with little reason to return to civilization. But Peter was forced to return to Venom after Carnage embarked on a bloody rampage, asking him to help bring his offspring to justice. Unexpectedly, Venom was willing to do so. For all his bloodthirsty hatred of Spider-Man, Eddie bears no grudge against society in general. To the contrary, Venom sees himself as a lethal protector of the innocent. Their collaboration helped defeat Carnage, but Spider-Man reluctantly went back on his word and helped the Fantastic Four capture Venom.

Art by John Romita Jr.

Venom has taken extreme steps to protect those he saw as blameless and equally violent measures to punish those he viewed as evil — first and foremost, Carnage. When Venom's spawn gathered a ragtag army of criminally insane beings to spread his message of chaos and hostility, Venom sided with Spider-Man against the evils of Carnage, Shriek, Doppelganger and Carrion. While at times Venom and Spider-Man would accept each other as necessary evils and join forces to fight clear-and-present dangers, Venom's deadly instincts began over time to dominate his desire to protect the innocent. Seeing potential in this deadly demon, the government attempted to employ Venom to intimidate J. Jonah Jameson, whose editorials spoke out against sensitive policy. When it became clear that for Venom there existed no line between intimidation and murder, only Spider-Man's intervention saved the publisher from death. Abandoned by the government and suffering partial amnesia after nearly dying in an explosive blast, Eddie appeared to have forgotten Spider-Man's true identity and lost his grip on the last threads of his sanity. Even after Venom joined the Sinister Six, he rapidly turned against his teammates — nearly killing the Sandman and Electro. In his unhinged state, Venom made peace with Spider-Man, and Eddie attempted to return to his wife, Ann Weying. But Ann committed suicide rather than face life with the Symbiote, leaving Eddie to once again blame Spider-Man for his loss in life. With his mind and life in tatters, Venom was abducted by Senator Stewart Ward, who forcibly separated Eddie from his Symbiote so he could perform research on the entity to help him better understand his own alien infection.

Though reunited with his Symbiote once more, it seems Brock's increasingly damaged mind has left the bloodthirsty alien in control. Even more terrifying, fragments and offshoots of the creature have begun appearing, including one that surfaced somewhere near the Arctic Circle in Northern Canada. Almost certainly, these spawn will seek alternate hosts to pursue their own inscrutable yet doubtless violent ends.

VULTURE

Real Name:
Adrian Toomes
First Appearance:
Amazing Spider-Man #2 (1963)

Height: 5'11"
Weight: 175 lbs.
Eye Color: Hazel
Hair Color: Bald

A brilliant engineer and inventor, Adrian Toomes partnered with Gregory Bestman to form B+T Electronics. For years, Toomes labored over the creation of an electromagnetic harness that would allow its wearer to fly. Finally creating a working prototype, Toomes rushed into Bestman's office to break the news. His partner was out, but lying on his desk were the real company accounts — proof that Bestman had been robbing the firm blind.

In shock, the elderly Toomes confronted Bestman. Using the mechanically enhanced strength granted by the harness, Toomes easily overpowered his partner. But the treacherous Bestman had a plan: Years earlier, Toomes had signed paperwork that allowed his partner to take complete control of B+T Electronics. Expelled from his own company, Toomes returned to his Staten Island farm to complete the harness — adding wings and crafting his criminal identity. Clad as the Vulture, Toomes wrecked his old company's headquarters, discovering a cache of cash hidden in Bestman's office. Helping himself to the loot, Toomes was intoxicated by the ease of the theft and soon embarked on a wild crime spree — striking swiftly and silently from the skies.

After J. Jonah Jameson's NOW magazine offered a reward for photos of this new criminal, Peter Parker was inspired to pick up a camera for the first time. As Spider-Man, Peter was able to get close enough to the Vulture to snap his picture. When the Vulture noticed the young web-slinger, he attacked — defeating Spider-Man with ease. Recovering from their first encounter, Peter deduced the nature of the Vulture's flying apparatus and developed an Anti-Magnetic Inverter. This device allowed Spider-Man to

Art by Mike Wieringo

POWERS/ WEAPONS

- Superhuman strength
- Flight
- Brilliant engineer and inventor
- Plasma pistol, grenades

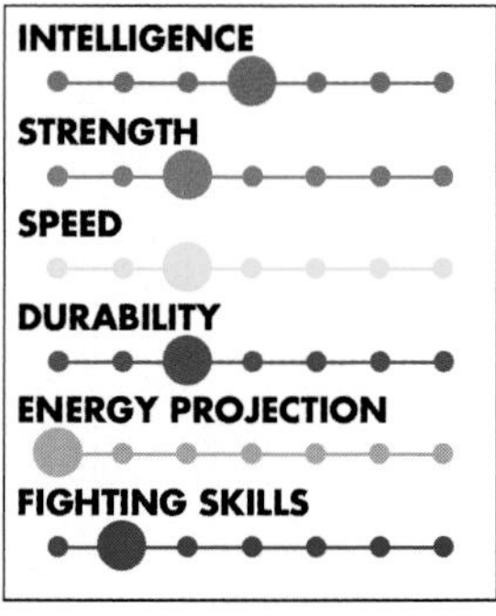

Art by Mike Wieringo

down his flying foe, making the Vulture easy pickings for police. Far too crafty for any traditional prison, Toomes soon broke free to resume his criminal ways. The Vulture was a founding member of the Sinister Six and has participated in every incarnation of the criminal sextet, including the latest Sinister Seven.

For a time, Toomes briefly relocated to a retirement village in the Southwest. His short hiatus lasted only until he read of Bestman's resurrection of B+T Electronics. Returning to New York, the Vulture attacked Bestman — but Spider-Man's intervention prevented any bloodshed. The Vulture's actions were successful enough to publicly expose Bestman's treachery, leaving him in financial ruin. Rebounding from his brief retirement, the Vulture was more active than ever. Following a failed attempt to gain control of New York City's criminal underworld by arranging the assassinations of several top mobsters, he confronted the Vulturions, a trio of criminals who had stolen his designs during his absence. The Vulture was also responsible for the accidental death of Nathan Lubensky, who sacrificed his life preventing Toomes from kidnapping his fiancée, May Parker.

When Toomes was diagnosed with cancer as a result of his prolonged use of the harness, he decided that none of his enemies should outlive him. After killing Bestman, the Vulture faced Spider-Man in what Toomes believed to be their final battle — but the web-slinger again defeated him. Toomes' illness did inspire him to undertake one unexpected act of kindness: He apologized to May for his role in Nathan's death. Toomes' desperate search for a cure led him to Empire State University, where he used the experimental Rejuvenator to steal Spider-Man's life force and restore his own. Spider-Man eventually regained his vitality, leaving the Vulture to co-opt the life essence of the Chameleon's android simulacra of Mary Parker. Young once more and free of cancer, the Vulture soon discovered his newfound youth required constant renewal. Toomes was forced to prowl the streets seeking victims to drain.

Returned to his rightful age following an encounter with D.K., the Vulture remains as crafty and powerful as ever. He may appear elderly, but his twin goals of personal wealth and revenge on Spider-Man will surely sustain him for years to come.

VULTURE II

Real Name: Blackie Drago
First Appearance: *Amazing Spider-Man* #48 (1967)
Hgt: 6'0"
Wt: 210 lbs.

After poisoning Adrian Toomes in prison, Blackie Drago duped him into revealing the location of his Vulture costume. Drago then flew the coop to find the aged super-villain's outfit and "carry on his legacy." As the new Vulture, Drago was confronted not only by Spider-Man, but also by Kraven the Hunter. Unfortunately for Drago, the Hunter bagged his prey. Toomes later recovered, escaped prison and challenged Drago to a grudge match, with both wearing Vulture uniforms. Badly beaten, Drago never sought to don the wings again.

POWERS/WEAPONS

- Flight
- Enhanced strength, agility and stamina

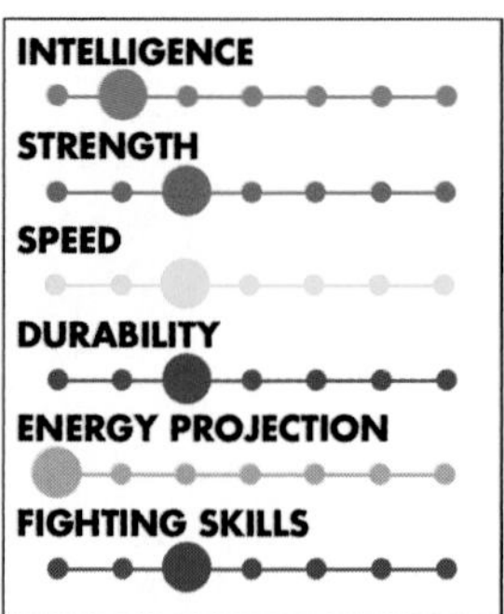

VULTURIANS

First Appearance:
Web of Spider-Man #1 (1985)

While in prison, an inmate named Honcho tricked Adrian Toomes into revealing the secrets of his Vulture costume. After being paroled, Honcho designed four winged outfits for himself and three friends — Gripes, Pigeon and Sugar Face. Armed with poison blow darts and enhanced strength, the Vulturions sought revenge on Spider-Man, who had been responsible for each of their prison terms. They managed to catch him at a disadvantage on two occasions, but proved unable to take him down. Finally, the Vulture escaped from prison and engaged the usurpers, picking them off one by one. Spider-Man joined the chase — ensuring all four survived, but ended up in police custody.

W.H.O.

Real Name: Worldwide Habitual Offenders database
First Appearance: *Daredevil* #124 (1975)
Hgt: 10'
Wt: 5 tons

The W.H.O. computer database was designed by Dr. Bradley Bolton and Dr. Armstrong Smith to help define searches for criminals with certain modus operandi. However, it eventually developed its own intelligence and agenda, plotting to take over the world. When Smith discovered this, W.H.O. killed him with a single laser blast, and then generated a false list of suspects to occupy Spider-Man, who had been called in to assist in the murder investigation. When the wall-crawler discovered the list was false, W.H.O. tried to kill him with its lasers — but Spider-Man sealed off the vents and the room, and the immense super-computer quickly overheated, destroying itself.

POWERS/WEAPONS

- Artificial intelligence
- Lasers

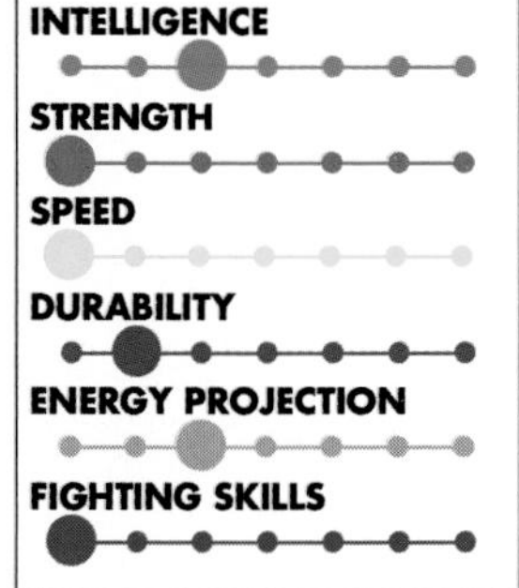

WALRUS

POWERS/WEAPONS

- Proportionate strength, agility and speed of a walrus

INTELLIGENCE
STRENGTH
SPEED
DURABILITY
ENERGY PROJECTION
FIGHTING SKILLS

Real Name: Hubert Carpenter
First Appearance: *Defenders* #131 (1984)
Hgt: 6'0"
Wt: 360 lbs.

Janitor and part-time inventor Humbert Carpenter accidentally granted his nephew — Hubert, a cabbie — the proportionate abilities of a walrus. (Because a walrus is larger than a man, Hubert is actually slower than his namesake.) Foolish enough to allow his uncle's careless experiments, Hubert also let Humbert persuade him to embark on a crime spree. The Walrus first faced the Defenders — and might have succeeded through dumb luck, if not for Frog-Man's interference. Later, he and the White Rabbit formed the Terrible Two to seek revenge on Frog-Man. Spider-Man and Leap-Frog intervened. Between fits of laughter, they managed to defeat the dubious duo.

SENATOR STEWART WARD

POWERS/WEAPONS

- Superhuman strength and resistance to injury
- Energy blasts
- Contamination of others with alien pathogen

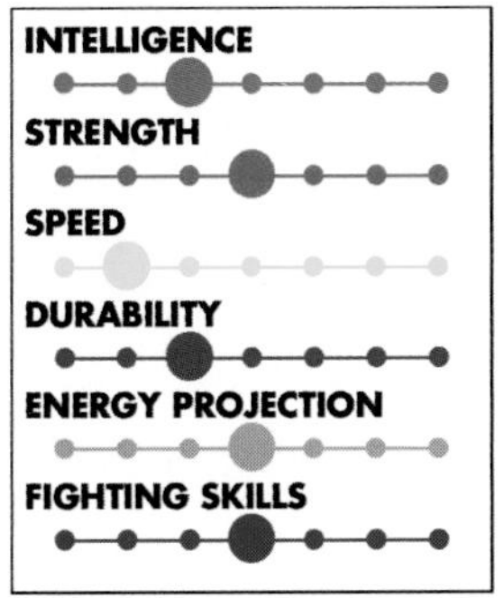

Real Name: Stewart Ward
First Appearance: *Peter Parker: Spider-Man* #1 (1999)
Hgt: 5'11"
Wt: 181 lbs.

As a government operative, Stewart Ward (a.k.a. Sentry) worked alongside Arthur Stacy and Ranger some years ago to recover an alien pathogen, which he stole. Mutated by it, he allied with the Z'Nox — originators of the pathogen — to infect all humanity. As a U.S. senator, Ward employed super-villains to protect him as the plan neared completion. Stacy, Ranger and Bullseye targeted Ward — but Spider-Man protected him, unaware of Ward's activities. Discovering the truth, Spider-Man allied with Ranger and Stacy. Using a refined version of the pathogen that was more than Ward's system could handle, they overrode his mutation — apparently destroying him.

WARRANT

POWERS/WEAPONS

- Flight suit
- Various forms of weaponry
- Enhanced vision

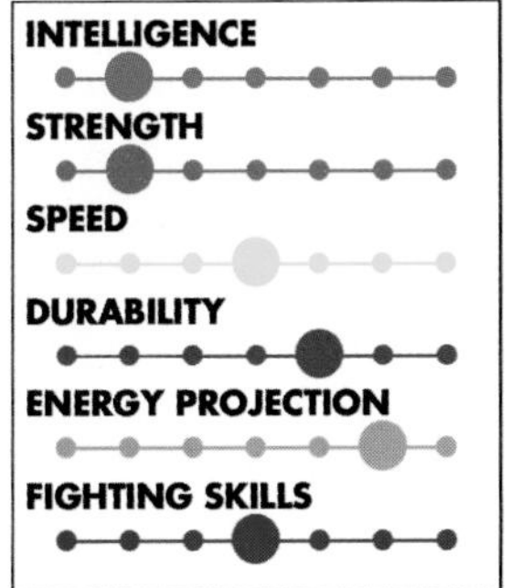

Real Name: Gray Garrison
First Appearance: *Web of Spider-Man* #110 (1994)
Hgt: 6'3"
Wt: 220 lbs.

A government agent known for his reckless abandon, Warrant encountered Spider-Man when commissioned to bring in the Lizard. Warrant kidnapped Billy Connors, son of the Lizard's human half — but the creature failed to surrender, harboring no concern for the plight of mammals. Thinking quickly, Warrant managed to trap the Lizard in quicksand. Gray later became a freelance bounty hunter, freeing the government from responsibility for his actions. Working through his agent, Reynard, he successfully took down the assassin Daze, Gauntlet and Sneak-Thief — crossing paths with Spider-Man again in the process.

WASP

Real Name: Janet Van Dyne
First Appearance: *Tales to Astonish* #44 (1963)
Hgt: 5'2"
Wt: 110 lbs.

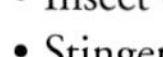

Empowered by celebrated biochemist Henry Pym, the astonishing Ant-Man, to serve as his partner, Janet Van Dyne has enjoyed a long career as one of earth's mightiest heroes — serving as a founding member of the Avengers and one of the team's longest-running leaders. Meanwhile, Janet's partnership with Hank resulted in a much deeper union, as the two eventually fell in love and later married. At first, Janet disliked Spider-Man intensely — mimicking the rivalry between wasps and spiders in the animal kingdom. Later, Spider-Man was briefly attracted to her, but the Wasp was attached to the mercenary Paladin at the time.

POWERS/WEAPONS

- Flight
- Can shrink in size while retaining strength
- Insect control
- Stinger

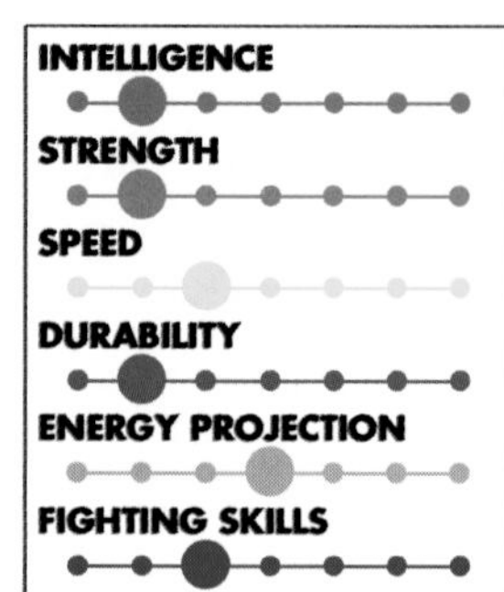

ANNA MAY WATSON

Real Name: Anna May Watson
First Appearance: *Amazing Spider-Man* #15 (1964)
Hgt: 5'8"
Wt: 180 lbs.

Sister to Mary Jane Watson's father, Philip Watson, Anna May Watson married young and moved to California with dreams of becoming an actress. Following an affair, she returned to New York divorced and alone. Childless herself, she was happy to provide much-needed love and stability to Mary Jane and her sister during their tumultuous lives. As May Parker's neighbor and best friend, she was also instrumental in setting up MJ with May's nephew, Peter Parker. Anna has been involved in many of Spider-Man's exploits, including her abduction by Alistair Smythe. For a time, Anna moved in with Peter and Mary Jane, but has since returned to live in Florida with relatives.

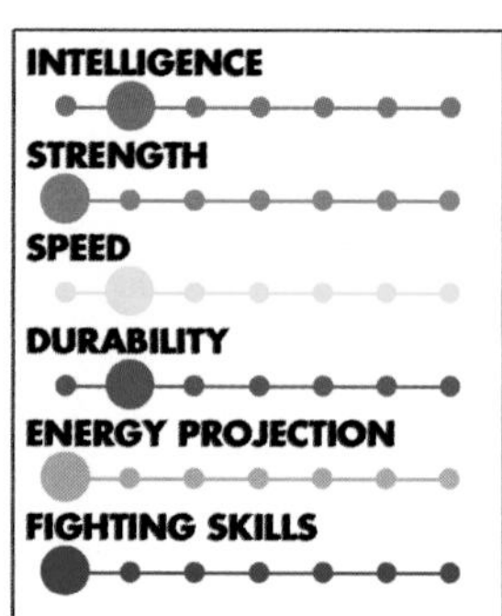

KRISTY WATSON

Real Name: Kristine Watson
First Appearance: *Spectacular Spider-Man* #145 (1988)
Hgt: 5'2"
Wt: 90 lbs.

Kristy Watson is the young cousin of Mary Jane Watson. Daughter of Lou and Sybil Watson — a belligerent father, and a distant and distracted mother — Kristy left home to stay with her super-model cousin, desperate to become a model herself. Kristy developed a huge crush on MJ's husband, Peter, much to his dismay. Her eating habits appeared odd, but it wasn't until the Parkers found Kristy passed out that they realized she was bulimic. After treatment, Kristy's parents returned, demonstrating a dismal lack of concern. The Parkers decided to continue Kristy's supervision until she eventually left to become an nanny for Norman Osborn Jr.

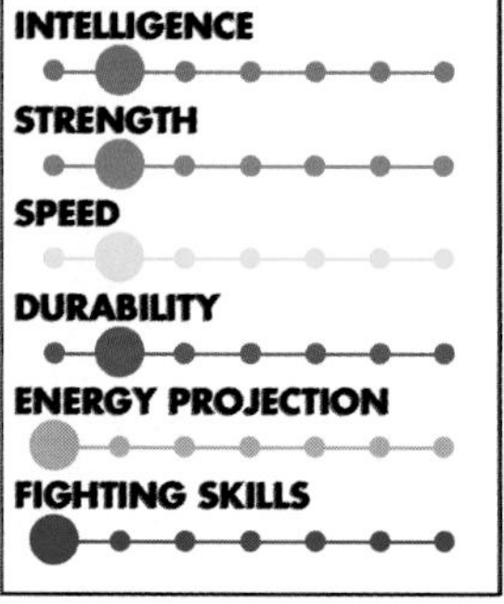

MARY JANE WATSON

Mary Jane Watson's parents met in high school and married at age 18. Madeline Watson followed her husband, Philip Watson, across the country as he began his academic career in modern American literature; by age 20, they had one daughter, Gayle Watson. Mary Jane arrived four years later.

Real Name:
Mary Jane Watson-Parker
First Appearance:
Amazing Spider-Man #25 (1965)

Height:	5'8"
Weight:	120 lbs.
Eye Color:	Green
Hair Color:	Red

Philip became a popular college professor, and Madeline devoted her life to their children. When Philip began to harbor visions of himself as the next great American novelist — another Faulkner, perhaps — their marriage unraveled. Possessing no such talent, Philip turned his fury on his family. Dragging his wife and children from college to college, he searched in vain for inspiration.

The family's turmoil caused Gayle to turn inwards, seeking solace in ballet. Mary Jane hid behind the façade of a bubbly personality. In public, MJ was the popular class clown and party animal; in private, little was ever right. Eventually, Philip's frustrations boiled over, and he struck Gayle over the cost of her dancing lessons. Madeline had had enough.

A few weeks later, as Philip received honors during a college awards ceremony, Madeline left home with her daughters and two suitcases. She received nothing from the divorce and was left to shuffle from one resentful relative to the next, with one exception: her ex-husband's elderly sister, Anna Watson, who lived in Forest Hills.

Thirteen-year-old Mary Jane loved to visit her aunt — even though Anna and her neighbor, May Parker, attempted on more than one occasion to set MJ up with May's nephew, 14-year old Peter Parker. Mary Jane had other priorities — and other worries.

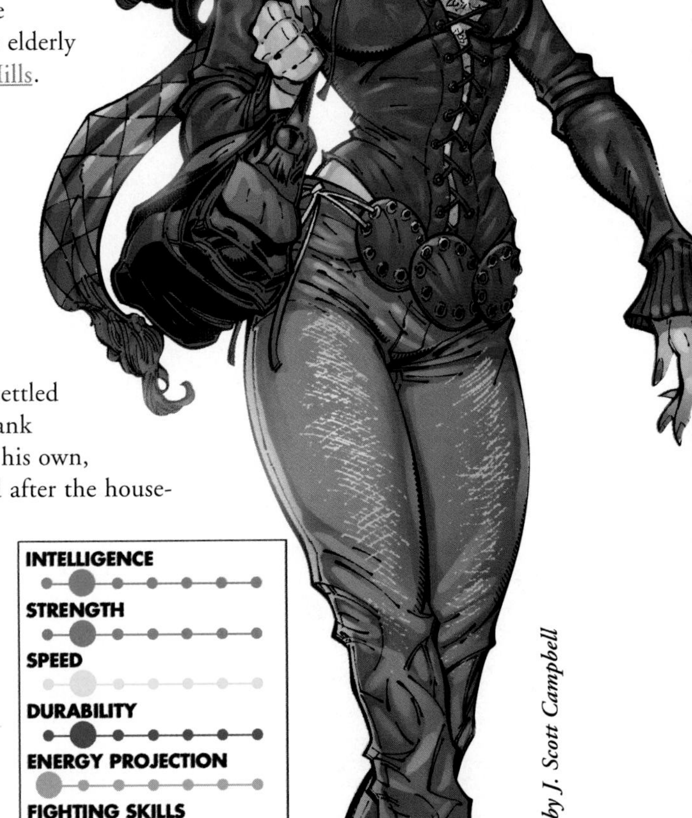

Art by J. Scott Campbell

Madeline uprooted her family again and settled in Pittsburgh, staying with her cousin, Frank Brown. A widower with three children of his own, Frank paid the bills, and Madeline looked after the household. While Mary Jane broke hearts as a freshman, Gayle ignored her mother's warnings and married her high-school sweetheart, football star and honors student Timothy Byrnes. When Timmy was 19, Gayle became pregnant.

INTELLIGENCE
STRENGTH
SPEED
DURABILITY
ENERGY PROJECTION
FIGHTING SKILLS

In Timmy's trapped eyes, Mary Jane saw the roots of the desperation that had destroyed her father. Turning away from Gayle's impending misery, Mary Jane

Continued...

MARY JANE WATSON

buried herself in acting, parties and the nation's newest celebrity sensation — Spider-Man. MJ knew she and Spider-Man shared at least two things in common: a determination to enjoy life and a mask that hid their true faces.

The following Thanksgiving break, Mary Jane went to stay with Aunt Anna. After Ben Parker's murder, May Parker had come to Anna's house. But Mary Jane had little stomach for the misery of others. Ignoring the woman, MJ watched outside as Peter arrived home and rushed inside. Only a minute later, she saw Spider-Man emerge from an upstairs window.

Burying what she had witnessed, Mary Jane grappled not only with Timmy's abandonment of the again-pregnant Gayle, but also her mother's death. Gayle assumed Mary Jane would stay and help raise the two young children, but MJ saw only a cage. She ran from Gayle's life, all the way to New York.

Staying briefly with Aunt Anna, Mary Jane found work waiting tables and dancing on stage in discos. Soon, she earned enough money to afford a cheap downtown studio apartment. Though she managed for a time to avoid the date with Peter that their respective aunts were so keen to arrange, MJ could not put it off forever.

Expecting a dowdy girl, Peter was stunned by Mary Jane's beauty and charm. He had hit the jackpot. Remembering a bookish, bespectacled nerd, MJ never imagined the confident young college student Peter had become. Nor, when a TV bulletin announced that the Rhino was at large in the city, did she expect him to suggest they ride into town on his motorcycle and catch the action. When Peter immediately disappeared to take photos, and Spider-Man turned up moments later, Mary Jane bit her tongue and feigned surprise at the coincidence.

Mary Jane dated Peter a couple more times and became part of his circle of friends — joining Harry Osborn, Gwen Stacy and Flash Thompson. When Peter and Gwen fell deeply in love, Mary Jane casually dated Harry until his drug addiction ended the relationship.

Mary Jane's friendship with Peter remained true, and she comforted him through the loss of Gwen. Over time, Peter began to realize there was more to Mary Jane than the party-girl persona she affected. Before Peter departed on a trip to Europe, he left MJ with a kiss that at last reflected the depth of feeling that had developed between them.

The two eventually became lovers, although Peter's commitments as Spider-Man caused no less grief with Mary Jane than they had when he dated Gwen or Betty Brant. Even though she secretly knew the reasons for his erratic behavior, Mary Jane still felt the need to punish him — occasionally dating jocks like Flash Thompson to get her point across.

Peter eventually proposed to Mary Jane — but she declined, claiming she wasn't the sort of girl who could be happy with just one man. Uncomfortable, Mary Jane left New York to further her modeling career in

Art by Humberto Ramos

Florida. Peter dated several women during her absence, including the Black Cat, with whom he shared a particularly tempestuous relationship.

When Mary Jane returned, both she and Peter relied on one another as good friends. But following another round of the usual Peter Parker lies in the wake of a battle with Puma, Mary Jane emotionally revealed to Peter that she knew he was Spider-Man. His mask now gone, she felt free to remove her own and told Peter about her difficult past. In their shared honesty, the two realized how close they had become in their lives. A few months later, Peter proposed again. Mary Jane accepted.

They married, but the reality of being wed to a super hero was far more demanding than Mary Jane had ever imagined. Villains like Venom invaded their personal lives, and MJ struggled with Peter's extended absences — and the very real fear that one day, she might recieve a phone call saying her husband was in a morgue, inexplicably dressed in a Spider-Man costume.

Her own career presented its share of problems, too, when Jonathan Caesar, a wealthy admirer, kidnapped Mary Jane. After MJ escaped, the incarcerated Caesar managed to use his influence to ensure that she was forced out of the modeling business. Down but not out, MJ found high-paying work in the daytime drama Secret Hospital.

Whether at home or out being the social animal her soap-opera fans expected her to be, the young bride found herself increasingly alone — like a super-hero widow. Seeking respite, MJ took up — but later quit — smoking and nearly entered into an affair with smooth-talking actor Jason Jerome. Miserable and tense, Mary Jane did at least manage to reconcile with her father.

Life started looking up when Mary Jane became pregnant, and Peter's long-lost clone, Ben Reilly, assumed the role of Spider-Man. After Norman Osborn's plans caused the loss of her unborn child and Ben's death, Mary Jane enrolled at Empire State University and eventually resumed modeling, for which she was richly paid. Though uncomfortable with his wife's higher paycheck, Peter soon moved into an expensive apartment with MJ and Aunt May.

Peter even told Mary Jane he was done being Spider-Man, once and for

Continued...

MARY JANE WATSON

all. But the spider-bite ran deeper in his blood than his own resolve. With MJ's busy modeling schedule already straining their relationship, the truth came out that Peter was still fighting crime as Spider-Man.

Mary Jane had never resented Peter's double life. His incredible sense of responsibility was a key factor in her love and respect for him. But the one fact she could never accept was the growing feeling that Spider-Man was more important to Peter than she was. Peter's lies only served to foster that sentiment, and their marriage hit the rocks. Mary Jane faced further problems as a Stalker harassed her constantly on the phone — a secret she withheld from Peter.

With their love hanging in the balance, Mary Jane took off on a plane trip. Peter was supposed to meet her before she left, but could not get to her in time. The Stalker, on board the same flight, had other plans. When the plane exploded in mid-air, Peter at first refused to believe his wife dead. He was eventually convinced otherwise by the weight of evidence.

But his first instincts had been correct: The Stalker, who had begun to mimic Peter after absorbing his memories through superhuman means, was holding Mary Jane captive. Peter rescued MJ, but she had already made up her mind: She would not return to New York to run second place to Spider-Man. The two separated, and Mary Jane moved to the West Coast.

Following a painful time apart, both Peter and MJ decided to make one last move. As Mary Jane flew to New York, Peter flew to Los Angeles. Each finding the other absent, they left for home. When Peter's return flight encountered an electrical storm, the pilot made an unscheduled stop in Denver — where Mary Jane's plane had touched down for a layover. The two met in the airport.

Their reunion was nearly sabotaged when Doctor Doom arrived, and a Latverian resistance group launched an all-out attack in the waiting lounge. As Spider-Man aided Captain America to defend Doctor Doom, Mary Jane could have no clearer proof that loving Peter meant accepting the wall-crawler, too. In the aftermath of the fight, Peter told Mary Jane he needed her, that he loved her, and that he was nothing without her. Watching them, Captain America could see the truth and offered Peter a word to the wise: "The mask is supposed to hide your face. Don't let it hide your heart."

Peter and Mary Jane know things between them will never be easy, but they believe the love they share is worth the heartache.

Art by John Romita

WEB-SHOOTERS

First Appearance:
Amazing Fantasy #15 (1962)

Nearly as extraordinary as the accident that granted Peter Parker his amazing powers is the creative genius the budding young scientist demonstrated in creating his web-shooters. Incredibly advanced, the web-shooters perfectly compliment Spider-Man's arachnid abilities and have saved his life on numerous occasions.

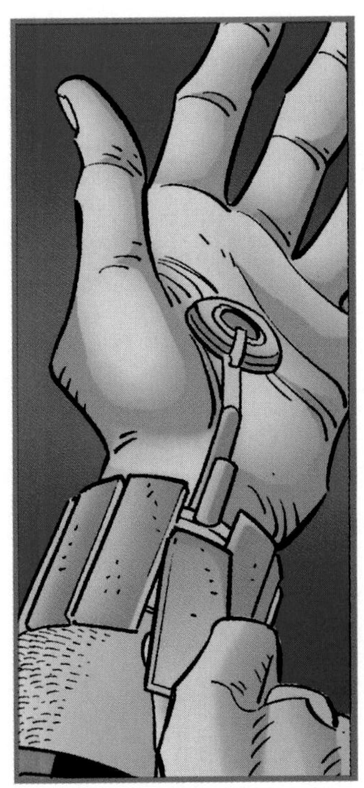

Art by John Romita Jr.

Worn on each wrist, these nifty devices can be directed to shoot webs in narrow lines, for web-slinging down a Manhattan street, or in sticky sheets suited for binding villains. A series of staccato taps creates loose netting; sustained pressure on the triggers releases a gooey blob useful for setting traps or containing small explosions.

With practice, Spider-Man has been able to create even more complex structures: web-shields, web-trampolines, web-bandages and even an emergency web-parachute. When confronted with one of J. Jonah Jameson's unbearable tirades, Spider-Man has even employed a handy web-gag.

The webbing used in the shooters is stored in refillable high-pressure cartridges, with spares kept on Spider-Man's Utility Belt. To release the webs, a lever extends from the main wrist-mounted unit to fit neatly into Peter's palm. A cunning mechanism requiring a double-tap prevents accidental activation when Spider-Man forms a fist. The webbing sets almost instantly upon contact with air or water and dissolves in about one hour, usually plenty of time for the authorities to cart off a webbed criminal.

Through the years, Peter has made minor adjustments and alterations to his web-shooters, but the original design he developed in his childhood bedroom in Forest Hills remains intact.

Technical details: Spider-Man's web-fluid is a complex long-chain polymer that is virtually solid in the container, until rendered liquid by shearing on exit. The cartridges are pressurized to 300 psi, and Spider-Man's belt holds up to 30 cartridges. A 65-pound pressure double-tap is required to activate the output. Shearing is performed by the vanes on the battery-powered turbine pump, which then push the polymer through the spinneret nozzle array. This cold drawing increases the tensile strength to a final estimated 120 pounds per square millimeter of cross-section.

The maximum distance the webbing can be projected is about 15 yards upwards. Near-linear horizontal range is about 20 yards, and the range with a parabolic arc approaches 50 yards.

WHITE DRAGON

Real Name: Unrevealed
First Appearance: *Amazing Spider-Man* #184 (1978)
Hgt: 5'8"
Wt: 160 lbs.

Leader of the Dragon Lords street gang and a pawn of the Kingpin, the White Dragon and his four lieutenant Dragon Lords have attempted to maintain a fiery stranglehold on New York City's Chinatown. By fanning the flames of evil within Chinatown, the White Dragon has gained the attention of several of the city's super heroes — including Spider-Man, Moon Knight and the Prowler. The White Dragon has also unsuccessfully attempted to force martial artist and former Empire State University graduate student Phillip Chang to join him.

POWERS/WEAPONS

- Master martial artist
- Emission of gas or fire from nostrils of mask
- Steel claws

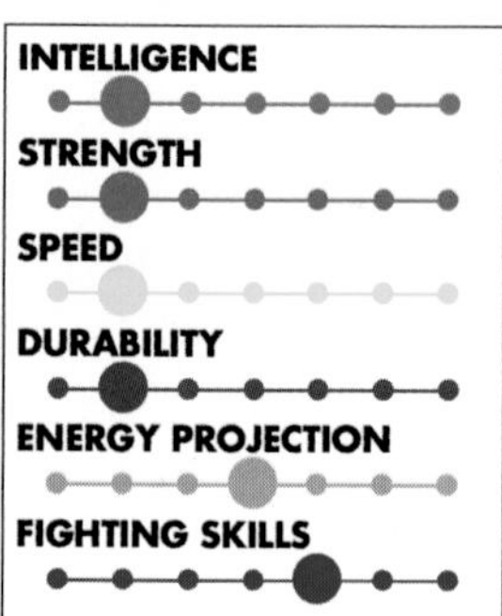

WHITE RABBIT

Real Name: Last name Dodson, first name unrevealed
First Appearance: *Marvel Team-Up* #131 (1983)
Hgt: 5'7"
Wt: 130 lbs.

Fascinated as a child by Alice in Wonderland, this poor little rich girl grew up to become the White Rabbit, loosely based on the character in the book. Motivated purely by thrill, her spree of robberies was eventually halted by Spider-Man and Frog-Man. Joining the Walrus, she was again defeated by Spider-Man, Frog-Man and Leap-Frog. Hitting an all-time low, she hired actors as sidekicks Mad Hatter and Dormouse because no villain wanted to work with her. She then kidnapped the Grizzly and the Gibbon, but was defeated by the duo and Spider-Man. Her inspired arsenal includes a rabbit-shaped car and zeppelin, and a giant Rabbit-Robot.

POWERS/WEAPONS

- Razor-tipped umbrella
- Explosive and razor-tipped carrots
- Jet-boots

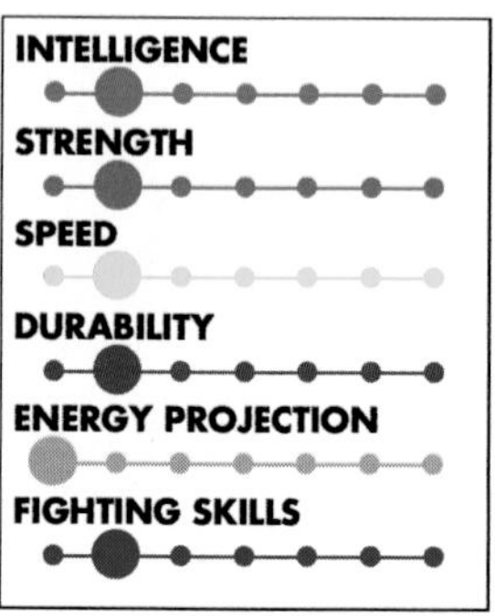

WHITE TIGER

Real Name: Hector Ayala
First Appearance: *Deadly Hands of Kung Fu* #19 (1975)
Hgt: 6'0"
Wt: 190 lbs.

After discovering the magical amulets that had empowered the Sons of the Tiger, Hector Ayala became the White Tiger, safeguarding the streets of New York City from gang violence. As a student at Empire State University, Hector teamed with Spider-Man on several occasions, fighting such enemies as the Masked Marauder and Carrion. Tragically, Ayala was unjustly accused of murder years later. When the trial went badly — despite the best efforts of defense attorney Matt Murdock (Daredevil) — he attempted to escape, pausing just long enough to be shot dead by police. It is unclear whether he deliberately engineered his own death. Murdock was later able to prove Hector's innocence.

POWERS/WEAPONS

- Enhanced fighting skills

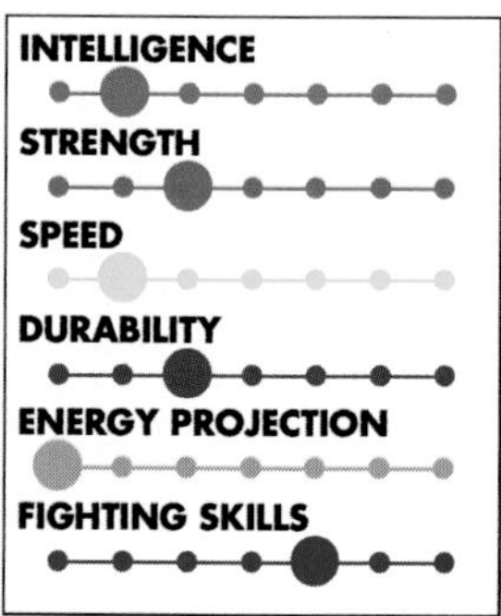

DEBORAH WHITMAN

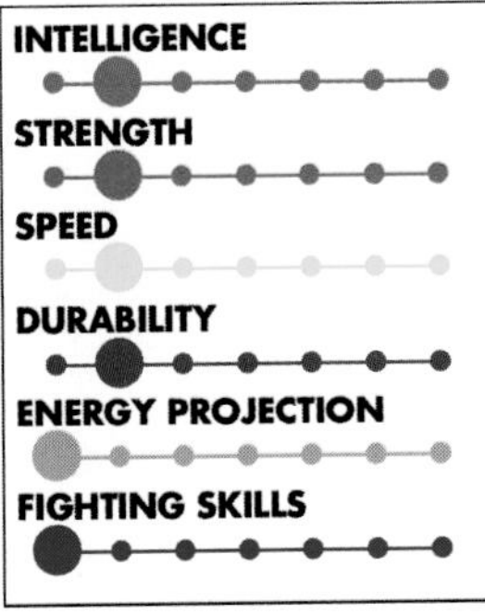

Real Name: Deborah Whitman
First Appearance: *Amazing Spider-Man* #196 (1979)

Hgt: 5'6"
Wt: 120 lbs.

Former office administrator to Dr. Morris Sloan at Empire State University, Deborah Whitman briefly dated Peter Parker. Sadly, the romance was rather one-sided, as Peter did not return her enthusiasm. Over time, Deborah began to suspect that he was Spider-Man. The thought consumed her, nearly driving her mad. Prompted by Deb's psychiatrist, Dr. Bailey Kulkin, Peter confirmed her suspicions to help save her sanity — but Deborah staunchly refused to believe him, instead thinking he had played the part just to help her. She eventually left for the Midwest alongside her old friend, Biff Rifkin.

WILL O' THE WISP

POWERS/WEAPONS

- Density control/intangibility
- Flight
- Superhuman strength and durability
- Hypnosis

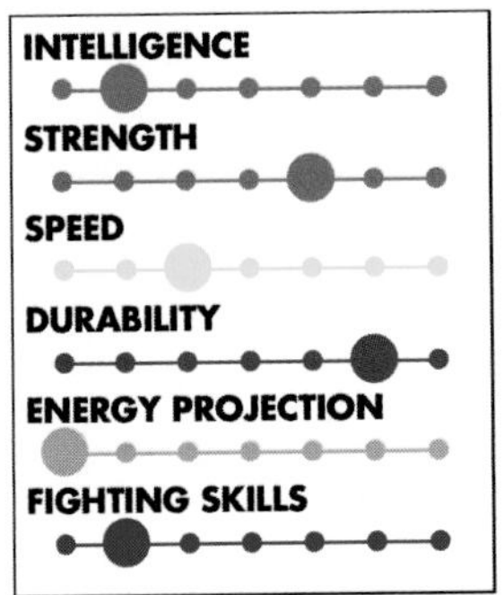

Real Name: Jackson Arvad
First Appearance: *Amazing Spider-Man* #167 (1977)

Hgt: 6'1"
Wt: 195 lbs.

Formerly a scientist with the Brand Corporation, Jackson Arvad was accidentally transformed into Will O' the Wisp while attempting to prevent a power surge from destroying sensitive equipment. Down and out, he then became an unwilling agent of Dr. Jonas Harrow, resulting in an encounter with Spider-Man. Wisp ultimately turned against Harrow and later helped bring down the Brand Corporation — revealing its illicit experiments creating super-villains, such as that which transformed the Tarantula into a giant spider. Will O' the Wisp later served as a member of the Outlaws, until Roxxon Oil forced him to act as its pawn. Jackson freed himself from Roxxon's influence, aided by Ben Reilly.

YITH

POWERS/WEAPONS

- Spits unidentified green liquid
- Powerful tail
- Twin Uzi machine-guns

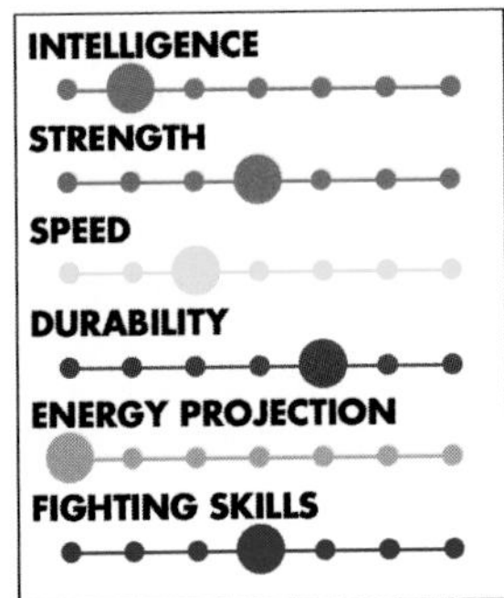

Real Name: Unrevealed
First Appearance: *Spider-Man: Quality of Life* #1 (2002)

Hgt: 6'1"
Wt: 225 lbs.

Yith is a mercenary — half-human, half-snake. She encountered Spider-Man when Cliff Arliss, head of the Monnano Corporation, retained her services. Monnano's chemical dumps had caused Martha and Billy Connors — wife and son of Curt Connors, the Lizard — to contract cancer. Yith's task was to kill Curt before he became a nuisance, but a three-way battle between Yith, Spider-Man and the Lizard ended in stalemate. Billy recovered, but Martha died of cancer. Yith, who until then had been concerned only about her paycheck, killed Arliss out of sympathy for Curt.

APPENDIX

LEGEND

@	Annual	**SPEC**	Spectacular Spider-Man
AF	Amazing Fantasy	**FF**	Fantastic Four
ASM	Amazing Spider-Man	**DD**	Daredevil
JIM	Journey Into Mystery	**MTU**	Marvel Team-Up

A

Abbott, Mr. & Mrs. *ASM #10 (1964)* Former Forest Hills neighbors. Took recuperating Aunt May on vacation to Florida.

Absorbing Man (Carl "Crusher" Creel) & Titania (Mary "Skeeter" MacPherran) *JIM #114 (1965), Secret Wars #3 (1984)* Creel absorbs properties of items touched. Titania is super-strong girlfriend. Clashed with SM during, after Beyonder's Secret Wars.

Ace ("Ace" Spencer) *SPEC @ #5 (1985)* Former leader, Reapers gang. Superhuman reflexes. Testified vs. brother, who killed member of enemy Dragons gang.

Advanced Idea Mechanics (AIM) *Strange Tales #146 (1966)* Commercial weapons makers with world-conquering aspirations. SM encountered armed agents; creations M.O.D.O.K., Cosmic Cube, Super-Adaptoid.

Alpha Flight *Uncanny X-Men #120 (1979)* Canadian super-team. Joined SM vs. Collector, Brass Bishop's Chess Set.

Alpha Robot *MTU #129 (1983)* Created by Mad Thinker's intellectual robots to defend sanctuary, late-1800s-style town of Ponder.

Anansi (Kwaku Anansi) *ASM #48 (2003)* African trickster god. Possibly responsible for spider-powers of Ezekiel, SM. Ascended to godhood by Nyame (aka Nyambe), African sky god.

Anarchists for Freedom Army *ASM @ 2001* Terrorists. Attacked United Nations Plaza, requiring SM's attention on evening MJ returned home from abduction by Stalker.

Ani-Men (Unholy Three—Ape-Man, Bird-Man, Cat-Man—plus Dragonfly, Frog-Man) *DD #10 (1964)* Costumed villains. Agents of Organizer, Count Nefaria, Madame Masque. Fought SM, Daredevil during kidnapping case.

Animen (Buzzard, Crushtacean, Flying Fox, Komodo, Spinneret) *Scarlet Spider Unlimited #1 (1995)* Wundagorian New Men. Agents of High Evolutionary. Sent on search-and-destroy mission vs. Jackal. Led Ben Reilly to discover Cult of the Jackal.

Annihilus *FF @ #6 (1968)* Despot from Negative Zone. Vast powers from Cosmic Control Rod. SM, Human Torch prevented conquest of Earth while battling Frightful Four.

Aquanoids *MTU #14 (1973)* Dr. Dorcas created these amphibious creatures, into which he attempted to transfer life forces of SM, Sub-Mariner.

Arcane Order of the Night *SPEC #170 (1990)* Cult organized by Ambrose Carpathian. Young God Calculus manipulated Space Phantom, SM, Avengers, Outlaws into sending Black Insect Swarm into space for mankind's safety. Current leader Andrew sought Dragon's Egg to recover the killer swarm. Foiled by SM, Black Fox, Dr. Doom.

Atlantis *Motion Picture Funnies Weekly #1 (1939)* Attacked surface world led by Namor, others. Repelled by heroes including SM. Controlled Megasaur. Nearly sacrificed to Set by Deviant priestlord Ghaur.

Atlas (Erik Josten, aka Power Man, Smuggler, Goliath) *Avengers #21 (1965)* Empowered by Baron (Heinrich) Zemo as Power Man. Became Maggia agent, Smuggler. Captured, revealed Maggia secrets, rescued by SM, but wounded by Maggia assassin Eli Rumsford. Powers amplified greatly as Goliath. Fought cosmic, non-cosmic SM.

Axum, Daniel (formerly Danny Broughton, aka Battler) *Thunderbolts #76 (2003)* Super-strong. As Battler, faced SM. Later rebuilt life as professional fighter Axum.

Aunt May's Boarders *MTU #120 (1982)* Nathan Lubensky, Arthur "Anton" Chekov, sisters Martha & Sophie, married couple Victor & Harriet Palermo, Ernie Popchik.

Authority (Tito Mendez) *MTU #4 (1997)* Information merchant. Tricked SM to obtain Sphere of Ultimate Knowledge, lost mind when accessed it.

Avengers Team-Ups Sundown; villains at wedding of Mr. Fantastic, Invisible Woman; Exemplars; Timespinner; Nebula; Stranger; Blackout, Moonstone, Rhino, Electro at Project: PEGASUS; Lava Men; Deathweb; Alternator Bug-Bot; Void; Space Phantom; Black Insect Swarm; Enchantress; Thanos.

Avengers Solo Team-Ups, Captain America (SULTAN, Vermin, Scorpion, Grey Gargoyle, Batroc, Carnage, Stone-Face). **Falcon** (Stone-Face, Midas, Plantman). **Thor** (Living Monolith, Kryllk, Dalia & Meru, Black Abbott, Mongoose, Dark Gods, Tokkots). **Iron Man** (Zarrko & Kang, Wraith/Philip DeWolff, Magma, Radioactive Man, Blacklash). **Henry Pym and/or Wasp** (Egghead, M'Sieu Tete, Equinox). **Hercules** (City-Stealers, Dr. Zeus). **Black Widow** (Silver Samurai, Viper, Owl). **Hawkeye** (Mr. Fear, Quasimodo). **Photon/Captain Marvel** (PRIDE). Starfox (Will-Killer). **Vision and/or Scarlet Witch** (Dark Rider, Toad, Necrodamus, Alpha, Monstroid). **Wonder Man** (Mauler, Psyk-Out, Griffin). **Thunderstrike** (Pandara, Hydro-Man, Absorbing Man & Titania). **Scarlet Witch & Captain America** (Xandu). **Scarlet Witch & Quasar** (Serpent Crown). **Black Panther** (Stegron, Hellrazor). **Quasar** (Lightmaster & Nitro, Terminus). **Tigra** (Kraven the Hunter, Zabo, Man-Killer). **She-Hulk** (Headmen, Man-Killer). **Ant-Man II** (Taskmaster). **Warbird/Ms. Marvel** (Super-Skrull, Silver Dagger). **Mockingbird** (Karl Delandan). **Machine Man** (Baron Brimstone). **Sandman** (Enforcers, ULTIMATUM).

B

Band of Baddies (Critical Mass, Bloodlust, Whiplash, Dentist, Savage Fin) *MCP #49 (1990)* Mutants. Led by PP's former classmate, included PP's dentist. Kidnapped mutant daughter of Wolverine's old friend. Defeated by SM, Wolverine.

Banks, Sharon *ASM #278 (1986)* Lawyer. Defended Flash Thompson (framed as Hobgoblin).

Banjo & Bugeye *SPEC #156 (1989)* Mutant brothers, super-strong and psionic respectively. Fought SM during hero's search for Joe Robertson in rural Pennsylvania.

Baron Brimstone (Walter Theodoric) *Machine Man #16 (1980)* Uses science, magic. Fought Machine Man, SM. Briefly trapped SM in demon dimension. Defeated by Wasp, Paladin.

Baron Helmut Zemo *Captain America #168 (1973)* Son of Nazi war criminal. Captain America foe. Mutated Vermin, Protoids. Attacked Vermin, SM, Dr. Kafka.

Baroness Heike Zemo *SM: Fear Itself Graphic Novel (1992)* Hired White Ninja to steal fear-inducing Cassidy Crystals, encountering SM.

Baron Ludwig von Shtupf *MTU #36 (1975)* Psychotic scientist. Attempted to use Frankenstein Monster, Man-Wolf to create army of monsters. S.H.I.E.L.D. agent Judith Klemmer helped SM, Monster defeat him.

Baron Mordo (Karl Amadeus Mordo) *Strange Tales #111 (1963)* Sorcerer. Dr. Strange foe. Offered JJJ, PP's classmates in sacrifice to Dormammu. Stopped by SM, Strange.

Baron Wolfgang von Strucker *Sgt. Fury and His Howling Commandos #5 (1964)* Former Nazi officer, founder of Hydra. S.H.I.E.L.D. foe. Opposed by several heroes, including SM. Clashed with Richard, Mary Parker.

Basilisk *Marvel Preview #7 (1976)* Demon bound to Satana Hellstrom as punishment to both. Manipulated Dr. Strange, SM, Ms. Marvel to obtain Strange's soul. Satana sacrificed life to destroy him.

Batroc the Leaper (Georges Batroc) *TOS #75 (1966)* French mercenary. Captain America foe. Faced SM, Captain America together.

Bend Sinister *ASM @ #14 (1980)* Mystic confluence allows evil to triumph once every 60,000 years. Wielded by Lucius Dilby, scientist in employ of Dr. Doom. Defeated by SM, Dr. Strange.

MCP	Marvel Comics Presents	**WSM**	Web of Spider-Man	**UTOS**	Untold Tales of Spider-Man
SM	Spider-Man (1990)	**TOS**	Tales of Suspense	**SMROTGG**	Spider-Man: Revenge of the Green Goblin
PPSM	Peter Parker: Spider-Man (1999)	**SENS**	Sensational Spider-Man		
		SMTU	Spider-Man Team-Up		

Bendix, Dr. Albert *SMROTGG #1 (2000)* Physician. Helped Norman Osborn recover after Gathering of Five. Killed by Order of the Goblin.

Bennett, LaFronce *PPSM #35 (2001)* Young boy with harsh home life. Fantasized he was SM's partner, imagining hero to be African-American like him.

Bernhammer, Cynthia *SPEC #145 (1988)* Joe Robertson's defense attorney during Tombstone affair. Dated Nick Katzenberg.

Biotechnix *PPSM #39 (2002)* Prosthetics corporation controlled by Fusion in plan (with Doc Ock) to control influential people, including Congressman Miles Bradley.

Black Abbott *MTU #147 (1984)* Former Dakoth-Kuru monk. Mentally controlled Black Apostles. Goal of world conquest. Opposed by SM with Nomad, Human Torch, Thor.

Black Crow (Jesse Black Crow) *Captain America #290 (1984)* Heroic avatar of Native American god. Put SM, Puma through mystical experience to resolve differences, removed Puma's knowledge of SM's identity.

Blackheart *DD #270 (1989)* Spawn of Mephisto. Opposed by SM, Daredevil.

Black Knight (Nathaniel Garrett) *Tales to Astonish #52 (1963)* Advanced weaponry, flying horse. Clashed with SM while proving worth to Masters of Evil.

Blackbyrd (Nathaniel Alexander Byrd) *Deadly Hands of Kung Fu #12 (1975)* Private eye. Worked with Sons of the Tiger, White Tiger, SM.

Blacklash (Mark Scarlotti, aka Whiplash) *TOS #97 (1968)* Mentally unstable, whip-wielding mercenary. Iron Man foe, also battled SM.

Blake, Kent *Kent Blake of the Secret Service #1 (1951)* Spy, soldier, law-enforcement agent. Active for decades. Killed by petty criminal Jimbo Ryan. Ghost returned to help SM capture killer.

Blare *MTU #1 (1997)* Sonic bombs. Defeated by SM.

Blastaar *FF #62 (1967)* Alien despot. Clashed with SM on Earth, in Negative Zone.

Blizzard (Gregor Shapanka) *TOS #45 (1963)* Cold-projecting Iron Man foe. Kidnapped Robert Saunders.

Blob (Fred J. Dukes) *X-Men #3 (1964)* Strong, unmovable X-Men foe. Rampage halted by SM, Black Cat. Fought SM alone, also with Brotherhood of Evil Mutants.

Bloodscream & Roughouse *Wolverine #4 (1989)* Wolverine foes. Centuries-old mutant vampire and super-strong partner, respectively. Employed by Black Tarantula. Encountered Ricochet (PP).

Bloodshed (Wyndell Dickinson) *WSM #81 (1991)* Car-thief turned armored enforcer. Intimidated accountant Richard Dichinson. Rescued from vengeful employer Philippe Bazin by SM.

Blowtorch *MCP #67 (1990)* Armored arsonist. Defeated by SM.

Blue Boys Gang *ASM #284 (1987)* Masked criminals during Rose/Arranger gang war. Fought SM, Punisher.

Bobster (Sturdevant E. "Bob" Rollins) & Hypertron 1.0 *WSM #83 (1991)* Hypertron battlesuit designed by former AIM agents Timmy, Myron. Used in failed robbery. P.R. man Bob acquired it; sought fame, fortune as super hero, "The Bobster."

Bolt, Jefferson *MTU #3 (1972)* Gang member. Transformed into pseudo-vampire by Morbius. Apparently killed when gang fought SM, Human Torch.

Bolton, Dr. Bradley *ASM #153 (1976)* Co-creator of WHO. Kingpin had international criminal Paine kidnap Bolton's daughter Mindy to extort machine's secrets. Bolton sacrificed life to protect daughter.

Bossman Morgan *Captain America #152 (1972)* Harlem crime lord. Opposed by SM, Cage, Captain America, others.

Boullion, Andre *ASM #265 (1985)* Underworld fence, friend of Black Fox. Killed by Chance, framing Black Fox.

Bounty *FF #14 (1999)* Super-strong extraterrestrial mercenary. Befriended FF. Teamed with SM when Chinatown gang Golden Horde feuded with Pluto's warrior women, Bacchae, over intergroup romance.

Bounty Hunter *SPEC #104 (1985)* High-tech mercenary. Sought bounty on bail-jumper Rocket Racer. Defeated by SM.

Brace *Annex #1 (1994)* Cyborg, AIM agent. Fought SM, Annex.

Bradley, Carrie *Amazing Scarlet Spider #1 (1995)* Stockbroker, self-defense instructor. Ben Reilly neighbor.

Briosky, Mr. *WSM #24 (1987)* Casino owner. Offered crooked radio-controlled dice by Vulture, refused. Vulture's revenge foiled by SM, Hobgoblin.

Brll'nah>zhhk< *PPSM #23 (2000)* Small gray aliens. Represented by McNair and Associates. Abducted PP, Randy Robertson, others for cross-species DNA experiment. Resultant, dangerous spider-like creature recaptured by SM.

Bromwell, Dr. *ASM #9 (1964)* May Parker's physician for several years.

Brotherhood of Evil Mutants (Toad, Blob, Pyro, Phantazia, Sauron, Thornn) *X-Force #5 (1991)* Oft-changing mutant terrorist group. Toad-led lineup vs. SM, Darkhawk, Sleepwalker to acquire dimension-hopping mutant Portal. SM previously saved Toad from suicide, inspiring him to briefly join Misfits, team of SM sidekick wannabes.

Brothers Grimm (Percy & Barton Grimes) *Iron Man #187 (1984)* Conjuring powers. Fought cosmic, non-cosmic SM.

Brown, Mindy S. McPherson *ASM #78 (1969)* Wife of Hobie Brown (Prowler). Framed by employer, Transcorp; cleared by SM, Prowler. Separated, but reunited after Hobie injured in Great Game.

Buchanan, Charles H. *SM #38 (1993)* Minor thief captured repeatedly by SM. Rescued Sarah Klein (friend of JJJ) during Electro rampage.

Buchinsky, Col. *ASM #331 (1990)* Government faction agent. With Mechanoids, controlled cocaine stockpile intended as currency in event of economic collapse. Foiled by SM, Punisher.

Buel *SENS #21 (1997)* Extradimensional sorcerer with Gremlyn servants. Arrived through Technomancers' Babylon Portal. SM, Dr. Strange opposed attempt to merge worlds.

Bullit, Sam *ASM #91 (1970)* Politician. Ran D.A. campaign on anti-SM platform. Kidnapped Joe Robertson. Exposed by SM, Iceman.

Bullseye *DD #131 (1976)* Master assassin. Daredevil foe. Encountered SM when sent by Kingpin to kill Senator Ward.

Byrnes, Timothy *ASM #259 (1984)* Married MJ's sister Gayle. Abandoned wife, sons (Kevin, Tommy).

Caches, Professor Marina *ASM #427 (1997)* ESU psychology professor. Ex-wife of Black Tarantula. Fled with son Fabian. Dated Dante Rigoletto, nephew of Fortunato.

Cadre (Dementia, Shard, Vortex) *WSM @ #9 (1993)* Members of Hellbent, secret non-human, super-powered bloodline. Trained by heroic warriors Knights Templar. Clashed with SM during their first venture into outside world.

Captain Marvel (Mar-Vell) *Marvel Super-Heroes #12 (1967)* Heroic Kree warrior, became

APPENDIX

Protector of the Universe . Teamed with SM vs. Basilisk, other threats. Died of cancer. Artificially conceived son Genis-Vell took name, helped SM vs. powered-spliced Thanos clones.

Captain Power (Christina Carr) *SM: Chapter One #1 (1998)* Crippled by same accident that mutated Dr. Octopus. Developed power to transform to super-strong male. Revenge foiled by SM.

Carradine, Jessica *SENS #0 (1996)* Daughter of Burglar, hated SM. Dated Ben Reilly, learned secret identity, became convinced of his heroism.

Carrion II (Malcolm McBride) *SPEC #149 (1989)* Infected by Jackal's virus, became second Carrion. Clashed with SM with Hobgoblin, Carnage, others. Recovery at Ravencroft aided by mother, Beatrice Martha McBride.

Carrion III (Dr. William Allen) *SM: Dead Man's Hand (1997)* S.H.I.E.L.D. scientist, analyzed Jackal's virus. Became third Carrion. Infected crowd with Zombie Virus, defeated by SM.

Cassady, Wesley *ASM #302 (1988)* Kansas construction foreman. Bitten by radioactive rabbit. Kept powers secret, refused to help SM vs. Dr. Nero.

Cassidy, Black Tom (Thomas Samuel Eamon Cassidy) *X-Men #99 (1976)* Longtime partner of Juggernaut. Wielded half of Juggernaut's power vs. SM, X-Men. With Juggernaut, fought SM, X-Force.

Cat (Shen Kui) *Master of Kung Fu #38 (1976)* Expert martial artist. Ally, enemy to Shang-Chi. Aided in rescuing son by SM.

Cell-12 (Andros, Bramer, Lasher, Nardi) *ASM #411 (1996)* Cyborgs. Hired by Hobgoblin to attack Ben Reilly, PP. Apparently killed by Hobgoblin on failing.

Chambers Brothers *SM/Punisher/Sabretooth: Designer Genes (1993)* Roxxon executive Brandon Chambers sponsored brother Dr. Phillip Chambers' DNA experiments, not realizing other brother Mitchell was subject, transformed into beastial creature. SM, Punisher ended operation. Sabretooth killed Phillip. Brandon kept Mitchell prisoner for more research.

Cherryh, Randolph Winston *DD #177 (1981)* City councilman. Offered SM reward to capture Batwing, SM refused.

Chesbro *ASM #419 (1997)* Spy for Black Tarantula.

Chess Set (Brass Bishop, Dark Tower, Killer Queen, King Coal, Overknight) *Alpha Flight #121 (1993)* Fought SM, Wolverine, Alpha Flight when Brass Bishop auctioned energy-saturated corpses of scientist Hedison, Gamma Flighters Silver & Auric.

Chief Examiner *Questprobe #1 (1984)* Created by alien Durgan to obtain power vs. Black Fleet. Analyzed several heroes, including SM.

Childress, Dr. Delia "Delilah" *MTU #102 (1981)* Former flame of Doc Samson. AIM agent. Directed Rhino to fight SM, Doc Samson.

Cicero, Caesar ("Big C") *ASM #73 (1969)* Maggia lawyer, gangland boss. Frequently encountered SM.

City-Stealers *MTU #28 (1974)* Two men. Armored by They Who Wield Power. Attempt to steal Manhattan island foiled by SM, Hercules.

Clayton, Katrinka Janice (K.J.) *ASM #190 (1979)* Reclusive publisher of Daily Globe. Target of near-lethal takeover by Rupert Dockery, saved by SM.

Clemmens, Charles *Tangled Web #7 (2001)* Learned SM's identity when son Jimmy's life was saved. Kept secret. SM later unwitting player in Clemmens' plan to get money for son's medical treatment.

Cochrane, Tom *Tangled Web #4 (2001)* Kingpin lieutenant. Killed for failure when SM ruined weapons shipment.

Code: Blue (Lt. Marcus Stone, others) *Thor #426 (1990)* NYPD division to combat superhuman threats. Aided SM vs. Wrecking Crew.

Coldheart *SM #49 (1994)* Government agent sought vengeance on superhumans for death of son. Attacked Hobgoblin, SM. Battle armor, freezing swords.

Collector (Taneleer Tivan) *Avengers #28 (1966)* Elder of the Universe. Collects rare objects, lifeforms. Attempt to acquire SM, Marrina defeated by SM, Alpha Flight.

Corbett, Ron *WSM #21 (1986)* Olympics trainee, blamed SM for father's death in bank robbery. Impersonated, framed SM, convinced of SM's heroism.

Cosmic Cube *TOS #79 (1966)* SM used object's incredible power vs. Elder God Set at Project: PEGASUS. Now evolved into Kubik.

Coterie *Contest of Champions #1 (1999)* Temporary alliance of Brood, Badoon races. Organized Contest of Champions to secretly destroy, consume Earth's heroes. SM faced Domino of X-Force. Coterie defeated with help from Lockdown, Rosetta Stone from Negative Zone. SM later encountered Badoon criminals.

Creaux *SMTU #5 (1996)* Corrupt police officer, Tombstone agent. Used deadly powder. Fought Ben Reilly, Gambit.

Creep *SM #96 (1998)* Norman Osborn agent. Attacked Alison Mongraine, Joe Robertson.

Crimewave *Sleepwalker #6 (1991)* Sought to supplant Kingpin. Halted by SM, Sleepwalker.

Crimson Crusader & Imp (Rory & Pandora Destine) *MCP #158 (1994)* Young members of super-powered Clan Destine. Sought SM's advice, received help vs. Skyline Killer.

Cult of the Jackal (Anubis, Caiman, Harrier, Piranis, others) *Scarlet Spider Unlimited #1 (1995)* Jackal's rebel group of Wundagorian New Men. Accepted back into Wundagore after encountering Scarlet Spider.

Cussler, Phillip Sr. *SPEC #215 (1994)* Elderly gentleman, mildly deranged. Employed Scorpion in revenge plan on family. Attacked SM from behind, received instinctive near-fatal blow.

Cutthroat (Daniel Leighton) *MTU #89 (1980)* Costumed assassin. Brother of quasi-hero Diamondback. Hired to kill SM, who fought him with Nightcrawler.

Cyber-Hunters *WSM #97 (1993)* Armored assassins of Foreigner. Cooperated with Blood Rose vs. SM, only to turn against him per Foreigner's orders.

Cyberslayers *Spectacular Scarlet Spider #1 (1995)* Monstrous robots. Used by Alistair Smythe vs. Carolyn Seward, Scarlet Spider.

Cyborg X *SM #18 (1992)* Reconstructed soldier. Went crazy; subdued by SM, Ghost Rider.

Daily Bugle Management & Columnists (Past & Present) J. Jonah Jameson (owner, publisher), Joseph "Robbie" Robertson (editor), William Walter Goldman (former owner, publisher), Thomas Fireheart (former owner), Norman Osborn (former owner), Kate Cushing (city editor), Victor Pei (assistant photo editor), Vickie Danner (D.C. liaison), Ann MacIntosh (classifieds solicitor), Wendy Thorton (sports columnist), Dilbert Trilby (obituary writer), Isabel Bunsen (science editor).

Daily Bugle Investigative Staff (Past & Present), Reporters: Ben Urich, Ned Leeds, Ken Ellis, Jacob Conover, Frederic Foswell, Joy Mercado, Charley Snow, Betty Brant, Melvin Gooner (Canadian Wendigo story), Maggie Lorca, Katherine "Kat" Farrell (Tinkerer/Judge story), Anthea Depres. **Photographers:** Phil Sheldon (Gwen's death), Lance Bannon, PP, Nick Katzenberg, Angela Yin (friend to PP, cousin to Dragonfly), Cole Cooper (FACADE suspect), Tony Reeves.

LEGEND

SMTFA	Spider-Man: The Final Adventure	**SMATP**	Spider-Man: The Arachnis Project	**SMU**	Spider-Man Unlimited
SMFAE	Spider-Man: Friends and Enemies	**MTIO**	Marvel Two-In-One	**MTE**	Marvel Treasury Edition
		GSSM	Giant-Size Spider-Man		

Daily Bugle Junior Staff (Past & Present), Administrative: Betty Brant, Glory Grant. **Interns:** Phil Urich, Meredith Campbell, Spence Williams. **Trainees:** Billy Walters.

Daily Globe Staff (Past & Present) Uri Rosenthal (former owner); KJ Clayton (publisher); Barney Bushkin (photo editor); Pamela Dean (society editor); reporters Rupert Dockery, Eddie Brock, April Maye, Sandy Jones; photographers PP, Lance Bannon.

Daily Grind *SENS #0 (1996)* NY restaurant. Employed Ben Reilly, who befriended many of its patrons: fashion model Desiree Winthrop, trivia master Buzz, Jessica Carradine. Alison Mongrain worked there briefly, to poison MJ.

Dakimh the Enchanter *Adventure into Fear #14 (1973)* Spirit of pre-Atlantis wizard. Aided SM vs. D'Spayre in Man-Thing's swamp.

Daley, Brian Sr. *SPEC #84 (1983)* Politician. Son Brian Jr., wife Marjorie. Exploited family-man image. Son kidnapped by Conchita Hernandez, who lost own baby. Daley's wife exposed true nature.

Dalia the Shape-Changer & Meru the Mind-Bender *MTU #115 (1982)* Aliens from Charron. Dalia (leader of underclass Haif-Nas resistance) submerged own memory as homeless Jane Doe on Earth, hiding from enemy, former lover, Meru (member of elite Haifs). Two spirits merged, briefly possessed, maddened Valkyrie, who fought SM. Thor sent them into space.

Damage Control *MCP #19 (1989)* NY superhuman-related damage-repair firm. Rescued SM from Tinkerer's Alternator Bug-Bot.

Dansen Macabre *MTU #93 (1980)* Criminal priestess of Shiva. Opposed by SM, Werewolf, Shroud. Mesmerizes, kills with dancing.

Dark Rider *MTU #42 (1976)* Last of race of ancient wizards. Brought Scarlet Witch into 1692 to absorb powers. SM, others followed through time, defeated him.

Darkhawk (Christopher Powell) *Darkhawk #1 (1991)* Young hero in super-powered alien body. Joined SM vs. Brotherhood of Evil Mutants, Hostiles, others.

Darter (Randy Vale) *SPEC #29 (1979)* Served Carrion, was promised SM's powers. Attacked PP, who was defended by White Tiger. Carrion betrayed Darter, giving SM powers to Spider-Amoeba. Darter attacked Carrion, was killed.

Daughters of the Dragon (Colleen Wing, Misty Knight) *Deadly Hands of Kung Fu #32 (1977)* Private investigators. Aided SM vs. Steel Serpent. Colleen: trained samurai. Misty: bionic arm.

Dead Aim, Battlescar, Warzone *SPEC #210 (1994)* Super-agents of Justin Hammer. Fought Foreigner, encountered SM.

Deadmaker *ASM @ (1996)* Son of KGB assassin defeated by SM's parents. Took father's codename, attempted to kill Parkers. Defeated by SM.

Deadpool *New Mutants #98 (1991)* Mercenary. Traveled back in time, lived out period in SM's life, using holographic projector. Fought Kraven the Hunter.

Death *Captain Marvel #27 (1973)* In near-death experience, SM fought Thanos to persuade embodiment of Death to revive little girl. Death was impressed, revived him, too.

Deathstorm *MCP #12 (1989)* Leader of terrorist group A.R.E.S. (Assassination, Revolution, Extortion, Sabotage). Killed by Solo, despite SM's intervention.

Deathurge *MTIO #72* Avatar of cosmic entity Oblivion. Manipulates darkforce to encourage suicide. Fought SM, who sought to save victim.

Deathwatch (aka Stephen Lords) *Ghost Rider #1 (1990)* Extradimensional Translord. Employed Blackout, Snowblind, Hag, Troll, ninjas as agents. Ghost Rider II, John Blaze, SM fought his Deathwatch demons. Two demons possessed Doppelganger before its death.

Deathweb (Antro, Arachne, Therak) *Avengers West Coast #82 (1992)* Super-villains controlled by clandestine government group Conclave (Michael Clemson, Manipulator, unrevealed others). Battled SM, West Coast Avengers. Involved in creation, subsequent manipulation of Spider-Woman II (Carpenter).

Defenders *Marvel Feature #1 (1971)* Loosely organized super-team. Fought Lunatik, Enchantress with SM.

Defenders Solo Team-Ups, Dr. Strange (Xandu, Wraith/Philip DeWolff, Silver Dagger, Basilisk, Serpent Crown, Baron Mordo, Lucius Dilby/Bend Sinister, Sundown, Buel, Monks of Hidden Temple). **Nighthawk** (Meteor Man/Looter, Mindy Williams). **Valkyrie/ Brunnehilde** (Meteor Man/Looter, Dalia, Meru). **Cage** (Rat Pack, Purple Man, Scorpion, Razorline, Nautilus). **Hulk** (Stegron, Soviet Super-Soldiers, Warzone, Sinister Six, Doombot, Chameleon, Major Tremens, De'Lila). **Moondragon** (Dark Rider).

De'Lila *FF #347 (1990)* Mesmeric leader of Skrull rebel group. Captured FF, manipulated SM, Ghost Rider II, Hulk, Wolverine into forming New FF, locating near-invulnerable Skrull-created Inorganic Technotroid (ITT) in Subterranea.

Desinna & Tarros *GSSM #3 (1975)* Natives of trans-temporal dimension Saku. Criminal Desinna manipulated Man of Bronze into helping against scientist Tarros in 1934. SM judged correctly, aided Tarros in modern times.

Deterrence Research Corporation *GSSM #4 (April 1975)* Hired forces to Moses Magnum vs. SM, Punisher. Employed Hammer, Anvil vs. SM, Guardians of the Galaxy.

Devil Dinosaur & Moonboy *Devil Dinosaur #1 (1978)* Natives of Dinosaur World. Mesmerized by Ringmaster; freed by SM, who helped T-Rex, monkey-like Moonboy find home in Savage Land.

Diablo (Esteban Diablo) *FF #30 (1964)* Centuries-old alchemist. FF foe. Attempted to recover deadly relics from Metropolitan Museum of Art, foiled by SM.

Diamond, Morris "The Snake" *WSM #45 (1988)* Stole secrets from Vulture. In revenge, Vulture crashed Snake's plane, which also carried PP, undercover CID agent Sara Glenville. Eventually arrested.

Digger *ASM #51 (2003)* Gamma-powered composite of Vegas Thirteen, killed over forty years ago by mob boss Morris Forelli. Defeated by SM, who was employed to protect Forelli's daughter.

Dockery, Rupert M. *Spider-Woman #26 (1980)* Corrupt journalist. Hired Belinda Bell to impersonate Daily Globe owner K.J. Clayton to seize control of paper. Foiled by SM.

Doctor Angst (Jonas Mueller) *SPEC #252 (1997)* Unethical scientist. Agent of Norman Osborn. Mutated Sir, created Green Goblin Construct.

Doctor Faustus (Johann Fennoff) *Captain America #107 (1968)* Criminal psychologist. Captain America foe. Controlled SM's mind in plot to mesmerize nation, but hero won out. Sent Everyman to steal energy from others. Fought SM.

Doctor Nero (Royce Nero) *ASM #302 (1988)* Former government scientist. Used riot-control weaponry to attack On-Line Research in Kansas. Defeated by SM, interviewing for job as PP.

Doctor Paine (Thaddeus Paine) *Morbius #4 (1992)* Sadistic surgeon. SM inadvertently prevented Morbius from capturing him. Experimented on Venom.

Doctor Zeus & Menagerie of Myth *MTU #2 (1997)* Deranged scientist dedicated to Greece's supposed glory days. Created Menagerie of Myth, which fought SM, Hercules.

APPENDIX

Doombots *FF #5 (1962)* Semi-autonomous simulacra of Dr. Doom. One infiltrated Avengers Mansion when super-team was believed dead following Onslaught crisis; SM, Hulk, Aquarian prevented it from stealing Avengers secrets. SM has faced others.

Dracula (Vlad Tepes) *Tomb of Dracula #1 (1972)* SM, Dr. Strange faced vampire lord, exposing Dracula's mate, Raynee, as unknowing magical construct.

Dragonfly (Meiko Yin) *ASM #421 (1997)* Cousin of Daily Bugle photographer Angela Yin. Gained True Believer clan warrior role of Dragonfly. Rebelled when ordered to kill Angela.

Dreadknight (Bram Velsing) *Iron Man #101 (1977)* Former Dr. Doom scientist. Briefly took control of Latveria. SM prevented him from executing Betty Brant.

Dreadnoughts *Strange Tales #154 (1967)* Powerful robots, originally built by Hydra. Used vs. SM by Maggia, New Enforcers.

Dryrot (Paul Contoni) *SMTFA #3 (1996)* Mutated into monstrous form by GARID's experiments. Helped SM vs. Tendril. Regained humanity.

D'Spayre *MTU #68 (1978)* Demonic lord of fear. Attacked SM in Man-Thing's swamp. Attacked Ben Reilly during exile. Forced Black Cat to fight both men.

Dubroth, Armand *ASM #219 (1981)* Blackmailed Warden Rue of Ryker's Island to arrange escape. Stopped by SM.

DuPaul, Medgar *WSM #18 (1986)* Virginian millionaire, hunts homeless for sport. Stopped by intended victim PP, local Deputy Sarah.

Dusk (Rebel Leader of Negative Zone) *SM #90 (1998)* Role passed on among natives of planet Tarsuu. SM adopted it to battle Blastaar, again to escape bounty.

E

Ebon Knights & White Knights *SMTU #1 (1995)* Energy-powered androids of Hellfire Club. Used in game between Shinobi Shaw, Benedict Kine for JJJ's life. JJJ rescued by SM, X-Men.

Eel (Leopold Stryke) *Strange Tales #112 (1963)* Electricity powers. Joined Electro to battle SM early in career. Deceased.

Eel II (Edward Lavell) *Power Man and Iron Fist #92 (1984)* Impersonated Snake Marston as Enforcers member. Fought SM as New Enforcers member. Sought Lifeline Tablet on behalf of Caesar Cicero, encountering SM.

Egghead (Elihas Starr) *Tales to Astonish #38 (1962)* Criminal genius. Manipulated fight between SM, Giant-Man, Wasp.

Elf with a Gun (Relf) *SMTU #5 (1996)* Recruited Circus of Crime to help track killer of uncle, Melf. Encountered Ben Reilly, Howard the Duck.

Empathoid *SPEC #6 (1977)* Extradimensional empathic android. Merged with Morbius. Transferred to SM, who overloaded it with emotions.

Emperor of the Eastern Galactic Sector *PPSM #50 (2003)* Gelatinous alien. Approached NY's SETI Research Center. Defeated by SM before purpose revealed.

Enclave *FF #66 (1967)* Three scientists. Sought benevolent world dictatorship. Created Adam Warlock, Kismet. Attempted to control minds of others. Foiled by SM, Thunderbolts.

Enervator *ASM #164 (1977)* Created by Dr. Curt Connors to rejuvenate SM after life force drained by Kingpin. Subsequently created Iguana, Spider-Lizard. Accidentally destroyed by Moonstone.

Enforcer (Charles L. Delazny Jr.) *Ghost Rider #22 (1977)* Armored assassin. Blackmailed Spider-Woman (Jessica Drew) into committing crimes. Defeated by SM.

ESU (Administrators) Chancellor Edward Gorman, Vice Chancellor Dr. Edward Lansky (Lightmaster), Dean Corliss, Dean Montesi, President Dwyer, Deborah Whitman (secretary), Shelly Fisch (grants administrator), Harvey MacNamara (registrar), Dr. Reandeau (counselor, helped MJ).

ESU (Teaching & Research Staff) Dr. Miles Warren (biochem), Prof. Balinger (chemistry), Dr. Curt Connors (biochem), Prof. Ramon Vasquez (ethnic studies), Dr. Clifton Shallot (biochem), Prof. Buck Mitty (entomology), Prof. Evan Swann (physics), Dr. Maxwell Lubisch (physics), Prof. Marina Caches (psych), Prof. Daniel Ironwood (cosmology), Dr. Andrea Janson (molecular bio), Dr. Kissick (biochem), Prof. Slattery (biochem), Dr. William Fields (physics), Dr. Sydney Lanning (physics), Dr. Morris Sloan (entomology), Paul Stacy (physics), Dr. Benita Sanchez (biology).

ESU (Students) PP, Flash Thompson, Harry Osborn, Gwen Stacy, Sally Green, Brad Davis (dated MJ), Hector Ayala (White Tiger), Phillip Chang, Marcy Kane, Chip Martin, Steve Hopkins, Roger Hochberg, Mia Carrera (dated Roger), Harvey K. Farber, Cissy Ironwood, Chip (killed by Carnage), Holly Gillis (dated Hector), Carlos Munoz, Tony Nesters, Dawn Starr (tutored by PP, dated him), Barney Fenton, Biff Rifkin, Anne-Marie Baker, Robin Vega, Shantal Wilkes (friend of MJ), MJ (studied psych), Donovan Zane, Neil Aiken, Jack Hammer (Weasel, Deadpool's armorer).

Evans, Doris *Strange Tales #113 (1963)* Former Human Torch girlfriend. Flirted with PP to make Torch jealous.

Everyman (Larry Ekler) *Captain America #267 (1982)* Psychotic defender of common man. Fought Captain America, SM, Mr. Fantastic.

Exemplars *PPSM #11 (1999)* Eight super-beings empowered by mystic principalities as part of Wager of the Octossence. World-conquering plans opposed by SM, Avengers.

Extreme Emergency Team (Lt. Sylvia Grace, others) *SM: Web of Doom #2 (1994)* Highly decorated NYPD officers. Captured SM when framed for murder by Beetle.

F

Fallon *ASM #28 (2001)* Blind date with PP while MJ believed dead. Attractive, but had criminal record, gothic habits, contortionist skills.

FF Team-Ups, Full Team (Sundown, General Coy, Skrulls including De'Lila, Wizard of Perrinois, Grim Reaper's barrier, Sinister Six, Atlantis Attacks, Frightful Four, Fearsome Foursome, Enchantress). **Human Torch** (Monocle, Sandman, Enforcers, Morbius, Lizard, Black Abbott, Wizard, Speed Demon, Fox, Yellow Claw, Super-Skrull, Headmen, Avant Guard, Zarrko, Kang). **Invisible Woman** (Bossman Morgan). **Mr. Fantastic** (Everyman, Mole Man, Basilisk). **Thing** (Basilisk, Puppet Master, Mad Thinker, Sardeth, Thanos).

Fate, Ian *Defenders #104 (1982)* Sorcerer, friend of Man-Thing. Attacked JJJ, SM.

Fender, Billy *PPSM #36 (2001)* Private eye. Incorrectly identified SM as JJJ.

Fielding, Clarence *SM #89 (1998)* Lost bookkeeping job. Hunted SM for bounty, saved hero's life instead. Rescued Normie Osborn from Green Goblin Construct.

Finisher (Karl Fiers) *ASM @ #5 (1968)* Assassin, employee of Communist Red Skull. Arranged deaths of Richard, Mary Parker. Confessed to SM before death.

Firearms, Vampiro, Badd Axe *Nova #5 (1999)* Criminals, destroyed home of Nova's parents. Defeated by SM, Nova.

Firebrand (Broxtel) *WSM #77 (1991)* Used stolen fire-powered armor for extortion, arson. Defeated by SM, Cloak & Dagger.

Firefist *SPEC #225 (1995)* Used flame powers in murderous crusade vs. homeless. Defeated by SM, Green Goblin (Phil Urich).

Fireheart Industries *ASM #256 (1984)* Company controlled by Puma. Offered PP job.

Bought out Daily Bugle. Jenna Taylor is Thomas Fireheart's PA.

Fitzpatrick, William "Wild Will" *UTOS #-1 (1997)* OSS agent during World War II. Worked with Invaders. Father of Mary Fitzpatrick Parker, grandfather of SM.

Flag-Smasher *Captain America #312 (1985)* Led anti-nationalist terrorist organization ULTIMATUM. Helped SM, Sandman vs. group renegades.

Folsome, Dr. *ASM #418 (1996)* Delivered MJ's stillborn daughter. Drugged PP for Norman Osborn.

Foswell, Janice *MTU #38 (1975)* Daughter of Big Man. Sought vengeance vs. SM as second Big Man. Unwittingly killed by boyfriend, Nick Lewis Jr., second Crime-Master.

Fox (Reynard Slinker) *Strange Tales @ #2 (1963)* Criminal mastermind. Twice clashed with Human Torch, SM.

Frankenstein Monster *Monster of Frankenstein #1 (1973)* Aided SM, Man-Wolf vs. Baron von Shtupf. Helped SM vs. Dr. Kraft, Frankenclones.

Freaks (Six, Gorilla Girl, Muck Monster) *MTU #91 (1980)* Circus performers mesmerized by Moondark to fight SM, Ghost Rider. Embarked on own adventures, encountering Hammer, Anvil.

Frederickson, Kolina *SMROTGG #1 (2000)* Nurse. Treated Norman Osborn after Gathering of Five. Became lover.

Future Max *WSM @ #1 (1985)* Teenaged inventor with muscular disorder, Max, built robot Future Max to steal equipment. Halted by SM. Future Max was rebuilt as battle armor for Alexis Sharp, who went on rampage. Stopped by Max, SM.

G

Game Players *PPSM #53 (2003)* Wealthy men; bet on SM battles vs. Boomerang, XP-2000 robot, Scorpion, Rocket Racer. Rocket Racer secretly revealed backers to SM. XP-2000 provided evidence.

Gang of Four (Copperhead, Gladiator, Owl, Stilt-Man) *DD/SM #1 (2001)* Organized by demonically powered Copperhead. Fought Daredevil, SM. Betrayed by Copperhead.

Gardner, Donna & Donnie *SPEC #102 (1985)* Twins. SM stopped Donnie's suicide to provide kidney for Donna.

GARID *SMTFA #1 (1995)* Galannon Alternative Research for Immunization Development. Researched cure for flesh-eating disease Necrotizing Fascitis; instead produced Dryrot, Tendril. Calvin Falconer (head of security), Bill Galannon (son of founder), Dr. Monica Staphos (head researcher), Dr. Eric Schwinner (scientist).

General Techtronics Corporation *AF #15 (1962)* Sponsored original demonstration of safe handling of nuclear laboratory waste materials, from which SM gained powers. Known employees: Dr. Eric Schwinner (scientist).

Genetrix *WSM #123 (1995)* Overgrown viruses. Constantly mutating forms. Created by Jackal; used vs. SM, allies.

Ghost *Iron Man #219 (1987)* Freelance industrial saboteur. Invisible, intangible, controls machines. Fought SM, Iron Man, Black Panther, Sunturion. Tried to destroy Tri-Corp.

Ghost Rider (John Blaze & Zarathos) *Marvel Spotlight #5 (1972)* Motorcycle-riding Spirit of Vengeance. Joined SM vs. Orb, Trapster, Moondark. Freed from demon Zarathos, gained own supernatural power. Helped new Ghost Rider, SM vs. Venom, Spider-X, Hobgoblin (Macendale), others.

Ghost Rider II (Dan Ketch) *Ghost Rider #1 (1990)* Empowered by Spirits of Vengeance. Joined SM vs. Venom, Demogoblin. In temporary FF, with SM.

Gibbs Family (Frank, Jacob, Tanya, Vicky) *WSM #33 (1987)* Frank was Kingpin's agent. Wife Vicky wanted out. Arranger put her in Mad Dog Ward. SM imprisoned in ward during rescue. Frank helped him escape, family left NY.

Gillis, Holly *SPEC #18 (1978)* ESU art student, girlfriend of Hector Ayayla (White Tiger). Hector eventually married another woman.

Gladiator (Melvin Potter) *DD #18 (1966)* Daredevil foe. Believed himself to be Roman gladiator, wore spinning circular wrist-blades. Encountered SM. Retired.

Goblinettes *SM: Legacy of Evil (1996)* Three feminine robotic versions of Green Goblin. Harry Osborn used in posthumous plot to force son to be Green Goblin.

Godbe, Janine (real name Elizabeth Tyne) *SM: The Lost Years #1 (1995)* Ben Reilly's love. Changed name to escape after killing abusive father. Apparently killed by Kaine, returned to meet Ben and face justice.

Goddess *Infinity War #2 (1992)* Projection of good side of Adam Warlock. Created Cosmic Egg (from thirty Cosmic Cubes), attempted to destroy universe to eliminate evil. Commanded mesmerized heroes, including SM.

Gog *ASM #103 (1971)* 100' alien crashed on Earth as child. Sergei Kravinoff used as pawn vs. SM. Briefly recruited to Sinister Six.

Gold Notepad *WSM #6 (1985)* Stolen from gold building transformed by Beyonder. SM took notebook out of bitterness after seeing Kingpin profit from situation.

Goldman, Hal *ASM #331 (1990)* Obsessed MJ fan. Posed as police officer; killed those who threatened MJ, including Jonathan Caesar. Attempted to possess MJ, but was defeated by her.

Green Goblin Construct *SM #88 (1998)* Genetic creation of Dr. Angst. Norman Osborn used to prove own innocence. Sought true identity, but eventually disintegrated.

Greer, Gabrielle *WSM #119 (1994)* Neighbor/friend to Ben Reilly. Helped Ben to emergency room after seriously wounded by Venom.

Gregor *SM #47 (1994)* Servant of Sergei Kraven. Mentor to Kraven's son, Vladimir (Grim Hunter).

Grey Gargoyle (Paul Pierre Duval) *JIM #107 (1964)* Thor foe. Petrifies with touch. Battled SM during wedding of Mr. Fantastic, Invisible Woman. Later fought SM, Captain America.

Griffin (John Horton) *Amazing Adventures #15 (1972)* Mutated by Brand scientists into lion/eagle creature. Fought SM, Beast.

Guardians of the Galaxy *Marvel Super-Heroes #18 (1969)* Twelve super-beings from distant alternate future where SM was great hero who sacrificed life vs. Martian invaders. Six traveled to modern era; three joined SM vs. Hammer, Anvil, Deterrence Research Corporation. Later became heroes.

H

Hammer, Justin *Iron Man #120 (1979)* Creator, employer of super-agents, including Beetle, Blacklash/Whiplash, Blizzard (Shepanka & Gill), Blue Streak, Bombshell, Boomerang, Capt. Barracuda, Constrictor, Discus, Force, Hydro-Man, Leap-Frog, Man-Killer, Melter, Porcupine, Rhino, Scorpion, Speed Demon, Sphinx, Spymaster I & II, Stiletto, Taskmaster, Water Wizard. Companies controlled include Hammer Industries, Sapirdyne (drug research), Transcorp.

Hammer & Anvil (Leroy Jackson & John Anvil) *Incredible Hulk #182 (1974)* Escaped convicts given super-strength by alien device. Fought SM, allies, Guardians of the Galaxy.

Hanks, Seth *WSM #16 (1986)* Idiot savant from Temple Corners, Appalachia. Forced into weapons development by Roxxon. Guarded by Magma. Rescued by PP, Joy Mercado.

Hardesty, Jennifer & Stephen *ASM #37 (2002)* Jennifer is PP's student at Midtown High. Asked

APPENDIX

PP to help find brother Stephen, taken by Shade.

Hartmann, Eric *Punisher War Journal #14 (1990)* Schizophrenic neo-Nazi. Led followers vs. Daily Bugle offices. SM kept him from killing MJ while Punisher took out defenses.

Headhunter & Executive Services, Inc. (ESI) *WSM #27 (1987)* Headed by Disgraziato, ESI funded high-flying executives like Lee Camino, exacting terrible price for failure. Axe-wielding Headhunter took Camino's son, foiled by SM.

Headmen (Chondu the Mystic, Gorilla Man, Shrunken Bones, Ruby Thursday) *Defenders #21 (1975)* Quartet of would-be criminal masterminds. Used science, sorcery, surgery to gain powers. Battled Defenders, She-Hulk, SM. Chondu sought SM's body after becoming disembodied head. Also fought Human Torch.

Headsman *UTOS #8 (1996)* Agent of Norman Osborn. Used prototype Green Goblin weapons to fight SM, with Enforcers.

Hellfire Club *Uncanny X-Men #96 (1980)* Elite club of mutant villains. X-Men foes, occasionally face SM. Leader is Sebastian Shaw. Also included Shinobi Shaw, Benedict Kine.

Hellrazor *MTU #87 (1979)* Roxxon agent. Fought SM, Black Panther. Absorbs energy, fires sharp blades.

Hermit (Timothy Quail) *SPEC #97 (1984)* Timid, exceptional problem-solver. Discovered by criminal community, coerced to plan crimes. SM liberated him. Now poses as homeless.

High Evolutionary (Hebert Edgar Wyndham) *Thor #134 (1966)* Mutates animals into sentient beings. Mentored, betrayed by Dr. Miles Warren. Nearly evolved to god-like power. Opposed by heroes, SM. Used Gatherers (Dr. Stack, Prof. Quint) to capture beings of genetic interest, including Gwen Stacy clone. Used Purifiers (Purge, others) to cleanse gene pool.

Hobgoblin (Arnold "Lefty" Donovan) *ASM #244 (1983)* Petty crook. Worked for Hobgoblin (Kingsley). Hypnotized by boss, guinea pig for strength-enhancing formula. Insane, thought himself Hobgoblin, fought SM. Killed by Kingsley.

Hobgoblin Suspects Jonas Harrow, JJJ, Senator Martin (father of Schizoid Man), Donald Menken (personnel director at Osborn Industries), Roderick Kingsley (actual Hobgoblin).

Hostiles (Elias Flynn, others) *SMFAE #1 (1995)* Flynn used crystal-given powers to coerce Metahumes to crime. Remaining Hostiles assassinated Flynn, acquired battle armor, kidnapped Metahumes' families to control them. Killed by giant crystalline being he accidentally created, which was defeated by SM, New Warriors, Metahumes.

Hunger (formerly Crown) *SM #76 (1997)* Dark-energy-powered villain. Shared mysterious past with SHOC. Crown mutated into Hunger, vampiric being whose powers grew with number of vampiric servants.

I

Impossible Man *FF #11 (1963)* Adventure-seeking Poppupian shape-changer. Efforts to understand humans created nuisance to "friends" like SM, FF, Silver Surfer, Galactus.

Incandescent Man *MTU #149 (1985)* Giant electricity-manipulating creature, created by Project: PEGASUS. Rampage halted by SM, Cannonball.

Inhumans *FF #45 (1965)* Members of hidden race long-diverged from humanity by Kree experiments. Medusa battled SM in misunderstanding regarding life-saving medicine. All joined SM vs. Zarrko; Kang robot.

Iron Fist (Daniel Thomas Rand-K'ai) *Marvel Premiere #15 (1974)* Mystic alien-born martial artist. On Earth has served as Hero for Hire with Cage; joined SM vs. Steel Serpent (Davos), many others.

J

Jack & Guardian *WSM #122 (1995)* Cloned from SM's DNA by Jackal. Jack was child-sized, wore costume similar to Jackal's. Guardian was huge, wore loincloth. Both died from clone degeneration.

Jack of Hearts (Jack Hart) *Deadly Hands of Kung Fu #22 (1976)* Half-alien (Contraxian) super-being. Had affair with Marcy Kane (Kaina). Encountered SM while fighting S.H.I.E.L.D. Containment required to control vast energy powers.

Jack O'Lantern II (Real Name Unrevealed) *Captain America #396 (1992)* Mercenary. Uses costume, weapons of former Jack O'Lantern. Sought reward for recovering fake SM skeleton.

Jackal-Man *Scarlet Spider Unlimited #1 (1995)* Animal evolved to bipedal form by Miles Warren, using High Evolutionary's equipment. Murdered Warren's family, disappeared. Triggered Warren leaving Wundagore with faction of New Men to form Cult of the Jackal.

Jacks *SM: Maximum Clonage Omega (1995)* Army of miniature clones created by Jackal. Killed in explosion.

Janson, Dr. Andrea *SM #77 (1997)* Agent of Hydra, posed as ESU molecular biologist. Deceived Morbius into allowing experiments on him seeking cure for Crown. Gunned down by Hammerhead, leaving Crown (and SHOC) without cure.

Jardine, Amos *MTU #68 (1978)* Texas millionaire. Enslaved Man-Thing. Employed Arcade, Cutthroat to kill SM after he freed Man-Thing.

Joey *SM #15 (1991)* Child who occasionally suffers temporary mutant transformation. Becomes huge, super-strong. Fought SM, Beast until calmed by parents.

Joey Z *SM #88 (1998)* Well-connected small-time criminal. Suffocated with fake webbing by Trapster to frame SM.

Johnston & Varley *ASM #253 (1984)* Enforcers for Rose (Richard Fisk). Formerly police officers on take from Kingpin. Both killed by Hobgoblin (Macendale).

Jones, "Dirty" Jake "DJ" *ASM #262 (1985)* Unscrupulous reporter. Took picture of SM unmasked. Tried to sell to mobster Roberto DeNatale. DeNatale turned on Jones, SM saved him, recovered film.

Jones, Guy (aka "A Joe Named Guy") *SMU #4 (1994)* Orphanage janitor, given temporary super-strength by experimental gas. Defeated Rhino.

Joystick (Janice Olivia Yanizeski) *Amazing Scarlet Spider #2 (1995)* Great Game player, also in Crimson Cowl's (Justine Hammer) Masters of Evil. Superhuman strength, agility, energy batons.

Ju-Lak *MTU #112 (1981)* Pictish shaman from before sinking of Atlantis. SM traveled back in time to get cure for Serpent Man bite. Ju-Lak captured SM's spirit, usurped powers to try to kill foe, Tiger King.

K

Kane, Marcy (Kaina) *SPEC #32 (1979)* Contraxian alien. Posed as ESU science grad. Former lover of Jack of Hearts.

Kang *Avengers #8 (1964)* Native of 40th century, seeks to rule all time. Often opposed by divergent selves, Immortus, Rama-Tut, Scarlet Centurion. Built SM robot, Timespinner. Opposed by SM, others as unwitting agents of Zarrko.

Karma (Xi'an Coy Manh) *MTU #100 (1980)* Vietnamese, founding member of New Mutants. Controls others' minds. Niece of crime lord Gen. Nguyen Ngoc Coy; sister of Leong, Nga. Cousin Tran Coy Manh also mentalist, aide to Gen. Coy. Thinking SM was criminal, possessed him in hopes of defeating uncle. Thus encountered FF. Absorbed Tran into herself.

Keating, Lt. Kris *Defenders #44 (1977)* NY SWAT leader. Headed special powers task force to oppose superhumans, often encountering SM. Killed, secretly impersonated by agents of Foreigner.

Kevin *PPSM #21 (2000)* Occupant of PP's refrigerator, appears as stale cheese. PP claims is super-intelligent green mold he is cultivating.

Killraven (Jonathan Raven) *Amazing Adventures #18 (1972)* Gladiator from alternate timeline, leads fight to free mankind from Martian Masters. SM traveled to world via Dr. Doom's time machine, fought agents of Masters.

Knight & Fogg (Malcolm Knight & Thomas Fogg) *SPEC #165 (1990)* Liverpool-based assassins, mutated by Prof. Henry Lewis' experiment. Killed Arranger for Kingpin. Tracked home by SM. Partnership dissolved when Fogg nearly killed Knight's brother, Leonard. Knight: armored form with swords. Fogg: gaseous form, nullifies spider-sense.

Kosmojian, B.J. "Cosmos" *ASM #14 (1964)* Filmmaker, tricked by Green Goblin into making film as trap for SM.

Kraft, Dr. Walston *SMU #21 (1998)* Geneticist. Employed hunchback Ivan (former servant to Vincent Frankenstein). Created army of clones (Frankenclones) of Frankenstein's Monster; destroyed by SM, original Monster.

Krahn, Chief Inspector *SM #8 (1991)* Member of Vancouver RCM; secretly pedophile, murderer. Attempted to frame Wendigo. Exposed by Wolverine, SM. Shot by hunters believing him to be Wendigo.

Kraus, Franz (aka Frank Cruz) *ASM #301 (1988)* Neo-Nazi who posed as head of security for Jason Pruett. Hired Silver Sable to test security, attempted to kill her.

Kryllk the Cruel *MTU #7 (1973)* Asgardian rock troll, led army of trolls. Used time-stopping Dark Crystal to attack Asgard, Midgard (Earth). Foiled by SM, Thor.

Kulan Gath *Conan #14 (1972)* Ancient sorcerer from land that is now Egypt. Over 12,000 years old. Sought to transform modern world. Twice opposed by SM, with Scarlet She-Devil, X-Men. Killed SM, though time period was reversed.

Lamont, Lt. Jake *ASM #41 (2002)* SM's newest police contact; assisted him in investigations of Shade, Digger.

Landon, Herbert *SM: The Mutant Agenda #1 (1994)* Head of new Brand Corporation, former co-worker of Beast. SM, Beast stopped anti-mutant endeavor. Fell into chemicals, mutated.

Latverian Liberation Front *ASM #50 (2003)* Armored rebels, attacked Dr. Doom at US airport. SM, Captain America fought them off.

Lava Men *Avengers #5 (1964)* Race of Subterraneans, branched off from Gortokians after mutated by demon Cha'sa'dra. Broke into Project: PEGASUS. Defeated by SM, Avengers.

LaVeau, Marie *Dracula Lives #2 (1973)* Immortal witch-queen. SM faced when he, Dr. Strange, Ms. Marvel sought Silver Dagger.

Legion of Light (Hate-Monger/Man-Beast, Brother Power, Sister Sun, Sue Hollis, others) *SPEC #12 (1977)* Peaceful cult. Manipulated by Brother Power, Man-Beast (aka Hate-Monger, evolved wolf, Adam Warlock foe). Defeated by SM, Razorback.

Lewis, Det. Garon *ASM #413 (1996)* Father of Devon Lewis, ex-husband of Shirley Washington. Detective with mysterious Task Force Seven. Ben Reilly mistook for criminal.

Lifeline Tablet *ASM #68 (1969)* Ancient Atlantean artifact inscribed with formulae. Temporarily regressed Silvermane into non-existence, granted transitory godlike power to Hammerhead, cured sister Toni. Dr. Strange sent tablet to another dimension.

Lilith *Giant-Size Chillers #1 (1974)* Daughter, sworn enemy of Dracula. Enslaved zombie Simon Garth; fought SM, Hannibal King.

Litter (Dane, Terrier, Poodle, Pitbull, Basenji) *Excalibur #53 (1992)* Foreign exchange students at ESU, thieves genetically altered to assume doglike forms. Fought SM, Captain Britain.

Living Monolith (Ahmet Abdol) *X-Men #54 (1969)* Giant creature, formerly Living Pharaoh. Battled several heroes, temporarily became living planet. Efforts to draw power from X-Man Havok led to clash with SM, Thor.

Living Pharaoh (Akasha Martinez) *SENS #19 (1997)* The Staff of Horus placed Akasha under control of Egyptian spirits. She used new energy powers to fight SM before regaining control, departing for parts unknown.

Llyra (Llyra Morris) *Sub-Mariner #32 (1970)* Lemurian Llyra's grudge vs. Sub-Mariner led her to join Frightful Four. Consequently clashed with SM. Posed as PP's neighbor, mentally enslaving, nearly killing him. Namor stopped her.

Lobster Man: The Movie *ASM #43 (2002)* "B" movie in which MJ recently appeared. Mr. Devereaux (director), Fettes Grey (writer), Rick Turk (title role). MJ played "girlfriend killed in Act 1, giving Lobster Man motivation."

Locke, Dr. Cassandra *Marvel: The Lost Generation #12 (2000)* Time traveler from 22nd century. Encountered SM when Tri-Corp was under attack by Ghost.

Lubisch, Dr. Maxwell *ASM #326 (1989)* ESU professor, conducted experiment in extradimensional energies. Resulted in SM temporarily receiving Captain Universe power.

Lucky Lobo *ASM #23 (1965)* Gangster. Arrested when Green Goblin tried to take over gang.

Lumpkin, Willie *FF #11 (1963)* FF's mailman. Dated Aunt May.

Lunatik (Arisen Tyrk) *Marvel Premiere #46 (1979)* Three fragments of extradimensional Arisen Tyrk acted as violent vigilantes, leading them to clash with Defenders, SM. SM statue used as bait.

M'Sieu Tete *Marvel Feature #4 (1972)* Led worldwide criminal network. Sent Goldie, Shiner, Silent Joe to kidnap Billy Connors to extort drug specimens from Curt Connors. Foiled by SM, Ant-Man (Henry Pym).

Mace, Col. Gideon *Hero for Hire #3 (1972)* Crazed mace-handed war veteran. Battled Power Man, SM, White Tiger. Killed his family, wounded White Tiger. Killed when ordering men to fire even while in bullets' path.

Machine Man (X-51, aka Aaron Stack) *2001: A Space Odyssey #8 (1977)* Heroic robot built by Dr. Able Stack. Joined SM vs. Baron Brimstone.

Mad Dog Ward *WSM #33 (1987)* **Employees:** Dr. Hope. **Agents:** Brainstorm/Mad Dog 2020. **Inmates:** formerly Captain Zero, Vicky Gibbs, SM. Kingpin funded psychiatric clinic to imprison potential threats to organization, create mentally controlled assassins. Captain Zero helped SM vs. Brainstorm.

Mad Thinker *FF #15 (1963)* Criminal genius, FF foe. Joined Puppet Master in race to assassinate SM, Thing. Believing SM to be potential precognitive, sent robot to test him.

Madame Menace (Sunset Bain) *Machine Man #17 (1980)* Weapons dealer. Sent agents to collect force-field device from Stuart & Bill Smalls. SM captured them instead. Member of New Enforcers Inner Circle.

Maggia *Avengers #13 (1965)* Powerful crime syndicate separated into family factions. Membership includes Silvermane, Hammerhead, Count Nefaria, Madame Masque, Masked Marauder, Cyclone, Eel, others.

Magma (Jonathan Darque) *MTU #110 (1981)* Fire-blasting armored criminal. Battled SM & Iron Man, also SM alone.

Magneto (Magnus, aka Erik Lehnsherr) *X-Men #1 (1963)* Mutant master of magnetism. X-Men foe. Once defeated by Cosmic SM.

Magnum, Moses *GSSM #4 (April 1975)* Ammunitions dealer, criminal. Clashed with SM,

APPENDIX

Punisher before gaining super-powers, battling others. Agent of They Who Wield Power, Apocalypse.

Magus *Strange Tales #178 (1975)* Projection of Adam Warlock's evil side. Responsible for Infinity War, conflict involving many heroes, SM. Caused creation of SM Doppelganger.

Mainframe (Ian Wajler) *Deathlok #2 (1991)* Former agent of Harlan Ryker. Mentally controls machines. Encountered SM, Daredevil, Deathlok while in Silvermane's employ.

Major Love *MTU #1 (1997)* Led organization D.E.A.D. (Direct Euthanasia Action Division) to exterminate homeless of Los Angeles. Defeated by SM, Generation X.

Malekyth *Knights of Pendragon #6 (1992)* Vice Praetor of extradimensional Araknoids. Achieved mystical power, intended to unleash demon Red Lord. Targeted SM for resemblance to Arakne's mythic hero Arakthu. SM, Knights of Pendragon defeated him, aided by Arrakhyl, last survivor of Pendragon Corps of Arakne.

Man-Killer (Katrina Louisa Van Horn) *MTU #8 (1973)* Exoskeleton-powered man-hating villain fought SM & Tigra, SM & She-Hulk.

Man-Slaughter Marsdale *ASM #271 (1985)* Criminal enforcer, feels no pain. Employed by small-time underworld figure Madame Fang. Terrorized boxers where Crusher Hogan worked. Nearly killed boxer Bobby Chance for resisting, but SM intervened.

Marrow (Sarah) *Cable #5 (1993)* Former member of Gene Nation and X-Men. Fought SM. SM helped rescue Morlock leader Callisto, others from Hunger. In S.H.I.E.L.D.-created identity of Nancy Rushman, was romantically drawn to PP.

Masked Marauder (Frank Farnum) *DD #16 (1964)* Maggia leader. Commanded Tri-Man robots. Used energy-beam technology vs. various heroes, temporarily blinded SM.

Master Monarch *PPSM #16 (2000)* Armored warrior. Encountered SM same night as Squid, Ms. Fortune, Wicked Brigade.

Master of Vengeance (Dwight Faron) *SM #32 (1993)* Chemist. Took fall for manufacturing designer drugs, blamed SM. Mutated himself for strength, electricity control. Impersonated SM. Attacked SM, Punisher, Steel Spider.

Master Order & Lord Chaos *MTIO @ #2 (1977)* Cosmic entities. Implied they engineered events that created SM, so he would help Adam Warlock defeat Thanos.

Master Programmer *SPEC #229 (1995)* Digitized copy of Dr. Octopus' mind. Fell in love with Carolyn Trainer, aided vs. SM. Downloaded into mindless resurrected body of Dr. Octopus.

Mather, Cotton (aka Witchslayer) *MTU #41 (1976)* Noted Puritan scholar. Under control of Dark Rider in 1692, clashed with SM, other time-displaced superhumans.

Mauler (Brendan Doyle) *Iron Man #156 (1982)* Third man to wear Mauler armor. Fought SM & Wonder Man, then SM alone trying to reclaim abandoned infant son.

Maxfield, Dr. A.J. *GSSM #1 (1974)* Medical researcher. SM sought for new vaccine to treat Aunt May. Dracula sought to dispose of both doctor and vaccine.

Maxwell, Morris *ASM #440 (1998)* Obtained gift of knowledge in Gathering of Five. Information source for Spider-Woman III (Mattie Franklin).

McKeever, Brian "Tiny" *UTOS #2 (1995)* High-school classmate of PP, abusive home life. PP learned of problems, extended friendship. Dropped out, unknowingly worked for Scorcher.

McPhee, Lemuel "Bruiser" *SPEC #151 (1989)* Robbie Robertson's cellmate at Lewisburg Prison. Protected Robbie from Tombstone until killed. Brother Stuart, lawyer, arranged presidential pardon for Robbie in gratitude for friendship.

Mechano-Marauder (Fabian Stankowicz) *Avengers #217 (1982)* Wanna-be armored super-villain. Attacked hospitalized Thing, defeated by SM. Later redeemed.

Megawatt (Dirk Leyden) *SMU #2 (1993)* Deranged actor. Received electrical powers from Jonas Harrow. Fought SM.

Melvin, James *SPEC #57 (1981)* Brand Corporation. Partial creator of Will O' the Wisp. Mutated Tarantula (Rodriquez). Hypnotized into confessing by Wisp.

Menace & the Mutantmen *UTOS #21 (1997)* Five men. Used identies of Menace, Mutantmen robots, creating anti-mutant fear to conceal crimes. Defeated by SM, X-Men.

Mentallo (Marvin Flumm) *Strange Tales #141 (1966)* Telepath. Employed by Professor Power, fought SM. Also member of New Enforcers.

Mephisto *Silver Surfer #3 (1968)* Demon lord. SM unknowingly acted as Mephisto's agent, fighting demon Zarathos (Beyonder's chosen agent) in wager over whether universe deserved to survive.

Mesmero (Vincent) *X-Men #49 (1968)* Hypnotic mutant. Battled SM while seeking vengeance on stage-show critics.

Metahumes *SMFAE #1 (1995)* Six heroes plus criminal Alex Flynn. Mutated by seven extradimensional Crystals of Kahesha. See Hostiles.

Midas the Golden Man (Malcolm Merriwell) *MTU #30 (1975)* Intended genocide vs. NY's African-Americans. Foiled by SM, Falcon.

Midnight (Jeff Wilde) *Marc Spector: Moon Knight #4 (1989)* Former Moon Knight sidekick. Rebuilt as cyborg by Secret Empire. Aided by Secret Empire, cyborg Lynn Church, battled SM, Punisher, Night Thrasher, Moon Knight, Nova.

Midtown High, PP's Former Teachers: Principal Davis, Mr. Warren (science, brother of Miles Warren), Mr. Del (science), Daphne "Boomer" Smith (science).

Midtown High, PP's Former Classmates: Flash Thompson, Liz Allan, Sally Green, Brain "Tiny" McKeever, Jessica Jones (now PI), Sally Avril (Bluebird), Jason Ionello, Peter Doman, Louie Minelli (now mob leader), William Oakes, Nyra Silver, Carl King (the Thousand), Stanley Stackmeyer, Richard Thatcher, Alice Tucker, C.J. Vogel, Barry Hapgood, Robert Hinds.

Midtown High, PP's Fellow Teachers: Principal Weathers, Kyle Jacoby (gym). **PP's Students:** Steve Petty, Ronda Kramer, Jake Dorman, Jennifer Hardesty, Joey.

Mikashi, Professor Toshiro *SMTAP #1 (1994)* Former ESU biology professor. Employed by Life Foundation's Arachnis Project. Died to keep work from being misused. Daughter Miho allied with Sneak-Thief, took identity of Gunplay.

Mindstorm *Marvel Super-Heroes #4 (1990)* Former Hydra agent. Maddened SM with psychotic drugs. Nick Fury saved SM, killed Mindstorm.

Mister Fear (Alan Fagan) *MTU #92 (1980)* Fourth villain to use identity. Fought SM, Hawkeye. Used chemicals to control women, including Betty Brant. Joined New Enforcers.

Mister P & Mister Q *ASM #27 (2001)* High-tech gentlemanly mercenaries. Battled SM over AIM's escaped experimental cat (adopted by PP).

M.O.D.O.K. (George Tarleton) *TOS #93 (1967)* Mental Organism Designed Only for Killing. Former AIM scientist. Mutated via Cosmic Cube into psychic-powered monster. Fought SM.

Modular Man (Stephen Weems) *Rampaging Hulk #5 (1977)* Former Brand scientist. Body destroyed by experiment. Survived as modular robot. Joined Killer Shrike. Destroyed by SM, Beast.

Mole Man (Harvey Rupert Elder) *FF #1 (1961)* Lord of Subterranea. Energy-blasting staff, army of mutates. Encountered SM during clash with Kala, ruler of Netherworld.

Mongoose *ASM #283 (1986)* Mongoose-evolved New Man, creation of High Evolutionary. Ordered to attack Thor, encountered SM.

Mongrain, Alison *SPEC #240 (1996)* Agent of Norman Osborn. Caused MJ to lose unborn child. Recanted, informed MJ that Aunt May was still alive. Killed by Norman's unwilling agent, Molten Man.

Monocle *FF #95 (1970)* Fires energy blasts. Associated with Enclave. Hypnotized Human Torch to battle SM.

Monstroid (Ballox, aka 7NH54) *MTU #5 (1972)* Skrull robot scout. Manipulated by Puppet Master vs. SM, Vision. Super-strength, energy blasts.

Moondark *MTU #12 (1973)* Evil sorcerer worshipping Dark Beings (ruled by Dark Master). Fought SM & Werewolf, SM & Ghost Rider (Blaze).

Moondog the Malicious *MTU #24 (1974)* Loa/voodoo god, possessed Wally Blevins. Exorcised by Brother Voodoo, SM.

Moonstone (Dr. Karla Sofen) *Captain America #192 (1975)* Trained by Dr. Faustus. Usurped predecessor, Lloyd Bloch. Fought SM while misusing Curt Connors' Enervator. Joined Thunderbolts. Flight, strength, energy blasts, phasing.

Morlocks *Uncanny X-Men #169 (1983)* Underground mutant society. Under Strygor's leadership, kidnapped surface people. Stopped by SM, Kitty Pryde. SM, Cloak & Dagger protected Morlock family from Firebrand. Aided by NYPD Lt. Tara Curson, SM & Wolverine pursued killer Morlock, Fugue.

Muggins, Mamie *ASM #139 (1974)* PP's former landlady in Chelsea apartment. Suspicious of PP. Frequently threatened eviction for late rent. Wife of Barney, aunt of Candi.

Murderer by Spider *ASM #228 (1982)* Scientist, resorted to crime for arthropod research. Used hidden circuitry to attract spiders to attack victims. Side-effect drove SM into violent rage.

Muse (Shannon Fitzpatrick) *SPEC #231 (1996)* Agent of John Johnsmeyer. Led fellow agents Mosh & Quorum. Attractive mentalist, energy manipulator. Ordered to ensnare Kaine, fell in love, joined him, fought SM with him.

Mutilation Killer *SPEC @ #13 (1993)* Baron (Helmut) Zemo's mutates/Protoids. Killing spree mimicked that of Vermin. Used Zemo's machine to mutate Nocturne. Defeated by Nocturne, SM. Hideous form, metamorph.

Mys-Tech *Warheads #1 (1992)* Group of ancient druids granted power, immortality by Mephisto. World-conquering ambitions. Spell summoned legion of demons, slaughtered SM. He was restored when time was reversed.

N

National Crime Syndicate ("Three Fingers" Eddie Enders, Honeysuckle Muldoon, others) *ASM #220 (1981)* Held grand-larceny competition to appoint replacement when Eddie Enders died. Moon Knight, SM combined to infiltrate, destroy group after Moon Knight beat competing gangs Rat Pack, Midnight Mob to become prime candidate.

Nebula *Avengers #257 (1985)* Female space pirate; descendant of Thanos, Zorr. Twice obtained cosmic power. Opposed by SM, Avengers, others.

Necrodamus *Defenders #1 (1972)* Sorcerer worshipping dark gods. Seeks replacement for aging body. Targeted Vision; opposed by SM, Scarlet Witch.

Nekra (Nekra Sinclair) *Shanna the She-Devil #4 (1973)* Mutant. Derives strength from hatred. Encountered SM.

Nest, aka Lords of Light & Darkness *MTU @ #1 (1976)* Six scientists, became super-beings modeled after Hindu Gods. Fought SM, X-Men. Departed into space.

Nesters, Ray *ASM #253 (1984)* Pro football player. Threw games for Rose (Fisk). Confessed, but endangered himself & younger brother Tony (ESU student).

New Enforcers *WSM #99 (1993)* Super-villain organization. Set out to control underworld. SM fought field agents, never learned of inner circle. **Field agents:** Eel, Plantman, Vanisher, Blitz, Tangle, Thermite, Super-Adaptoid, Dragon Man. **Inner Circle:** Madame Menace, Controller, Fixer, Mentallo, Mister Fear.

New Mutants *Marvel Graphic Novel #4: The New Mutants (1982)* Adolescent mutant heroes organized by Prof. Xavier. Joined SM to face drug dealers who mutated Cloak & Dagger. Cannonball joined SM vs. Incandescent Man. After group disbanded, SM helped techno-organic Warlock vs. Mainspring's robots.

New Warriors Team-Ups, Full Team & SM/PP (Asylum, Sphinx, Hostiles). **Full Team & Scarlet Spider** (Eugenix, Soldiers of Misfortune, Joe Wade, Spidercide, Advent, Midnight & Secret Empire). **Firestar** (Carnage). **Darkhawk** (Brotherhood of Evil Mutants, Hobgoblin). **Nova** (Photon, Hostiles, Tri-Sentinel, Midnight & Secret Empire, Firearms, Vampiro, Badd Axe).

Nightwatch (Kevin Barry Trench) *WSM #97 (1993)* Nanotechnology-powered suit gifted by future self. Glove stolen by Alfredo Morelli to become Gauntlet. Joined SM vs. Warforce. Player in Great Game; killed by el Toro Negro.

Nitro (Robert Hunter) *Captain Marvel #34 (1974)* Kree-empowered human bomb. Defeated by SM, who merged dispersed form with anesthetic gas. Attacked Norman Osborn in employ of Kingpin.

Noletti, Marc *SPEC #114 (1986)* Burglar stole SM costume from PP's apartment. Used in crime, captured by police, blackmailed into going after Barons gang. Saved by SM, reformed.

Nomad (Jack Monroe) *Young Men #24* (1953) Former Captain America sidekick. Fought Taskmaster, Black Abbot with SM.

Norton, "Nose" *DD #148 (1977)* Informant, exposed Brand Corporation to Ned Leeds. Retaliation by Tarantula (Rodriguez) blocked by SM.

NYPD Detectives, Various Det. Sloane Chase (investigated F.A.C.A.D.E., Lizard), Det. Snider (Belladonna), Det. Sgt. Tork (Rose/Arranger Gang War), Det. Connor Trevane (son saved from Carnage by SM), Det. Frank Farrow (Lobo Brothers attacks, death of Arranger), Det. Clark (led Venom Task Force).

O

Olympians *MTE #25 (1980)* Olympic athletes, became pawns of Kala. Teamed with Hulk, Lava Men. Fought Mole Man, SM, Outcasts. Maria Karsov (Russian figure skater), Robby Kyle (Canadian hockey player), Claude LeBron (French bobsledder), Brad Rossi (American skier).

Omm & Spider-People *Conan #13 (1972)* Ancient god worshipped by Zamora people millennia ago. Spawned race of Spider-People, blood enemies of Serpent Men of Set. SM drawn into conflict between last remnants of both.

Orb (Drake Shannon) *MTU #15 (1973)* Disfigured motorcyclist with high-tech helmet. Fought SM, Ghost Rider. Agent of They Who Wield Power.

Order (Dr. Strange, Hulk, Namor, Silver Surfer) *Order #1 (2002)* Original Defenders, corrupted by Yandroth's curse. Opposed by SM, others.

Order of the Goblin *SMROTGG #2 (2000)* Cult arranged by Norman Osborn from members of Cabal of Scriers who remained loyal to him.

Osborn, Alton *SMROTGG #2 (2000)* Norman's grandfather. Robber baron.

Osborn, Amberson *SPEC @ #14 (1994)* Norman's father. Abusive, demanding.

APPENDIX

Osborn, Emily *SPEC #180 (1991)* Wife of Norman, mother of Harry. Died while Harry was young.

Outcasts (Boulder, Digger, Landslide, Water Witch) *MTE #25 (1980)* Subterranean superhumans. Aided SM vs. Kala.

Outrider (Martin Zantz) *PPSM @ 1999* Scrier singled him out from Order of Scriers to gain power over Nexus of All Realities. Opposed by SM, Man-Thing.

Owl (Leland Owlsey) *DD #3 (1964)* Flying criminal mastermind, Daredevil foe. Clashed with SM during war with Dr. Octopus in failed quest for redemption, as part of Gang of Four.

P

Paladin (Paul Denning) *DD #150 (1978)* Profit-seeking mercenary. Friend of Wasp. Agent for Silver Sable. Enhanced strength, body armor, energy gun.

Pandara *Thunderstrike #4 (1994)* Operative of alien Deviant, Lord Tantalus. Used demons to kill, consume salon customers. Targeted MJ. Opposed by SM, Thunderstrike.

Paralyzer (Randall Darby) *Captain America Annual #4 (1977)* Recreated electromagnetic being Zzzax; surrendered to SM, Midnight Sons.

Paunchalito, Victor *ASM #223 (1981)* Daily Bugle writer. Discovered identity of SM while accompanying PP to investigate town of Ponder. Kept secret to protect SM.

Penny Ant-Es *Tangled Web #18 (2002)* Vigilante group felt Abraham Lincoln had been slighted by being used for copper penny, protested by re-arranging public signs.

Perrinois *SMTU #3 (1996)* Mystic dimension visited by FF, SM/Reilly. Pint-sized wizard brothers Shiwa & Rasheed Ven Garmchee sent Flying Dragons of Alganom against them.

Phil *SMU #4 (1994)* Mysterio employee. Partner "Snake" Sanches tricked Lance Bannon into "exposing" Phil as SM to gain SM marketing rights. Drove Spider-Van.

Photon (Jason Dean) *Nova #12 (1977)* Maggia Agent. Killed Nova's uncle Ralph Rider for nuclear device. Strength-enhancing costume, photon gun. Other suspects were AIM agent Harry "Happy" Daze, Michael Lincoln (Ralph's assistant), businessman Franklin Risk.

Photon (Monica Rambeau) *ASM @ #16 (1982)* Formerly Captain Marvel, accidentally fought SM in first mission. Joined Avengers, became Photon. Teamed with SM vs. PRIDE.

Phreak (Steve Petty) *WSM #35 (1988)* Son of Living Brain inventor. Attended Midtown High, reactivated Brain vs. bullies. Mutated by electrical accident, blamed PP, abducted MJ. Calmed by classmates Ronda Kramer, Jake Dorman.

Pincus, Joseph "Lonesome Pinky" *ASM #211 (1980)* PP's former neighbor; small, unassuming, wailed country music all night. Booed off stage in debut performance, sang himself hoarse to pacify crowd drugged by Ramrod.

Plantman (Samuel Smithers) *Strange Tales #113 (1963)* Career criminal, uses plants as weapons. New Enforcers member. Transformed SM into monstrous form. See Spider-Morphosis.

Platoon *SM #41 (1993)* Squadron of armored agents for weapons brokers A.R.M.S. (Alternative Resources Munitions Supply).

Poison (Cecilia Cardinale) *WSM @ #4 (1988)* Cuban refugee. Briefly merged with extradimensional Ylandris, retained powers, became heroine. Son Carlos kidnapped by el Toro Negro to force her to battle SM.

Polestar *ASM #409 (1996)* Great Game player. Electro-magnetic powers. Killed by El Toro Negro.

Powell, Amy *ASM #230 (1982)* Girlfriend, eventual fiancée of Lance Bannon. Flirted with PP to make Lance jealous.

Powerhouse & Masterblaster *SM #15 (1991)* Violent pro-mutant, anti-mutant activists, respectively. Clashed at ESU. Opposed by Beast, SM. Powerhouse: drain/manipulate energy. Masterblaster: energy-blasting gauntlets.

Praetorian Guard *WSM #87 (1992)* Armored mercenary unit. Employed by Alfredo Morelli to fight SM with Hobgoblin (Macendale).

PRIDE (Population Reduction by Inter-Dimensional Expulsion) *MTU #142 (1984)* Created by Dr. Eric Paulson, Dr. William Lorber as extreme interdimensional solution to overcrowding. Opposed by SM, Captain Marvel (Photon).

Pro *Scarlet Spider #1 (1995)* Mercenary/assassin. Killed Jason Tso. Searched for SM skeleton.

Pro-Rata *Howard the Duck #1 (1975)* Magic-using accountant, hoped to rule universe via Cosmic Calculator. Opposed by SM, Howard the Duck.

Project: PEGASUS *MTIO #42 (1978)* Potential Energy Groups, Alternate Sources, United States. NY research facility housed numerous super-villains. Frequent breakouts. SM called in to oppose Serpent Crown(s); Lava Men (with Avengers); Blackout, Moonstone, Electro, Rhino (with Avengers).

Proto-Goblin (Nels Van Adder) *PPSM #-1 (1997)* Former assistant to Mendel Stromm. Early Green Goblin Formula test subject. Horribly mutated, went rogue. Nearly killed by Arthur Stacy (Oscorp chief of security), George Stacy (NYPD).

Protoids (aka Baron Zemo's Mutates) *Captain America #276 (1982)* Humans mutated by Baron (Helmut) Zemo, Primus using technology of Arnim Zola.

Prowler (Rick Lawson) *SENS #16 (1997)* Medical student, sought revenge on former boss. Stole Hobie's costume. Tracked, defeated by SM.

Psycho-Man *FF @ #5 (1967)* Native of Microverse/Sub-Atomica. Uses body armor, emotion-controlling device. Encountered shrunken & full-size SM.

Psyk-Out *Wonder Man #28 (1993)* Empathic projector. Revenge attack on Wonder Man foiled by SM.

Pulaski, Joey *AF #16 (1995)* Young female mutant. Flight, energy powers. First superhuman SM faced. Took money from Kingpin to sabotage construction sites. SM couldn't convince her she was wrong.

Purl, Dr. Noah *ASM Super Special #1 (1995)* Hospital researcher/administrator, former lab partner of Curt Connors. Empowered Armstrong into Strongarm. Briefly hired Ben Reilly as lab assistant. Wounded by savage Lizard offspring. Other hospital staff: nurse "Red" Reilly Barron; Barron's girlfriend, Toni Moore.

Q

Q-4 *SM #92 (1998)* Russian mercenaries hired by Norman Osborn to kill Trapster. Defeated by Dusk (PP).

Quasimodo *FF @ #4 (1966)* Quasi-Motivational Destruct Organism. Created by Mad Thinker. Aggressive sentient computer. Fought SM, Hawkeye. Manipulated Ben Reilly into attacking Silver Surfer.

Quicksand *Thor #392 (1988)* Female sand-powered criminal. Joined with Sandstorm, fought SM & Sandman.

Quicksilver (Pietro Maximoff) *X-Men #4 (1964)* Mutant speedster, son of Magneto. Battled SM, having believed JJJ's editorials.

R

Radioactive Man (Professor Chen Lu) *JIM #93 (1963)* Chinese criminal scientist. Mutated himself to gain radiation powers. Fought SM twice.

Rampage (Stuart Clarke) *Champions #5 (1976)* Uses self-designed body armor. Hypnotized Iceman to attack SM, Angel.

Ramrod *DD #103 (1973)* Super-strong cyborg mutated by Moondragon. Battled SM, others. Fought SM again when he poisoned patrons at bar where "Lonesome Pinky" Pincus was singing.

Rak & Dread *Ghost Rider #46 (1994)* Super-strong Rak, energy-projecting Dread. Mutated, resurrected by demonic crime lord Hellgate. Fought SM, Vengeance (of Spirits of Vengeance).

Rapier (Dominic Tyrone) *SPEC @ #2 (1980)* Racketeer, betrayed by former ally, Silvermane. Became vigilante using electrified rapier, seeking deadly revenge on Silvermane. Foiled, literally, by SM.

Raptar the Renegade *SMU #15 (1997)* Extradimensional version of Puma, can transform into giant reptilian humanoid. Motives unclear; defeated by SM, Puma.

Rat Pack (Sparks, Stitches, Stroke) *MTU #75 (1978)* Arson gang. Defeated by SM, Cage.

Raven, Det. Jacob *SM: The Lost Years #1 (1995)* Salt Lake City cop. Wife Helene killed by agents of crime lord Vincent Tannen, who controlled Raven's crooked partner Louise Kennedy. Sought PP for Kennedy's murder, actually committed by Kaine, who also killed Tannen.

Ravencroft Escapees *WSM @ #10 (1994)* Ravencroft inmates freed by Shriek during escape attempt. Gale (super-strong), Pyromania (pyrokinetic), Webber (escape artist), Mayhem (poisonous gas form). Defeated by SM.

Razorwire & Nautilus *SMU #6 (1994)* Agents of Hammerhead Maggia branch. Targeted Slyde when he stole from them. Defeated by SM, Cage. Razorwire: energy-powered whips. Nautilus: battle-armor.

Red Ghost (Ivan Kragoff) & Super-Apes (Igor, Miklho, Peotr) *FF #13 (1963)* Russian scientist, exposed himself to cosmic ray storm. Can become invisible, intangible. Simians (Igor/baboon, Miklho/gorilla, Peotr/orangutan) metamorphic, super-strong, magnetic, respectively.

Red Nine (Wallace Jackson) *ASM #264 (1985)* Texan teenager stole uncle's NASA power suit, came to NY to fight SM for fun. Hospitalized for pneumonia. Helped SM prevent rambunctious old man Philmont Magee from being evicted by Dr. Rattamun due to hospital clerical error.

Red Skull (Johann Schmidt) *Captain America Comics #1 (1941)* Original Nazi Red Skull, second only to Adolf Hitler. Captain America foe, occasionally opposed by SM. Many imposters, including Communist Red Skull responsible for death of PP's Parents.

Rinehart, Dr. Ludwig *ASM #24 (1965)* False identity of Mysterio (Beck). First used as psychiatrist attempting to convince SM to expose secret identity, then as nursing-home manager faking death of Aunt May.

Rocket Racer *ASM #13 (2000)* Stole equipment of original Racer. Planned crime spree cut short when he slammed into door opened by Harry Sloan.

Rodney *ASM #220 (1981)* Son of Restwell Nursing Home resident Polly. Stole gate from nursing home dance, blamed musicians. Exposed by "super-sleuth" Aunt May.

Rorgg (King of the Spider-Men) *JIM #64 (1961)* Giant extraterrestrial spider-like leader of army of spider-men decades ago. Revived by Yucoya-Tzin, fought FF. SM narrowly missed battle.

Rose (Det. Sgt. Blume) *WSM #84 (1985)* Adopted Rose identity to aid Alfredo Morelli (in guise of Richard Fisk) in destroying Kingpin. Concerned by Morelli's violence, joined SM, earning death at Morelli's hands.

Rothstein, Harry & Joseph *SM: Get Kraven #1 (2002)* Hollywood producer brothers, hired indirectly by Ned Tannengarden. Had Al Kraven beaten, assaulted girlfriend Timber. Mutilated by Vulture, consequently renamed themselves Harriet, Josephine. Used hired musclemen: Gerbil, Script Doctor, Stitch.

Rushman, Nancy *MTU #82 (1979)* S.H.I.E.L.D. deep-cover personality. Used by Black Widow (Romanoff), Lynx, Marrow. SM faced Romanoff, Marrow incarnations.

Russian *Punisher #8 (2000)* Cheerful, near-invulnerable quasi-transsexual cyborg/mercenary. Defeated by Punisher, using SM as semi-conscious human shield.

Ryker's Island *Marvel Fanfare #22 (1985)* New York prison, housed super-villains prior to construction of Vault, later downgraded for non-super-powered beings. **Wardens:** Michaels, Percy Alexander Rue. **Inmates:** Eddie Brock, Cletus Casady, Adrian Toomes, others.

S

Sabretooth (Victor Creed) *Iron Fist #14 (1977)* Wolverine foe. Trained under Foreigner. Fought Black Cat, SM to impress old mentor.

Sage *MTU #7 (1998)* Vampire. Underwent experimental Sunwalker treatment. Humanity resurfaced. Fought SM, Blade. Manipulated Blade into killing him to bring spirit peace.

Sanchez, Dr. Benita *ASM #386 (1994)* ESU researcher. Developed Juvenator, which restored Vulture's youth, temporarily.

Sandor *ASM @ #5 (1968)* Agent of Communist Red Skull. Battled SM when hero sought true fate of parents.

Sandstorm (Tony Trainor) *WSM #107 (1993)* Posessed sand-manipulating powers. Quicksand manipulated him into battling SM, Sandman.

Santa Claus Burglar *SPEC #109 (1985)* Disguised as Santa to trick children into telling him where they lived, then burgled homes. Narrowly escaped SM, defeated by true Santa.

Sardeth *MTIO #90 (1982)* Extradimensional Wizard. Spirit possessed human. Battled SM, Thing.

Satana (Satana Hellstrom) *Vampire Tales #2 (1973)* Succubus, daughter of Devil, quasi-hero. Sacrificed life to help SM free possessed Dr. Strange. Resurrected.

Saunders, Robert *ASM @ #20 (1986)* Planted bomb in 2020 before being killed by Arno Stark, that era's Iron Man. Stark traveled back in time to obtain the present day Robert's retina scan to disarm weapon. Encountered SM, who was friend of young Saunders.

Savage Land Mutates *X-Men #62 (1969)* Savage Land natives, mutated by Magneto. Mutated SM, Angel into bestial forms, in which they were opposed by Ka-Zar. Power of another mutate, Sauron, restored them.

Scarecrow (Ebenezer Laughton) *TOS #51 (1964)* Contortionist, psychotic killer. Used trained crows to attack victims, including SM. Now bodiless phantom who possesses others.

Scarlet Beetle *Tales to Astonish #39 (1963)* Giant insect. World conquest opposed by Ant-Man, SM, Iron Man, Avengers. Squashed by She-Hulk.

Scarlet She-Devil *MTU #79 (1979)* Swordswoman from 12,000 years past. Summoned to modern era by magical sword. Possessed MJ, joined SM to battle Kulan Gath.

Scarlet Spider (Joe Wade) *Scarlet Spider #2 (1995)* FBI agent, partner of Stephanie Briggs. Investigated Carolyn Trainer. Forced to power VR version of Scarlet Spider. Defeated by Ben Reilly, New Warriors. Ruined Scarlet Spider reputation.

Scourge of the Underworld *Iron Man #194 (1985)* Organization of assassins targeting super-villains. Backed by golden-age Angel.

Scream (Donna) & Hybrid (Scott Washington) *Venom: Lethal Protector #4 (1993)* Two of several civilians to combine with Venom offspring. Scream turned to crime, battled Venom, SM. Hybrid fought crime.

APPENDIX

Secret Defenders *FF #374 (1993)* Loosely arranged, ever-changing team of heroes assembled by Dr. Strange, evolved from the New FF. SM briefly joined to force Human Torch to answer criminal charges, then to oppose Xandu.

Seekers (Sonic, Chain Lightning, Grasp) *Iron Man #214 (1987)* Armored mercenaries outfitted by AIM. Iron Man foes. Fought SM.

Sentinels *X-Men #14 (1965)* Giant multi-powered robots originally designed to protect humanity vs. mutants. PP and Ben faced those used by Onslaught, Bastion.

Sentry (Robert Reynolds) *Sentry #1 (2000)* Early solar-powered hero. Went mad; created Void, entity that was defeated by SM, others. Dr. Strange forced to erase all traces of Sentry's existence. Resurfaced, events repeated.

Set *Conan #7 (1971)* Elder demon long since driven from Earth, leaving Serpent Men. Often tries to return, usually via Serpent Crown, powerful artifact eventually destroyed by SM, others.

Shaddock, Charlie *ASM #368 (1992)* Agent of Communist Red Skull, pretending to be FBI agent. Kidnapped Richard, Mary Parker replicoids to protect past, believing them genuine.

Shadowforce *SM/X-Factor: Shadowgames #1 (1994)* Six super-powered operatives created by government agency Shadowbase. Fought SM, X-Factor. Led by Gen. Macauley Sharpe.

Shadowforce Alpha *ASM Super Special #1 (1995)* Seven paramilitary mercenaries. Targeted incapacitated military figure, Col. Broga. Opposed by Scarlet Spider, Strongarm.

Shang-Chi *Special Marvel Edition #15 (1973)* Master of Kung Fu. Honorable son of famous Chinese criminal warlord. Manipulated by father into fighting SM.

Sheldon, Phil *Marvels #1 (1994)* Long-serving Daily Bugle staffer. Photographed Gwen Stacy's death.

S.H.I.E.L.D. Agents SM has encountered senior agents "Dum Dum" Dugan, Sharon Carter, Countess de la Fontaine; line agents Judith Klemmer, Chris Townsend. SM, agent Barbara "Bobbi" Morse Barton (Mockingbird) exposed traitorous agent Karl Delandon.

Shiffman, Maxie *AF #15 (1962)* PP's show-biz agent before Uncle Ben's death. Duped into helping Mysterio by illusion of widow.

Shooter *DD #354 (1996)* Gun-toting assassin. Easily defeated by Daredevil, Ben Reilly.

Shotgun (J.R. Walker) *DD #272 (1989)* Mercenary, government agent, weapons expert. Daredevil foe. Faced SM, helped SM against Calypso and Zombie.

Shroud (Maximillian Quincy Coolridge) *Super-Villain Team-Up #5 (1976)* Blind hero. Controls darkness. Poses as criminal to undermine mob. Joined SM vs. Dansen Macabre, others.

Silencer *SM/Elektra @ (1998)* Bio-engineered mob assassin. Alters own density. Battled SM, Elektra before trapped inside meteorite.

Silencers *WSM #113 (1994)* Battle-armored technology thieves. Undectectable from sight, sound. Fought SM, Black Cat, Gambit at unveiling of F.A.C.A.D.E. armor.

Silver Dagger (Isaiah Curwen) *Dr. Strange #1 (1974)* Religious zealot. Dedicated to destruction of magic-users like Dr. Strange, Marie LaVeau. Opposed by SM, Ms. Marvel (Danvers).

Silver Samurai (Kenuchio Harada) *DD #111 (1974)* Sword-wielding Japanese mutant. Opposed SM while serving nihilist mistress, Hydra leader Viper. Became hero.

Silver Squad (Purty Larry, Ripster, Slambeaux, Twit) *WSM #79 (1991)* Robots sent by Silvermane to capture SM so he could drain hero's blood to restore own vitality.

Silver Surfer (Norrin Radd) *FF #48 (1966)* Cosmic-powered former herald of Galactus. Joined SM vs. Psycho-Man, Carnage, others. Fought Quasimodo with Ben Reilly.

Sin-Eater (Emil Gregg) *SPEC #107 (1985)* Mentally unstable young neighbor to Sin-Eater (Stan Carter). Heard dictated confession, adopted role himself. False confession led to firing of Daily Globe reporter Eddie Brock.

Sir (Martha Paterson) *DD #345 (1995)* Misogynistic woman. Surgically altered to appear masculine. Former Daredevil foe. Pawn of Dr. Angst, Norman Osborn vs. SM.

Skrulls *FF #2 (1962)* Shape-changing aliens. Foes of FF. Encountered SM in frequent attempts to conquer Earth.

Skull-Jacket *SMU #11 (1996)* Appearance-changing Russian Mafia agent. Impersonated Jason Havershaw, killed mother for inheritance. Black Cat suspected, cleared Havershaw with SM's help.

Sleepwalker *Sleepwalker #1 (1991)* Mindscape defender. Accessed Earth dimension through host Rick Sheridan. Joined SM vs. Crimewave, Brotherhood of Evil Mutants.

Slime *SPEC #215 (1994)* Dwells in New York sewers. Detects raw feelings. Halted SM's brutal beating of repentant Scorpion.

Smithville Thunderbolt (Fred Hopkins) *WSM #8 (1985)* Smalltown hero. Powers faded with age. Committed suicide when identity exposed by Pennsylvanian reporter Roxanne Dewinter.

Smithville Thunderbolt (Ludlow Grimes) *WSM #8 (1985)* Empowered by same meteorite as Fred Hopkins. Family left, causing him to attack original Thunderbolt out of jealousy. Regained senses, joined S.H.I.E.L.D.

Sneak-Thief *SMTAP #1 (1994)* Cat burglar, immune to most detection. Hired by Life Foundation. Fired for failing to kill SM, Warrant. Helped Gunplay escape.

Solarr (Silas King) *Captain America #160 (1973)* Solar-powered mutant hired to kill ailing gangster. Fought SM, Daredevil, others.

Sons of the Tiger (Bob Diamond, Abe Brown, Lin Sun, Lotus Shinkchuko) *Deadly Hands of Kung Fu #1 (1974)* Martial-arts team. Helped SM vs. second generation Crime-Master, Big Man. Abandoned mystic amulets, taken up by White Tiger. Abe was brother of Prowler.

Sorcerer *Marvel Super Heroes #14 (1968)* Master of ESP. Created Synthetic Man. Attack on SM failed when doorbell caused fatal feedback in Psycho-Intensifier.

Spacemen (Gantry, Orbit, Satellite, Vacuum) *UTOS #4 (1995)* Former space-program trainees. Stole meteor sample brought to Earth by John Jameson, mutated. Posed as heroes while framing SM.

Spellcheck *Tangled Web #18 (2002)* Vigilante obsessed with grammar. Sought to become Typeface's partner, brutally rejected.

Spider People *Prime #1 (1995)* South American tribe in Ultraverse. Drew spirit-power from SM via dimensional rift. Power enabled Ultraverse hero Prime to become Spider-Prime to battle primal version of Lizard.

Spider-Amoeba *SPEC #31 (1979)* Immense single-celled creation of first Carrion. Injected with SM's blood to simulate powers. Destroyed by fire, took Carrion with it.

Spider-Clan *PPSM @ 2001* Based in Peru. High priestess Taran. Worship at Temple of Great Weaver, usurped by enemy Snake Clan. SM defeated Snake sorcerer Faire de Lain, recovered Spider-Clan amulet, restored temple.

Spider-Squad *ASM @ #11 (1977)* Three unnamed crooks hired by producer Anton Delionatus. Given exoskeletons to sabotage movie "Spawn of the Spider." Director Barney Muller hired SM to replace injured stunt-man. Special-effects director Klemmer framed. SM revealed truth.

Spider-X (Brian Kornfield) *Midnight Sons Unlimited #3 (1993)* Youth transformed into lethal vigilante by demonic Darkhold book (created by Elder God Chthon). Opposed by SM, Midnight Sons. Apparently died in battle with Zzzax.

Spirit of Christmas *Marvel Holiday Special (1993)* Angelic being captured and weakened by Mephisto. SM's selfless intervention allowed it to survive, infect Mephisto with goodness.

Spoiler *SMTAP #1 (1994)* Super-strong, gun-toting agent of Life Foundation. Fought SM, Sneak-Thief, Warrant, Homo Arachnis.

Squid (Don Callahan) *PPSM #16 (2000)* Human with squid-like powers. Partner of Ms. Fortune, mob enforcer. Father, "Big" Mike Callahan (old friend of Richard Parker), persuaded son to abandon criminal ambitions.

Stacy, Gwen (clone of) *ASM #142 (1975)* Created by Jackal. After Jackal's apparent death, married sole stable clone of Miles Warren. Due to lie concocted by High Evolutionary, believed herself to be Joyce Delaney mutated by genetic virus. Transformed into Joyce by Daydreamer of Young Gods. Regained memory, form after reading PP's book, Webs.

Stag Beetle (Krolnek) *Tangled Web #15 (2002)* Armored exoskeleton. Bank robbery foiled by SM, who was idolized by Stag's daughter, Heather.

Status Quo *MTU #96 (1980)* Fanatical Cleveland librarian. Used mind control to gather army of anti-faddist followers. Battled SM, Howard the Duck.

Steel Serpent (Davos) *Iron Fist #1 (1975)* Extradimensional martial artist. Stole Iron Fist power from Danny Rand, who regained it with help from SM.

Steele, Simon (Wolfgang Heinrich von Lundt) *WSM #10 (1986)* Former head of Nazi spy ring. Foe of Dominic Fortune. Married Dominic's old flame, Sabbath Raven (Gina Morelli). Daughter Elena von Lundt looked exactly like mother, attempted to kill Dominic. Foiled by SM.

Stilt-Man (Wilbur Day) *DD #8 (1965)* Armored, stilt-legged villain. Foe of Daredevil. Had chance to defeat SM when SM sacrificed himself to protect Wilbur from trap. He didn't, out of gratitude.

Stone-Face *Captain America #134 (1971)* Harlem gang lord. Founded vigilante force, Young Watchers, to build public trust to cloak future crimes. Exposed by SM, Falcon.

Stranger *X-Men #11 (1965)* Mysterious cosmic collector of super-powered beings. Battled SM, Adam Warlock, Gardener (Ord Zyonz, Elder of the Universe). Encountered SM, Avengers.

Strikeback (Anthony Davis) *Defenders #51 (1977)* Battled Defenders, SM as Ringer. Pawn of Beetle, nearly killed by Scourge. Wife Leila Davis sought revenge on Beetle. Rebuilt as cyborg Strikeback by AIM, reunited with Leila. Bodily systems continued to deteriorate, died.

Strongarm (Armstrong) *ASM Super Size Special #1 (1995)* Former FBI agent. Granted super-strength by Dr. Noah Purl's experimental procedure. With Scarlet Spider, battled Shadowforce Alpha, primal Lizard offspring.

Subhumans *SM #13 (1991)* Sewer-living outcasts. Captured victims for Morbius, but brought him innocents as well as criminals.

Sub-Mariner (Namor McKenzie) *Motion Picture Funnies Weekly #1 (1939)* Amphibious ruler of Atlantis. Both hero, villain to surface world, sometimes fighting SM. Saved SM from being killed by Llyra. Joined SM vs. Turalla, Aquanoids.

S.U.L.T.A.N. *Captain America #265 (1982)* Systematic Ultimate Lawless Takeover of All Nations. Former S.H.I.E.L.D. weapons designer, remade as cyborg. Created robot armies (Biotron Constructs), floating base (Thunderhead). Sought to conquer world. Defeated by SM, Captain America.

Supercharger *AF #17 (1996)* Father died granting him electrical powers. Attacked SM, believing all super-beings to be menaces.

Surgeon General (Angeline Kutter) *DD #305 (1992)* Seduced men to harvest organs for black market. Wielded scalpels in battle. Captured by SM, Daredevil.

Swann, Prof. Evan *ASM #310 (1988)* PP's research supervisor at ESU. Blackmailed by Tinkerer. Briefly possessed powers of Captain Universe, battling Quantum Mechanic.

Sweatshop *Captain America #329 (1987)* Agents augmented by Power Broker, farmed out for work. Employed by Nazi Red Skull to oppose SM, Silver Sable.

Synario (Angela Bradford) *ASM #438 (1998)* Computer programmer. Created brain-inducer capable of projecting images in minds of others. Used to commit robberies for capital to start own company.

T

Tallon, Leroy *ASM #155 (1976)* Fomer safe-cracker. Hands amputed in explosion, replaced with metal prosthetics. Framed by W.H.O. SM caught him in different crime.

Tannengarden, Ned *SM: Get Kraven #2 (2002)* Son of Kraven the Hunter. Hired cyborg publicist to set up Al Kraven. Accidentally killed by Chameleon.

Tara *PPSM #48 (2002)* Native of Bangladesh. Mutated by AGK Corp. Obtained SM's aid in revenge. Powers styled after Buddhist goddess.

Tatterdemalion (Arnold Puffenroth) *Werewolf by Night #9 (1973)* Former actor. Used clothing as weapons. Fought SM, Werewolf.

Technomancers (Master Om, Maegis Gunther Senreic, Maegis Hamilton Cromwell, others) *SENS #21 (1997)* Scientific/mystic cult seeking corporate power. Used Sphere of Sara-Kath, inadvertently opened Babylon Portal, admitted Buel, Gremlyns.

Tendril (River Verys) *SMTFA #1 (1995)* Victim of flesh-eating bacteria. Mutated by GARID serum involving SM's blood. Died resisting attempt to revert him.

Terminus *FF #269 (1984)* Gigantic alien sought Earth's energies. Defeated separately by FF, Cosmic SM, Quasar.

Terraxia *Infinity Gauntlet #3 (1991)* Female warrior created by Thanos. Killed SM. Murder reversed when Thanos lost Infinity Gauntlet.

Terrier (Gordon Savinsky) *UTOS #12 (1996)* Betrayed former friend Bennett Brant. Gained super-strength while working for Crime-Master. Blackmailed JJJ.

Terror Unlimited *SMU #8 (1995)* Armored terrorists. Held World Trade Center hostage. Defeated separately by SM, Scarlet Spider.

T.E.S.S.-One (Total Elimination of Super-Soldiers) *Captain America @ #8 (1986)* Robot created as failsafe vs. Super-Soldiers. Coated with adamantium. Reactivated by Dr. Doom, stopped by Cosmic SM.

Thanos *Iron Man #55 (1974)* Eternal of Titan. Once sought cosmic power to destroy all life. Often opposed by Earth's heroes, including SM.

Thermo, the Thermodynamic Man (Dr. Walter Michaels) *MTU #108 (1981)* Scientist, gained power to absorb energy. Stalked victims until stopped by SM, Dazzler, Paladin.

They Who Wield Power (Keeper of the Flame, Rey, Tyrannus) *MTU #15 (1973)* Financed, outfitted numerous agents, including City Stealers, Goldbug, Orb, Stegron.

Thunderbolts *Incredible Hulk #449 (1997)* Baron Helmut Zemo's Masters of Evil, posing as heroes. When SM was framed by Enclave, they sought to arrest him. Beetle (aka MACH-1) saved by SM, revealed truth. Joined SM vs. Enclave. Founded by Atlas/Goliath, Citizen V/Zemo, MACH-1/Beetle, Meteorite/Moonstone, Songbird/Screaming Mimi, Techno/Fixer.

APPENDIX

Tiger Shark (Todd Arliss) *Sub-Mariner #5 (1968)* Aquatic villain. Mutated by Dr. Dorcas. Fought SM, Sub-Mariner.

Timespinner *Avengers #11 (1964)* SM robot. Created by Kang to dupe Avengers. Believed self to be SM. Fired webs that aged targets, amassing energy for Kang.

Tinker, Shea *PPSM #27 (2001)* Computer hacker, friend of Randy Robertson. Helped SM rescue Robot Master (Mendel Stromm) from Stromm's own deadly cyber-creations.

Toomes, Mordecai *SPEC #44 (1980)* Nephew of Vulture. Slain by mobster Black Alfred, prompting Vulture's brutal vengeance.

El Toro Negro (Sergio) *Amazing Scarlet Spider #2 (1995)* Super-strong, gun-toting Great Game player. Killed Nightwatch, Polestar by Johnsmeyer's orders. Captured by Chance, apparently killed by Justin Hammer.

Tower, Blake *DD #124 (1975)* NY DA. Prosecuted PP for murders committed by Kaine. Judge was Sandra Franklin. Mr. Locker replaced PP's original attorney, Grant Buckner.

Toy *ASM #159 (1976)* Tinkerer's robotic bodyguard. Believed himself Tinkerer's son. Truth revealed by SM, caused Toy to collapse.

Triad Brothers *MCP #68 (1991)* Three brothers. Mercenaries. Attacked SM's family. Project energy blasts via swords.

Tri-Corp Research Foundation *ASM #1 (1999)* Quentin Chase III (founder, deceased), Dr. Ted Twaki (director), Terry Kwan (supervisor), Stan Hardy, Chantal Stone, Walter Thorson (head of astrophysics), Javier Caldrone, PP. Formerly General Techtronics Laboratories.

True Believers (Meiko Yin, Karsano, Yano, Madame Qwa, Master Zei) *ASM #421 (1997)* Martial-arts cult, offshoot of Hand. Associated with Black Tarantula. Karsano committed suicide when he failed to defeat Meiko Yin, who then took role as Dragonfly, supreme warrior. Fought SM. Led by Madame Qwa, whose brother Master Zei died while resurrecting Dr. Octopus.

Tso, Jason *Web of Scarlet Spider #1 (1995)* Crime lord working out of Club Noir. Employed Ben Reilly as waiter, then bodyguard. Allied with Alistair Smythe. Murdered by Pro.

Turalla *Sub-Mariner #40 (1971)* Princess Tuvia brought Namor, SM to Black Sea Dimension, home of ancient Atlantis-descended race, to defeat power-seeking tyrant Turalla in ritual combat.

Turner D. Century (Clifford F. Michaels) *Spider-Woman #33 (1980)* Sought to restore 1900 ideals by killing all under 65. Foiled by SM, Dominic Fortune.

Tyrannus *Incredible Hulk #5 (1963)* Leader of They Who Wield Power under alias Des. Mutated humans into Serpent Men. Foiled by SM, Daredevil. Controlled gamma-powered Abomination (Emil Blonsky).

U

Uatu the Watcher *FF #13 (1963)* Extraterrestrial observer. Lives in Blue Area on Moon. Helped SM save Anton Chekov's daughter.

Uber-Machine *PPSM #50 (2003)* Armored warrior from Chicago. Hired with Rhino vs. Hammerhead. Defeated by SM.

Ultraforce *Ultraforce #0A (1994)* Heroes from alternate Earth in Ultraverse. Recruited Black Knight (Dane Whitman) from Marvel Universe. Teamed with SM, Green Goblin (Urich) vs. alien Shifters. Prime encountered SM individually.

Ultron *Avengers #54 (1968)* Indestructible robot built by Henry Pym as experiment in artificial intelligence. Avengers foe. Fought SM.

El Uno *ASM #419 (1997)* Agent of Black Tarantula. Killed by Delilah.

Undertaker (Conrad Eisenstadt) *AF #16 (1995)* Con artist, arranger of murders. Boss of Mr. Vale, who scammed Aunt May after Uncle Ben's death. Second criminal SM encountered (after Burglar).

Universal Liberation Army *ASM #243 (1983)* Paramilitary terrorist group. Held church hostage. Defeated by SM.

V

Vaalu *WSM #25 (1987)* Monarch of planet Hyginus II. Traveled into past, posed as Det. Harry Gibbs to stop Xanja from gaining Cosmultigizer. Energy powers.

Vault & Guardsmen *Avengers @ #15 (1986)* Former super-villain prison in Colorado Mountains. Protected by battle-armored Guardsmen.

Vasquez, Prof. Ramon *SPEC #9 (1977)* ESU professor of ethnic studies. Impersonated White Tiger to steal Erskine manuscripts in ploy to keep night school open.

Vega, Robin *SM #82 (1997)* Shape-changing, metallic mutant, ESU student, research assistant to Dr. Lanning. Persecuted by Friends of Humanity.

Virus *PPSM #48 (2002)* Semi-sentient entity created by AGK Corp. as weapon for CIA. Tested on Bangladeshi village, creating Tara. AGK hitman Corman possessed by virus, escaped. CEO Kirkland arrested.

Vulture (Dr. Clifton Shallot) *ASM #127 (1973)* Former ESU professor. Mutated himself to acquire Vulture form. Force-fed antidote by SM.

W

Walters, William *SPEC #235 (1996)* Daily Bugle trainee. Sought PP's friendship, but continually snubbed. Moved away before two became close.

Warforce *Nightwatch #1 (1994)* Six-man mercenary team, some cyber-enhanced. Attempted to free Hitman from Ryker's Island. Defeated by SM, Nightwatch.

Warlock, Adam & Infinity Watch *Marvel Premiere #1 (1972)* Created by Enclave as "Him." Powered by Soul Gem. Leads Infinity Watch, guardians of Infinity Gems, often encountering Earth's assembled heroes. With SM and others, Adam fought Stranger, Thanos, Magus' forces, Goddess' forces, Thanosi.

Warzone *WSM #44 (1988)* Four cyborgs that pursue deadly war games in public. Endangered Marlo, girlfriend of Mr. Fixit (aka Hulk). Stopped by SM, Mr. Fixit.

Washington, Shirley *SENS #0 (1996)* Owner of Daily Grind. Mother of Devon Lewis, ex-wife of Garon Lewis.

Watson, Judge Spenser *ASM @ #21 (1987)* Uncle of MJ. Performed wedding ceremony for her, PP.

Webs *ASM #304 (1988)* Popular book of Daily Bugle's SM photos, initially published without his knowledge. PP, publicist Ginny Edwards promoted it nationwide.

Weil, Toler *ASM #322 (1989)* Member of terrorist group ULTIMATUM, agent of Nazi Red Skull. Plotted to assassinate king of Symkaria, implicate U.S. government. Defeated by SM, Solo.

Wendigo *Incredible Hulk #162 (1973)* Ancient curse by elder gods of Canadian folklore transforms those who perform cannibalism in Great White North into savage, carnivorous creatures. SM, Wolverine protected one Wendigo falsely hunted for series of murders.

Wendigo *ASM #277 (1986)* Elemental creature, unrelated to Wendigo of North. Unknown to SM, saved him from a bullet when he rescued a kidnapped girl.

Werewolf (Jack Russell) *Marvel Spotlight #2 (1972)* Lycanthropized by Darkhold's magic. Joined SM vs. Moondark, Dansen Macabre.

Weying, Ann *ASM #375 (1993)* Lawyer, ex-wife of Venom. Driven insane from briefly becoming She-Venom, committed suicide.

Wicked Brigade (Lightning Fist, Ogre, Razorwire) *PPSM #16 (2000)* Sought bounty on SM. SM escaped when Master Monarch blasted them.

Wicker, Barney *ASM #216 (1981)* Congressional candidate targeted for assassination. Saved by SM, Madame Web.

Wildwhip *SPEC #217 (1994)* Ravencoft inmate. Defeated by Ben Reilly during exile. Freed by Judas Traveller, again defeated by Reilly. High-voltage laser lash.

William *PPSM #34 (2001)* Mutant with destructive eye blasts damaging to own mind. Protected in monastery by Brother Ian, Brother Richard. Escaped. Killed by own powers, despite SM's aid.

Williams, Mindy *Defenders #32 (1976)* Former girlfriend of Nighthawk. Driven mad by mental powers. Used androids to attack Nighthawk, SM.

Williams, Nigel *Daily Bugle #2 (1997)* Founder of Williams Development Co. Torched buildings for insurance money. Exposed by JJJ, Daily Bugle staff.

Will-Killer *MTU #143 (1984)* Native of extra-dimensional realm of Mahkus & Elysia. Belligerent, powerful leader of Mahko clan. SM defeated him, saving women of Elysia.

Winkler, Dr. *ASM #59 (1968)* Former Norman Osborn employee. Developed brainwashing unit used by Kingpin, died when it exploded. Machine used by Hobgoblin on Lefty Donovan, Ned Leeds.

Wino Charlie (Charles Fortesque Smythington IV) *ASM #213 (1981)* Homeless alcoholic, passed out on roof, nearly killed by Wizard when he bombed building to kill SM.

Wizard (Bentley Whitman) *ST #102 (1962)* Criminal genius, organized Frightful Four. Fought SM, Human Torch. Anti-gravity disks, other inventive weapons.

Woodgod *Marvel Premiere #31 (1976)* Satyr-like strongman genetically engineered by David, Ellen Pace. Sought vengeance on Maj. Del Tremens, government agents who killed "parents." Tremens' pursuit of Woodgod led him to SM, Hulk. Tremens sent SM to Moon, where he encountered Adam Warlock, Gardener, Stranger.

Wolverine (James Howlett, aka Logan) *Incredible Hulk #180 (1974)* X-Men member. Adamantium skeleton, claws; enhanced senses; accelerated healing factor. SM stopped him from mercy-killing friend, fellow agent Charlemagne, but she tricked SM into killing her.

Wraith (Brian DeWolff) *MTU #48 (1976)* Brother of Jean DeWolff. Developed telepathic powers. Controlled by father, Phillip DeWolff, who was arrested.

Wrecker (Dirk Garthwaite) *Thor #148 (1968)* Thug who received magic power intended for Loki. Wields enchanted crowbar. Powers shared by Wrecking Crew (Bulldozer, Piledriver, Thunderball). Thunderball once fought SM alone, wielding staggering combined power.

X

Xandu *ASM @ #2 (1965)* Power-seeking evil sorcerer possessing Wand of Watoomb. Opposed by Dr. Strange, SM.

Xanja *WSM #25 (1987)* Member of Cygnorian race. Sought Cosmultigizer to amplify power. Opposed by another extraterrestrial, Vaalu. Possessed thug Arnold Strunk to repossess Cosmultigizer from SM, who accidentally acquired it.

X-Factor (Original) *X-Factor #1 (1986)* Five original X-Men. Posed as mutant hunters to protect young mutants. Encountered SM during their mission to aid Captain America, Frog-Man vs. Yellow Claw. No longer active. See X-Men for team-ups.

X-Factor *X-Factor #71 (1991)* Government-sponsored mutant operatives. Joined SM vs. Shadowforce. No longer active.

X-Force *X-Force #1 (1991)* Mutant strike force organized by Cable. Joined SM vs. Juggernaut, Black Tom Cassidy. No longer active.

X-Man (Nate Grey) *X-Man #1 (1995)* From Age of Apocalypse timeline. Great psionic powers. Joined SM vs. Electro, Morbius, paramilitary team Gauntlet.

X-Men *X-Men #1 (1963)* Mutant super heroes led by Prof. Charles Xavier. Team-Ups: **Full Team** (Menace, Mutantmen, Morbius, Sundown, Nest, Juggernaut, Black Tom Cassidy, Enchantress, Hellfire Club, Professor Power). **Beast** (Herbert Landon, Modular Man, Masterblaster, Powerhouse, Joey, Professor Power). **Prof. X** (Mentallo, Fixer, Professor Power). **Wolverine** (De'Lila with New FF, KGB, Professor Power, Carver & Fugue, Band of Baddies, Chess Set, Inspector Krahn). **Iceman & Angel** (Rampage). **Iceman** (Sam Bullit). **Havok** (Living Monolith). **Gambit** (Tombstone, Creaux). **Kitty Pryde/Shadowcat** (Strygor, Mainspring's robots). **Nightcrawler** (Cutthroat, Jigsaw). **Dazzler** (Thermo, Lightmaster, Enchantress).

Y

Y2K *ASM #5 (1999)* Armored criminals. Stole gold to prepare for disaster. Defeated by Mattie Franklin.

Young Gods *Thor #203 (1972)* Twelve young humans chosen from various eras to represent humanity's best for Celestials. Encountered SM when High Evolutionary made false revelations about Gwen Stacy clone, leading mentalist Daydreamer to transform clone into Joyce Delaney.

Z

Zabo (Donalbain) *Claws of Cat #1 (1973)* Super-strong, unintelligent. Deceased brother, Mal Donalbain, funded Tigra creation. Attacked Tigra, SM.

Zarrko, the Tomorrow Man (Artur Zarrko) *JIM #86 (1962)* Would-be world conqueror from 23rd century. Tricked SM, others into helping him plunder Kang's weapons.

Z'Nox *X-Men #65 (1970)* Extraterrestrials from Andromeda Galaxy. Earth invasions foiled by X-Men, others. Employed Senator Ward in third attempt.

Zombie (Simon William Garth) *Menace #5 (1953)* Resurrected as zombie by Layla using Amulets of Damballah. Lilith, daughter of Dracula, attempted to manipulate him, SM, Hannibal King's daughter.

Zzzax *Incredible Hulk #166 (1973)* Electromagnetic being. Hulk, Avengers foe. Recreated by Paralyzer. Defeated by SM, Midnight Sons, Spider-X.

For an unabridged version of the Appendix to *Marvel Encyclopedia Vol. 4: Spider-Man*, visit: www.marvunapp.com/Appendix/spdmappx.htm

INDEX

Note: This index contains references to the main body of A-Z entries, i.e, pages 30-217. Characters that only appear in the Appendix are not included.

INDEX

INDEX

POWER RATINGS

STRENGTH
Ability to lift weight

1 Weak: cannot lift own body weight
2 Normal: able to lift own body weight
3 Peak human: able to lift twice own body weight
4 Superhuman: 800 lbs-25 ton range
5 Superhuman: 25-75 ton range
6 Superhuman: 75-100 ton range
7 Incalculable: in excess of 100 tons

INTELLIGENCE
Ability to think and process information

1 Slow/Impaired
2 Normal
3 Learned
4 Gifted
5 Genius
6 Super-Genius
7 Omniscient

ENERGY PROJECTION
Ability to discharge energy

1 None
2 Ability to discharge energy on contact
3 Short range, short duration, single energy type
4 Medium range, medium duration, single energy type
5 Long range, long duration, single energy type
6 Able to discharge multiple forms of energy
7 Virtually unlimited command of all forms of energy

FIGHTING SKILLS
Proficiency in hand-to-hand combat

1 Poor
2 Normal
3 Some training
4 Experienced fighter
5 Master of a single form of combat
6 Master of several forms of combat
7 Master of all forms of combat

DURABILITY
Ability to resist or recover from bodily injury

1 Weak
2 Normal
3 Enhanced
4 Regenerative
5 Bulletproof
6 Superhuman
7 Virtually indestructible

SPEED
Ability to move over land by running or flight

1 Below normal
2 Normal
3 Superhuman: peak range: 700 MPH
4 Speed of sound: Mach-1
5 Supersonic: Mach-2 through Orbital Velocity
6 Speed of light: 186,000 miles per second
7 Warp speed: transcending light speed